INQUIRY AND CHANGE

Charles E. Lindblom

INQUIRY AND CHANGE

The Troubled Attempt to

Understand and Shape

Society

Yale University Press

New Haven and London

and Russell Sage Foundation

New York

Published with assistance from the
Louis Effingham deForest Memorial Fund.

Designed by Barbara Werden
Set in Trump Medieval type by Cambridge PrePress Services,
Cambridge, Massachusetts.

Printed in the United States of America by Vail-Ballou Press,
Binghamton, New York.

Library of Congress Cataloging-in-Publication Data

Lindblom, Charles Edward, 1917–
    Inquiry and change: the troubled attempt to understand and
shape society/Charles E. Lindblom.
        p. cm.
    Includes bibliographical references and index.
    ISBN 0-300-04794-0 (cloth)
    0-300-05667-2 (pbk.)
    1. Social problems. 2. Social sciences—Methodology.
    3. Social scientists. I. Title.
    HN28.L56 1990
    361.1—dc20

A catalogue record for this book is available from the British
Library.

The paper in this book meets the guidelines for permanence and
durability of the Committee on Production Guidelines for Book
Longevity of the Council on Library Resources.

10 9 8 7 6 5 4 3 2

Contents

Part IV Toward Prescription

Preface

     This book is a study of how people in contemporary industrialized societies, competently or not, go about gathering and analyzing information in grappling with social problems. By people I mean all kinds: among them ordinary citizens, politicians and other public officials, heads of private organizations, opinion leaders, and experts of various kinds, including, for special attention, social scientists.

     I look into how these persons set or define problems, think about and establish goals, find opportunities, cope with complexity, seek or take advantage of information and helpful analysis, inform and misinform each other, and create answers when they cannot discover them. These topics call for discussion of other aspects of social problem solving, such as the relations between leaders and ordinary citizens; the variety of sources of information and analysis, of which social science is one; the significance of likemindedness for problem solving; and the ways in which ordinary people, their leaders, and social scientists and other experts search for coherence in their thinking about society.

     The point of my study is not merely to observe knowledge and analysis as they are employed in social problem solving, but to analyze some difficulties and causes of failures. In no nation does social problem solving work as well as would seem possible. Problems, threats, and missed opportunities abound: among others, nuclear destruction, environmental warming, third-world squalor, depletion of natural resources, nutritional deficiencies, irresponsible governments, and, in some countries, civil war, widespread drug use, racial conflict, and severe educational inadequacies. Although one might attribute these problems not to any lack of information and analysis but to failures or conflicts of political will, this study proceeds on an assumption that inadequate information and analysis are an important part of the story. Even some failures or conflicts of will can be traced to our failures to inform ourselves and analyze those very problems.

Not with an eye solely on contemporary problems do I examine human inquiry and knowledge as they are employed in social problem solving. Their use and misuse are important phenomena in all ages, past, present, and future. When today's social problems abate, as some will, others will appear, endlessly into such futures as we can imagine. And we might be expected to come to understand that even well-fed and secure populations need inquiry and knowledge in order to formulate new aspirations. One can think of people in a society as not only curing their social ills but also as positively developing capacities and opportunities, some of which they have been unaware of.

The present study introduces new issues and reexamines others discussed in David Cohen's and my *Usable Knowledge* (Yale University Press, 1979). I began this project in the frame of mind represented by the earlier book, but the ensuing journey or struggle has produced a book other than the one I set out to write.

Some of the theses or themes voiced here are worrisome. My study calls into question, for example, widespread veneration for agreement or consensus in society. It makes more room for power and less for intelligence than do many studies of problem solving. It displays the dark side of the human accomplishment that we call culture, and the dark side as well of the socialization of children into law-abiding adults, both of which create impairments of people's capacities to think. To some readers the study will appear to deprecate the value of truth, but that is not my intention. It raises questions about the special abilities of social scientists and other experts. It suggests that the social scientific passion for testing hypotheses and models is excessive. It argues that social scientists try too hard to escape from their dependence on ordinary or nonprofessional knowledge.

Rather than bashing social science, I have tried to give a discriminating account of its distinctive strengths and weaknesses. After fifty years in social science, none regretted, I do not apologize for it as a profession. But if social science were near perfection, it would be the only human institution that had achieved that status.

To ask how inquiry and knowledge are used in problem solving might be to raise epistemological questions: for example, how to find ground for holding any belief to be true or false, or whether or how to distinguish empirical from evaluative statements. This mill is not designed for that grist, and other mills grind it finely. This is a study neither of epistemology, nor of scientific method, nor of philosophy of science (though some questions in those categories creep in) but of the sociology, social psychology, politics, and economics of inquiry into social problems. Consequently, I do not analyze the idealized circumstances in which, hypothetically, people can closely approximate knowlege of the true, the beautiful, and the good. Instead I examine how various kinds of people in actual practice do or might accomplish useful inquiries into their problems, recognizing that the meaning of "useful" itself requires attention.

In inquiring into the social processes through which knowledge is employed in problem solving, I do not fly so high as, for example, the abstractions of Jacques Ellul or Herbert Marcuse on how "technical domination" corrupts the way people think about their problems, Gramsci's "ideological hegemony," or Habermas's "ideal speech situation." Those powerfully suggestive lines of analysis link abstract concepts with less sustained reference to concrete behavior and social process than the present analysis contains. Not to deprecate but to supplement that heady kind of analysis, such a study as this seems appropriate.

For the specific purposes of my argument, I sometimes dispose of complex methodological and philosophical issues on which debate can be expected to rage for the next thousand years no less vigorously than it has for the past two thousand. My strategy is deliberate: I do not try to settle the issue but to extract from it the core consideration needed for my present limited purposes. Because this calls for sentences or paragraphs instead of pages or chapters, it will leave some readers undernourished.

A few who have already read the manuscript have reacted to my worrisome themes by taxing me for not dwelling on certain reassurances. For example, a major line of argument in these pages is that many shared beliefs and attitudes that are widely argued both in political rhetoric and in social science scholarship to be necessary for social stability are attributable in large part to socially caused impairments of people's capacities to think straight. The critics reply that I fail to acknowledge the benefits of consensus and stability. But my point is that however small or large the benefits, society pays a price for them in the form of impaired thinking. Rather than know the price or discuss it, the critics wish to turn their attention and mine back to recounting the benefits themselves.

Concerned with impairments in our capacities to think our way to ameliorating our social problems, I of course acknowledge that my own thinking, like everyone else's, is to a significant degree defective. I am sure that I have been captured by some faddish elements of contemporary thought; that I am deeply influenced by the legacy of mid-twentieth-century liberal and social democratic thought with their subsidiary Marxist elements; and that I am, with most of my countrymen, parochially American, as a consequence never fully understanding my country's atypicality and, on many counts, its extremism. But if these are all constraints, I would add that classical nineteenth-century liberalism is my prison. It is not the most inhumane of prisons; its cells are by far larger than those of any other prison I know. Indeed, its construction is such that inmates often succeed in persuading themselves that they are wholly free. But the care that has gone into its construction and maintenance makes it almost impossible for me and the other inmates to break out.

Society's probe of a social problem is at best open-ended and pursued by a multiplicity of methods. It achieves, with good fortune, illumination without conclusiveness. This study is itself a probe in each of these three respects. Consequently, it intends neither to prove my argument nor to win the agreement of all readers. On issues such as are here discussed, broad agreement is impossible, except as many people fall into the same error. No one engaged in social problem solving or in observing the process as an ordinary citizen, official, or expert can claim to know, to be able to demonstrate, or to command agreement on how problem solving can best be done. But many people—of diverse opinions—have informed and thoughtful views about how to do it well. I hope that this book will contribute to our growing understanding, although it cannot even approach a tight proof that this or that line of thought on problem solving is right or wrong.

Acknowledgments

I dedicate this book to an elite of graduate students, members of which appeared irregularly (and not in every year) over the course of half a century. The conventional "I am deeply grateful" would understate how much I prize what I have learned from them in the interchanges of seminar and study. Beyond my indebtedness to them, also to teachers whose influence remains strong fifty years later, also to both identifiable and anonymous or untraceable creators and transmitters of scholarship and culture for at least three thousand years, and also to my contemporary academic colleagues at Yale and elsewhere, I record my great appreciation of and profit from the help of the following, who have responded to my requests for information or offered helpful counsel, often also taking on the chore of reading and commenting on the manuscript or sections of it: Oliver Avens, Michael Barzelay, Mark Blaug, David K. Cohen, John S. Cornell, James S. Fishkin, Jane Fountain, Kenneth P. Fox, Christopher Jencks, Ronald L. Jepperson, Ira Katznelson, Brian Ladd, Robert E. Lane, Donald N. McCloskey, James G. March, Richard R. Nelson, Paul Pierson, David Plotke, Cathy Potter, Rune Premfors, Harry Redner, Wolfgang Reinicke, Erik Ringmar, Ian Robinson, George Rosen, Barnett R. Rubin, Alan Ryan, Michael J. Sabia, James C. Scott, Ian Shapiro, Miriam Smith, Rogers M. Smith, Steven B. Smith, Carol H. Weiss, Philip Wexler, Aaron Wildavsky, Edward J. Woodhouse, and Ross Zucker. Of these, some, like Barzelay, Jepperson, and Lane, I have repeatedly turned to; but I am indebted to all.

For clerical and secretarial help over roughly ten years spent on this study, I give thanks to more persons than can be listed. At risk of injustice to others, I single out Barbara Boggs, who brought successive near-final drafts of the entire manuscript through repeated revisions with exemplary goodwill and extraordinary intelligence and skill, and, earlier, the excellent work of Beverly Denoyelle, Robin Ellis, and Claire (now Sister) Lavoie.

I have had much-appreciated help from the Ford Foundation, the German Marshall Fund, the John Simon Guggenheim Foundation, the William and Flora Hewlett Foundation, and the Institution for Social and Policy Studies at Yale University. The Russell Sage Foundation I thank for its especially patient and encouraging support.

INQUIRY AND CHANGE

CHAPTER 1

Knowledge and

Social Problems

If paved roads, pensions for the elderly, and curbs on industrial air pollution provide evidence of some success in social problem solving in the industrialized nations, on many problems similar success eludes them. Most of us say we want to stop inflation. But we—or our governments—seem unable to do so. We want better schools but remain dissatisfied with efforts to improve them, and want peace but lack confidence that we can maintain it.

Explanations of our apparent incompetence often fall into standard patterns. Human nature or perversity: we would rather leave some problems unsolved—alcoholism, for example—than accept the constraints on behavior that would eliminate them. Irresponsive government: having created Leviathan, we have not yet found sufficient methods to make it an obedient servant. Social conflict: for any given problem not everyone wants it solved, because some stand to gain by its continuation—an unfavorable balance of payments, for example. Inadequate knowledge: we do not know how to solve the problem— how to accelerate the education of some slow learners, for example.

Explanations as rough as these patently overlap. Perhaps governments act irresponsively because people—including their political leaders—do not know how to make them responsive. Or because of social conflict about appropriate tasks for them. Or perhaps those who obstruct a solution do so because they do not know better. Hence, any one of the explanations appears both as one aspect, among the others, of a complete explanation and as an illumination of the others.

This study explores knowledge: how in the world's industrialized societies it helps social problem solving, how ignorance and faulty analysis get in the way, and whether and how people can do better.

Why choose to study knowledge rather than, say, defective governmental organization? Because it is fundamental to problem solving, as just illustrated. One reason that government and other institutions disappoint people is that we lack the knowledge required to improve them. And one reason that interpersonal conflict often obstructs betterment is that no one knows enough about curbing or channeling it. More immediate and practical, though lesser, reasons also encourage the study of inquiry and knowledge. Relative to the study of governmental and other institutions, inquiry as a method for social problem solving lies neglected.

One can, however, dismiss as superficial all such justifications for choosing one field of study over another. I believe that the core reason for choosing to study inquiry and knowledge derives from a commitment to information and intelligence in human affairs—indeed, a suspicion that people have, for all their cognitive shortcomings, no better resources even when their intelligence sometimes leads them to foreswear certain lines of inquiry. This claim grounds the case for investigating inquiry and knowledge on a particular though not narrow perception of human beings, their cognitive capacities, and the value of using them. Thus it brings us back to substantive elements in a social philosophy. But the elements will appear only in the course of the study. For that reason, the root justification for studying knowledge and inquiry lies in what the study can produce, the proof of the pudding in the eating.

Enmeshed as it usually is in the examination not of knowledge but of government and other institutions, the study of social problem solving usually asks questions about how bureaucracies or, say, legislative committees employ or fail to employ information and analysis in discharging their functions. As a consequence, the study of social problem solving looks like political science viewed from a particular perspective. The present study departs from that pattern. It will ask instead such questions as how not only officials but ordinary people make use of information and discussion in formulating problems and the positions they take on problems. It moves closer to the sociology of knowledge—closer perhaps to the philosophy of science—than to the institutional concerns of political science.

Beginning in an ancient world of extreme inequality, political philosophy identified the key problems of society as maintaining order, authority in the hands of elites, obligations to obey on the part of all others, subservience of the individual to societal needs, and an inequality that could be rationalized as justice. These have come to be the standing concerns of Western political philosophy, a traditional set of power-oriented topics that continues to hold much of the center stage in philosophic discourse. Other issues that now seem of no less importance have been neglected—and it might have been premature to address them in predemocratic times: the deployment of human intelligence in social problem solving, the dissemination of information, and the social processes by which people set social goals. These intelligence-oriented topics—the subject matter of this book—now begin to force themselves into philosophical discourse, which, however, often remains indifferent to them, leaving much of their cultivation to other, less reputable branches of scholarship.

It follows that I intend to explore social inquiry or the production of social knowledge as a vast social process in which even relatively uninformed, ordinary people play significant parts along with political and opinion leaders. It is a larger and more heterogenous social process than problem solving at the hands of social scientists, although their roles also loom large. The process embraces more than the production and dissemination of information, vast as that appears. For it also includes the production and dissemination of misinformation and all those interchanges among people that as often leave them confused as enlighten them.

Where common understandings permit launching into analysis without defining terms, I shall take advantage of that happy opportunity. Prudence, however, requires that the very concepts of problem and problem solving quickly be nailed down (because of old disputes about the terms), that some words be addressed to those who dismiss the concepts as less useful than concepts of interest adjudication or conflict resolution, and that some widespread understandings be recorded as reminders that social problem solving cannot be reduced simply to scientific problem solving. Not exciting tasks, these three nevertheless get the study under way on a sound footing.

By such terms as *social problem solving, guided social change,* or *betterment,* I mean all those processes that people regard as failing or succeeding in converting one social state into another that is by some standard better. An ordinary citizen voicing dissatisfaction, a researcher trying to formulate a solution to recommend to someone with authority to act, a civil servant or functionary in a business or other organization making a decision, and a legislator voting on a bill all take part in these processes.

A social problem arises only when people look at a state of affairs in a particular way: specifically, with a desire for its improvement. It follows that a state of affairs—say, inequality of wealth—constitutes a problem to some people but not to others. Moreover, what counts as a solution or betterment will vary from person to person. And people dispose of problems in many ways: solving, exacerbating, giving up, forgetting, and so on. Economists declared that "fine tuning" the economy was a problem in the 1960s when they thought they could do it. Earlier they had not so aspired, and later they abandoned the attempt. Much problem solving also takes the form not of altering any state of affairs but of altering people's perceptions and evaluations.[1]

The term *problem solving* is a misnomer; one ought to speak of problem *attacking* or *grappling.* Even those words regrettably restrict by implying intention or deliberateness. Some problem solving lacks intent. Idiomatically, one sometimes says of a social change that it solved a problem—for example, that World War II solved for a time the unemployment problem—without meaning that anyone intended a war in order to reach that outcome. Broadly defined, the idea of problem solving, sometimes successful and sometimes not, corresponds roughly with the idea of social betterment. Often but not always it corresponds with the idea of guided social change, which, again, may fail or succeed.

It is worth remembering that "problem solving," like "betterment" or "guided social change," often—in many contexts—denotes not just action but suitable or successful action. Like the verbs *cure* or *persuade,* and unlike *fall* or *pull,* it denotes an activity successfully accomplished.[2] If one asks, say, for a specification of the necessary

1. This point is developed in Murray Edelman, *Words that Succeed and Politics that Fail* (New York: Academic Press, 1977).
2. The distinction is from Gilbert Ryle, *The Concept of Mind* (New York: Barnes and Noble, 1962), p. 130.

steps in problem solving, one actually wants to know what makes it succeed.

Ordinary people, officials, and intellectuals all seem to like to assign blame, fault, or responsibility. They consequently ask such questions as who did it? who made the decision? whose idea was it? For social problem solving, these are foolish questions, for whatever the outcome, it follows from complex interactions of countless influential participants, most of them at a great distance from the place and hour of decision. The attitudes and behavior of millions of ordinary citizens constitute part of the explanation of the present condition and policies of NATO.

As a consequence, one finds that outcomes often seem not to have been decided upon but simply to have happened somehow. How, for example, will the Soviet Union solve its problems of divisiveness and regional demands for political autonomy? One can only answer by outlining a variety of processes in which millions engage: villagers making or withdrawing demands; their local leaders stimulating or dampening popular agitation; state and party officials bargaining, cajoling, threatening, and commanding; and military and other functionaries deploying whatever influence they can bring to bear. No one ever decides on each series of interim solutions that emerge.

Conflict Resolution

But some students of problem solving say that social problem solving differs from problem solving in the customary sense of the words *problem* and *solving*. They say it is a process of resolving conflict among groups each of which already knows its preferred solutions.[3] It follows, then, that one group's failure often implies another's success. The failure of a proposal to make abortions illegal implies the success of those who do not want to outlaw them. Problem solving as conflict resolution, in this view, does not call for knowledge; it simply requires that some causes, interests, or groups prevail over others in a contest of power.

In one variant of this view, each conflicting hard-headed group knows what serves its own interests. In another variant, each conflicting group holds to an ideology, less a structure of knowledge than one of faith, belief, and value, to a great degree impervious to information and analysis. Either way, so the argument goes, finding solutions or achieving desirable change calls not for knowledge but for political procedures ranging from violence to the invocation of rules

3. See James B. Rule, *Insight and Social Betterment* (New York: Oxford University Press, 1978), chap. 1.

that provide for adjudication through courts, legislatures, cabinets, or elections.

Both variants seem inadequate. Interest groups, as well as more diffuse ideological groups, frequently rethink their positions in order to form alliances and render themselves less hostile to potential adversaries. Management and union, for example, find common ground in tariff protection for their industries or in governmental loans for the industry to expand or protect itself against adversity. If the resolution of some conflicts at some point necessarily requires such machinery as elections and authoritative governmental decisions, no less does it require that the adversaries search for additional information and analysis that might permit them to move toward agreement.

Probably more frequent by far than direct and explicit conflicts, half-hidden conflicts proliferate. Everyone wants better schools but conflict arises because some want a reduction in their taxes even more intensely. Although no one objects to export promotion, some people will object on principled or ideological grounds to government's exercising the very powers it proposes to use to promote exports. Others will urge cabinet or legislature to busy itself instead with problems that they consider more urgent. In the U.S., for example, endless complaints about the quality of public school teaching reveal the continuing inability of state and local governments to impose taxes sufficient to raise teachers' salaries. Common aspirations for day care for infants, occupational retraining for adults, better police patrolling in dangerous urban locations, and development assistance to the third world appear to be, among countless other examples, policy areas in which common or widespread aspirations cannot carry programs over the resistance of those who do not wish to pay for them.

One can say, consequently, that there exist countless social problems for which no adequate solutions come into sight unless and until people reconsider the positions they have taken and consequently alter them. Short of that, the state lacks the capacity to act. It follows that in such conflict situations, ubiquitous in society, the only prospect of solution lies in further inquiry. The path to a solution is through inquiry and knowledge that will make a politically imposed solution not now possible eventually possible. Little question, then, that in every such situation, all parties to the conflict have a problem on their hands calling for investigation and knowledge. Not typically a search for solutions to problems that fit existing dispositions or positions, problem solving becomes instead a process of bringing inquiry and knowledge to bear in such a way to alter dispositions and positions so that they make a solution possible later.

A utopian prescription for problem solving? In hard fact, a critic might argue, solutions have to be found—and often imposed by appropriate authorities—without altering prevailing dispositions and positions taken by parties to the conflict, for they cannot be altered or they alter only unpredictably over time. The critic is at least half right: often they cannot or will not alter. But that sorry fact does not necessarily make authoritative imposed solutions possible. Instead it promises inaction, stalemate. Resistance to change in disposition and position taken often explains why problems like ethnic discrimination, inflation, threat of war, civil disorder, urban decay and congestion, and poverty persist indefinitely. The choice for a society often comes down to making a new inquiry into attitude and belief, difficult as that may be, or finding no adequate solution at all. On a hardheaded view, there is no other alternative.

PROBLEM SOLVING AS UNENDING INQUIRY

Social problem solving, it will become clear, requires widespread inquiry and knowledge that even at their best will not look very scientific in the conventional sense. Inquiry is more varied than investigations by Plato's philosopher-king or by contemporary social scientists, systems specialists, or policy analysts. The required inquiry proceeds in a broad, diffuse, open-ended, mistake-making social or interactive process, both cognitive and political.

"Inquiry" is not quite the right label for the process, suggesting as it does the rigors of scientific inquiry. But I shall often use it for lack of a better word. "Probing" captures much of the flavor of the process, since it emphasizes persistence and depth of investigation, uncertainty of result, and possible surprise; but it suffers, for present purposes, from its medical connotations. Again, however, for lack of a better term, I shall very often use it. "Examination," "investigation," and "search" imply looser forms of inquiry than those prescribed by scientific canons; and that is their advantage for present purposes, their disadvantage perhaps lying in too strong a suggestion of superficiality. I shall use all the terms, treating them as synonyms, though sometimes in a particular context choosing one rather than another because of nuance.

In any case, the process cannot be less than a continuing varied, diffuse, and interactive process, never less than a variety of inquiries persisted in by functionaries and other specialists as well as by ordinary citizens—and by social scientists and other experts when they go beyond their distinctive scientific methods.[4] No one ever stops thinking; it persists without interruption. One's attention to social problems will vacillate, remain superficial, or, on the other hand, go off on a tangent. But whatever the imperfections of one's thinking, thoughts—whether of ordinary citizen or functionary—become, especially in a democracy, part of the inputs into and constraints on social change. Consequently, the study of social knowledge in social change calls for a study of amorphous inquiry, probing, investigation, or search as practiced by many kinds of people in various roles. The specialist contributions of those who engage in professional scientific discovery and testing have a place in such processes, but only a limited one.

That society's employment of knowledge cannot do more or better than inquiring or probing requires some explanation. For this allegation conflicts with the view that problem solving can be and ought to be greatly more scientific—a process more of proving than of probing—and put into the hands of experts rather than of functionaries and ordinary citizens. Espousal of more scientific problem solving has declined pari passu with the slow decline of positivism in the twentieth century and with disillusionment in the 1960s with applied social science. Yet scientific problem solving still commands a following, and the case for it provides a hook on which to hang an examination of the reasons why societies cannot, rare exceptions aside, do better than engage in what we call probing, inquiry, investigation, and search, though not without help from science and social science.

The Questionable Case for Scientific Problem Solving

Thanks largely to virtuosity in the natural sciences and engineering, and, among other things, to the increased interdependency among persons that a consequent technology has both facilitated and urged, social relations have become, so the argument goes, complex to a degree never before seen. The economies of nations intertwine. The political decisions of even the most powerful lose some of their autonomy. Within each nation or society, a person can survive only by

4. I use the awkward term *functionary* to refer to any person who takes on or is assigned a specialized, highly influential or powerful function in social problem solving. It constitutes a smaller category than "activists." Functionaries are ordinarily called leaders. But we impair our thinking in applying the term *leader* without respect to whether the designated person is actually leading, following, manipulating, frustrating, or exploiting an ostensible following. So-called democratic "leaders" spend at least some of their time deceiving and manipulating the electorate. A refreshing view of "leaders" is in F. G. Bailey, *Humbuggery and Manipulation* (Ithaca, N.Y.: Cornell University Press, 1988).

finding a place within a division of labor of extreme intricacy. Moreover, attacks on any one problem—say, air pollution—produce myriad consequences throughout the social system. For example, they may render some industries unprofitable, drive some workers into unemployment, constrain traditional liberties, create budgetary problems for a government carrying the cost of the new policies and hence possibly destabilize the economy, and so on. The technology also pushes scientists and engineers into intricate new problems such as those associated with genetic engineering, to say nothing of such poignant problems as deciding which person on the point of death deserves the available donated kidney or heart.

Then, too, a technological revolution in communications, in computation, and in the storage and retrieval of information places many analytical tasks exclusively in the hands of persons who can operate the new technologies.[5] For many tasks, the revolution has pushed aside the political official or other functionary as well as the ordinary citizen.

As a result, the familiar argument continues, neither ordinary citizens nor government officials can master much of the knowledge about society that is required to understand the subtleties of contemporary social organization. They cannot go more than a short way. Responsibility consequently shifts to experts of various kinds (loosely controlled, of course, by appropriate political authorities)—among others, economists, environmental experts, planners, systems analysts, and management consultants. Their scientific knowledge, their information, and their analytical capacity make possible more effective use of knowledge about society to guide society.

This is a good argument, up to a point. In our era, one can hardly imagine a world that does not rely on the natural sciences and engineering, or deny the necessity of comparable social scientific experts in communications and information, in the intricacies of money, credit, and the economy, in psychology and psychiatry, and in some emerging fields like administration and management.

There remain, however, fundamental aspects of social problem solving that not even a revolution in the technology of computation and information processing can turn into scientific problems lying within the competence of persons of sufficient expertise. Any claim

5. For a characterization of the revolution, see Daniel Bell, "The Third Technological Revolution," *Dissent*, Spring 1989. For a summary of and comment on a diversity of views of the relation of technology to knowledge, see John G. Gunnell, "The Technocratic Image and the Theory of Technocracy," *Technology and Culture* 23 (July 1982).

that social problem solving is now largely a task for social scientists or other scientists obscures the ordinary citizen's role as well as the role of the political official in producing and disseminating knowledge. In the first place, it underestimates the inconclusiveness of empirical social science. A later chapter will show, if anyone doubts it, that, even given well defined goals and other values, social scientific analysis usually cannot demonstrate empirically the efficiency of one means over several others with which it competes. Will an increase in the interest rate accomplish what is intended by it? It is never conclusively established that it will, and controversy on its effects abounds. Will more discipline in the schools raise educational achievement? Experts will often endlessly dispute.

If social scientists and other experts cannot approach conclusiveness on empirical questions about the appropriateness of means to given ends for complex social problems, then inquiring citizens and functionaries must choose, with the help of experts willing to probe rather than to hold tightly to conventional scientific inquiry.

Inquiry will displace conventionally scientific investigation for another familiar reason: ends as well as means call for choice. If the choice of ends and other constraining values goes beyond scientific competence as conventionally defined and must be made by a political process, that process turns out to embrace a wide variety of inquiries by experts, functionaries, and ordinary citizens. Even if they do so superficially, voters investigate before casting their ballots. Interest group leaders, party officials, bureaucrats, and legislators all investigate before exercising their authority or other powers. To say that a society sets policy goals and other constraining values politically is not to say that the participants in the process do so mindlessly; they all probe.

One can think of lists of problems that appear to deny the need to inquire into ends, especially when agreement on them seems evident. These include "technical" problems that require conventional scientific analysis of means only: controlling epidemics, improving nutrition, raising the educational achievements of schoolchildren, or maintaining a high level of employment. For does not almost everyone agree on suppressing epidemics, improving nutrition, educating the young, and providing jobs for all?

If this is true, people nevertheless disagree on how much of the nation's resources should be allocated to epidemic control, nutrition, education, or the pursuit of full employment. Problem solving requires informed analysis of how far to go toward ends that are only loosely agreed on. And on many ends, neither citizens nor functionaries agree even loosely: whether one is better red than dead, or whether abortion, euthanasia, gender equality, and genetic engineering are acceptable. Probing these issues calls for information and analysis, for inquiry that goes beyond conventional scientific testing of fact.

The AIDS epidemic makes clear how greatly people dispute not only goals or ends but side or constraining values. How much disclosure is to be required? Should there be compulsory testing? What about employment rights of the afflicted? In what extreme circumstances should AIDS patients be restricted in mobility, or even confined? These constitute more than simply technical or means questions. Or consider the policy questions that arise in the pursuit of employment opportunities. One could simply require employers to give a job to any applicant, but such a program violates customary standards of free choice and promises extraordinarily inefficient labor in any case. On further investigation in later chapters, it will turn out that almost all social problems are easily remedied if one disregards constraining values; the presence of constraining values obstructs solutions more than do purely technical difficulties. Many different participants in social problem solving have to probe those values.

Another reason that the natural and social sciences cannot bear the large burdens of problem solving envisaged in scientific problem solving is that their standards are too high. Consequently, they often shrink from giving answers when answers are desperately needed. They stop their inquiries or put them on hold while they debate epistemological—even ontological—issues: How do I or we know that I or we exist? How do we know anything? What justifies belief? Meanwhile, ordinary people and functionaries are compelled to go on making commitments on how to live and how to solve social problems without waiting for answers to so fine a set of questions. Necessarily, they go beyond where science and philosophy can take them; they must leave their escorts behind.

No Case for Ideology

The questioning of scientific problem solving does not call for a return to ideological thinking on the part of those, if any exist, who have shed it. To be sure, many social scientists and other commentators on social problem solving have fallen into believing that decision makers can approach problems in only one of two ways: either technically, as means to ends, or with all the rigidities, obfuscations, and imprecisions of ideology. But a third option is available: selective and varied probing of both means and ends, as well as of other values.

This now seems obvious at least as an ideal and, for all the superficialities and other shortcomings of its practitioners, as a practice.[6] It calls for inquiry, admittedly inconclusive, into questions about how people choose to live and organize their societies. Even habitual ideologues need that kind of information and analysis. People are taught to think ideologically by communications received since birth. If what they read and hear can make them into ideologues, perhaps it can again change their style of thought to one that is less constrained.

Probing Because of Social Change

For one final reason, ends, goals, and other values require profound new probing, broader and more varied than conventionally scientific inquiry. Established beliefs on ends and values decay in the industrialized societies, indeed throughout the world. Post–World War II anticolonialism called into question white supremacy, liberalism, democracy, conventional deference to authority, and "Western" materialism. In the West, changes in family life and sexual mores have combined with feminist movements to upset a whole structure of once-accepted norms. The widespread yet far from universal legitimization of the once-outcast homosexual shows how far the erosion of old values has gone. On dress, language, forms of personal relationships, and politics, old habits of thought give way to new inquiries.

While one might deplore this erosion, one might also rejoice in the opportunities afforded for investigating values in a search for better ways to live. Either way, the phenomenon of erosion opens up numerous consequential questions for both lay and professional inquiry. The questions need inquiry either to save civilization from decay, if one fears that, or to take a long step toward a more humane future, such as that represented by the invention of liberal democracy, if one hopes for so great a step. (But perhaps no society can probe so intensely as to bring about either its ruin or achieve human transformation. The feasible accomplishments of inquiry may be more modest.)

The challenge to old values now so conspicuous in the world raises to new prominence a particular kind of means question that is habitually neglected: political strategy as a means problem. Consider this means problem as it appears to radical thought. Assume, for purposes of argument, that a radical finds the social inequalities of

6. For a line of analysis parallel to the above but with specific respect to the professions, see Donald A. Schön, *The Reflective Practitioner* (New York: Basic Books, 1983), esp. chap. 2, "From Technical Rationality to Reflection-in-Action."

the world intolerable, liberal democracy largely a sham, and governments almost wholly exploitative—that, in short, only a society drastically different from any existing society deserves an ethical defense. What is to be done? Rejecting an existing society as intolerable and elevating a hypothetical society into an ideal makes no advance at all on the inescapable great strategic questions: By what means is this ideal society to be brought into existence? Revolution? It is impossible in some countries and unpredictable in outcome in any case. By piecemeal reform? If so, what should our priorities and sequence be? What other strategies, if any, should be employed? By what means can one— or an organization, or even a state—transform a society? The radical wrongness of what exists endows neither radicals nor anyone else with the wisdom to improve it. The simple assumption common in radical thought that radical defects and radical goals call for radical means or steps will not hold water. They may or may not. Nor will the simple assumption that if a goal can be formulated, means will be available. Rejecting both assumptions, one confronts a formidable problem of devising strategic means to radical ends. And demonstrably correct or even highly probable answers are impossible. More difficult tasks of inquiry for ordinary citizens, functionaries, and experts alike are hard to imagine.

Nonradical reformist thought needs, it would appear, to approach much the same question of strategic means, especially because it is vulnerable to the radical charge that it is unacceptably slow or even futile. To solve, say, a problem of the growing technological obsolescence of a society's capital equipment requires not only a probe of such means as tax write-offs that if adopted might solve the problem, but a probe of effective strategies to form a coalition or in some other way to bring about the enactment of tax write-offs or other intended remedies. That kind of strategic means problem goes beyond a problem culminating in a conventionally scientific solution produced by experts.

This sketch of issues places this study. It will inquire not so much into institutions as into the probing of society at the hands of ordinary citizens, functionaries such as government officials, and specialists. Precisely of what does social probing or inquiry consist? What do people look for when they probe: the "good," their own interests, or what? Are there standards by which a solution or amelioration of a problem can be judged to be less or more successful? What are the major defects of or obstructions to probing? How can we reduce them? What role does social science play in inquiries that either displace or enrich probing? What are the possibilities of improving both inquiry and social science's contribution to it?

Again, the significance of probing lies in the possibility that people can change themselves to a degree, that they can achieve at least small betterment, that they can ameliorate some problems. They in fact often fail and in some dimension always fail. For between the complexity of the social world and human thinking capacity, there exists a tragic discrepancy. But the possibility remains that sometimes in some circumstances people can to some degree succeed. I confess that the tattered flag of the Enlightenment still stirs a deep response.

By training and acquired habit, social scientists often avoid topics not because they consider the topics unimportant but because they are unable to assemble sufficiently conclusive evidence. They often leave relatively unexplored many lines of investigation on which, because of the inconclusiveness of analysis, a scholar is more likely to damage his reputation than to reach a widely applauded new finding. In effect they ask, why not leave the more speculative inquiries to journalists and nonacademic pundits and save the skills of professional social science for tasks that are scientifically approachable? To ask such a question wisely acknowledges limits to the feasibility of the scientific study of society.

Yet there is a case for some social scientists' tackling questions, such as those about social knowledge in social change, about which they can offer no proof but can themselves only probe, and on which they accept, in their search for illumination, a lower level of conclusiveness than social scientists usually intend. One might even argue that none of the most important questions of social science lend themselves to conventional scientific pursuit of relatively conclusive answers, that coming to grips with fundamentals always frustrates conclusiveness.

In this study, consequently, the tie between method and substance is extremely close. I shall myself do no more than probe how people probe and how their probing might be improved.

PART I

Probing Volitions

CHAPTER 2

Volitions

In most treatises on social problem solving in our time, good problem solvers are ordinarily expected to pursue not the will of God or some abstract ideal derived, say, from the human telos but the satisfaction of human dispositions variously called preferences, wants, needs, or interests. Some disagreement persists on whose dispositions are to matter. Advocates of democracy usually say everyone's; others will specify a class, race, or some elite. But the whole problem-solving process is anchored in the dispositions of some category of human beings.

If, roughly speaking, such a formulation serves the purposes of this study, it needs refining—or even amending—on some points. Neither preferences, nor wants, nor needs, nor interests sufficiently specify just what it is that people pursue when engaged in problem solving. A long-standing objection to the way in which these concepts appear in the literature of social science says that social scientists err in treating preferences, wants, needs, and interests as given or fixed, and thus escape explaining how they are in fact socially formed and variable. An invalid criticism as it stands, it seems to deny that a social scientist might for simplicity's sake usefully assume fixity for some analytical purposes. The criticism that I offer here takes another tack. It questions the frequent assumption that, whether fixed or variable, preferences, wants, needs, and interests are discoverable to a degree that warrants searching for them.

Those who argue that they are discoverable do not necessarily believe that empirical inquiry dispenses with the need for ethical and other evaluative thought. They do believe, however, that the foundation of social problem solving lies in uncovering or discovering what it is that people prefer, want, need, or what it is that serves their interests. The alternative view taken here is that they are not discoverable—not even to a degree that warrants an attempt at discovery. Hence the foundation of social problem solving lies somewhere else. The consequence for later chapters of this line of argument is great, for they will have to describe problem solving in terms that make sense despite the impossibility of searching for and discovering preferences, wants, needs, or interests.[1]

THE IMPOSSIBILITY OF DISCOVERY

A familiar obstacle to discovering preferences, wants, needs, or interests is that the actual choices that people make do not reveal them. People distinguish their actual choices from their preferences, wants, or interests when they regret a wrong choice, saying, for example, that it would serve one's own interest to (choose to) stop smoking, or that it would have suited the nation's needs better if in the last election voters had chosen the other party. But not only do people regret actual choices as insufficiently indicative of their "real"

1. Debate continues on the usefulness of these concepts. All are both defended and attacked. For an excellent depiction of social scientists' frequently thin treatment of preferences as no more than tastes (and objections to their so doing), see James G. March, "Bounded Rationality, Ambiguity, and the Engineering of Choice," *Bell Journal of Economics* 9 (March 1978), pp. 593–604. See also Amartya Sen, "Rational Fools," *Philosophy and Public Affairs* 6 (Summer 1977) and Sen, "Behavior and Concept of Preference," *Economica* 40 (August 1973).

On the inadequacy of the concept of preferences, see Nicholas Rescher, "The Role of Values in Social Science Research," in Charles Frankel, ed., *Controversies and Decisions* (New York: Russell Sage Foundation, 1976), pp. 36–39. On wants, see Michael S. McPherson, "Want Formation, Morality and Some 'Interpretive' Aspects of Economic Inquiry," in Norma Haan et al., eds., *Social Science as Moral Inquiry* (New York: Columbia University Press, 1983). On contemporary dispute about the meanings of "interests," see Grenville Wall, "The Concept of Interest in Politics," *Politics and Society* 5 (November 1975). A short history of the term is in Albert O. Hirschman, *The Passions and the Interests* (Princeton, N.J.: Princeton University Press, 1977), pp. 28–52. On needs, see David Braybrooke, *Meeting Needs* (Princeton: Princeton University Press, 1987).

preferences, needs, or interests, they sometimes reject the "real" ones as unsatisfactory. They sometimes wish to upgrade their own preferences. They might wish, for example, to be more caring persons.[2]

In democratic societies, many people, including many social scientists, hold that whether people themselves know their own wants, preferences, needs, or interests, the correct procedural rule specifies that the society be governed by what they actually choose. People should decide which party or candidate for office will most probably satisfy their preferences, wants, needs, or interests. They also should choose for themselves among consumer goods in the market. But the question of what constitutes a good procedural rule differs from the question of how to ascertain wants or interests. How do we define or ascertain wants, preferences, needs, and interests so as to include those implicit in such sentences as "I made the wrong choice; I did not get what I wanted," or "The result of the election is not in anyone's interest," or "I think we should reconsider our needs"?

Objective Wants and Interests?

People who use the terms *preference, wants, needs,* and *interests* often assume that they refer to some objective attributes of human beings, such as a person's metabolic rate, which are in principle "there" and observable if one could only find them. These are bedrock facts about "real" preferences or interests which expressed preferences or beliefs about interests only approximate. An ambitious statement of the position proposes "to study [the human being's] inner nature scientifically and to discover what it is like." Such a study promises "a court of ultimate appeal of good and bad."[3] On this view, people who wish to improve their understanding of their own needs, wants, or interests must call on highly sophisticated empirical inquiry. Alone, or with the help of other empirical investigators, they must look into themselves to discover or uncover essential facts about themselves. They look for a biologically imprinted bedrock of dispositions.

Since this is not a study of ontology or epistemology, I skip over reasons for doubting that such a bedrock exists. Biologically imprint-

2. For implications, see Harry G. Frankfurt, "Freedom of the Will and the Concept of a Person," *Journal of Philosophy* 58 (Jan. 14, 1971). See also Martin Hollis, "Rational Preferences," *Philosophical Forum* 14 (Spring–Summer 1983); Jon Elster, ed., *The Multiple Self* (Cambridge: Cambridge University Press, 1986); and Donald N. McCloskey, *The Rhetoric of Economics* (Madison: University of Wisconsin Press, 1985), pp. 66–68.

3. A. H. Maslow, *Toward a Psychology of Being*, rev. ed. (Princeton, N.J.: Van Nostrand, 1968), pp. 3f.

ed drives and other attributes, yes; but sufficient to specify wants or interests for guiding problem solving? No. One cannot, it would seem, derive a guiding position on the right to strike, the case for a tough line in foreign policy, the merits of a multiparty system from biological drives.

But for present purposes, the endless epistemological question can be set aside in favor of questioning whether in fact one can un- or dis-cover a bedrock set of preferences, wants, needs, or interests. No one has yet discovered such a bedrock. People continue to dispute its possible components. Hence, epistemology aside, the actual human situation in social problem solving is uncertainty about preferences, wants, needs, and interests that discovery cannot in fact remedy, irrespective of whether it can in principle.

In addition, one must question the relevance of a bedrock if it were discovered. For much of social betterment consists of suppressing or denying certain categories of ostensible biologically imprinted wants and interests even if they in fact exist—for example, a perhaps biologically imprinted desire to inflict cruelty on others in some circumstances, or a desire not to share when social peace urgently requires sharing.

For everyone options abound: when and under what circumstances to reduce one's longevity; what risks to accept; whether to live a long, lean life or a short, happy one. Of many possible reconciliations or resolutions of conflicting wants or interests, none can be observed to meet a person's needs or interests.

Moreover, even if there existed "inherent" or biologically imprinted sets of conflicting desires for life itself, for health, for sociability and for privacy, for adventure and for security, for challenge and for release from challenge, such desires conflict with each other. And neither self nor observer can observe—can discover the bedrock empirical existence of—a wanted resolution of the conflicts. Suppose that self or an observer could see that some resolutions of the conflicts leave one serene, others restless. Of the two sets of consequences, which accords better with want, interest, or welfare? No observation that self or observer can make can answer that question. Even observing that serenity lengthened life, neither self nor observer could observe that a serene long life serves a person's interest better than a shorter, more challenging or active life. One's basic needs, some have argued, derive from whatever one requires in order to function. But a person can function in many different ways.[4]

4. Raymond Geuss, *The Idea of a Critical Theory* (Cambridge: Cambridge University Press, 1981), p. 46.

For the specification of wants and interests, presumably whoever tries to specify them would need a very large body of facts about human biology as well as about how society forms human beings. But all that information taken together will for all these reasons fall short of specifying wants, needs, preferences, and interests that are appropriate for guiding problem solving.

VOLITIONS CREATED, NOT DISCOVERED

For everybody, then, those wants and interests suitable to guide problem solving are not data in fact discoverable by any possible observation of their inherent selves, of some bedrock within them, although observation will take them partway. "Wants" and "interests" appropriate to guide social problem solving consist of those that each person, with more information, thoughtfulness, and discourse than guide present choices, would choose, formulate, or will (as a result of inquiry, reflection, discourse, and other social interchange). They would consist of considered and chosen dispositions ranging from choice of attire to complex judgments on prudent and moral conduct. They would vary in depth and implication of commitment from "I'll take vanilla" to embracing a lifetime of sacrifice.

Building on a foundation of fact, poorly or well constructed, people (never alone but always in social interaction) form, create, decide, will. In ethical theory, the same point sometimes appears, usually more narrowly: we "are making rather than finding, creating morality rather than discovering it."[5] On how to live—what wants and interests to pursue—at every point and for every facet of this question, people create rather than find. Call what they create a volition. It might be called a judgment, but "volition" has the advantage of stressing commitment or will.[6]

What an informed and thoughtful person would decide to pursue may, if one wishes, be called a want (or preference, or need, or inter-

5. Richard Rorty, "Method and Morality" in Norma Haan et al., eds., *Social Science as Moral Inquiry* (New York: Columbia University Press, 1983), p. 174.

6. Psychologists use the term *volition* in another meaning I do not intend: a bodily change, like raising one's arm. On various meanings of *judgment*, the variety of which suggests that "volitions" is preferable for our purposes, see Ronald Beiner, *Political Judgment* (Chicago: University of Chicago Press, 1983), esp. pp. 4–6.

In these pages, I am trying to use some familiar words in their familiar senses: terms like *judgment, choice, create, will,* and *problem solving* itself. In no case do I mean to tap into the specialized meanings that some of these words have taken on in some branches of the social sciences: "choice," for example, as in rational choice theory. In some very few cases, I then give a word a more carefully defined meaning for present purposes: "volitions" is an example.

est); but the decision does not derive from the want. Instead, the want derives from the decision. The decision does not respond to a want; it decides what the want is to be. Alternatively, one's hypothetical informed and thoughtful decision on what to pursue does not derive from his interests; his decision creates his interests.

That conclusion is not quite identical with the familiar idea that policy-making should be guided by enlightened preferences or enlightened self-interest or enlightened wants or needs.[7] As those terms are often used, an enlightened preference or interest is one that, being informed and studied, is for that reason closer to bedrock. By contrast, the present concept of an informed and thoughtful choice is just that and nothing more: informed and thoughtful. It does not assume the existence of a bedrock that enlightenment can approach. An enlightened preference, although an improvement over an unenlightened preference, remains in error until and unless the bedrock is discovered. An informed and thoughtful volition, by contrast, is never in error for such a reason, although always subject to challenge and reformulation. The one concept finds the point or rationale of social problem solving in responding to observable human attributes approximated as well as possible, the other in human choice, will, or volition.

The difference between discovered want, preference, need, or interest, all regarded as fact, and probed volition regarded as a commitment or creation goes beyond mere terminological difference. To say that problem solving pursues the satisfaction of well-probed volitions is to see human beings as burdened with aesthetic, prudential, moral, and ethical choices that they, on the rejected view, escape. It is to understand that they write rather than read the human scenario: to cast them in the role of designers or creators of selves and society.

Some Objections

Obviously, one might reply, a large category of needs (wants, preferences, or interests) lies well established in simple fact: food, shelter, medical care, and education, for example. People who form their choices and volitions with informed thoughtfulness as well as those who form them more superficially will agree on volitions of this kind so predictably that observers can take them as fact, whether thoughtfully examined or not. But social betterment or social problem solving does not face such choices as whether or not to provide food or medical care. Instead it must decide how much of what kind

7. As in Jane J. Mansbridge, *Beyond Adversary Democracy* (New York: Basic Books, 1980).

of food should be provided to what categories of people, as well as making the same difficult choices for all the other presumed good things of life. Facing these choices, the best that societies can do is to build social decisions and outcomes on informed and thoughtful judgments, choices, or volitions—the terms are synonymous in this context—by each person on how he or she wants to live, wants society organized, and wants other people to live. No empirical observation can render those volitions unnecessary, irrelevant, or even secondary.

But surely, one might protest, an expert in nutrition can competently make a judgment on behalf of any person or group about the quantity and kinds of food that are necessary to life. Indeed, a nutritionist can tell anyone who asks what the trade-offs are: for example, how certain foods will reduce one's risk of heart attack though simultaneously increasing that of stroke. That falls short, however, of competence to tell anyone how long to try to live, or how to live, or what risk is worth trading off against another risk.

The position taken here approaches an alternative from which it nevertheless differs, a concept of interest that goes beyond many formulations of enlightened self-interest. The alternative defines interest as what people would choose if they possessed not only perfect knowledge but were also uninfluenced by coercion or deprivation, even if influenced by gentler social forces. There appears to remain in such a concept an implicit postulate that a determinate set of choices alike for all people would be reached under those hypothetical circumstances—again, therefore, a discoverable finding about what would be good for the human animal in these ideal circumstances. According to the present analysis, even such hypothetical circumstances would leave everyone with options—with a question as to what alternatives to formulate, create, or will. If so, interests would remain undiscoverable for, again, they are not data waiting to be discovered. A person's interest would be whatever that person thoughtfully chooses or wills in such ideal circumstances, not foreordained.[8]

Notwithstanding, it may look as though I believe that there exists at least one objective interest: the human interest in the use of the mind to attack problems, an intent central to my study. I do indeed make a commitment to the use of the mind to understand the world and to attack social problems, addressing readers who form a similar volition. But I do not allege that as a matter of fact their objective interest or anyone else's requires that people use their

8. On the alternative in its varied presentations, among them some by members of the Frankfurt School, see Raymond Geuss, *The Idea of a Critical Theory* (Cambridge: Cambridge University Press, 1981), chap. 2.

minds to attack social problems. Instead, to use the mind is my volition and that of some others.[9]

Kinds of Volitions

One forms volitions of many degrees of stability and scope: at
one extreme, stable or standing attitudinal volitions, such as for personal freedom or for close family ties, and, at the other extreme,
transitory action volitions, as for a candidate for office. Some volitions are closely tied to others: for example, a standing or an action
volition opposed to government funds in support of universities because of a standing volition against governmental subsidies to middle-
class families. A volition can be expressed either in language or in
action.

Although one values anything for which one forms a volition,
"volition" in some contexts differs from "value." For example, to say
that a person forms an action volition by probing a conflict of values
and resolving it by value trade-offs is to distinguish the two concepts
from each other. Nor in all contexts is "volition" synonymous with
"decision" or "choice," for sometimes the two latter terms refer only
to action volitions, such as a volition for or against a new tax bill, and
exclude the formation of standing volitions like those for or against
race discrimination.[10]

WHOSE VOLITIONS ARE TO COUNT?

One can duck the difficult question Whose volitions should
count? only by believing that on a sufficient study of volitions, interpersonal conflicts among them will disappear to be replaced by a
natural harmony of volitions so that it no longer matters whose
counts. A Platonic conception, it reappears in various forms in contemporary thought. Thus, "any critical theory will see the lives of its
audience as composed of two levels of being: the manifest, in which
there is confusion and frustration; and the latent, in which there is an
underlying order." Analysis then seeks to "discover" the latter.[11]

The argument appears as another facet of the doctrine of objective or in-principle-observable preferences or interests—"there" to
be uncovered or discovered. But if objective interests do not exist or

9. For a similar position, see Rogers M. Smith, *Liberalism and American Constitutional Law* (Cambridge: Harvard University Press, 1985), pp. 205–208, and 216f.

10. For fuller discussion of the concept, see Edgar Taschdjian, "On Volition,"
Revue européenne des sciences sociales et cahiers Vilfredo Pareto 17 (June 1979).

11. Brian Fay, *Critical Social Science* (Ithaca, N.Y.: Cornell University Press,
1987), p. 69.

are in any case undiscoverable, there cannot exist a discoverable objective harmony. Problem solving consequently has to cope with volitions conflict, not assume it away, and hence must face the question of whose volitions are to count. One can of course observe some areas or issues on which volitions appear harmonious. Even there, it is not that harmonious volitions have been uncovered but that people have formulated them, often in order to avoid or resolve conflict. An objective harmony does not give rise to unconflicted volitions. Instead, people form unconflicted volitions in order to achieve harmony.

Among professional intellectuals, the commitment to a roughly equal regard for the volitions of all seems strong. Ask social scientists what they mean by a good solution to a problem, and they will probably reply that it means one that has taken into account as equally worthy of consideration the volitions of all.[12] To think otherwise would usually appear to violate scientific neutrality (although it would seem that social scientists often violate it by in fact limiting their regard for volitions largely to those of their countrymen).

In my own volition for regarding the volitions of all members of my nation-state in rough equality, I estimate that I am like most readers of this book and like most social scientists and philosophers. For some purposes, however, all of us regard as roughly equal in claims on social problem solving the volitions of everyone of all nations and must confess to deep-seated biases that prevent our doing so more often.

Absent Volitions

On most of the never-ending decisions made by any government, most citizens do not form volitions at all. Clearly, problem solving in those cases does not therefore become impossible, nor do solutions reached bear no relation at all to popular volitions. Citizens form many volitions that bear on choices of solutions even if they do not form a volition on the solution itself. Not having formed volitions, say, on a new tax proposal, citizens will have formed earlier volitions with respect to sharing tax burdens or acceptable forms of collection that may guide this decision. Often, too, when citizens have not formed volitions on the problem at hand, problem solving calls for finding futures that accord with other volitions formulated by masses of people, including their volitions with respect to the process by which functionaries, to whom they often delegate responsibilities,

12. That does not imply an egalitarian outcome. A social scientist is likely, for example, to hold that for the good of all, equally regarded, certain economic and other inequalities are wise.

choose. Citizens will form volitions for throwing certain decisions into the hands of a legislature, others into the bureaucracy. In specifying process, they often form a volition for requiring authorized persons to whom choices are delegated to estimate what mass volitions would be if only they were formed and to make their decisions accordingly. Hence, to conceive of problem solving as bringing futures into line with well-examined volitions requires no fanciful situation in which almost everyone carefully forms a volition on almost every issue. Problem solving is a process in which solutions accord sometimes only distantly and loosely with thoughtful volitions.

Information and thoughtfulness never place anyone's judgment or volition beyond challenge and beyond a possibility of reconsideration. Up to a point of overload, and with exceptions, the more informed and thoughtful the volition is, the more valid it is as a guide to problem solving. Nothing finally or ultimately meets the requirements of problem solving fully. No judgment or volition is good enough, it is only all we have.

IN ANTICIPATION OF SKEPTICS

The certainty that many citizens and functionaries will not probe well might be a ground for skepticism about the usefulness of the concept of volitions. Assume that formulated volitions rather than discovered wants or preferences constitute the appropriate guides for social problem solving. Assume also that in principle each person has to formulate volitions for one's self. Notwithstanding, one might add, in actual fact most people will investigate their possible volitions poorly, and hence expert observers (say, both political and other functionaries and social scientists) can better formulate volitions for the great mass of people, where "better" denotes volitions toward which masses would move if they in fact probed much better than they do.

The objection raises a pivotal issue. Is the concept of a well-examined volition useful only for specifying an ideal of social problem solving and otherwise of little consequence? Or does the examination of possible volitions constitute an important aspect of problem solving, so important that to understand problem solving one must understand how ordinary citizens and functionaries go about it, how they are obstructed from doing so, and how their examination of volitions might be facilitated? This study supports the latter argument.

Chapter 1 has already indicated one powerful reason for believing that, unless many millions of ordinary citizens and functionaries reexamine their volitions, a multiplicity of social problems lie beyond adequate solution. Discordant volitions, say, on inflation, race relations, day care, or European economic integration block action on them. For that large category of social problems, the prime requirement for their significant amelioration is a reconsideration and consequent alteration of what I have referred to as attitudes and positions taken, thus of volitions. Yet quite aside from that urgent reason for probing volitions, they need reexamination in order to set goals for problem solving even when existing volitions are not in discord. Presumably, not just discord but ill-considered agreed volitions stand in the way of problem solving.

The case for better-probed volitions does not make a case for a broad and actively participatory democracy or for ignoring either the traditional incompetence of citizens or such new forms of incompetence that lie, for some groups, say, in drug addiction or in the commercial advocacy or huckstering of candidates and parties in election campaigns. However one might defend participatory democracy if only volitions were greatly more examined, for the time being they are not; nor do designs for more participation assure the required improvement. The case for probing does not settle the question of what practical arrangements for social and political decision making should here and now—and in the foreseeable future—be relied on or attempted. That question remains open.

Evidence that more thoughtful and informed volitions might greatly matter to human betterment will come in the course of exploration of both probing and its obstacles. Depending on what the obstacles turn out to consist of and whether they can or cannot be reduced, I shall make or fail to make a case for the importance of more carefully formulated volitions in social problem solving. More information and analysis at the hands of functionaries, experts, and ordinary citizens brought to bear on both their standing and their action volitions might help people cope with the social world that they have made and that they sometimes seem about to destroy. The recent emergence of atmospheric threats to welfare and survival provides one more of many historical examples of opportunities to put information and analysis to good use. At this date in the history of civilization, we do not know enough, for example, about how to organize the international cooperation that appears to be necessary to cope with atmospheric threats, nor do we know enough about the costs and whether we are willing to bear them. And when I say *we* do not know, I mean that I do not know, you do not know, and neither do presidents, prime ministers, cabinets, legislatures, and civil servants. Our volitions need a great deal of investigation.

The case for more carefully examined volitions does not rest, however, solely on the urgency of conflict resolution and the possibility of avoiding catastrophe from atmosphere or bomb. In some subtle dimensions of human life most valued by the architects of Western and other traditions in thought—dimensions denoted by such expressions as cultivating the most distinctly human (and social) qualities of life—societies are not yet far advanced. Since thinking about what that cultivation might become derives largely from the thinking of intellectual elites, especially the great philosophers, one might suspect a bias toward defining progress as turning ordinary citizens into intellectuals or inducing masses of people to venerate art galleries as they are venerated now in highly educated circles. Because we cannot be confident that we know what specific content to pump into such expressions as self-development, the pursuit of self-development in society, the good life, and the good society, all call for clarified volitions. For in this cold universe, the only blueprint for utopia or any human betterment is what human beings themselves draw, and the path ahead may be longer than the path already walked.

Yet to a skeptic who observes that no one has ever been able to prove that more information and intelligence brought to bear discriminatingly on human personal and social problems will raise human competence in problem solving, pay off, or be a "good thing," I must say that I agree. With the arrival of the Bomb, we came to understand as never before that knowledge can be deadly. In this study, I do not try to make the case for information and intelligence, instead addressing myself to those who think the case, appropriately qualified, is either valid or worth considering. I try only to examine how people use and misuse intelligence and information in solving their problems, on an assumption that their use and misuse is consequential.

CHAPTER 3

Probing

If discoverable preferences, wants, or interests could guide problem solving, then the key players might consist of those capable of discovering them—perhaps social scientists. If, on the contrary, only formulated, created, or willed volitions can provide the guidance—each person formulating his own volitions—the key players include the great mass of ordinary citizens as well as functionaries. But then again, if ordinary people probe poorly, a case might be made for permitting an elite—either a political elite or an elite of knowledgeables—routinely to estimate presumed volitions for them, keeping popular participation in problem solving to the minimum level required for democracy. For these and other reasons, how ordinary people and their associated functionaries go about the task of investigating possible volitions becomes a large part of an account of how a society accomplishes problem solving. Consider, then, certain specifics of their task, saving for later chapters the many obstructions to their inquiries. I shall not ask epistemological questions about how inquiry best proceeds or how belief can ideally be tested, but questions instead about how people proceed in a real world to work their way to beliefs and volitions.

For a skeptic who doubts that ordinary people often engage in probing, a simple proposition, only slightly overstated if at all, makes a good beginning: Everybody always probes. However badly, all of us engage in examining volitions, even while asleep and both consciously and unconsciously in waking hours. We supplement the most casual inquiries with scattered active investigation. We may discuss with friends the merits of competing candidates for office. We speculate from time to time about the patterns of our lives and changes we might attempt. We look among our acquaintances for models. We may take a poll in the form of asking acquaintances whether they have ever tried cocaine. We may seek help from persons to whom we attribute a more specialized capacity for inquiry than ours: a physician, auto mechanic, priest, or astrologer. In some societies people might disembowel a chicken to read its entrails.

Inquiry mixes with and advances through action, for we do not first probe and then act but continue to probe and learn in every action we take. For complex personal and social problems, we practice, among other strategies of inquiry, trial-and-error, realizing that we cannot know very much until we act, must consequently learn from the consequences of the act, and use the new knowledge for another fallible step.

It takes all kinds. Among those at a great distance from a periphery of passive or superficial probers lie those assigned or self-selected to take on special responsibilities for social problem solving: opinion leaders, heads of some organizations, business executives, researchers, and government officials. Of these, some examine at least two sets of volitions: their own private volitions and volitions governing their special responsibilities. But the multiple roles that everyone plays may occasion a multiplicity of sets of volitions for anyone.

One probes in the midst of social interchange, profoundly influenced by a life history of it. Every "self" is socially formed, an obvious point but worth making to dispose of the notion that each of us automatically or freely chooses what and how to think. Society thrusts on everyone a language, concepts, beliefs, values, and the like before one has the time or capacity to make a selection. In other ways, as well, we are induced to ask certain kinds of questions while wholly blinded to others. It will not occur to many Catholics that the confession serves, and over the centuries has been designed to serve, as an instrument of elite control over masses, specifically through enforcement of such conformity in thought and action as an elite hierarchy, from priest up to Pope, wished to impose.[1] Depending on what one means by "reality," reality itself is socially constructed.[2]

Probing or inquiry is deeply social or interactive in another sense. Tell people engaged in probing unemployment among young American black males that roughly 40 percent of them are unemployed, compared to 16 percent for young white American males, and they will not understand the problem![3] Tell them that these young blacks show various signs of anomie and demoralization, and their understanding will advance a little but still fall short of an adequate understanding. Tell them that in anticipation of unemployment many young blacks drop out of school early and cripple their earning capacities for life, and, again, they will advance their understanding, which, however, will still fall short. They will not fully grasp the unemployment problem as it afflicts young black males unless, as is improbable, they know some of them, talk with them, observe them and begin to sense such feelings in them as cynicism, despair, anger, or resentment. Because young black males are significantly isolated from the world of whites as well as from significant segments of black society, few people understand their difficulties well enough to care to do anything about them. For most Americans, their unemployment constitutes either no problem at all or one not significant enough to stimulate an effective attack on it.

Perhaps this example oversimplifies and overstates. But the point is that to identify or formulate a social problem requires not simply cold rationality but some sensitivity of feeling or affect, with respect to other people; and it develops only in social interaction or in some dramatization of cold, objective phenomena. A high infant mortality rate becomes a problem because some people not only count the number of infant deaths but have had experiences that make them feel disturbed. The deaths offend sensitivities ranging from immediate and deeply felt emotions to moral sentiment, and they include even the limited sensitivities of people for whom high infant mortality is intolerable only because they see it as a waste, to them abhorrent. Whatever distinctions between belief and feeling or between cognition and affect may be drawn, probing or inquiry has to

1. Thomas N. Tentler, "The *Summa* for Confessors as an Instrument of Social Control," in Charles Trinkaus and Heiko A. Oberman, eds., *In Pursuit of Holiness in Late Medieval and Renaissance Religion* (Leiden: E. J. Brill, 1974).

2. Peter L. Berger and Thomas Luckman, *The Social Construction of Reality* (New York: Irvington, 1966).

3. *U.S. Economic Report of the President* (Washington, D.C.: U.S. Government Printing Office, January 1987), table B-38, p. 288.

be recognized as, among its other aspects, an inquiry into one's reactions of love, hate, revulsion, sympathy, admiration, or horror, among many other possibilities, as one actually experiences the many aspects of social life. Because most people do not directly experience all the things about which they develop sensitivities, feelings, or emotions, they get the experience once removed, through literature and the arts; the impact of personal experience and feeling reported by family members, friends, and acquaintances; and the drama of vivid media reporting.[4]

THE VARIETIES OF PROBING

Forming volitions pushes people into a richer variety of probes than show up, say, in some theories of decision making. For example, as some theorists see it, the main empirical or factual inquiry in social problem solving asks: What means will probably achieve a given end? But means-end questions constitute only one category—probably only a small category—of inquiry, and even of empirical inquiry. The empirical probes of both functionaries and citizens run overwhelmingly in a different direction: into inquiries, often amorphous, that will help to set ends or goals. These include empirical investigations of one's own capacities and limits and similar questions about what the physical and social environment forbids or permits. Everyone asks such varied questions, far removed from means-to-end questions, as What am I like? Are frictions between the USSR and the U.S. going to provoke war? or What are people thinking about these days?

To countless empirical inquiries, people of course add countless evaluative inquiries. The question at least as old as Socrates, "What shall we do and how shall we live?"—which Tolstoy declared was "the only question important to us"—deeply engages the inquiring mind. Evaluation itself embraces a variety of inquiries: aesthetic, moral, ethical, and prudential. Moral and ethical questions proliferate over a range from personal conduct to such complex issues as "man's inhumanity to man" or the ethics of competition. Ethical questions often

4. What I say here about probing or inquiry will strike some readers as reminiscent of John Dewey. But his concept of a social process in which citizens could join in inquiry appears limited, in his words, to "face-to-face intercourse" in the "neighborly community." But that identifies only one of the arenas in which people inquire and accomplish a social interchange of ideas. Then, too, Dewey excluded vast areas of inquiry from popular participation, advocating "on questions of most concern" inquiries to be "carried on only by those especially equipped." See John Dewey, *The Public and Its Problems* (1927; Chicago: Gateway Books, 1946), pp. 211, 213, 124f.

slide into prudential questions. Shall we settle it by a show of hands? remains an ethical question to some, but becomes only a prudential one to others.[5]

Ethical and other evaluative questions require probing irrespective of whether Hume, Nietzsche, and Weber did or did not err in asserting a distinction between facts and values. A person need not decide that issue or even recognize it as an issue, nor be troubled if the distinction seems to break down because evaluative inquiries repeatedly at some point turn empirical. Since, when a person can establish a criterion for evaluation, the rest of the task of evaluation will consist largely of empirical inquiry, and since, even without a criterion, evaluation largely takes the form, as Hume saw it, of an empirical examination of consequences, an intermix of evaluation and empirical inquiry spawns many kinds of probes.

Everyone also inquires—again, however incompetently—into concepts and cognitive organization. Some people think God a pertinent entity about whom or which to ask questions; others probe or reject the concept. Some people ask questions about democracy; others think it important to substitute the concept and word *republic* for *democracy*, thus shrinking the concept in ways that suit their purposes. Similarly we all probe elaborate cognitive frameworks or systems—or, more precisely, reconstruct inheritances from parental and other influences—such as those that lead us to regard, say, human affairs as a simple struggle between good and evil or (for some people) social change as a Hegelian movement to an Absolute.

One might think that on concepts and cognitive organization, most people simply passively absorb. In fact, everyone is "creator and initiator as well as receptor."[6] A student of political socialization finds that "children do not simply reproduce the communications that reach them from the adult world. They work them over, detach them from their original contexts, and assimilate them to a general conception of what government is about."[7] A psychologist writes: "The growth toward expertise (whether in perceiving the world as a child or chess situations as an adult) involves far more than the mere

5. An illuminating comparison of (Talcott Parsons on) moral evaluation and (Erving Goffman and Alan Garfinkel on) prudential evaluation is in Alvin W. Gouldner, *The Coming Crisis of Western Sociology* (New York: Basic Books, 1970), chaps. 7 and 9.

6. Stanley Allen Renshon, "Assumptive Frameworks in Political Socialization Theory," in Renshon, ed., *Handbook of Political Socialization* (New York: Free Press, 1977), p. 30.

7. R. W. Connell, *The Child's Construction of Politics* (Carlton, Australia: Melbourne University Press, 1971), pp. 27f.

accumulation of information. Rather, the frameworks used to analyze input information change."[8]

One also underestimates the richness of everyone's inquiries by overlooking the pervasiveness of methodological inquiry of many kinds. A probing mind does not merely ask if acid rain despoils forests, but also asks, "Who am I to believe about acid rain?" Questions abound about what to believe and what kind of evidence, if any at all, to require as a condition of belief, as well as practical questions of how to go about structuring questions to be attacked.

One can identify many other kinds of inquiry. But those mentioned already make the point: probing ventures out in many ways and directions. Kant might regroup probes into those categories suggested by his three key questions: What can I know? What ought I to do? What may I hope?[9] But a classification would threaten epistemological dispute that is better avoided here.

All the inquiries engage both functionaries and ordinary citizens, with little division of labor between them, despite such proposals as that citizens inquire into moral issues, political leaders into technical issues.[10] Obviously, both often inquire into both. Some theorists also suggest that while functionaries formulate alternative policies (action volitions, in our terms) in response to general aspirations (standing volitions), ordinary citizens formulate the general aspirations or commitments. But, obviously, functionaries also deal heavily in standing volitions, which they urge on their constituents; and sometimes, too, ordinary citizens formulate action volitions. No easy generalization seems to apply except that citizens depend heavily, at some peril to themselves, on help from functionaries.[11]

Alike in their methods of inquiry, ordinary people and functionaries do not usually engage in scientific research, though they pick up directly or indirectly many results of scientific inquiry and feed them into their own inquiries. To describe what they do calls for an emphasis on the varied, open, never-ending, and inconclusive character of their investigations of a social world in motion: exploration rather than conclusion, variety of method rather than formal technique,

8. Rand Spiro, "Understanding and Remembering Verbal Information," in Spencer A. Ward and Linda J. Reed, *Knowledge Structure and Use* (Philadelphia: Temple University Press, 1983), p. 112.

9. Immanuel Kant, *Critique of Pure Reason*, trans. Norman Kemp Smith (1787; London: Macmillan, 1973), p. 635/B833.

10. Locke, *An Essay Concerning Human Understanding*, ed. Peter H. Nidditch (1690; Oxford: Clarendon Press, 1975), p. 646.

11. For an early but still excellent formulation, see Anthony Downs, *An Economic Theory of Democracy* (New York: Harper and Brothers, 1959), chap. 12.

intermittence rather than professional persistence, and unpredictability of outcome rather than task completion. Probing does not seek the degree of conclusiveness of knowledge to which scientists have conventionally aspired; instead, it seeks enough knowledge to warrant this volition instead of that in a world in which one must choose while knowing one's own fallibility. One might speak of inquiry or probing as Cassirer spoke of reason, "not as a sound body of knowledge, principles, and truths, but as a kind of energy."[12] It chips away at a mountain of belief or habitual thought that cannot withstand the chisel where applied, although the mountain remains largely untouched, so great its size, so small the chisel.

Whether much aware of doing so or not, everyone pursues probing strategies. Everyone knows, though not with the same degree of awareness, that everyone else probes; that action on collective or social problems requires some agreement on volitions; and that one must therefore adapt one's own volitions to others', preferably in ways that induce others to adapt theirs as well. On this count alone, every prober becomes something of a games strategist. In addition, one may probe strategies for exercising even greater influences on other people's investigations of their volitions. And finally, as a strategist one probes alternative institutional routes to problem solutions, commonly forming a volition for action by national, regional, or local government but often instead for private action by family, labor union, business enterprise, or other organization.

Inquiry or probing is a large concept. Skeptics might think it too large to be useful. But I intend to discuss a range of problems that confront people—ordinary citizens, functionaires, experts, of various kinds, including social scientists—when they try to use their intelligence to solve or ameliorate social problems. One could make "knowledge" the core concept. But, as already observed, it seems better to emphasize the activity of inquiry than take stock of findings. Then why not simply identify "thinking" as the focus of this study? My choice of terms like *probing* and *inquiry* is simply a matter of emphasis and nuance. I want to call attention to thinking that is engaged in real-world problem solving, to the relation, consequently, between thinker and the world thought about, and to the open-ended and exploratory quality of thought. I also want to call attention to interplay between thought and action as part of the process of probing or inquiry itself. And, not the least, I want to play up aspects of systematic and productive thinking about real-world problems that de-

12. Ernst Cassirer, *Philosophy of the Enlightenment* (Princeton: Princeton University Press, 1951), p. 13.

part from conventional scientific methods; and for that I think of no better word than *probe*, especially when it is set in contrast to *prove*. Probing is not some distinctive category of thinking but thinking looked at in a way that both calls attention to its many dimensions and gives prominence to certain of them.

Probing to Define a Problem

From where do the probed problems come? Because a social problem derives from a state of affairs seen or interpreted as regrettable or as a possible opportunity for improvement, a high infant mortality rate becomes a problem to one who sorrows over the deaths but not necessarily to another who sees in those deaths a curb on excessive population growth. Consequently, formulating a problem calls for inquiry no less than does formulating a solution to a formulated problem.[13] The origin of a social problem lies in the probes that declare it to be a problem.

Everyone who is not simpleminded formulates problems in packages, that is, formulates no one problem independently of formulations of other related problems. Why did many Brazilians of the 1980s point to debt as their great national problem? Among other reasons, they conceived of declining economic growth as a problem, and they believed that debt stood in the way of reversing the decline. And why did they see weak political leadership as so urgent a problem, given that many nations often fear excessive strength rather than excessive weakness in government? Because they did not see that any but strong leadership would cope with the debt problem. But there were other Brazilians who formulated "the" problem as gross inequality of income and wealth, and others who formulated the problem as how elites can best keep masses politically docile despite their poverty.

Significantly, and for good reason, people simplify their inquiries broadly and generally by never thinking about more than a fragment of all that they experience, never formulating any whole as a problem but only some of its parts. Some critics complain. Effective problem solving, they say, requires that "the problem as a whole" be formulated and attacked. One can quickly see that any formulated social problem consists of a part of some larger problem: for example, a problem

13. Problem solving for a problem already defined calls for what has been labeled "single-loop learning." When the formulation of a problem itself is in question and when its reformulation compels a broader and deeper reconsideration of volitions, including a cognitive reorganization, it calls for double-loop learning. See Chris Argyris and Donald A. Schön, *Organizational Learning* (Reading, Mass.: Addison-Wesley, 1978), pp. 18–26.

of discipline in the classroom becomes a part of the problem of failures in child-rearing practices in the family, and that in turn becomes part of the problem of family disorganization, which becomes part of the problem of ethnic conflict, and which becomes part of the problem of defective economic institutions. And so on. The only whole problem, at least in the absence of communication with possible life on other planets, becomes that of how to make earthly society better.

But that "whole" is too big for anyone's brain and too big for effective social action. Little wonder, then, that all of us consequently formulate no more than pieces or fragments of so impossible a "whole problem." Holists formulate larger problems than nonholists, but never "the whole problem." And larger does not necessarily mean better.

People fragment problems logically—that is, disassemble large problems into manageable parts. Societies and history also fragment them chronologically: problem solvers at any given time in fact usually do no more than work on fragments of problems bequeathed them by earlier problem solvers. The problem of unemployment, for example, is not the imaginable large problem of finding useful roles for every adult. For that, labor markets have long been in place, and the contemporary problem reduces to a fragment: how in some respect to make the market work better.[14]

THE MEANS-END RELATION AND PROBING FOR COHERENCE

When people try to tackle the greatest issues, the highest values, the most general and fundamental propositions about the good society, they often blunder into a morass. Yet they also often find some strategies for coping with difficulties that might seem beyond their competence. To understand them, observe first what they do not do, and why not.

One version—I think a mistaken one—of how they struggle with the most abstract problems of ultimate values describes them as forming volitions at each of various levels into a hierarchy or pyramid, testing each volition regarded as a means against a higher volition at the next higher level regarded as an end; and so on up to an apex value, which serves as the ultimate value from which all lower-level values are derivable. A long though disputed tradition in philos-

14. On how a social problem comes to be defined—usually poorly—and how it becomes a public problem, see Joseph R. Gusfield, *The Culture of Public Problems* (Chicago: University of Chicago Press, 1981), chap. 1; and Murray Edelman, *Constructing the Political Spectacle* (Chicago: University of Chicago Press, 1988), chap. 2.

ophy postulates the existence of an apex value, principle, purpose, or objective, an example being Aristotle's *eudaimonia*, conceived of as what human beings tend toward in the fullest development of a nature unique to human beings.

Now, whether omniscient minds could find a workable apex value or not and whether they could then convert all other tasks in probing into means-end analysis or not, apparently relatively few people believe that mortals can in practice do so. Nor, unable to uncover a single apex value, can they formulate, create, or will one as a volition. Most people appear to grapple with the lower-level values and volitions more directly than by tracing them up to or down from a created apex. They will often feel more competent at the lower levels closer to life's concrete experiences. There they deal with means in relation to a variety of ends far below an apex.

Even at the lower levels, however, they encounter familiar difficulties in testing means against ends.[15] For complex social problem solving, they cannot establish a sufficiently verified empirical relation between a means and postulated end because they lack either sufficient information or sufficient analytic capacity or both. That only begins their difficulties, all well known.[16] They find, for example, that they choose ends to suit means, not merely means to ends. "A cook is not a man who first has a vision of a pie and then tries to make it; he is a man skilled in cookery, and both his projects and his achievements spring from that skill."[17] Men landed on the moon only when means to do so first made the end attractive. Or they cannot trust an end to stay put. It may fail when tested as a means to a higher end. Or they find the means to reach it too expensive, hence abandon the attempt and turn to other ends. Up and down a rickety ladder of means-end relationships, reciprocate relations between the two show more complexity than a means-end pyramid.

Multiplicity of ends also confuses a probing of a means-end pyra-

15. Even for policy analysis, the means-end pattern is often inappropriate because it neglects "distributive ends, procedural and historical principles, and the values . . . associated with personal rights, public goods, and communitarian and ecological goals" (Laurence H. Tribe, "Policy Science: Analysis or Ideology?" *Philosophy and Public Affairs* 2 [Fall 1972], p. 105).

16. See Max Weber, " 'Objectivity' in Social Science and Social Policy?" in Edward A. Shils and Henry A. Finch, eds., *The Methodology of the Social Sciences* (New York: Free Press, 1949); Gunnar Myrdal, "Ends and Means in Political Economy," in *Myrdal: Social Theory*, (London: Routledge and Kegan Paul, 1958); and John Dewey, "Means and Ends," in Leon Trotsky, John Dewey, and George Novak, *Their Morals and Ours* (New York: Pathfinder Press, 1973).

17. Michael Oakeshott, *Rationalism in Politics and Other Essays* (New York: Basic Books, 1962), p. 91.

mid.[18] Conflicts among the multiple ends require trade-offs, or complementarities among them require certain combinations of them, any one of the ends by itself being unacceptable. As an end, full employment, for example, would be easy to achieve simply by paying employers to hire the unemployed, were it not for other ends or constraining values that probers see in conflict with it or necessary to combine with it. "It is doubtful whether decisions are generally directed toward a goal. It is easier and clearer to view decisions as being concerned with discovering courses of action that satisfy a whole set of constraints. It is this set, and not any of its members, that is most accurately viewed as the goal of the action."[19]

Probing for Coherence

Given these difficulties, no matter how hard one tries from time to time, no one arranges volitions in a linear means-end chain, hierarchy, or pyramid, or even approaches such an accomplishment. Instead, it appears that one examines many interrelationships among volitions in all directions and achieves at best a greatly flawed consistency that might be called coherence. People seek only a modest coherence within sets of volitions;[20] how much they actually achieve we do not know. For personal problem solving, they try to work out feasible ways to live, some not excessively conflicted life-style in which they choose many varied volitions in some accommodation to each other. For volitions on social problems, it is not idiomatic to speak of a life-style or way to live, but more customary to speak either of a social philosophy or ideology. But no articulated social philosophy or ideology can represent the full complexity of a structure of social volitions.[21]

Coherence is admittedly a loose concept, but its obvious alternative, "consistency," is too rigid. That people make trade-offs implies

18. And multiple ends cannot always be subordinated to an overarching single value, even if not an apex. See Thomas Nagel, *Mortal Questions* (Cambridge: Cambridge University Press, 1979), chap. 9.

19. Herbert Simon, "On the Concept of Organizational Goal," *Administrative Science Quarterly* 9 (June 1964), p. 20.

20. S. E. Taylor, "The Interface of Cognitive and Social Psychology," in J. H. Harvey, ed., *Cognition, Social Behavior, and the Environment* (Hillsdale, N.J.: Erlbaum, 1981), pp. 189–195. See also, on "reflective equilibrium," John Rawls, *A Theory of Justice* (Cambridge: Harvard University Press, 1971), pp. 20, 48–51.

21. Patterns in individual beliefs and attitudes that reflect at least a weak coherence have been documented, especially for political activists and leaders. See, for example, Sidney Verba and Gary R. Orren, *Equality in America* (Cambridge: Harvard University Press, 1985), chap. 5; and, on Sweden, the U.S., and Japan, Sidney Verba, *Elites and the Idea of Equality* (Cambridge: Harvard University Press, 1987).

that they combine volitions that interfere with each other, volitions they cannot satisfy without sacrificing others. In that sense, inconsistency of volitions appears everywhere, and consistency they do not seek. Within their competence, which inevitably falls short of what the complexities of volition formation require, people to some significant degree seek to adjust volitions to each other mutually or reciprocally, and in all directions. They will often locate and sometimes remove conflicts for which they can find no satisfactory justification. Similarly, they will sometimes locate and rectify unnecessary failures of volitions to support each other. But they will not know—even distantly—what either a consistent or an optimum set of volitions would consist of.

What ordinary people do to achieve coherence does not greatly differ in main outline from what scientists do in their scientific work. "The totality of our so-called knowledge or beliefs . . . is a man-made fabric which impinges on experience only along the edges. . . . A conflict with experience at the periphery occasions readjustments in the interior of the field. . . . There is much latitude as to what statements to reevaluate in the light of any contrary experience."[22]

This would be the common situation even in a static world. But technology and other forces constantly change society in ways that pose new choices to everyone. And people themselves grow, mature, and decline. All the more, consequently, will they form new volitions that do not square with old ones. Any particular consequent discord they may or may not remedy as new experience, new volitions, and consequent new discords crowd in.[23]

The structure of one's volitions, then, takes the form of a web rather than a hierarchy, a web "stretched across the ground of experience, serving as one of the structures that unifies it."[24] An example of a search for coherence: suburban house or inner-city apartment? The choice carries immediate implications for choosing methods of transportation, schooling for children, sociability with neighbors, and leisure-time activity. These implications in turn develop further implications for the family budget, hence for all other activities and

22. W. V. Quine, *From a Logical Point of View* (New York: Harper Torchbooks, 1953), pp. 42–43.

23. Leon Festinger, *A Theory of Cognitive Dissonance* (Stanford, Calif.: Stanford University Press, 1957).

24. On values not as hierarchically structured but in a web in which tremors at one point have repercussions elsewhere, see Michael J. Shapiro, *Language and Political Understanding* (New Haven: Yale University Press, 1981), pp. 85f; and Michael Scriven, "Science, Fact, and Value," in S. Morgenbesser, ed., *Philosophy of Science Today* (New York: Basic Books, 1967), p. 180.

purposes on which the family might spend its income. The choice of house or apartment becomes, consequently, a choice of a way of living of many dimensions, and a choice that calls for no simple linear means-end analysis but one marked by all the complications outlined.

For any one person, the search for coherence becomes an extension of the task not of finding but of forming, creating, or willing, even to the point of so altering volitions as to become a "different person."

Means-End Analysis as a Heuristic

Given a web rather than a hierarchy or pyramid, means-end analysis of a modest kind becomes a simplifying cogitative strategy for dealing with parts of a volitions structure. In contemporary Western cultures, when people are called upon to give reasons—even to themselves—for choosing a volition, they often find it difficult to maintain sustained thought about it other than by exploring connections between it regarded as means and some other volition as end. Often they cannot think, cannot analyze, cannot debate except about means to assumed ends. If, at the end of the line, they consider a possible volition as an end only and cannot cast it as means to a still further end, their minds stop working on the issue; they fall silent, have nothing to say or think. Their analysis, even if incomplete, terminates. Even sophisticated intellects often cannot define rational thought other than as thought that appropriately connects means to end.[25]

By disaggregating an impossibly complex volitions analysis into pieces—each cast as a means-end problem—which they take up one at a time as occasions arise, without assuming or attempting a pyramid or hierarchy of means-end relations, people sometimes find a practicable solution to the age-old problem of justifying end-of-the-line or ultimate values. In effect, they deny they exist by temporarily converting the ultimate value, for purposes of a partial analysis at hand, into a means to some end seized upon for that purpose at hand. Why a volition for democracy? Because it allows for the fullest possible development of distinctly human qualities. Many people see the latter as an end-of-the-line volition, an end in itself and justified by no further end. But challenged by themselves or others, they will, to

25. In attempts to describe or theorize about policy analysis, for example, the choice of means appropriate to end is characterized as a problem calling for rationality, but the choice among ends is often characterized as calling not for rationality but for survey of the opinions of government officials or citizens and the use of political or other processes for resolving their disagreements. An example is Michael Carley, *Rational Techniques in Policy Analysis* (London: Heinemann, 1980), pp. 16–19.

avoid having to fall silent, argue individual development as a means, say, to (the end of) happiness. Hence, for some piece of analysis at hand, the end-of-the-line value is demoted to the status of means. For another example, people sometimes see equality of opportunity as an end, thinking about various policies to achieve it. But on other occasions they position it as a means to the end, say, of efficiency. Then again, they may position efficiency as a means to reduce poverty. And even so broad a purpose as the reduction of poverty they can position as only instrumental to so relatively specific a purpose as reduction of costs of welfare programs.[26] No matter that the means-end relation has shifted or even reversed from one analysis to the other. A makeshift tactic such as this one they find helpful for formulating a coherent structure of volitions.

Probing as "Immanent Critique"

For these reasons and others, people in their inquiries appear closer to the practice of Hegelian immanent critique than to the practice of foundationalism, although few of them are professional philosophers and, strictly speaking, none strictly practices either.[27] A foundationalist, beginning at a high level of abstraction and generality, would propose to begin inquiry with either an apex value or some other key principle or concept to which volitions can be anchored. By contrast, immanent critique, beginning at and working up from a low level of abstraction or generality, finds no such key concept, value, or principle and does not propose to spend its energies in the search for one. It begins, consequently, with relatively concrete questions and propositions. If one intends to form a volition about euthanasia, instead of trying to deduce it from a principle about, say, the value of human life, one asks: Who are the people for whom euthanasia is a possibility? What is their situation? What do they think about it and why? What do others think about it and why? Can I find relatively concrete persuasive reasons for agreeing or disagreeing with either? On what grounds might my line of thought then in turn be challenged? The one method descends, the other ascends.[28]

Despite powerful feelings in many minds that one ought to begin

26. For documentation of just how such a rotation proceeds in social science itself, see chap. 9.

27. Again, this chapter is not a study of epistemology but one of how people in fact probe. On immanent critique in Hegel, see Steven B. Smith, "Hegel's Idea of a Critical Theory," *Political Theory* 15 (February 1987). On foundations, see Hans Albert, *Treatise on Critical Reason* (Princeton: Princeton University Press, 1985), chap. 1.

28. As these methods are represented esoterically in scholarly probing, in or near the foundationalist camp are, among others, Plato, Aristotle, Aquinas and other

with foundations—how else to be logical?—the practical difficulties of doing so, we suggest, repeatedly drive people into an inquiry immanent in that it arises from experience confronted. Presumably, significant elements of both styles mix in most probes. But the large component of immanent critique, in which inquiries move out like an exploratory party into new terrain, making do with what they have and coping, sometimes in makeshift ways, with whatever difficulties appear, again makes the term *probing* apt for how people go about forming volitions.

Understandably, then, no satisfactory model of the ideal society, the ideal life, or the ideal personal character meets the needs of probing. Some thinkers have proceeded partway toward one or more of such models; but none has completed the task, and their results, like Plato's in *The Republic*, stimulate endless dispute. Even ideal models of limited aspects of the social system fail. A common consequent strategy, then, identifies ills to escape rather than ideals to approach.[29] In examining social problems, many people form with some confidence a volition, for example, for eliminating some of the most severe forms of poverty but not one for any ideal distribution of income and wealth. Unable to describe an ideal tomato, they identify the inedible.

Similarly, no one can specify the ideal practice of inquiry itself. Examining everything is a path to madness. Examining in depth every issue probed at all goes far beyond human capacity. Too much inquiry into public affairs can be dangerously divisive. Or it may divert energy from personal problems (and vice versa). Of the ancient city-states, it has been suggested that "the more perfect their democracy, the poorer the citizens became."[30] Yet most of us would say with considerable confidence that misinformation constitutes an obstruction to

---

Roman Catholic thinkers, Descartes, Kant, Strauss, MacIntyre, and many other contemporary social scientists who, though they cannot in practice find foundations, are constrained by their training in orderly thought to assume their existence. In or near the immanent critique camp are, among others, ancient medical writers, Sophists, Skeptics, Polybius, Thucydides, Machiavelli, Montaigne, Locke, Montesquieu, Hume, Marx, James, Dewey, pragmatists, Collingwood, and Quine.

Aristotle, however, distinguishes between the need for foundations for theoretical analysis and the dispensability of foundations for practical discourse. "Rational arguments and decisions regarding the proper conduct of life and the order of the *polis* were not to be derived from theoretical-analytical thinking but from what Aristotle called 'topical' thinking ... from *topikos*, meaning local" (Werner Ulrich, *Critical Heuristics of Social Planning* [Bern: Verlag Paul Haupt, 1983], p. 68).

29. As social scientists themselves often do. See Barrington Moore, Jr., *Reflections on the Causes of Human Misery* (Boston: Beacon Press, 1972).

30. Giovanni Sartori, *Democratic Theory* (New York: Praeger, 1965), p. 254.

good probing (not to deny some exceptions); and so also deprivation of information in many circumstances, intimidation that constrains thought, or personal demoralization.

At this point, every reader may nevertheless want an answer to the question: What are the most important things to probe? At this stage in human thought, no one is competent to answer. What is most worth inquiry itself calls for inquiry and might—but it is not to be assumed—be among the questions most worth probing.

Chapter 4

Inquiry, Imposition, and

Partisanship

According to a common complaint, societies turn prematurely to "power" to reach solutions to social problems; they do not push the use of information and analysis in probing far enough. Of course, anyone who engages with anyone else in discussion or dissemination of information exercises the "power" of persuasion. The complaint, more precisely characterized, points to power other than that of information and honest persuasion: thus deceit, obfuscation, threats, commands, and authority. A common aspiration is to raise the level of informed analysis and persuasion in policy making, and to reduce the use of other powers seems laudable. Yet beyond a point it becomes foolish, for reasons worth stating as cautions against an excess of confidence in the potential of probing.[1]

1. Of many possible examples of the aspiration, one formulated with great sophistication as a program—without, I believe, a sufficient place for imposition—is Donald T. Campbell, "Reforms as Experiments," *American Psychologist* 24 (April 1969). For a brief characterization and documentation of the aspiration, see Douglas Torgerson, "Between Knowledge and Politics," *Policy Sciences* 19 (July 1986), pp. 34–36.

A solution reached wholly by inquiry and persuasion and without any exercise of power (of the other forms) is by implication one on which people have thought their way through to a voluntary agreement, all convinced of its merits. For, short of such voluntary agreement, some exercise of power will always be required in order to proceed over objections from those who do not agree. Obviously, a persisting absence of unanimity of volitions calls for an exercise of authority or other power.

For other familiar reasons, too, the exercise of power can move a society further toward a solution when fuller analysis cannot. Sustained thinking becomes time-consuming, costly, and sometimes painful. Or, given the complexity of problems, people sometimes distrust their own competencies to formulate sufficient appropriate volitions. Especially the evaluational aspects of probing may discourage them. Or misinformation and obfuscation may distort or block analysis. Any such circumstances may at one point or another require not further inquiry but an imposed solution, say, by vote or by delegation to an authorized decision maker.

Beyond these limits on the efficacy of inquiry hide other, more profound ones. When people think about social problems, they in fact think about how to escape from or adapt to power. Aside from flights into the most fanciful of utopias, one cannot even conceive of a solution or outcome reached wholly by examining its merits. For all participants in problem solving live in a network of existing impositions and coercions, born as they are into an economy, polity, and culture that they never chose. When, then, they examine such a question as the case for higher taxes, for new environmental controls, or for new governmental programs for midcareer occupational retraining, they approach the problems from their imposed-upon condition, asking themselves whether they would find proposed new programs an improvement on their present imposed-upon condition. Their analyzed solutions or outcomes never constitute an alternative to an imposed solution. They constitute instead a different set of impositions. Inquiry not in that way constrained by power would represent problem solving ab nihilo, starting from scratch, assuming nothing. It would

---

The aspiration to dampen power and enlarge analysis often identifies politics with power, as though political persuasion or discourse, inquiry, and probing were not part of politics. I pose the choice not as politics versus analysis but as power in politics versus analysis in politics.

be impossible, except for a god, and one free from the power of other gods.

The difficulties invalidate the idea of resolution of a conflict or achievement of a solution through no other influence than the force of the best argument, a venerable concept in the history of thought.[2] The best argument and all the other arguments as well never go beyond analysis of how best to adapt an outcome to prior continuing impositions, the outcome then no more the result of the arguments than of the impositions.

Inquiry and the impositions of power intermix in yet another way. Volitions for outcomes or solutions commonly though not always take the form of volitions for imposing: imposing, for example, taxes, restrictions on discharging pollutants into the air, or housing codes; or imposing various obligations on the bureaucracy to carry out legislated programs. The cry for more brain and less brawn in problem solving often in effect turns into a demand that people— especially functionaries—think more and harder about how to impose rather than a demand to reduce the imposition of power.

Probing for Interpersonal Conflict Resolution

Notwithstanding, on other counts the scope for inquiry goes beyond what first appears possible. A frequent social science error holds that when the volitions of various people or groups of people conflict with each other a reconciliation must be imposed. In the face of interpersonal conflict, what else is there to do? But, of course, there exists an "else"—as already noted, more probing, more discussion. At any point at which conflict exists, more inquiry and mutual persuasion continue to be a possibility. That suggests a hypothesis about past and current inquiry, unfamiliar in some contexts but wholly consistent with what anthropologists and sociologists say about how collections of people become societies and how people live together in tolerable harmony. The principal conflict-resolution mechanism of most (all?) societies is not governmental or state imposition but various social interchanges that move people toward agreed volitions. They persuade, cajole, and threaten, both with words and with harsher forms of influence. Of these interchanges, some intimidate and coerce, some obfuscate and deceive, but some exchange informa-

2. Given contemporary prominence by Jürgen Habermas, "Wahrheits-theorien," in H. Fahrenbach, ed., *Wirklichkeit und Reflexion: Festschrift für Walter Schultz* (Pfullingen, 1973), p. 219; for English commentary, see Thomas McCarthy, *The Critical Theory of Jürgen Habermas* (Cambridge: MIT Press, 1981), pp. 305–308.

tion and counsel helpful to reconsideration of volitions. As indeed has already been noted, inquiry itself consequently serves as a major method of conflict resolution, along with the many social interchanges in which people impose on each other more than they join with each other in probing.

One can easily miss the importance to a society of probing in the direction of agreement because of the impossibility, rare cases aside, of probing all the way to agreement. The former persists inexorably in most societies, the latter remains only a utopian aspiration. Probing constitutes a vast social process in which people—ordinary citizens and functionaries—endlessly reexamine their volitions not in a vain hope for unanimity but in a practical ambition to reduce volitions conflict to the point at which an imposed solution through a vote or legislative enactment becomes feasible. Probing often makes the difference between a collection of people and a society.[3]

As a method of conflict resolution, the vast scope of probing consequently contrasts with an only residual (which is not to say unimportant) process of conflict resolution through power in the hands of government and other institutions.[4] Inquiry continues without end, always a possible source of new agreements. The Dutch came to their distinctive social welfare program largely because they probed or talked their way to an agreement, not because that government imposed the program to resolve earlier discordance. And it may turn out that such deep conflict as separates Protestant from Catholic in Northern Ireland will be resolved, if ever at all, by discourse, so futile appear the attempts of the British government to impose or coerce a resolution.

THE STATE IN CONFLICT CREATION AND RESOLUTION

To identify an only residual role for state or governmental power in conflict resolution—a role to be played after inquiry, persuasion, and other social interchanges have made their great contributions to conflict resolution—does not, however, reduce the state to

3. On the difference, see Marvin Harris, 4th ed. *Culture, People, Nature* (New York: Crowell, 1975), pp. 290–298; and Leopold Pospisil, "Law and Order," in J. Clifton, ed., *Introduction to Cultural Anthropology* (Boston: Houghton Mifflin, 1968), pp. 200–224.
4. The "aggregation of individual preferences"—that is, aggregation without their reconsideration—so widely studied by social scientists since the publication of Kenneth J. Arrow's *Social Choice and Individual Values* (New York: Wiley, 1951), is an aggregation that copes with the problem of residual resolution.

a secondary role. The residue remains large, the state being a major determinant of its size. And, among other things, the state shapes inquiry itself. Its position in society and its impact on inquiry raise further questions about the crude doctrine that problem solving suffers from too much power and not enough intelligence.

Given the centrality of the nation-state in modern social life, it of course greatly shapes the probing that people do in pursuit of conflict resolution. But state power does not much engage in resolving what might be called a Hobbesian conflict among ordinary people. Hobbes saw the state as organized to resolve preexisting conflict among men over their "wives, children and cattle"; and political science has been on a wrong track ever since, perpetuating the idea of a state serving primarily as an adjudicator of personal conflicts among its subjects or citizens; thus Lasswell's concept of politics as deciding "who gets what, when, and how" or Easton's concept of politics as the "authoritative allocation of values."[5] If nothing like the state—not even the Athenian *politeia*—existed, presumably it would have to be developed in order to cope with Hobbesian conflict. But the Hobbesian conflict problem is often largely solved by the mere existence of the state, except for continuing peripheral Hobbesian conflict. For the most part, the state once established puts Hobbesian conflict out of its mind and attends to other things.

The conflicts that the state today attempts to resolve through authority and other power consist largely of such conflicts as those over possession of office, taxes, highway construction, negotiations with other states, control of the bureaucracy and the military, and disposition of government funds. These conflicts arise only after the establishment of a state. These reveal not the causes of a state but its consequences.

Moreover, they make clear that the state, among other things, engages in a variety of cooperative tasks, such as educating the young; keeping peace or fighting wars with other states; and providing transportation, communication, and other services. These tasks do not reconcile conflict; they create conflicts, especially over how to carry out the cooperation and who shall have what powers over how it is carried out. These conflicts the state then helps to resolve, but the origin of its tasks of conflict resolution lies largely in the cooperative tasks it undertakes.

5. Harold Lasswell, *Politics: Who Gets What, When, How* (New York: McGraw-Hill, 1936); and David Easton, *The Political System* (New York: Knopf, 1960), pp. 129–134.

The state serves as a mechanism for the varied purposes of various people, of which the resolution of Hobbesian conflict counts as no more than one. Resolution of conflict among created private organizations has become a major task. Another is the encouragement of private organizations through which groups of citizens can pursue purposes common to the group, and another the creation of governmental organizations with assigned function and authority to implement social cooperatism.

Nor is the state a bench to which problems are brought from society for resolution or solution. For the very existence of a state or something like it transforms society. Even tribal authority transforms group life. So much more, then, does the nation-state create forms of social cooperation, facilitate individual and group purposes, and raise for every person questions about relations with others in society, including but not limited to relations with officials of the state. In all these specific senses, state or government merges with society or intimately intermixes with all other aspects of society. If it is the existence of the state that accounts for the very conflicts that the state must then try to resolve, it is also the existence of the state that in large part accounts for the world of frustrations and opportunities that each person probes. To volitions the state responds one way or another, but perhaps no more so than the volitions respond to the state as a pervasive social influence, as a core aspect of society.

Much of every person's ingenuity goes into probing ways to reduce the constraints of, or adapt to, the multitude of impositions that guide his life. People try to break out of or diminish the constraints of their limited income, the discipline of their jobs, some of their obligations to family, their tax burdens, even the rules of highway traffic. They never, as noted, probe from scratch but always from the constraints that enmesh them. From where do these constraints come? It is the state that lays down rules on what income is whose, on what authority can be exercised over whom by whom, on one's obligation to family, on taxes, and, of course, on the highway speed limit. A principal task of every investigator is to examine the state in which he is enmeshed and its powers, from which he cannot escape.

PARTISAN PROBING

For inquiry to make its best contribution to social problem solving, especially to conflict resolution, one might hope that it would be high-minded, cooperative, and to a degree altruistic—in short, not partisan. In fact, its frequent partisanship is apparent, even if not to the complete exclusion of altruism or principle.[6] Hence, a continuing contrast between, on one hand, the idealized cooperative public-spirited "government by discussion" of earlier democratic theorists[7] and, on the other hand, the uglier aspects of inquiry and public discourse, calls for a reconsideration of partisanship.

With respect to partisanship, how might one proceed in probing? First, one may search for wholly shared volitions on the assumption that sufficient investigation and discussion will bring everyone into agreement, as many exponents of "government by discussion" advocate. Second, one may withdraw into a familiar kind of partisanship: formulate volitions that take into account one's self and a few close others of one's kind, disregarding any larger group.

A third alternative? As in the first case, in one's inquiry one takes everyone into account—or at least everyone in one's own nation or society. But one discards as impossible a successful search for shared volitions. One thus formulates one's own volition for the common good, a proposed resolution of the disagreements, while not denying either that they continue to exist or that others will not agree with one's formulated concept of the common good. You construct a liberal vision of the common good. Others do not. Or hers gives a special consideration to the volitions of the intelligentsia, his weighs more sympathetically the volitions of the poor.

People who take the third alternative often see themselves as nonpartisan—concerned with the welfare of all. Not ignorant, narrow, excessively self-regarding, opinionated, or bigoted, they nevertheless in fact play a partisan role in espousing a version of the common good that is inevitably different from many other versions of the common good. Not narrow partisans, they can be called common-good partisans.

Common-good partisanship often wears a disguise. A British Conservative declares: "Our policy is to work for the nation as whole—town and country, employers and employed, professions and Unions, pensioners and youngsters, working class and middle class— respecting and balancing the interests of all sections, but without

6. But cautions against overstating the partisan component in public policy making are sounded in Steven Kelman, *Making Public Policy* (New York: Basic Books, 1987) and Robert B. Reich, ed., *The Power of Public Ideas* (Cambridge, Mass.:Ballinger, 1987).

7. Ernest Barker, *Reflections On Government* (Oxford: Oxford University Press, 1942), p. 61.

subservience to any one."[8] Presumably, in so writing he thinks of himself as nonpartisan. But like anyone else's, his idea of what constitutes a balance distributes gains and losses among competing groups; and his balance will differ from others' balances in favoring or depriving some groups rather than others. For their differing volitions for the common good, people are sometimes willing to kill or die, as illustrated in the intensity of dispute between partisans who have seen the common good in one nation's ascendancy and those who have seen it in another's.

Insofar as people in fact pursue successfully the first alternative—the identification of shared ends, goals, or volitions—it appears that they do so by first trying their partisan visions of the common good out on each other and then modifying their own visions to make them more attractive to others. Hence, they do so largely by first employing the third alternative. In short, even if they intend a nonpartisan conclusion to their probes, they begin it and long continue it as common-good partisans. "A steady accumulation of evidence" shows that the "influence of self-interest on political thought and action is tenuous." People reveal "concern for larger purposes that transcend their own immediate situation."[9] The judgment appears to confirm common-good partisanship rather than inquiry into shared values.

Partisan examination of versions of the common good would seem an inescapable and acceptable aspect of probing. But the narrow form of partisanship stirs anxieties. Often destructive to good social problem solving, it also deserves a brief note of appreciation. A common objection to narrow partisanship holds that "the aim of politics ought to be to promote the good of the whole community."[10] Yet good problem solving requires responses not only to many common volitions but also to many private and segmental volitions. Good problem solving requires attention to the special volitions of each of various subgroups—children, elderly, farmers, or disabled, for example—even at cost to other groups. Narrow partisan investigation does not by any means necessarily obstruct the achievement of appropriate solutions to segmental problems.

As for common or shared volitions, how might they be formed?

8. Robert McKenzie and Allan Silver, *Angels in Marble: Working-Class Conservatives in Urban England* (Chicago: University of Chicago Press, 1968), p. 23.

9. Sidney Verba and Garry R. Orren, *Equality in America* (Cambridge: Harvard University Press, 1985), p. 248.

10. Donald W. Hanson, "The Education of Citizens," *Polity* 11 (Summer 1979), p. 471.

Sometimes, following the first alternative, people engage in a deliberate attempt to formulate them explicitly. Alternatively, as just noted, they pursue their partisanship, whether narrow or seeking a common good, in a pragmatic way that induces them to move, whether they intend to or not, toward forming shared volitions. In the face of conflict over volitions on possible solutions to problems, even narrow partisans find themselves pushed toward examining their relations with others. Their search will raise at least some questions about their identification with, sympathy for, or fellow-feeling with various others. Even their narrowest investigation will also raise strategic questions about the relation of their volitions to those of others. Especially when social problem solving requires, as it usually does, alliances or cooperation, almost everyone will see some point in at least small strategic shifts in volitions in order to win allies.[11]

In addition to historical examples, evidence derives from the observation of small groups. A small-group study, for example, compares two ways of solving a problem of the group as a collectivity: one way through inquiry into "what is best for the group"; the other way through members' each taking a position, then trying to defend it, which is a form of what we call partisanship. The study concludes: "The personal commitment of a subject to an initial position motivates him to defend his choice by presenting all the information which supports his position. . . . Group search is stimulated in both extent and quality."[12] The groups observed were less successful problem solvers when solely concerned with "what is best for the group."

Shared volitions have emerged over centuries of interchange from partisan probing—gradually and with the participation at various levels of intensity of millions of people. Although a few social theorists bridle at such a conclusion, it is not a surprising one. Anthropologists tell us that norms have often developed from pragmatic efforts of people to solve their own problems, often from what we have labeled narrow partisanship.[13]

Indeed, both in anthropology and sociology a variety of interpretations explain the emergence of shared norms from partisan pursuits, just as in political philosophy concepts of the social contract

11. For further development and empirical detail, see Richard A. Smith, "Advocacy, Interpretation, and Influence in the U.S. Congress," *American Political Science Review* 78 (March 1984), pp. 47–49.
12. Joseph L. Bower, "The Role of Conflict in Economic Decision-Making Groups: Some Empirical Results," *Quarterly Journal of Economics* 79 (May, 1965), p. 273.
13. Elman Service, *Primitive Social Organization* (New York: Random House, 1971), pp. 41–45.

derive agreement from partisanship. For example: "Boundaries of rights, duties, and authority are . . . continually open to negotiation—with rules being created, broken, redefined, and elaborated . . . . It is cumulative individual deviations from a rule or norm that make possible the assertion of a new one."[14]

The shared terms and meanings that constitute a language are examples of how commonalities arise from the efforts of diverse persons to solve their own narrowly conceived problems, in this case, their problems of communication. "No individual or group of individuals ever sat down to plan the phonemic repertory of English or French or Kwakiutl."[15] An appreciation of the possibility that common norms or shared volitions can emerge from partisan self-interest rather than an intent to cooperate to discover a common good ranges from at least a hint of the possibility in Hume's comments on the origins of "agreement and convention" to contemporary applications of game theory to demonstrate the logic of the derivation of agreements from self-interest.[16]

Even for establishing questions of fact, narrow partisanship is not to be generally disdained. The approach to truth, in the words of John Stuart Mill, "has to be made by the rough process of a struggle between combatants fighting under hostile banners."[17] For analysis of specific issues, the merits of partisan probing in many circumstances have been widely recognized. An official in and scholarly observer of the U.S. Department of Defense writes that by "an adversary proceeding between opponents who each had a serious and genuine interest in proving their point (a procedure as old as Anglo-Saxon law) . . . the Secretary of Defense arrived at an answer to the question of how he could believe anybody's calculations."[18]

Probing, then, cannot carry people all the way to decisions or solutions on social problems. For conflict resolutions in particular, it has to be supplemented by the imposition of solutions, especially by the

14. Roger Keesing and Felix Keesing, *New Perspectives in Cultural Anthropology* (New York: Holt, Rinehart and Winston, 1971), p. 232.

15. Marvin Harris, *Culture, Man and Nature* (New York: Crowell, 1971), p. 134.

16. David Hume, *A Treatise on Human Nature*, ed. L. A. SelbyBigge (1740; Oxford: Clarendon Press, 1978), p. 490; and Robert Axelrod, *The Evolution of Cooperation* (New York: Basic Books, 1984).

17. John Stuart Mill, *On Liberty* (1859; New York: Appleton-Century-Crofts 1947), p. 47.

18. Alain C. Enthoven, "Analysis, Judgment and Computers," *Business Horizons* 12 (August 1969), p. 33.

state. Even so, probably most conflict resolution is achieved through the multiple interchange of people in a society, of which interchange probing is a part. The state is not to be seen exclusively or even primarily as a residual conflict resolver, for it is also a creator of conflicts and a fundamental formative influence on probing as well. Whatever the process of conflict resolution—state or not—people choose among or mix various roles; and in so doing they are always partisan in their inquiry. Their partisanship is both necessary and helpful to social problem solving, even if its narrower forms often are not.

PART II

Impaired Inquiry

Chapter 5

Impaired Probing

In some ways, the quality of inquiry appears to be improving. People are credited with an active "attempt to understand their social environment and their own place in it."[1] Their beliefs and volitions undergo what appear to be rational changes.[2] Even a generation ago, they were on some counts already probing more skillfully than did their parents.[3] At least some of them in all the democracies take advantage of "opportunities to discuss and debate political and social issues."[4] Systematic survey work in Western Europe and North America strongly suggests that "an increasingly

1. James R. Kluegel and Eliot R. Smith, "Beliefs about Stratification," *Annual Review of Sociology* 7 (1981). See also Rand Spiro, "Understanding and Remembering Verbal Information," in Spencer A. Ward and Linda J. Reed, *Knowledge Structure and Use* (Philadelphia: Temple University Press, 1983).

2. M. Kent Jennings and Richard G. Niemi, *Generations and Politics* (Princeton: Princeton University Press, 1981), pp. 380–382.

3. Robert E. Lane, "The Decline of Politics and Ideology in a Knowledgeable Society," *American Sociological Review* 31 (October 1966).

4. Gabriel Almond and Sidney Verba, *The Civic Culture* (Princeton: Princeton University Press, 1963), pp. 333–334.

large proportion of the public is coming to have sufficient interest and understanding of national and international politics to participate in decision making at this level."[5] In as short a period as 1950 to 1965, entry into institutions of higher education doubled in the U.S., more than doubled in West Germany, and tripled in France.[6] Survey research also indicates that people now take more critical or skeptical attitudes toward government and other institutions, again a significant change in as short a period as fifteen years and suggestive of improved policy.[7] Some social scientists believe that, even if functionaries need higher levels of capacity to probe, ordinary citizens can probe well enough to play their limited roles in social problem solving with only minimal probing.[8]

Yet we are all imperfect or defective investigators.[9] "Incompetent," says a contemporary political scientist who has examined a variety of studies of how people choose among candidates and parties.[10] Ordinary citizens possess only "inches of facts,"[11] prove incapable of logical inferences on complex personal and social issues,[12] lack a firm understanding of political abstractions,[13] and retreat from

5. Ronald Inglehart, *The Silent Revolution* (Princeton: Princeton University Press, 1977), pg. 3.

6. Other specific developments are suggestive of improvements in the prospects for probing: for example, the 1965 Vatican Council's Declaration of Religious Liberty and the growing independence from the Vatican of the U.S. bishops as a collectivity. See James Reichley, *Religion in American Public Life* (Washington, D.C.: Brookings Institution, 1985), pp. 289ff.

7. *Ibid.*, pp. 14–17. On competence in probing, often debated with respect to voters' competence to acquire and organize information, see the discussion of possible gains in John C. Pierce and John L. Sullivan, "An Overview of the American Electorate," in Pierce and Sullivan, eds., *The Electorate Reconsidered* (Beverly Hills, Calif.: Sage, 1980); reconsiderations of evidence in W. Lance Bennett, *The Political Mind and the Political Environment* (Lexington, Mass.: Lexington Books, 1975), esp. chap. 1; W. Russell Neuman, *The Paradox of Mass Politics* (Cambridge: Harvard University Press, 1986); and allegations of decline in Paul E. Corcoran, *Political Language and Rhetoric* (St. Lucia, Queensland: University of Queensland Press, 1979).

8. A widely circulating hypothesis since its statement in Pendleton Herring, *The Politics of Democracy* (New York: Rinehart and Company, 1940); and Bernard R. Berelson, Paul F. Lazarsfeld, and William N. McPhee, *Voting* (Chicago: University of Chicago Press, 1954), chap. 14.

9. For an overview of the political ignorance of U.S. citizens, for example, see Robert S. Erickson, Norman R. Luttbeg, and Kent L. Tedin, *American Public Opinion*, 2d ed. (New York: Wiley, 1980).

10. Giovanni Sartori, *Democratic Theory* (New York: Praeger, 1965), p. 78.

11. Aaron Wildavsky, "Choosing Preferences by Constructing Institutions," *American Political Science Review* 81 (March 1987), p. 8.

12. Richard E. Nisbett and Lee Ross, *Human Inference* (Englewood Cliffs, N.J.: Prentice-Hall, 1980).

13. Henry Brady and Paul Sniderman, "Attitude Attribution," *American Political Science Review* 79 (December 1985).

probing in apathy, among many other shortcomings. They do not approach qualities of inquiry widely regarded as necessary to rational problem solving and perhaps even necessary to the long-term survival of democracy.

The phenomenon of defective thinking about social problems by all categories of people has loomed large enough to stimulate many kinds of studies of certain aspects of it, some rooted in Marx:[14] among others, sociological studies of institutionalized social indoctrination of schoolchildren by their teachers or of both children and adults by the media;[15] and psychological studies of ignorance, bias, stubbornness, cognitive apathy, rigidity, and illogic.[16] Of such cognitive studies, some look for biologically imprinted patterns in thinking,[17] others for effects on thinking of personality differences,[18] and others for the effects of differences in attributes like age and gender.[19] Still another style of study—there are more than can be mentioned—has emerged from the study of power achieved through bending the mind rather than controlling behavior directly.[20]

IMPAIRMENT AS SOCIALLY CAUSED DEFECTS IN PROBING

Biology limits the human capacity to probe. It also programs everyone to indulge in various "irrationalities" for various reasons, including the pleasures of doing so. Although people devise ways to reduce the effects of biological limits on brain capacity—for example, paper and pencil, electronic computation, and the construction of theories to organize information—they never wholly override them.

14. At various distances from him in substance or method: Herbert Marcuse, *One-Dimensional Man* (Boston: Beacon Press, 1966); Nicholas Abercrombie, *Class Structure and Knowledge* (Oxford: Basil Blackwell, 1980); R. W. Connell, *Ruling Class, Ruling Culture* (Cambridge: Cambridge University Press, 1977); James C. Scott, *The Moral Economy of the Peasant* (New Haven: Yale University Press, 1976); Richard Sennett and Jonathan Cobb, *The Hidden Injuries of Class* (New York: Vintage, 1972).

15. A number of supporting studies are cited in chaps. 6 and 7.

16. Howard Margolis, *Patterns, Thinking, and Cognition* (Chicago: University of Chicago Press, 1987); and David Faust, *The Limits of Scientific Reasoning* (Minneapolis: University of Minneapolis Press, 1984), chap. 2.

17. For example, Richard Nisbett and Lee Ross, *Human Inference* (Englewood Cliffs, N.J.: Prentice-Hall, 1980); and Daniel Kahneman, Paul Slovic, and Amos Tversky, *Judgment under Uncertainty* (Cambridge: Cambridge University Press, 1982).

18. For example, Leon Festinger, *A Theory of Cognitive Dissonance* (Stanford, Calif.: Stanford University Press, 1957).

19. For example, many cognitive studies in Richard R. Lau and David O. Sears, eds., *Political Cognition* (Hillsdale, N.J.: Lawrence Erlbaum Associates, 1986).

20. Steven Lukes, *Power—A Radical View* (London: Macmillan, 1974); and John Gaventa, *Power and Powerlessness* (Urbana: University of Illinois Press, 1980).

If biologically imprinted defects call for some degree of acceptance or resignation, another enormous category of defects permits or requires a different response: the category of socially caused or exacerbated defects. Just as positive capacities for inquiry are socially formed, so also are many defects. Society gives and society takes away. Society teaches people to read, then circulates misinformation to them; or adults provide children with schooling, then use the classroom to indoctrinate them. Social influences may impair a specific investigation, as when a relevant piece of information is withheld, or impair a continuing capacity to investigate, as in illiteracy or in the intimidations of a bureaucrat by a superior who threatens to retard his advancement.

Socially caused incompetence in inquiry—yours and mine, that of ordinary people, but also of functionaries and even of the learned—has long been lamented: Plato's allegory of the shadows in the caves, Bacon's four "idols"; Kant's "tutelage" and Locke's "insinuations" on the mind;[21] Adam Smith's concern about the stultification of the human mind in the work environment of the factory;[22] Tocqueville's finding, when speaking of America, less "true independence of mind and freedom of discussion" than in any other country he knew;[23] Marx's "false consciousness"; Schumpeter's "manufactured will" in politics;[24] Schattschneider's wry comment that "the heavenly chorus sings with a strong upperclass accent";[24] and Habermas's "distorted communication."[26]

These and other commentators on the phenomenon have also observed that people do not acknowledge and often explicitly deny the severity of their impairment. If in the democracies people are tempted to claim that their legal freedoms protect them from impairment, Rousseau observed that "there is no subjugation so perfect as that which keeps the appearance of freedom. Thus the will itself is held captive."[27] And a distinguished contemporary scientist observes of

21. Neal Wood, *The Politics of Locke's Philosophy* (Berkeley: University of California Press, 1983), p. 95.
22. Adam Smith, *The Wealth of Nations* (1776; Homewood, Ill.: Richard D. Irwin, 1963), vol. 2, p. 284.
23. *Democracy in America* (1835–40; New York: Schocken, 1972), vol. 2, p. 310.
24. Joseph A. Schumpeter, *Capitalism, Socialism and Democracy*, 3d ed. (New York: Harper and Row, 1962), p. 263.
25. E. E. Schattschneider, *The Semi-Sovereign People* (New York: Holt, Rinehart and Winston, 1960), p. 35.
26. Jürgen Habermas, *Knowledge and Human Interest* (Boston: Beacon, 1971), esp. chaps. 3 and 9.
27. Jean-Jacques Rousseau, *Emile*, trans. Allan Bloom (New York: Basic Books, 1979), p. 120.

Americans that they "were free to say what they think, because they did not think what they were not free to say."[28] Conceding some impairing influences, people rarely go so far as to consider that impairment may cripple every culture.

A finding of impairment assumes—and I shall not argue the point—that there exists a real world "out there" even if no mind grasps it well. It also assumes that there are more and less valid methods of grasping it and that many minds, though fallible, have some knowledge of the difference between valid and impaired methods. However insufficiently defined, the valid methods include empirical observation, verification through interpersonal agreement, logic, and endless challenge and response. In the hands of professional investigators, these methods, practiced with greatly more care than by laymen, take the label of "the scientific method"; but the scientific method itself lacks precise definitions, undergoes historical change, and may itself on at least some points constitute a kind of impaired thinking. And even if "the scientific method" helps to define impaired probing by contrast, it cannot be identified with any one narrowed concept of science, such as logical empiricism.[29]

Hence, the concept of an impairing influence and a consequent impairment of inquiry promises great difficulties in analysis. One presumes that suppression of information or deliberate misrepresentation obstructs inquiry. But they do not always do so; or, alternatively, they do not always make a bad situation worse and may on some accounts improve it. A lie may supplant even more severely impairing misinformation. The escape from home into the ostensibly impairing influences of military training may, on balance, liberate someone whose mind has previously been intimidated by oppressive parents. Overload of information or analytic tasks will in some circumstances obstruct rather than improve an investigation. To put the last point in larger perspective, to think clearly about any question requires one to take a vast set of beliefs, attitudes, and values for granted—at least for the time being. Hence, too much inquiry, as well as too much information, disables.

28. Leo Szilard, *The Voice of the Turtle* (New York: Simon and Shuster, 1961), p. 42.

29. If an anthropologist wishes to persuade me that I am espousing without argument a culture-bound set of concepts of inquiry and knowledge from which some non-Western cultures would dissent, I shall not stop to argue. I would also note that the literature of anthropology that asserts the relativism of standards of inquiry, rationality, and knowledge is in practice itself committed to the same culture-bound set.

On relativism and its opponents, see Martin Hollis and Steven Lukes, eds., *Rationality and Relativism* (Cambridge, Mass: MIT Press, 1982); and Robin Horton and Ruth Finnegan, eds., *Modes of Thought* (London: Faber and Faber, 1973).

As children grow, they pick up necessary concepts that on some counts obstruct their thinking—clumsy concepts like evil, democracy, conflict, or success. Yet they cannot do without them. No one—child or adult—knows the surrounding world except through constructed images, and all contain elements of impairment.

> The features of the social image that everyone seems to agree to are: (1) It is expressed in symbols (mostly verbal) and their accompanying emotional affects; (2) it is often implicit and always incompletely articulated in linguistic form; (3) it is systematically instilled in each generation through various agencies of socialization and education; (4) it is an ordering device, ensuring common meanings and responses by means of stereotypical metaphors, models, myths, or other symbolic devices; (5) it is most difficult to recognize as something other than reality or experience; (6) it is impossible to test or evaluate as well as difficult to question; (7) it is anonymously authored; and (8) its absence would mean idiocy or insanity.[30]

Moreover, as I have already noted in chapter 3, not even in the course of a lifetime does anyone—citizen or functionary—significantly examine every possible object to which inquiry might hypothetically be applied. "Thinking is in the interstices of habit," wrote John Dewey.[31] How much probing of what kind a person can do or ought to do, no one very well knows. The question itself needs probing.

In assessing the scope of socially caused defects in inquiry, one must allow room for the alternative idea that people impair themselves. Quite aside from bio-imprinted impairments, they choose, for example, not to probe some issues, to probe some impulsively or whimsically rather than thoughtfully, or to indulge themselves in wishful thinking. The idea of self impairment is a valid one; yet because we are all socially formed, how we impair ourselves is in itself in large part socially determined. It is socially caused defects in probing that will occupy these pages, though this is not to deny biological impairment or the troublesome category of self-impairment.

No one can describe an ideal bicycle or explain how to classify or rank all bicycles with respect to their approximation to an ideal, or how to specify systematically all the features through which a bicycle comes closer to or remains more distant from an ideal. Often, howev-

30. Larry D. Spence, *The Politics of Social Knowledge* (University Park: Pennsylvania State University Press, 1978), p. 229.
31. *The Public and Its Problems* (New York: Holt, 1927), p. 160.

er, one can point to defects that make it unacceptable—for example, the rims are so warped that the wheels will not turn. So also with evaluation of impairing influences and consequent impairment. Evaluation most fruitfully forswears clarifying an ideal of nonimpairment or nonobstructive impairment to tackle the more modest task of identifying unacceptable impairments and circumstances. It cannot successfully pursue the question, say, of how much information of what kind a voter needs for his probing; but it can pursue the easier question of whether, say, systematic campaign misinformation designed to manipulate him results in an impairment.

Surely, some critics of this line of analysis will object, it must be acknowledged that societies cannot hold together—do not even constitute societies—without unifying shared attitudes and beliefs. The various influences on the mind here called impairing create the social bonds that make it possible for people to live together in peaceful order. I think it important to meet that allegation head-on at this point, although a fuller treatment of it waits for later chapters. Other than careless bald statement, there exist no findings, no formulated hypotheses, and no supporting argument or evidence (nor any persuasive common sense) alleging that all impairments serve such a purpose. The most that is claimed is that some do. Impairing influences constitute a broad phenomenon not limited to those that do. This study consequently pursues a fuller understanding of impairing influences and consequent impairments of probing or inquiry, subsequently returning to the question of which of various impairing influences or consequent impairments contribute to, or are indispensable for, social order, especially for a democratic order. I am never unmindful of many possible connections between impairments and social stability. But I do not allow those connections to stand in the way of a close look at the impairments and their sources.

When Weber describes the kind of rational man produced by money, markets, and capitalism, Herbert Marcuse alleges a "one-dimensional man," Jacques Ellul explains what technology is doing to the way people think, or Gramsci writes of hegemony, they too are discussing impairment. But they do so at a high-risk level of abstraction, generalization, and subjectivity in interpretation that invites an alternative method of inquiry that can challenge, amend, or supplement theirs. Fearful of analysis that flies very high, I take an alternative course: tracking impairment by looking, at a low level of abstraction, at how people influence each other in ways that obstruct probing, not to deny aggregative or system effects but to reduce the seduction of attractive abstractions. I pay a price for the gain intended; the analysis will not even attempt the richness of hypotheses and speculation of Gramsci, Ellul, Marcuse, and others.

Kinds of Impairing Influences

When I talk with my colleagues about impairment, they, not in the habit of using the term in this context, frequently shift to "indoctrination." But clearly, impairing influences are not limited to what is ordinarily called indoctrination. Some social scientists often reduce the scope of the phenomenon of impairing influences by identifying it only with indoctrination and then searching for sources of indoctrination only in deliberate attempts at "manipulation." Most of the phenomenon slips like water through their fingers. They miss impairing influences on children by well-intentioned parents who simply want their children to "fit in," those visited on schoolchildren by equally well intentioned teachers innocent of any awareness of "manipulation" who unwittingly teach children that some categories of questions are to be ruled out as disrespectful, and the confusions introduced into probing by an overwhelming flow of commercial messages that routinely rather than selectively offer a purchasable commodity, not some possible collective effort, as the solution to one after another of people's problems.[32]

The many ways in which people can impair each other's probing are so varied, so numerous, so complex—and so subject to alternative interpretations—as to escape satisfactory classification. They presumably include almost all of the ways in which people, for any reason, control or influence each other; and these too have so far escaped satisfactory classification. But some distinctions will quickly indicate the scope of impairing influences.

Impairments are both *deliberate* (censorship, some kinds of peer pressure, propaganda, police intimidation of dissenters, misrepresentations of sales promotion, political campaigning, among other examples) and *inadvertent* (some kinds of peer pressure, unintended misrepresentation, parental or school discipline that dampens the curiosity of children, among other examples).

They can employ either *word and symbol* (ceremonial oratory, propaganda, sales promotion, political campaigning, admonitions, slogans—and other instruments of what is often called indoctrination) or *deed* (social ostracism, threat of exile or incarceration, parental or

32. For an example, see Dennis Thompson, *The Democratic Citizen* (Cambridge: Cambridge University Press, 1970), p. 93. On the impairments of social scientists themselves, more is to be said in a later chapter.

school threat of discipline, invasion of the privacy of the mail, and telephone eavesdropping, among other examples).

They can *inculcate* (an ill-probed attitude, belief, or volition: for example, white supremacy, class war, capitalism, or socialism) or *obstruct or confuse* the forming of attitudes, beliefs, and volitions (governmental and corporate secrecy, false assurances from government officials, in broadcasting on public issues, fair-play norms that so carefully balance pros and cons as to obstruct reaching a conclusion, commercial and political huckstering that diverts attention from relevant issues to others, among other examples).

They include both positive acts or *commissions* (for example, censorship, intimidation, propaganda) and *omissions* (inadequacies in education or in the circulation of information, and failures of parental encouragement, among others).

Impairment through an Inadequate Competition of Ideas

Aristotle appreciated the contribution to social problem solving of contention among ideas. Of the thinking individual person, he wrote: "Each of them by himself may be of a good quality; but when they all come together it is possible that they may surpass—collectively and as a body, although not individually—the quality of the few best."[33] The idea reappears—among its many restatements—in liberal esteem for a contention among ideas, in Milton, Locke, and Mill, among others.[34] In nineteenth- and early to middle twentieth-century liberal democratic thought, democracy is often proposed as a design for improved probing (by other names), or, in the language of the times, as a "competition of ideas" or as "government by discussion," or as a "free market in ideas."[35] Later democratic theory brought political leadership, especially leaders of groups, more prominently

33. Ernest Barker, ed., *The Politics of Aristotle* (New York: Oxford University Press, 1962), p. 123.

34. Although it appears that many "liberals" have applauded such a competition to obscure their own acceptance of severe restrictions on it. See Benjamin Ginsberg, *The Captive Public* (New York: Basic Books, 1986), chap. 4.

35. For examples of use of these concepts and the liberal emphasis on interaction, see J. S. Mill, *On Liberty*; Walter Bagehot, *Physics and Politics* (New York: Collier, 1900), p. 158; James Bryce, *The American Commonwealth*, vol. 2 (London: Macmillan, 1888), p. 368; John Dewey, *The Public and Its Problems* (New York: Holt, 1927), p. 208; Walter Lippmann, *Essays in the Public Philosophy* (Boston: Little, Brown, 1955), pp. 124ff; Frank H. Knight, *Freedom and Reform* (New York: Harper and Brothers, 1947), pp. 190ff; Ernest Barker, *Social and Political Theory* (Oxford: Oxford University Press, 1951), p. 200; A. D. Lindsay, *Essentials of Democracy* (Oxford: Oxford University Press, 1929), pp. 34–50.

into the competition. Either way the theme persists: one can find the key to good problem solving, as well as good government in a democracy, in the interaction of mutually challenging minds.[36]

Because for some communications in our times, no voice except television's is loud enough, one can predict impaired probing when some of a set of rival ideas cannot win access to it. For other communications, impairment follows from the exclusion of certain ideas from the classroom. The daily repetition by American schoolchildren of "I pledge allegiance" to a government with "liberty and justice for all" leaves them perhaps forever impaired in capacity to probe an alternative; the desirability of bringing thoughtfulness or dissent rather than allegiance to one's role as a citizen. Any form of social inequality—whether in power or influence or in income and wealth—may impair the probing of everyone by permitting some messages to overwhelm or silence others: for example, the availability of funds to disseminate some ideas but not others.

Tracking Impairment

To understand impairment, one has to travel down both highways and byways. One has to reflect, for example, on implications of research that finds feelings of powerlessness, normlessness, self-estrangement, isolation, and meaninglessness, all presumably impairments, to be more pronounced among blue-collar than among white-collar workers, and inversely related to education and occupational status. Or research that has presented evidence, strong but not conclusive, that correlates low socioeconomic status—presumably an impairing influence—with a raised frequency of mental illness as an impairment.[37] Or research that finds higher levels of such feelings as powerlessness and self-estrangement not only at the very bottom of the scale but generally among the blue-collar employed, hence providing evidence that impairment caused by social inequalities constitutes a widely diffused phenomenon not limited to persons of conspicuous anomie or alienation.[38]

36. Giovanni Sartori, *Democratic Theory* (New York: Praeger, 1965), p. 75.
37. The research is reviewed with critical comment in Charles E. Hurst, *The Anatomy of Social Inequality* (St. Louis: C. V. Mosby Company, 1979), chap. 5. For an unusually thoughtful analysis of subtle class influences on individual autonomy with implicit consequences for impairment, see Julienne Ford, Douglas Young, and Steven Box, "Functional Autonomy, Role Distance, and Social Class," *British Journal of Sociology* 18 (December 1967).
38. At an extreme, is the impaired prober to be contrasted with the autonomous prober? Although some may find such a contrast useful, I do not want to have to make

In alleging a person's impairment, do I fall into the trap of claiming to know that person's mind better than that person does? No, nor can I probe for anyone better than one can for one's self. I assume only that an observer can point to a whole array of specific impairing influences, from false information through intimidations to brainwashing.

HISTORICAL IMPAIRMENT

The whole history of humankind reads in some large part as a history of impairment of inquiry: ignorance, superstition, barriers to inquiry, exile and execution of dissenters, the many intimidations of tyranny, illiteracy, the steady impositions of peer pressure, and the use of the media for propaganda, among many manifestations. This undeniable point invalidates the careless claim that contemporary attitudes, beliefs, values, and volitions are on the whole a rational product of a winnowing out process through which, over millennia and centuries, humankind comes to know what is true and valid. On some contemporary attitudes, beliefs, values, and volitions, there exists adequate confirming knowledge—people have learned that the earth is spherical, that some categories of people in authority can be removed through balloting, or that repression sometimes triggers violence. But countless other attitudes, beliefs, values, and volitions— as well as incompetences to probe—persist only because of the history of impairment through which humankind, or some segment of it, has passed: racial antagonisms are an example; so also the often simpleminded endorsements given by masses of people to their existing political and economic institutions. That the British endorse a parliamentary system while Americans endorse a presidential system testifies more to the inheritance of habits of thought than to their knowledge of the suitability of either system for either country.

That today's impairments are largely the consequence of earlier impairments often seems obvious: for example, ill-probed submissiveness to arbitrary authority "learned" from parents by each generation of children and then "taught" in their adult years to their children, over the course of a hundred generations. But the further

use of the questionable concept of an autonomous person. Regardless of how autonomous or socially influenced the mind is, we can distinguish in principle between some social influences that adversely affect probing and some that do not, of which some improve probing. Some influences do both.

proposition that from the effects of some impairing influences in earlier generations no one ever wholly escapes is less familiar.

If in the 1950s a government, fearful of appearing vulnerable to charges that it had carelessly endangered the health of many of its subjects, had suppressed information about the toxic effects of fallout from its atomic bomb testing, it would have impaired its affected but uninformed subjects in their capacities to cope with their own health problems. In addition, it would have deprived scientists of information that would have advanced their work. Only a generation later, when the suppressed information leaks out, can both popular thought and scientific work then engage in inquiry that otherwise could have been done many years earlier. The train of enlightenment forever runs behind. In the best of circumstances the train never reverses or runs off the track and it makes all the station stops. But it arrives at each stop late.

If enlightenment at best takes time, even when least encumbered, if it flows like a river fed by many tributaries, and if some gains in insight follow only when earlier insights make them possible, then retardation or blockage at any point will often guarantee that as many miles down the track as one can imagine, the train will run late. Today, at this late date, everyone may suffer more impairment on some counts—proceed less competently in probing—than, for example, if the church had not imposed its constraints on Galileo. Any person, even if of the highest intelligence and intellectual sophistication and even if extraordinarily informed, suffers from impairing influences that, however long ago, slowed the cumulation of knowledge in history, thus bequeathing less knowledge than might otherwise have been possible. Atilla and Saint Paul belong in the history of every person's impairment.

IMPAIRMENT IN SOCIALIZATION

While one can imagine people in a state of nature, very likely engaged in a "war of all against all," in the history of humankind people cohere in organized rule-regulated groups ranging in size from nuclear family or tribe to the nation-state. Each such groups becomes a "society." A question then arises: How does a mere collection of people come to be organized and maintained as a society? On the question of original organization, answers remain incomplete and disputed. But on the question of maintaining a society, the answer, useful though not wholly satisfactory, is something called socialization. Socialization means that each generation is taught a language, shared concepts, way of looking at the world, and a set of rules of the game that specify both the impermissible and the obligatory.

Regarding, as they do, socialization as necessary for the viability of society, many people see it as benign, often, for example, characterizing it as an educational process.[39] But societies "teach" ways of looking at the world not only by enlightening the new generation about life's many opportunities but by inducing or coercing the new generation not to consider some possibilities. They "teach" the rules of the game not solely by an illuminating instruction but by coercive enforcement that cuts off probing. In an anthropologist's words, socialization forges "shackles which bind and restrict and make it necessary that there be repression, suppression, and sublimation of basic impulses."[40] In short socialization proceeds in large part through impairing influences—for example, "censorship and deception that in turn promote ignorance."[41]

Convergences

Not all but much of socialization urges interpersonal likemindedness, conformism, or convergence in attitude, belief, value, and volition. In each society, because of socialization some ideas overwhelm or dominate others, relegating the others to infrequent probes or excluding them from discussion as inappropriate, irrelevant, even improper or immoral. Much socialization appears as "narrowing" or "conforming."[42] Socialization that produces convergences would seem to impair by undercutting the competition of ideas in addition to any other impairments it produces.

A convergence is a narrowed range of thought or attitude, sometime still wide, of variation in attitude, belief, value, or volition. Never or rarely does it approach a unanimity or a consensus. Given the conventions of identifying and classifying positions for survey re-

39. Some examples are in Diane Mitch Bush and Roberta G. Simmons, "Socialization Process over the Life Course," in Morris Rosenberg and Ralph H. Turner, eds., *Social Psychology* (New York: Basic Books, 1981), p. 135.

40. Florence Rockwood Kluckhohn and Fred L. Strodbeck, *Variations in Value Orientations* (Evanston, Ill.: Row, Peterson, 1961), p. 21.

On strong tendencies, however, for social scientists to underplay the impairing effects of socialization in their preoccupation with its benign effects, see the discussion and citations below in chapter 12, "Professional Impairment."

41. Larry Spence, *The Politics of Social Knowledge* (University Park: Pennsylvania State University Press, 1978), p. 60.

42. Edward Zigler and Irvin L. Child, "Socialization," in G. Lindsay and E. Aronson, eds., *Handbook of Social Psychology*, 1st ed. (Reading, Mass.: Addison-Wesley, 1969), vol. 3, pp. 451, 474.

search,[43] only infrequently in a convergence does agreement on any one position in a nation's population rise as high as 80 percent. Ordinarily, on no one position will agreement rise higher than around 50 percent, and it will often fall short of that. Some positions, however, will have no advocates at all or so few as to appear as only occasional eccentrics; the convergence lies in their rejection.

Convergence or conformity in attitude, belief, values, and volitions appears as a fundamental phenomenon in all societies. "The life-history of the individual is first and foremost an accommodation to the patterns and standards traditionally handed down in his community. From the moment of his birth the customs into which he is born shape his experience and behavior. By the time he can talk, he is the little creature of his culture, and by the time he is grown and able to take part in its activities, its habits are his habits, its beliefs his beliefs, its impossibilities his impossibilities."[44]

Convergences, especially evident in religious belief and attitude, appear in a variety of areas: dress, food, politics, family, and child care, as well as in ideas about individual responsibility and fault, rules for social interchange, and work ethic, among many others. Some societies believe in arranged marriages, others not. Some believe in science, others less so; some in honoring promises and contracts, others less so. In each society or group of societies, commitment, thought, and discussion fall largely within a characteristic narrowed or convergent range. In political science and political sociology, recent decades have seen much research on the distinctive political cultures of various societies.[45]

Some further illustrations: In the West, an agreement on equality as an abstract undefined value and at the same time a nearly unanimous rejection of approximations to equality of income and wealth.[46] In the West again, substantial agreement that endorses in-

43. The degree of agreement depends of course on how alternative positions are perceived by those expressing opinions. Unanimity on the desirability, say, of lower taxes is consistent with a 50-50 split on the desirability of tax reductions that would eliminate funding of specified governmental services.

44. Ruth Benedict, *Patterns of Culture* (1934; Boston: Houghton Mifflin, 1961), pp. 2f.

45. For example, Gabriel Almond and Sidney Verba, *The Civic Culture* (Princeton: Princeton University Press, 1963) and Sidney Verba, Norman H. Nie, and Jae-On Kim, *Participation and Political Equality* (Cambridge: Cambridge University Press, 1978).

46. Sidney Verba, *Elites and the Idea of Equality* (Cambridge: Harvard University Press, 1987). On the U.S., Herbert McClosky and John Zaller, *The American Ethos*, (Cambridge: Harvard University Press, 1984), chap. 3; and Sidney Verba and Gary R. Orren, *Equality in America* (Cambridge: Harvard University Press, 1985), chap. 8.

heritance of wealth and finds status differences to be the "natural order" of things.[47] Also agreement on the nuclear family, fraying at the edges in some societies. Many of the convergences are remarkable. A study of the U.K. discloses that 69 percent of respondents "claim never to have considered a law unjust or harmful"! And a convergence on political docility is strongly suggested by the finding, in the same study, that two-thirds of respondents had never gone beyond voting to any other kind of political activity, such as communicating with an elected or appointed official, signing a petition, or writing to a newspaper.[48]

In the U.S., interview respondents show such attitudes and beliefs as a hostility to socialism; endorsement of competitive personal relations; belief that freedom depends on private enterprise; and "'private' values, as distinguished from social-group, political, or religious-moral values."[49] The expressed agreements, sometimes embracing 90 percent of respondents, lead to such conclusions by students of the American ethos as "Most public debate in America . . . takes place within a relatively restricted segment of the ideological spectrum."[50] The existence of forty thousand units of local government in the U.S. might seem to promise the wide variety of inquiries and a vigorous competition of ideas. But their more than forty thousand probes fall within the "relatively restricted segment."

Abroad, in the democracies, the range of thought and discussion broadens. Yet characteristic narrowness appears in each political culture. A forty-country study finds, for example, characteristic national patterns in each with respect to beliefs and attitudes about inequality, power, hierarchy, and individualism, among other differences.[51] A ten-nation study of civic education in the schools discloses "striking differences" between countries in political attitudes.[52] A number of studies have shown that modal attitudes and beliefs about

47. For a case in point, see Sherry Cable, "Attributional Processes and Alienation," *Political Psychology* 9 (March 1988).

48. Roger Jewell and Colin Airey, *British Social Attitudes: The 1984 Report* (Aldershot, England: Gower, 1984), p. 21.

49. Gabriel Almond, *American People and Foreign Policy* (New York: Harcourt, Brace, 1950), p. 9. See also Calvin F. Exoo, ed., *Democracy Upside Down* (New York: Praeger, 1987), chap. 1.

50. Herbert McClosky and John Zaller, *The American Ethos* (Cambridge: Harvard University Press, 1984), p. 186.

51. Geert Hofstede, *Culture's Consequences* (Beverly Hills, Calif.: Sage, 1980), pp. 119, 176, 238, 294, and passim.

52. Judith V. Torney, A. N. Oppenheim, and Russel F. Farnen, *Civic Education in Ten Countries* (New York: Wiley, 1975), p. 12 and passim. See also International Studies of Values in Politics, *Values and the Active Community* (New York: Free Press, 1971).

authority of most citizens vary from nation to nation.[53] Survey research finds differences between Australians, West Germans, and Swiss, on one hand, and Americans, Britons, Finns, and Italians on the other with respect to their regard for the right to demonstrate or the right to free assembly.[54] The range over which the question, say, of deference to authority is probed in Iran does not include questions that such probing raises in Italy; nor does Italian probing of the question raise the range of questions probed in Iran. The same holds true for a comparison of probing, say, of the merits of corporatism in the U.K. and Sweden, given their many relevant differences in political attitudes and beliefs.

Societies do not practice a universal general consensus or agreement. Convergence operates selectively. If some abstract, deep-rooted values command near universal assent,[55] hundreds of questions posed by survey research to the populations of dozens of countries show dissension on thousands of social issues.[56] Nor do democratic societies necessarily share as full an agreement as envisaged in Gramsci's hegemony of ideas. They may do so, but such a claim is not necessary for present purposes. Nor is a "dominant ideology" claimed for each democratic society. Again, such an ideology may exist on some beliefs or attitudes, depending on the definitions of "dominant" and "ideology"; but by almost any of the preferred definitions a "dominant ideology" seems too strong a concept for Western democratic societies.[57] For present purposes, the claim goes no further than that discussion and thought fall within a narrowed range, the consequent narrowness of thought impairing by undermining a competition of ideas.

53. Alex Inkeles and Daniel J. Levinson, "National Character," in Gardner Lindzey and Elliot Aronson, eds., *Handbook of Social Psychology* (Reading, Mass.: Addison-Wesley, 1969), vol. 4, pp. 448–451. See the same on other national differences. See also Dean Peabody, *National Characteristics* (Cambridge: Cambridge University Press, 1985).

54. Edward N. Muller, Pertti Personen, and Thomas O. Jukan, "Support for the Freedom of Assembly in Western Democracies," *European Journal of Political Research* 8 (September 1980), pp. 267f.

55. For a list, see P. H. Partridge, *Consent and Consensus* (New York: Praeger, 1971), pp. 125f.

56. For detail on U.S. dissension, see Herbert McClosky and John Zaller, *The American Ethos* (Cambridge: Harvard University Press, 1984). On Italy, Joseph LaPalombara, "Italy: Fragmentation, Isolation, and Alienation," in Lucien W. Pye and Sidney Verba, eds., *Political Culture and Political Development* (Princeton: Princeton University Press, 1965). Also Richard M. Coughlin, "Social Policy and Ideology: Public Opinion in Eight Rich Nations," in Richard F. Tomasson, ed., *Comparitive Social Research*, vol. 2, (Greenwich, Conn.: JAI Press 1979).

57. On hegemony of ideas and the dominant ideology thesis, see Nicholas Abercrombie, Stephen Hill, and Bryan S. Turner, *The Dominant Ideology Thesis* (London

Narrowness in thought and attitude do not become evident exclusively in constrained, well-formed opinions but also in incapacities to think about some issues, such as might follow from obfuscating communications about them. A survey researcher reports from his study of American attitudes and beliefs on civil liberties, presumably an issue of importance, that the polls suggest that there is no "attitude about" or "commitment to" or "hostility toward" civil liberties one way or the other.[58] Retreats from probing by "burned-out" activists provides another example.[59]

Pseudoconvergences

Discussion often suffers from the constraint of pseudoconvergences, that is, prestigious or dominating ideas that constrain discourse independently of any genuine belief in them. Not to be confused with genuine convergences, they nevertheless display another kind of impairing influence. Some expressed attitudes, beliefs, or values become influential because they are regarded as commanding wide agreement, to the degree that one risks isolation or censure in challenging them. In many circumstances, especially in communications to mass audiences, one does not deny that one's society guarantees "equal justice under the law," despite palpable evidence that no society in fact does so. Even in one's own thinking, one may defer to the presumed convergence, accepting the burden that it places on the line of inquiry.[60] A corollary is that persons well situated to reach audiences can circulate expressions of attitude, belief, and value that may be influential even if no one, not even the source of the messages, ever comes to believe them. A great deal of public rhetoric, alleging society's achievements in liberty, justice, equality, and the like appears to have originated with people who did not believe their own disseminated claims.

and Boston: Allen & Unwin, 1980); T. J. Jackson Lears, "The Concept of Cultural Hegemony," *American Historical Review* 90 (June 1985); Goran Therborn, "The New Questions of Subjectivity," *New Left Review* 143 (January–February 1984); and C. A. Rootes, "The Dominant Ideology Thesis and Its Critics," *Sociology* 15 (August 1981).

58. John Mueller, "Trends in Political Tolerance," *Public Opinion Quarterly* 52 (Spring 1988), p. 22.

59. Stephen A. Kent, "Puritan Radicalism and the New Religious Movements," in Richard F. Tomasson, ed., *Comparative Social Research* 10 (Greenwich, Conn.: JAI Press, 1987), p. 21 and passim.

60. How discussion is regulated by each participant's perception of what others think and how these perceptions are often mistaken are explored at length in Elizabeth Noelle-Neumann, *The Spiral of Science* (Chicago: University of Chicago Press, 1984); James M. Fields and Howard Schuman, "Public Beliefs about the Beliefs of the Public,"

Pitfalls

In a too close association of convergences with socialization, ordinary people, political oratory, and at least some social scientists often fall into the same few pitfalls. To begin with, in varying degrees of sophistication, they deprecate the impairing effects of the convergences by seeing them as no more than indicators of a society's distinctive culture. That ploy transforms a disturbing phenomenon—narrowness of thought—into a reassuring one. But that each society possesses a distinctive culture constitutes no denial of narrowness and consequent impairment. Its distinctiveness is in fact nothing other than its distinctive narrowness, its distinctive pattern of impairment, a conclusion anything but reassuring.

They also deprecate, as already noted, the impairing effects of convergent attitudes and thought by dismissing them as a necessary price to pay for socialization and the social stability made possible by it. Social peace—and in the democracies, the viability of democracy—require, they say, likemindedness through socialization. They forget to ask how high the price may be. Assuming that likemindedness or narrowness supports social stability and democracy (which may or may not be the case), does the conclusion follow that only a severely impaired population can maintain an orderly or democratic society? The implications of impairment on this point loom great indeed. Democracy, it would appear, must forever operate under a low ceiling of competence, the price of democracy being its own incompetence.

They also incorrectly assume that impairing conformities or convergences can be credited with socializing members of society into ways of living together peaceably and democratically. But a convergence, say, on the inferiority of blacks does not necessarily serve either social stability or democracy. Clearly, as already noted, only some convergences do so, and others do not, the latter perhaps serving no purpose at all other than the impairment of those who share the convergence. On this count alone, the impairment of probing deserves the most careful study: what kinds of convergences under

Public Opinion Quarterly 40 (Winter 1976–77); and D. Garth Taylor, "Pluralist Ignorance and the Spiral of Silence," *Public Opinion Quarterly* 46 (Fall 1982). See also Karl Popper on the distinction between opinion as a subjective phenomenon and an "opinion" that circulates in some expressed and objective form, independently of the possibility that it exists in no mind as a subjective opinion. Such a distinction lies in his discussion of "three worlds" (*Objective Knowledge* [Oxford: Clarendon Press, 1972], p. 153).

what circumstances offer no aid to, and even perhaps obstruct, social stability and democracy?

Assume for the moment that only certain convergences aid stability and democracy. Societies then face the need for a trade-off; they need impairing convergences to maintain stability and democracy, but few enough to leave their citizens and functionaries competent to solve social problems. The fourth pitfall lies in the assumption that a society already operates in the vicinity of a defensible trade-off. If they have deprecated the impairing effects of convergences on the grounds that at least some are necessary, they do not know the magnitude of what they are trading and have no reason to believe that any existing trade-off is defensible.

For all these reasons, the impairments of probing, especially those of convergent or conformist thought, require meticulous examination, an examination on constant guard against smothering an acknowledgment of the adverse effects of convergences with assurances of the benignity of socialization. This group of chapters will continue to examine the severity and character of impairment. Only later, once the magnitude and character of impairment have been outlined, shall I turn explicitly to the question of what kind and degree of impairment ensure social stability and democracy, a question that can hardly be competently explored until then.

CHAPTER 6

Elite and Other Advantaged Sources of Impairing Influences

Five big but secure steps will quickly cover a great deal of ground to reach a major, even if familiar, thesis about impairment.

Understanding the social world depends on communication and other interchange. I take it as undeniable that what people think about the social world—belief, attitude, value, and volition—derives from social interchange far more than from direct observation. If you can directly observe that you have just lost your job, your understanding of unemployment will nevertheless derive largely from words and other interchanges. How many people are out of work, why they were discharged, what prospects they have for reemployment, whether only the one industry or the entire economy is affected—for answers to these questions you depend almost entirely on other people, including acquaintances, journalists, and other people who reach you through press and broadcasting.

Most of the social world is too far away for anyone to observe much of it. Each person can see, listen to, and touch only a small part of it. Its complexities also resist direct observation. Even social scientists find direct observation laborious and difficult, hence each specializes to no more than a few points of observation and sometimes none at all. No single economist can, for example, observe the causes of unemployment but instead pieces together an explanation in interchange with others, each testing by direct observation at most a few of the propositions they exchange with each other. While the economist and I may both claim that we observe the social world when we look at statistics about it, unless we ourselves observe and tabulate the items to be counted, both of us in fact draw our understanding from what others tell us.

Hence, everyone's volitions with respect to such issues as equality and inequality, democracy, private enterprise, the nuclear family, authority, cooperation, and honesty derive from social interchanges beginning in infancy. An advocate of democracy never directly observes more than small aspects of it, cannot possibly observe in any direct way the system as a whole, cannot make observations sufficient to test an endorsement of it, and consequently depends heavily throughout on incoming messages.

One is not puzzled, then, that research finds a person's political attitudes and voting less affected by experienced circumstances than by customary acceptance of interpretations. An unemployed person does not much differ from an employed person in judgments about the fairness of rewards or "more general concepts of the operation of the social world." On complex and abstract issues of this kind, what people directly experience cannot strongly compete with what they read and hear.[1]

Interchanges through which people form an understanding of the social world include verbal communications in all forms, both true and false, but also symbolic interchanges. A pat on the back at the right moment speaks as loudly and clearly as words. Or intimidations will alter—very likely reduce—one's understanding. The interchanges that give each person an understanding of the social world include, consequently, both educating or enlightening communications and all the kinds of impairing influences summarized in the schema in the preceding chapter. As noted there, any method by which one or more persons control one or more other persons is a method, intended or not, of altering the latter's understanding of the social world.[2]

1. See Kay Lehman Schlozman and Sidney Verba, *Insult to Injury* (Cambridge: Harvard University Press, 1979), pp. 142, 144, 355n.
2. Here is an opportunity to try to falsify my analysis: show that what people read and hear is not a major determinant of their attitudes and beliefs. Show that, though people send messages, people rarely receive them or are influenced by them.

People enter into interchanges in order to control others. I take it as also undeniable that when people enter into interchanges, only in limited circumstances do they do so in order to enlighten others. Teachers often do so in the discharge of their professional obligations. Friends will often offer helpful information to each other. Physicians, lawyers, and other experts provide helpful specialized knowledge. Typically, however, one communicates with others and enters into other interchanges with them in order to exercise control over them. Parents induce children to behave. One seeks help from a friend or tries to talk a friend into doing something one wants him to do. Business managers and advertisers tend to induce people to buy products; party spokesmen and political candidates, to win their votes; priests and pastors, to regulate their conduct. The most frequent purpose of entering into an interchange is to alter the behavior of others, not to educate or enlighten them. If sometimes enlightenment offers the best way to alter someone else's behavior, the world-be controller will subordinate it or sacrifice it to the intention to control. Even teachers commonly fall into controlling or manipulative communications in teaching children beliefs thought necessary, whether true or not, for their proper socialization, for in all the democracies the schools play a major role not only in education but in socialization.[3]

Interchange is consequently impairing. Because communicative and other interchanges intend control rather than enlightenment, almost all interchanges result in some impairment of probing. They may—often will—on some points enlighten, but simultaneously they carry a load of impairing influences. Given the intention to control, incentives to suppress information, dissemble, distort, and obfuscate play havoc with the truth content, validity, and potential for enlightenment of communication and other interchanges.

Everyone practices, even if constrained by some standards of honesty, silences, misrepresentations, equivocations, and distortions in order to persuade others to do as one wants. The familiar phenom-

---

For all the dispute over the relative efficacy, say, in influencing children of media, family, and school messages, my line of argument on efficacy is as indicated: that our interpretations of the social world derive in very large part from communications about it rather than direct observation of it.

3. The contrast between the manipulative or controlling and the enlightening interchange intends to call attention to the frequency of the former relative to the latter, not to deny other kinds of interchanges. Some intend, for example, neither to educate nor to control but simply to entertain, as in much of the content of newspapers and magazines, broadcasts, and films. Of course, the offer of entertainment, as in broadcasting, often prefaces an attempt at control or is intertwined with an attempt.

enon of the white lie serves as an example. So also flattery, hints of promises one only half intends to keep, and proffered assurances that one's self does not believe. In sales promotion, the manipulative use of communication and other interchange joins diversion and obfuscation to misrepresentation. Communications from political functionaries to each other and to ordinary citizens similarly impair their probing. Political functionaries lie, dissemble, and suppress information whenever it is to their advantage to do so, constrained only by loose conventions of honesty and candor.

Consequently, everyone—citizen and functionary alike—builds his understanding of the social world on impairing interchanges. Clearly, people engage less in mutual edification than in mutual impairment. Social life consists in large part in an exchange of impairing influences.

A competition of ideas offers some escape from impairments. So bleak a picture raises the question of how societies could avoid self-destruction from their impairments. The answer is that, despite the frequency of mutual attempts to control through strategic silences, misrepresentations, and obfuscations, each person could be protected by engaging in a multiplicity of interchanges of conflicting intent that challenge each other. You or I could enjoy at least a limited opportunity to form a reasonable judgment not wholly crippled by impairment, say, about the prospects for global warming or improved day care facilities for infants because the many people and institutions that attempt to control us—say, to win us over to this or that organization, party, or candidate—dispute with each other and give us the benefits, unintended, of their challenges to each other. In short, our hopes for some degree of competence—some abatement of impairment—and society's comparable hope, lie in a competition of ideas. They lie less in the goodwill, honesty, or competence of those who communicate to me and otherwise engage with me, than in a possible rivalry and mutual challenge among them. This constitutes an even stronger case for a competition of ideas than the conventional one on which I drew in the preceding chapter.

The five steps just taken now pose the question of how rigorously ideas in fact compete. The proposed twofold answer: (1) *the advantages in communication and other influences of some participants severely weaken and narrow the competition of ideas,* (2) *through a predominance of ideas that defend the varied advantages of the advantaged.* A familiar double thesis that many people see as obviously true, by no means does it win unanimous assent. And the thesis identifies processes that work more strongly in some societies than in others: the U.S. and Norway, for example, fall near opposite poles of a continuum.

As already briefly noted in the preceding chapter, many social inequalities weaken or rig the competition of ideas. A task for this chapter is to begin to explore the distribution of advantages in communication and other interchange and the pattern of effects. Such a task constitutes, among other things, a return to convergences and conformism in thought also noted in the preceding chapter to see how they derive from advantages that permit some groups to urge their messages and other influences on others without sufficient challenge.

ADVANTAGED PARTICIPANTS

As for the first half of the thesis, in both intended and unintended indoctrinations, obfuscations, misrepresentations, as well as in the practice of controls that have the effect of sabotaging probing, parents proceed with undeniable advantages over children, teachers over pupils, and, in those many societies in which females defer to males, males over females. No less advantageously does a race, ethnic group, or elite impair if its wealth or political position gives it disproportionately large control over the mass communications media, the school system, the police, or any other major channel of communication or intimidation. In the war of words on racial inferiority, advocates of white supremacy have, the world over, more frequently and coercively asserted themselves than advocates of black supremacy.

Historically advantaged capacities to impair have been, for one reason or another, institutionalized, as in gender differences and as in medieval European collaboration between secular and religious elites to attempt control of soul, mind, and body. In our age the institutionalization of impairing influences allows not only the teacher but both the local pastor and the television evangelist a special position to enlighten or impair (or both) the probing of followers. So also executives of press and broadcasting. But perhaps the most highly influential appear in two elites, government officials and business managers; and among their methods is their use of the press and broadcasting.

As for the second part of the thesis, the stronger do not simply exploit the weaker. In the parent-child relation, for example, parental affection and ambition for the child curb while also energizing parental impairment of the child. On the one hand, they hold parents to some standards of honesty and disclosure in child rearing and forbid the wholly instrumental exploitation of the child as servant. On the other hand, they induce parents to inculcate in the child conformist habits, attitudes, and beliefs thought to be efficacious in the child's advancement in adult life: deference to authority, obedience, "good" behavior, acceptance of inequalities of various kinds, and approval of the existing social structure of which the family is a part. The teacher-pupil relation is much the same: teachers employ their advantages of influence and power to develop and mold the student in both admirable and questionable ways, the latter including the conformist habits cited above. Political and economic elites also bring their influences to bear in a mix of purposes. Indeed, elites sometimes foreswear any defense of their advantages over those with respect to whom they hold elite status—a transitory reformist or revolutionary elite, for example. Yet elites and other advantaged groups, with exceptions, invest a great deal of energy in the defending of their own advantages and the established institutions that protect them.

To some degree, their themes or messages of order, authority, work, political docility, delegation of decision-making responsibility, and inequalities in influence and reward make sense. Most informed and thoughtful people form qualified volitions for them. The impairment lies both in frequent misrepresentation, obfuscation, and intimidation and in other influences producing a narrowed and weak competition, defensive messages or themes overwhelming and often silencing contrary or challenging communications, with the result that the themes are insufficiently qualified and challenged.

In the steady persistence of defense of advantages, long-ago—presumably in prehistory—elites enlisted allies including, in our day, parents and teachers, and turning interchanges among peers into a reinforcement of the attitudes and values of elites. These allies remain largely ignorant of their roles as inadvertent allies and, indeed, deny them on the rare occasions when the thought arises.

Elite attitudes and beliefs with respect to their own advantages consequently become in large part mass beliefs. Distinctions between elite and mass volitions are on many issues hardly distinguishable and on other issues small.[4] Consequently, no sharp contrast between

---

4. Thus, although elites are more defensive of their advantages in income and wealth, mass opinion accepts many of their advantages. That almost everyone now rhetorically decries poverty and extremes of income inequality, does not deny that they accept gross inequality between nations, that within many nations there is little political motion in the direction of reducing inequalities, that almost no one endorses an approximation to equality of income or of wealth, that fear of adverse effects on incen-

elite and mass thought provides unmistakable evidence of elite impairing influences.

The Complexity and Subtlety of Defense of Advantages

Defense of the advantages of the advantaged does not stand out clearly as a simple phenomenon in which the advantaged, with eyes open, deliberately defend their advantages. They may indeed do so, and historically they have often done so, as in elite explicit intent to exploit fear of a vengeful God to induce political obedience. But in a more common scenario the advantaged come to believe, whether for good reason or not, that the perpetuation of their own advantages is incidental and necessary to the maintenance of a good social order.[5] Thus they teach such "values" as authority, political acquiescence, deference to elites, the work ethic, trust, faith, hierarchy, the merits of the status quo, and the necessity for certain explicit inequalities such as those of income and wealth. Still other possibilities do not require either intent to defend advantages or self-awareness. Neither the teacher nor the political authority who intimidates pupils or subjects passive patterns of behavior need recognize the self-serving character of the intimidation and will often not do so because he is convinced of the abstract merit of the intimidations.

Hence, scenarios differ also in their consequences for the impairment of the advantaged themselves. They may inculcate what they do not themselves believe, or they may come to believe. In all societies, moreover, impairing influences that protect advantages have long ago passed into the "culture" of the society, crystallized in beliefs, attitudes and practices the origins of which have been lost. Even one skeptical of such an assertion may acknowledge that contemporary patriotism may be rooted in historical long-practiced elite indoctrinations once quite explicitly designed to maintain political obedience and passivity, though now perpetuated thoughtlessly by parent and teacher.

tives of reduction of inequality is something of a dogma in many societies, and that in recent years elites appear to have persuaded the mass of people in North America and Western Europe that there exists a "crisis" of the welfare state. See Sidney Verba and Gary R. Orren, *Equality in America* (Cambridge: Harvard University Press, 1985); Robert Kuttner, *The Economic Illusion* (Boston: Houghton Mifflin, 1984); A. Szirmai, "How Do We Really Feel about Income Equalization?" *Netherlands Journal of Sociology* 20 (October 1984); Sidney Verba et al., *Elites and the Idea of Equality* (Cambridge: Harvard University Press, 1987); and Fred Block, Richard A. Cloward, Barbara Ehrenreich, and Frances Fox Piven, *The Mean Season* (New York: Pantheon, 1987).

5. See Nicholas Abercrombie, Stephen Hill, and Bryan S. Turner, *The Dominant Ideology Thesis* (London: Allen & Unwin, 1980), pp. 70–72.

Nor is it implied in the defense-of-advantages thesis that the advantaged intransigently dig in, incapable of flexible strategies in their defenses. They often defend by yielding, surrendering some advantages to protect others, as in elite concession of voting rights to increasing proportions of the English population in the nineteenth and early twentieth centuries. In our day, elites in the third world do not simply protect all traditional advantages. On the contrary, some of them have taken up a rhetoric of equality and modernization.

Elites have broadly conferred among themselves about common courses of defensive action against popular unrest, England in the nineteenth century, for example: and the collusive defense practices of governmental elites—the British government's employment of the Official Secrets Act, as an example—indicate the frequency of contemporary small cabals. But defense does not usually occasion conspiracy or cabal. It is motivated by the self-interest of millions of advantaged persons who cooperate with each other only tacitly, if even that. And it comes to be reinforced by mass participation in it when almost everyone comes to believe and give expression to such values as authority, obedience, hierarchy, inequality, and the status quo.[6]

The history of the West and now the history of the world appear to record not only constant attacks on the advantages of the advantaged but their steady success. Many societies slowly become egalitarian. Those who defend and those who attack the advantages of elites and other favored groups engage in a never-ending struggle. Given the numbers of people engaged in the attack, they make slow and steady advances even in the face of the advantages of influence in the hands of the advantaged.

Neither belief nor discussion freezes on unchanging attitudes, beliefs, or volitions. Year by year, the defense of elite advantages shifts to take account of marginal concessions, by the advantaged and their allies, and the rise of new demands such as those pressed in recent

6. In contemporary social science, it appears to be a conclusive ground for rejection of an interpretation that it rests on "conspiracy theory," as though it were obvious that conspiracies either never existed or belong to an irrelevant past. But if we mean by conspiracy a deliberate, self-aware, and explicit social cooperation for achieving ends injurious to others, or ends that the cooperators dare not reveal to the others, then Watergate was a conspiracy, as is the frequent cooperation between government and press in the U.K.; French governmental control over broadcasting; the efforts of thousands of American businessmen to resist trade unionism; covert CIA operations; discussion and mutually informed action among American foundations and economic elites to resist communism; and in some circles in the McCarthy period discharge of governmental and private employees on dubious disloyalty charges.

years by women. And from time to time new inequalities are advocated: social Darwinism at one point, for example, or the inegalitarianness of the 1970s and 1980s. Probing is consequently constrained within a slowly moving narrow band.[7]

One might think of both adversaries as grasping and not highly competent. But if they are alike in limited competence, in impairment—even in stubbornness or avarice—they differ in their capacity to use money, wealth, power, influence, authority, established rules or habits of deference, the appeals of hierarchy and order, and other inequalities both to skew the competition of ideas and to employ intimidation and coercion to impair probing of the relevant issues.

THE HISTORICAL RECORD

In early predemocratic times, although not necessarily in small-scale primitive societies, and perhaps beginning with agrarian societies overrun by nomadic conquerors, word and deed both loudly asserted the merits of elites and hierarchy.[8] If today elites and other advantaged groups declare only with circumlocution the obligation on lower-class people to obey their betters, they still spoke plainly and explicitly in the nineteenth century. For example, they urged a belief in an afterlife because, for the masses, . . . "it atones for disobedience; it excites to obedience; it purchases strength for obedience; it makes obedience practicable; it makes it acceptable; it makes it in a manner unavoidable, for it constrains to it; it is, finally, not only the motive to obedience, but the pattern of it."[9]

In joining religious authority with secular authority, some societies, like the later Christian societies, elevated a hostility to popular probing into a moral virtue by calling for faith rather than reasoned skepticism. The word *heresy* tells the story. From the Greek *heiretikos*, meaning "able to choose," usage turns that admirable quality into a moral defect. These societies then took the next step of identifying faith in a supernatural power with faith in the rightness of religious

7. On a twenty-five-year U.S. shift, see James A. Davis and Tom W. Smith, "Have We Learned Anything from the General Social Survey?" *Social Indicators Newsletter* 17 (August 1982), p. 2.

8. See Alexander Rüstow, *Freedom and Domination* (Princeton: Princeton University Press, 1980); and Gunnar Landtmann, *The Origin of the Inequality of the Social Classes* (Chicago: University of Chicago Press, 1938).

9. From A. Ure, "Philosophy of Manufactures, 1835," in Patricia Hollis, ed., *Classes and Conflict in Nineteenth-Century England, 1815* (London: Routledge and Kegan Paul, 1973), p. 343.

and secular leadership. Thus the church's support of feudalism in Europe;[10] thus Geneva's Calvinistic theocracy; and thus colonial New England congregations, where "pulpit oratory was simply a voice of political orthodoxy."[11]

Sometimes elites practiced outright repression as a more effective social control than capturing minds, especially for illiterate populations. Yet significantly, they usually practiced repression not as an alternative to capturing minds but as a method of doing so: hence the use of selective repression—for example, jailing popular leaders or prohibiting meetings—to stop the spread of ideas, thus to impair many minds by repressing a few.

But perhaps democracy has now put an end to all that? The rise of political democracy has shaken the world. Political rhetoric now everywhere sings its praises and proclaims this to be the age of equality. Many thoughtful people fear not the failure to achieve greater equality but its excesses. It has already gone far.

Despite the many evidences of decline of elite advantages, political and economic elites and those who join with them in their impairing influences continue to retard further movement to reduce advantages such as in political power and influence, power and influence within the corporation, educational opportunity of many kinds, distribution of government benefits (for example, housing subsidies), and status and respect in both personal interchange and ceremony. They face perhaps inexorable social forces powered by popular volitions. Yet not only elites but almost everyone shows, despite abstract commitments to equality, hostility to many of its particular forms, among them high degrees of equality in income and wealth.[12] If Sweden, among the most egalitarian of societies, provides an example of the strength of contemporary egalitarianism, it also reveals both anxiety about redistribution's going too far and a continuation of long traditions of deference to authority and political passivity.[13]

The struggle over democracy in nineteenth-century England illuminates patterns of defense of advantages disguised by concessions

10. Marc Bloch, *Feudal Society* (Chicago: University of Chicago Press, 1961), chap. 5; and Walter Ullman, *Principles of Government and Politics in the Middle Ages* (New York: Barnes and Noble, 1974).

11. Paul E. Corcoran, *Political Language and Rhetoric* (St. Lucia, Queensland: University of Queensland Press, 1979), p. 121.

12. Herbert McClosky and John Zaller, *The American Ethos* (Cambridge: Harvard University Press, 1984), pp. 82–86.

13. Sidney Verba et al., *Elites and The Idea of Equality* (Cambridge: Harvard University Press, 1987), chap. 7.

to democracy. English middle and upper classes, frightened by disorderly working-class challenges to the established order culminating in the Chartist movement at midcentury, succeeded by 1860 in diverting the working class from what appeared to be a path toward revolution into acquiescence in the established order, a remarkable change from the first to the second half of the century. They achieved it in part through concessions, such as a slow expansion of suffrage, but also through resisting the egalitarian implications of democracy through indoctrination, intimidations, and coercions, including violence.

For indoctrination they proliferated Sunday schools, temperance societies, mutual improvement societies, mechanics institutes, and dozens of other kinds of organization through which they substituted the doctrine of individual self-improvement for earlier working-class practices of collective and even radical action.[14] And they succeeded in drawing skilled workers away from the unskilled, thus crippling the leadership of the unskilled and drawing the skilled closer toward middle-class values.[15] In these methods, elite voices in pulpit, press, and the new indoctrinating organizations overwhelmed contrary voices.

In both England and the U.S., early- to mid-nineteenth-century radicalism actually declined as elites faced up to the urgency of using their advantages in communication and intimidation to win the minds of a potentially rebellious populace. If some reformers thought of the vote as a way to empower citizens, many others intended it to deflect attempts at popular empowerment from dangerous to safer forms. The always present threat of revolutionary action that lies in demonstrations, riots, and other forms of disorder they could, they thought, diminish by conferring suffrage on citizens. Meanwhile, they could use their advantages of income and wealth, of social status,

14. Trygve R. Tholfsen, *Working-Class Radicalism in Mid-Victorian England* (London: Croom Helm, 1976), pp. 199–209 and chap. 8.
15. Geoffrey Crossick, *An Artisan Elite in Victorian Society* (London: Croom Helm, 1978), p. 253; and F. C. Mather, "The Government and the Chartists," in Asa Briggs, ed., *Chartist Studies* (London: Macmillan, 1965). The history and analysis of the remarkable nineteenth-century "turn-around" of the English working class has been much studied by scholars who disagree on the relative effectiveness of the various mechanisms of social control that were operative at the time. See, in addition, to works already cited, John Foster, *Class Struggle in the Industrial Revolution* (New York: St. Martin's, 1978); Francis Hearn, *Domination, Legitimation, and Resistance* (Westport, Conn.: Greenwood, 1978); and Richard Johnson, "Educational Policy and Social Control in Early Victorian England," *Past and Present* 49 (November 1970).

of education, and of access to other elites to prevent the vote from destroying elite advantages.[16]

Compelled to defend their advantages by "winning minds" and explicitly acknowledging that necessity, elites today continue to address a barrage of communications to citizens celebrating democratic political equality as though it were already achieved,[17] but a barrage at the same time intended to justify existing political institutions and practices advantageous to elites, as well as to deploy nonverbal controls to maintain their existing advantages.[18]

Nineteenth- and twentieth-century England, Western Europe, and North America were engaged in a vast economic expansion which, together with political concessions from elites compelled by democratic movements, greatly improved the welfare, by almost any standard, of the great mass of people. Not denying these mass benefits, I am simply pointing to a continued, insistent, and ubiquitous process of elite communication and intimidation to protect advantages against slow erosion—constant elite struggle to win minds to a commitment to such values as order, obedience, the status quo, deference, political docility, and inequalities of income and wealth, as they, the elites, saw that powerful historical forces were inducing challenges to them.

While professing political equality, its many opponents—and that probably includes not only elites but (consequently?) most people of all socioeconomic strata—oppose many lines of its fuller development, advocating in effect a democracy that instead of approximating political equality practices "a subtle screening of participants and demands."[19] Elite advantages in an ostensible competition of ideas and other harsher elite advantages achieve such a screening. "The 'aver-

---

16. For further discussion of the point, see Benjamin Ginsberg, *The Captive Public* (New York: Basic Books, 1986), pp. 48–57.

17. On the nineteenth-century English experience with such misrepresentation, see H. F. Moorehouse, "The Political Incorporation of the British Working Class," *Sociology* 7 (September 1973), esp. p. 346.

18. See Bruce C. Johnson, "The Democratic Mirage," *Berkeley Journal of Sociology* 13 (1968); Gareth Stedman Jones, "Languages of Class" (Cambridge: Cambridge University Press, 1983), chap. 4; Trygve R. Tholfsen, *Working-Class Radicalism in Mid-Victorian England* (London: Croom Helm, 1976), chap. 7; and David Roberts, "Tory Paternalism and Social Reform in Early Victorian England," in Peter Stansky, ed., *The Victorian Revolution* (New York: New Viewpoint, 1973).

19. Michael Crozier in M. Crozier, Samuel P. Huntington, and J. Watanuki, *The Crisis of Democracy* (New York: New York University Press, 1975), p. 12; see also pp. 25–30.

age' voter . . . has been socialized to believe that the citizen has more power than is actually the case."[20]

I have found in conversation with business elites that if one gently presses them on an apparent discrepancy between their conventional rhetorical commitments to political equality and their desire to play a special political role—as reflected, for example, in their assertion that "we have to be regarded as partners with government officials"—they finally acknowledge their opposition, principled as they see it, to political equality or any approximation to it. A confirming study of American business concludes that "many leading business executives, feeling the intense public pressures on them, have begun to wonder whether democracy and capitalism are compatible."[21] The struggle between elite defenses and egalitarian assaults on them continues; and, once more, the point is not that inegalitarianism is evidence of impairment but that on the issue of inequality the competition of ideas is narrow and weak.[22]

Equality of Opportunity

Elite defense of existing advantages seems not greatly undercut by contemporary elite commitment in the democracies—"almost unanimously"—to equality of opportunity.[23] Historically, equality of opportunity defends rather than attacks many elite advantages or, as in the Jacksonian period in the U.S., attacks only a limited array of elite advantages, mostly legal. Equality of opportunity looks much like a contemporary formulation of social Darwinism, a doctrine so savagely defensive of elite advantages, as some people saw it, as to have required its less harsh reformulation as equality of opportunity. A libertarian rather than egalitarian volition,[24] equality of opportunity among tadpoles guarantees that most will never live to become frogs.[25]

The commitment to equality of opportunity appears in any case to be itself greatly limited. At most, elites—and (consequently?) al-

20. The conclusion of a study by Robert D. Hess and Judith V. Torney, *The Development of Political Attitudes in Children* (Chicago: Aldine, 1967), p. 218.

21. Leonard Silk and David Vogel, *Ethics and Profits* (New York: Simon and Schuster, 1976), p. 189.

22. Here is an opportunity to falsify my line of analysis: produce evidence that historically elites did not engage in defense of their advantages, or never did so in ways that attempted to win the minds of masses of people.

23. Based on interviews with American elites, defined more broadly than here defined. See Sidney Verba and Gary R. Orren, *Equality in America* (Cambridge: Harvard University Press, 1985), p. 72.

24. Herbert Gans, *More Equality* (New York: Pantheon, 1973), pp. 63f, 77f.

25. R. H. Tawney, *Equality* (London: Allen & Unwin, 1952), pp. 108f.

most everyone else—favor only certain tightly limited approximations to equal opportunity that are consistent with the perpetuation
of the family as a source of advantage, including family advantages in
education. They do not favor equal job opportunities; on jobs they
favor no more than equality in nondiscriminatory hiring out of a pool
of qualified applicants, with no questions asked about how previous
inequalities account for who is or is not in the pool.[26]

DIFFUSION OF ELITE AND OTHER ADVANTAGING INFLUENCES

In resisting erosion of their advantages, elites make converts to
their own attitudes, beliefs, values, and volitions. Elite influences diffuse, permeate societies, and are sustained over time. Diffused as
their advocacy becomes, their sources become obscure; and some
skeptics will doubt any alleged connection between the current
themes and messages and older elite influences. Some detail on the
diffusion processes may help to confirm a connection. Two great dif-
fusing mechanisms are school and family. Teachers and parents, as
already noted, have their own reasons to employ their advantages to
impair children, deliberately or inadvertently. Consequently, one cannot in any empirical instance separate the "autonomous" impairing
influences of school and family from their impairing influences as
diffusion agents of elite impairing influences. School and family each
play both impairing roles.

Schools

An educational historian contrasts the two sides of "education":
"On the one hand, schooling, like every other agency of deliberate
nurture, socializes: it tends to convey the prevailing values and attitudes of the community or subcommunity that sponsors it. On the
other hand, schooling . . . liberates and extends . . . opens the mind to
new options and new possibilities. . . . It never empowers without at
the same time constraining."[27] The history of public education appears to begin not as one of enlightenment but as a history of elite
attempts to socialize the masses in a particular way: specifically, to
maintain elite favored positions by controlling dangerous mass un-

26. But, as abroad, the American meanings of equality of opportunity have been
slowly shifting to incorporate certain specific limited equalities. For a brief history and
analysis, see Herbert McClosky and John Zaller, *The American Ethos* (New York: Simon and Schuster, 1984), pp. 80–100.
27. Lawrence A. Cremin, *Traditions of American Education* (New York: Basic
Books, 1976), pp. 36f.

rest and potential. It consequently begins in dispute over whether any education at all should be offered to the great mass of people. In 1723 Bernard de Mandeville declares that they should be "Ignorant as well as Poor," for "Knowledge both enlarges and multiplies our Desires."[28] In 1778 Joseph Priestley extols the virtues of teaching the poor "contentment in their situation, and a firm belief in the wisdom and goodness of providence."[29] Hannah Moore in 1801 proposes to "train up the lower classes in habits of industry and piety."[30] Adam Smith's reflections on education for the mass of undereducated are full of concern for their potential for "disorder," "faction," "sedition," and "opposition."[31] Southey in 1817 wants the masses to be "fed the milk of sound doctrine" to induce "habits of Industry" and make the state and other institutions secure.[32]

Later in the U.S., business leaders, amid similar declarations from teachers, government officials, and the National Education Association, resolved that "it [is] our highest duty to pronounce enthusiastically, and with unanimous voice, for the supremacy of law and the maintenance of social and political order."[33] Employers have long desired to form an obedient or docile work force, committed to steadiness of habit, disposed, therefore, not to probe either workplace authority or such institutions as the market system, private property,

28. Bernard de Mandeville, *The Fable of the Bees*, 2d ed., containing *An Essay on Charity and Charity-Schools* (London: Printed for Edmund Parker at the Bible and Crown in Lombard Street, 1723), p. 328.

29. Brian Simon, *Studies in the History of Education 1780–1870*, (London: Lawrence and Wishart, 1960), p. 35.

30. R. Brimley Johnson, ed., *The Letters of Hannah Moore* (London: Bodley Head, 1925), p. 183.

31. Adam Smith, *The Wealth of Nations*, ed. Edwin Cannan (1776; Chicago: University of Chicago Press, 1976), p. 309.

32. Robert Southey, *A Letter to William Smith Esq., M.P., 1817* (London: John Murray, 1817), pp. 35f.

33. David B. Tyack, *The One Best System* (Cambridge: Harvard University Press, 1974), pp. 74f.

For further explicit statement and documentation on education to control the masses in the U.S. and other nations, see Ira Katznelson and Margaret Weir, *Schooling for All* (New York: Basic Books, 1985); Phillip McCann, ed., *Popular Education and Socialization in the Nineteenth Century* (London: Methuen, 1977); Mary Jo Maynes, *Schooling in Western Europe* (Albany: State University of New York Press, 1985); Anne Digby and Peter Searby, *Children, School and Society in Nineteenth-Century England* (London: Macmillan, 1981); W. D. Halls, *Education, Culture and Politics in Modern France* (Oxford, N.Y.: Pergamon, 1976); Marzio Barbagli, *Educating for Unemployment: Politics, Labor Markets, and the School System—Italy, 1869–1973*, trans. Robert H. Ross (New York: Columbia University Press, 1982), pp. 7f; Nubuo Shimahara, *Adapta-*

the corporation or elite advantages.[34] Possibly, employer concerns for a controllable workforce have long formed the dominant or shaping influence on public education.[35] That thesis has, however, been challenged; and the broader and perhaps more frequent interpretation sees business people as using their influence to join other elites to make of the schools an instrument for preserving the social order, including both economy and state.[36]

Again, it is not the message but its loudness and frequency of communication (as well as the methods by which communicated) that achieve the impairment. Only a rare eccentric dissents from a volition for some degree of social order. The impairment lies in teaching social order to pupils as a dogma or an article of faith, obfuscating the question of how much order is desirable, and in using the school as an instrument for shutting down rather than holding open a competition of ideas, if only one suitable for the competence of very young minds.

In the emphasis on docility, obedience, authority, inferiority of the lower classes, piety, and faith in providence, education appears to have intended to put a low ceiling over probing the advantages of the advantaged. It expresses also a fear of the common person's attempt to investigate his own volitions. And today, at the end of the twentieth century, the schools still reflect much of this early purpose and mani-

---

tion and Education in Japan (New York: Praeger, 1979); and Harold Silver, The Concept of Popular Education (London: MacGibbon and Kee, 1965), pp. 208f.

34. Herbert G. Gutman, "Work, Culture and Society in Industrializing America, 1815–1919," American Historical Review 78 (June 1973).

35. See, for the U.S., Samuel Bowles and Herbert Gintis, Schooling in Capitalist America (New York: Basic Books, 1976).

36. See Ira Katznelson and Margaret Weir, Schooling for All (New York: Basic Books, 1985); and, for the U.K., Brian Simon, The Politics of Educational Reform, 1920–1940 (London: Lawrence and Wishart, 1974), pp. 299f.

Business influence in U.S. schools is varied and deep. It embraces conferences that bring business people and teachers together, business-sponsored summer classes for teachers; production and distribution of films, displays, and text materials for the classroom; and, in recent years, a flourishing adopt-a-school movement by which a business enterprise takes on a continuing influential relation with a school, providing a variety of services, sometimes including curriculum planning. Many thousands of firms participate in many thousands of schools. See the New York Times, October 28, 1984, p. 34; Sheila Harty, Hucksters in the Classroom (Washington: Center for Study of Responsive Law, 1979); David Lindorf, "An Apple for the Banker," Working Papers Magazine 8 (July–August 1981); G. William Domhoff, The Powers that Be (New York: Random House, 1978), pp. 179–183; and a cautionary note sounded by Elizabeth L. Useem, "The Limits of Power and Commitment," in G. William Domhoff and Thomas R. Dye, eds., Power Elites and Organizations (Newbury Park, Calif.: Sage Publications, 1987).

fest it in new forms.[37] They remain strong themes, even if they erode slowly.[38] In the U.S. today, competent observers describe some of the consequences of instruction on children in words like the following: ". . . an unwillingness to accept social conflict, a learning of political slogans, an over-estimation of the effectiveness of the vote as a means to exercise political influence, an obedient orientation to authority, a failure to understand the meaning of democratic principles, and most importantly the failure to recognize the gap between certain ideal values and sociopolitical realities which deny these values. Political education thus becomes an effort to maintain the status quo or a vision of a past social order."[39]

A study of twelve thousand American elementary schoolchildren observed:

> Compliance to rules and authority is the major focus of civics education in elementary schools. . . . Teachers of young children place particular stress upon citizen compliance, de-emphasizing all other political topics. The three items rated as more important than basic subjects (reading and arithmetic) by a majority of second- and third-grade teachers were the law, the policeman, and the child's obligation to conform to school rules and laws of the community. . . . Political socialization at early age levels emphasizes behavior that relates the child emotionally to his country and impresses upon him the necessity for obedience and conformity. . . . The tendency to evade some realities of political life seems to be paralleled by the school's emphasis upon compliance.[40]

37. None of this denies that in recent years in the U.S. some departures from conventional conformities are conspicuous. Legal controversy over the separation of religion and state in public instruction has produced extraordinary and, I would agree, hostile silences rather than conformism in school textbooks on the subject of religion and on some related issues, such as those that fundamentalists refer to as "family values."

The pattern is documented in Paul C. Vitz, Censorship: Evidence of Bias in Our Children's Textbooks (Ann Arbor, Mich.: Servant Books, 1986). Vitz also shows that the schools are not evenhanded on attacks on evolutionary theory mounted by religious fundamentalists, as to him it seems obvious that they should be.

38. On continuities, see Michael B. Katz, Class, Bureaucracy, and Schools (New York: Praeger, 1971); and Reconstructing American Education (Cambridge: Harvard University Press, 1987), chaps. 1, 3, and 4.

39. A paraphrase of Robert D. Hess, "Political Socialization in the Schools," Harvard Educational Review 38 (Summer 1968), in Charles F. Andrain, Children and Civic Awareness (Columbus, Ohio: Merrill, 1971), p. 22.

40. Robert D. Hess and Judith V. Torney, The Development of Political Attitudes in Children (Chicago: Aldine, 1967), pp. 110f.

In civics courses, another study finds, "the instruction proceeds from emphasis on indirect and symbolic patriotism [pledging allegiance, singing patriotic songs] to explicit but shaded use of facts about American history and government.... This curriculum ignores events and conditions that contradict the ideal descriptions of the political system. The normative content emphasizes compliance with rules and authority while skimping citizens' rights to participate."[41]

A study of Italy, Sweden, the U.K., West Germany, and the U.S. found that "the courses are mostly non-reality oriented. Conflict, systemic difficulties, difficulties of institutional adaptation, and so forth are virtually ignored."[42]

A UNESCO international commission drawing on a mass of documents and visits to twenty-one countries expressed a variety of concerns: such tendencies in the schools as to "cultivate unthinking respect for hierarchies," "[make] people easy to govern," "inculcate conventional knowledge," and "[neglect] helping man to define his choices."[43] Of French secondary education, William Schonfield writes: "Like the proverbial bureaucrat or the modern worker in an assembly-line factory, pupils possess finely delimited models of what should be done and how they should do it. These models have been transmitted to them by outside authorities, who will also provide the appropriate cues to activate the relevant repertoire of behaviors."[44] In France, too, "most work is done from traditionally designed textbooks that cram the maximum material into the most memorable headings and sub-headings, that are dogmatic in style, that raise no problems or unanswered questions."[45]

Dozens of studies of many countries similarly document the use of public education to maintain challengeable features of the existing

41. Frederick M. Wirt and Michael W. Kirst, *The Political Web of American Schools* (Boston: Little, Brown, 1972), p. 29. See also Richard M. Battistoni, *Public Schooling and the Education of Democratic Citizens* (Jackson: University Press of Mississippi, 1985), p. 122; and Michael J. Shapiro, "Social Control Ideologies and the Politics of American Education," *International Review of Education* 20 (January–March 1974).

42. Russell F. Farnen and Dan B. German, "Youth, Politics and Education," in Byron G. Massialas, ed., *Political Youth, Traditional Schools* (Englewood Cliffs, N.J.: Prentice-Hall, 1972), p. 175.

43. International Commission on the Development of Education, *Learning to Be* (Paris: Unesco, 1972), pp. 58, 64f, 69.

44. *Obedience and Revolt* (Beverly Hills, Calif.: Sage, 1976), p. 21.

45. W. R. Fraser, *Reforms and Restraints in Modern French Education* (London: Routledge & Kegan Paul, 1971), p. 143. On West Germany, see R. L. Merritt, E. P. Flerlage, and A. J. Merritt, "Political Man in Postwar West German Education," *Comparative Education Review* 15 (October 1971).

social order,[46] to teach the dangers of criticizing it,[47] to repress conflict and recognition of it,[48] to obfuscate,[49] to define citizenship as passivity and conformity,[50] to idealize society, and to teach the merits alone of challengeable existing institutions.[51]

Many people defend the school's impairment of the child's mind. Many of the society's institutions, they will rightly say, are worth saving; civilization requires obedience to rules and authority; and young people have to fit into the available roles in society. For these purposes they need not critical enlightenment but such indoctrination and intimidation as the schools give them. The necessity of impairing young minds remains, until a later chapter, beside the point, which is simply the fact of the impairing influences of the schools.[52]

46. Barrie Stacey, *Political Socialization in Western Society* (New York: St. Martin's, 1977), p. 153; Ira Katznelson and Margaret Weir, *Schooling for All* (New York: Basic Books, 1985); Francis Fox Piven and Richard A. Cloward, "Social Policy and the Formation of Political Consciousness," in Maurice Zeitlin, ed., *Political Power and Social Theory*, vol. 1 (Greenwich, Conn.: JAI Press, 1980); and Michael W. Apple, *Ideology and Curriculum* (London: Routledge & Kegan Paul, 1979), pp. 69ff and chap. 4.

47. Robert E. Cleary, *Political Education in the American Democracy* (Scranton, Pa.: Intext Educational Publishers, 1971), p. 101.

48. Seymour Martin Lipset, *Political Man* (Garden City, N.J.: Doubleday, 1960), p. 291.

49. J. J. Patrick, "The Impact of an Experimental Course, 'American Political Behavior,' on the Knowledge, Skills, and Attitudes of Secondary School Students," *Social Education* 36 (February 1972); and Cleary, *Political Education*, p. 101.

50. M. K. Jennings and R. G. Niemi, *The Political Character of Adolescence* (Princeton: Princeton University Press, 1974), p. 272; W. H. Hartley and W. S. Vincent, *American Civics* (New York: Harcourt, Brace, Jovanovich, 1974); and John J. Patrick, "Political Socialization and Political Education in Schools," in Stanley Allen Renshon, ed., *Handbook of Political Socialization* (New York: Free Press, 1977).

51. Brian Simon, *The Politics of Educational Reform, 1920–1940* (London: Lawrence and Wishart, 1974), esp. pp. 299f; Charles Andrain, *Children and Civic Awareness* (Columbus, Ohio: Merrill, 1971), pp. 23f; and Jon Parker Higgin, "Political Socialization in a Discontinuous Setting," in Byron G. Massialas, ed., *Political Youth, Traditional Schools* (Englewood Cliffs, N.J.: Prentice-Hall, 1972). For further bibliography on the various effects of school socialization, see Stanley Allen Renshon, ed., *Handbook of Political Socialization* (New York: Free Press, 1977).

A study by Judith V. Torney, A. N. Oppenheim, and Russell F. Farnen, *Civic Education in Ten Countries* (New York: Wiley, 1975), opens with the statement: "In each of these countries the schools carry out a systematic teaching program *aimed* [my italics] at producing well-informed, democratically active citizens" (p. 17). The study finds that the objective "was not successfully attained in any of the countries" (p. 18). Nothing in the study demonstrates that the aim or objective of civics education is as characterized; and given the history of other aims in public education, one must doubt that such an aim is dominant, despite lip service to it. Little wonder, then, that the study finds that not one of the ten countries achieves such an objective.

52. Schools also discriminate by socioeconomic class. See, among other sources, Caroline Hodges Persell, *Education and Inequality* (New York: Free Press, 1977), chap. 7; Gabriel Almond and Sidney Verba, *The Civic Culture* (Princeton: Princeton Univer-

Parents

Themselves impaired probers, parents do not always realize that the habits of attitude, belief, and action that they inculcate in their children represent only one set among possible defensible sets. They plunge, often with little thought, into teaching religion, authority, obedience, and deference, the naturalness of inequality, often the inferiority of other ethnic groups, the belief that democracy has already been achieved, and such virtues as loyalty and patriotism. Since to them very little seems questionable about any of these teachings, they will not teach their children to be reflective about them and weigh alternatives.

"It is highly plausible that the family's principal influence may be in the domain of highly consensual attitudes and behaviors. At least in the United States, such dispositions as national identity, acceptance of the legitimacy of political authority, reverence for such concepts as 'democracy' and many core features of the political culture are *likely* to be transmitted from one generation to the next via the family."[53]

Hardly noteworthy, one may reply. The functions of parenthood include passing on to a new generation the rules and values of the society. Indeed so; but also impairing in the way done. Research on parental socialization of children has been relatively inattentive to whether it operates through opening or closing the child's mind. But in casting socialization as a process of turning undisciplined potential barbarians into civilized adults, the conception of socialization often at least hints at a process something like breaking a horse.

Statistics on parental violence against children prohibit the assumption that all parents mean to do well by their children. Let us, however, assume here that most do and, specifically that they mean well when they teach their children not explicit political values at all

sity Press, 1963), p. 337; A. Morrison and D. McIntyre, *Schools and Socialization* (Harmondsworth, England: Penguin, 1971), p. 74; Frances Fox Piven and Richard Cloward, "Social Policy and the Formation of Political Consciousness," in Maurice Zeitlin, ed., *Political Power and Social Theory*, vol. 1 (Greenwich, Conn.: JAI Press, 1980), pp. 131–137; Frederick Erickson, "Gatekeeping and the Melting Pot", *Harvard Education Review* 45 (February 1975); Frank Parkin, *Class Inequality and Political Order* (New York: Praeger, 1971), pp. 62f; James Rosenbaum, *Making Inequality* (New York: Wiley, 1976); and Edgar Litt and Michael Parkinson, *U.S. and U.K. Educational Policy* (New York: Praeger, 1979).

53. Robert Wiesberg and Richard Joslyn, "Methodological Appropriateness in Political Socialization Research," in Stanley Allen Renshon, ed., *Handbook of Political Socialization*, (New York: Free Press, 1977), p. 54.

but the formulas of good behavior: not talking back to adults, obedience, going along, not fussing, and the like. Abundant research says that even these superficially acceptable lines of indoctrination, depending on circumstances and the rigidity of the inculcation, can imprison the mind in lasting habits of subservience to authority and indisposition to indulge in critical thought.[54]

Research shows some differences between socioeconomic classes with respect to what they pass on to their children. A survey of studies concludes: "Working-class parents are more likely to be imperative in their control, showing more concern with obedience, external behavior and appearances than with internal states and feelings. They are less likely to give reasons for their commands or to encourage the child to make his own decisions in family matters. They appear to be less concerned with the child's opinion and to give him fewer alternatives for action or for thought."[55]

A number of studies have found that low self-direction in the parent's job strongly associates with low valuation of independence in children.[56] Research has also linked power-oriented socialization methods in the family with aggressive, dependent children whose development of conscience is impaired. Other research stresses the limited "role-taking" opportunities provided for children in working-class households.[57] English research argues that traditional working-class families do not encourage progression in the forms of conceptualization used by children; thus their children tend to fail to develop facility with the analytical thought that can offer them new political and problem-solving capacities.[58]

Whether through socioeconomic elites, school, family or other diffusions of elite messages, the subtlety of diffused impairment that defends the advantaged presumably often escapes attention. Since it is

54. For bibliography and comment on the research, see Viktor Gecas, "Contents of Socialization," in Morris Rosenberg and Ralph H. Turner, eds., Social Psychology (New York: Basic Books, 1981).

55. Robert D. Hess and Judith V. Torney, The Development of Political Attitudes in Children (Chicago: Aldine, 1967), pp. 126f. See also Claus Mueller, Politics of Communication (New York: Oxford University Press, 1973), pp. 62–72; and Dean Jaros, Socialization to Politics (New York: Praeger, 1973), p. 83.

56. For an excellent review, see Victor Gecas, "Contexts of Socialization," in Morris Rosenberg and Ralph H. Turner, eds., Social Psychology (New York: Basic Books, 1981).

57. Julienne Ford, Douglas Young, and Steven Box, "Functional Autonomy, Role Distance, and Social Class," British Journal of Sociology 18 (December 1967).

58. Melvin L. Kohn, Class and Conformity (Homewood, Ill.: The Dorsey Press, 1969), p. 200.

difficult to track, I acknowledge that its evidences are frequently debatable. What shall one make, for example, of attempts of social thought to invest "envy" with ugly connotations? One wonders if "envy" has come to denote any personal attempt at betterment that threatens the advantages of elites. Other forms of attempted betterment are given approving labels like "individual initiative" or "emulation."[59] Or consider a vocabulary that identifies elite status with moral worth, "noble" meaning both high elite status and high moral worth, and "vulgar" meaning popular or pertaining to the people (as in the Vulgate) but also low, or lacking in quality? Or what to make of the process by which "faith" contrasts not with skeptical reason but with dissent and heresy, to the discredit of the latter terms? They look like evidence, yet not conclusively so.[60]

Because language draws distinctions, accuses, punishes, decries, and evaluates in ways hidden by the ostensible meaning of words, phrases, and sentences, it becomes possible to entertain the hypothesis not simply that language impairs but that many of its impairments fall into the advantaging pattern. Common forms of classification—for example, such as these that refer to class, subclass, species, and genus—assume, some suggest, that order both in nature and in social life is hierarchical.[61]

59. For an example of discrediting envy in order to defend inequality, see Gonzalo Fernandez de la Mora, *Egalitarian Envy* (New York: Paragon House, 1987).

60. For the history of American struggle over political language, see David Green, *Shaping Political Consciousness* (Ithaca, N.Y.: Cornell University Press, 1987).

61. Gunter W. Remling, *The Road to Suspicion* (New York: Appleton-Century-Crofts, 1967), p. 11. On how concepts become in themselves impairments through which one joins with one's peers in perpetuating existing power relations in a society, the principal theorist is probably Michel Foucault, who finds in such terms as *patient* and *doctor* hidden admonitions for the one to obey and the other to exercise authority. His explorations of the relation between power and language, especially rules of discourse, and related other explorations by others are embryonic and disputed. But that they open up new avenues to the understanding of the profundity of social impairment can hardly be questioned. See Foucault, *The Archaeology of Knowledge*, trans. A. M. Sheridan Smith (New York: Pantheon 1972); *Power/Knowledge*, edited and translated by Colin Gordon (Brighton, Sussex: Harvester Press, 1980); and *Discipline and Punish*, trans. Alan Sheridan (New York: Pantheon, 1977). See also Alan Sheridan, *Michel Foucault* (London and New York: Tavistock, 1980).

CHAPTER 7

Contemporary Elites

Contemporary impairing influences go beyond an inheritance of older historical elite, class, and other influences now diffused and independently reinforced through school, family, and peers. They include, as everyone knows, a mixture of communications media, business, and state influences on contemporary thinking, consequential both for the competition of ideas and for the informational and analytical content of communications. In the democracies, civil liberties protect a competition of ideas much stronger than the emasculated competition of earlier fascist and contemporary communist systems. But that the democracies differ greatly from authoritarian systems does not deny the continuing impairing influences of elites or a continuing narrowness in the competition of ideas. The democracies are not all alike in this respect. In impairment at the hands of contemporary elites, the U.S. might be at one extreme—the most impairing—and the Scandinavian countries at the other—the least impairing.

LITERACY AND THE COMMUNICATIONS MEDIA

In literacy and the mass media of communication began a transformation of the possibilities of elite impairing influences still perhaps on the rise. However great on some counts is the contribution of mass literacy to human welfare, literacy offsets its own contribution to a degree by the shift it brought about from multilateral communication among acquaintances and friends in the give-and-take of small groups to unilateral communication in which one or a few commonly address thousands or millions. Mass literacy vastly expanded elite capacities to reach mass audiences, audiences larger than a voice could earlier reach from any pulpit. With broadcasting came a further expansion of elite capacity to disseminate on a vast scale misrepresentation, deceit, and obfuscation. No one can deny the exercise of these capacities by the Nazis in the first large-scale explicit systematic use of broadcasting to rule a nation, or their massive use in the democracies in advertising and politics.

Unilateral communication may specifically have undercut earlier capacities of people, stimulated by their multilateral discussions, "to develop relatively autonomous interpretations" of their world and their lives in it.[1] In addition, the version of the competition of ideas prized in nineteenth-century liberal thought may have envisaged nothing more than the control of public opinion by elites practicing a limited competition in their largely unilateral messages to masses.[2] And it is only slowly coming to be understood that conventional "free speech" does not at all insure a competition of ideas when mass communication requires a costly technology. Only recently have social scientists come to appreciate the significance of that obvious proposition for identifying impairment at the hands of religious, political, and business elites, as well as for defining free speech.[3]

The influence of the media was for many years missed by those social scientists who looked for evidence of effects through their studies of no more than short-term influences on voters and consumer choices. They have since found evidence of varied effects, both short-

1. Francis Fox Piven and Richard A. Cloward, "Social Policy and the Formation of Political Consciousness," in Maurice Zeitlin, ed., *Political Power and Social Theory*, vol. 1 (Greenwich, Conn.: JAI Press, 1980), p. 135. See also Terence H. Qualter, *Opinion Control in the Democracies* (London: Macmillan, 1985), pp. 198f.

2. Benjamin Ginsberg, *The Captive Public* (New York: Basic Books, 1986), chaps. 2, 3, and 4.

3. Three important books on the issues with respect to government are Mark G. Yudoff, *When Government Speaks* (Berkeley: University of California Press, 1983); Paul Corcoran, *Political Language and Rhetoric* (St. Lucia, Queensland: University of Queensland Press, 1979); and Ginsberg, *The Captive Public*.

run and long-run.[4] While seeking it, they came to understand as well "the power of the media to define normal and abnormal social and political activity, to say what is politically real and legitimate and what is not; to justify the two-party political structure; to establish certain political agendas for social attention and to contain, channel, and exclude others; and to shape the images of opposition movements."[5] They earlier missed but now better understand the media's role in explaining or interpreting events as distinct from media advocacy.[6] They also missed but now acknowledge the effectiveness of the media in confirming existing opinions, beliefs, and volitions[7] and the long-term effects of constantly repeated messages.[8]

State monopoly or regulation of broadcasting tries to curb the excesses of manipulation of audiences that is possible in commercial broadcasting and unregulated political advocacy. But in curbing some elites, they open up new possibilities for state elites. Western European broadcasting (and press) displays a variety of ways in which government enlists the media in defense of the advantages of governmental or state elites.[9] These elites achieve their control over the media less by direct censorship than by an intimidating authority held in reserve. Consequently, "the 'controls' are built into the assumptions inside the minds of producers and management."[10]

4. Benjamin I. Page, Robert Y. Shapiro, and Glenn R. Dempsey, "What Moves Opinion?" *American Political Science Review* 81 (March 1987).

5. Todd Gitlin, "Media Sociology," *Theory and Society* 6 (September 1978), p. 205.

6. Shanto Iyengar, "Television News and Citizens' Explanation of National Affairs," *American Political Science Review* 81 (September 1987).

7. See G. R. Miller and M. Burgoon, *New Techniques of Persuasion* (New York: Harper and Row, 1973), p. 5.

8. On this point, see the testimony of two leading figures in media research, Elihu Katz and Paul Lazarsfeld, in their *Personal Influence* (New York: Free Press, 1955), p. 23n13. And today we percieve the importance of an additional media phenomenon: the managers of the media, especially broadcasters, do not simply address audiences; they assemble them. They create through entertainment an audience that can then be put at the disposal of a seller of a product, a candidate for office, or a spokesperson for a cause. See Dallas W. Smythe, *Dependency Road* (Norwood, N.J.: Ablex Publishing, 1981).

9. Elizabeth Noelle-Neumann, "Mass Media and Social Change in Developed Societies," in Elihu Katz and Tamás Szecskö, *Mass Media and Social Change* (Beverly Hills, Calif.: Sage, 1981); Herbert Steinhouse, "Closing the Gap between Expanding Knowledge and Society through Television in the U.S.," in Kenneth Boulding and Lawrence Senesh, eds., *The Optimum Utilization of Knowledge* (Boulder, Colo.: Westview Press, 1983); Denis McQuail and Karen Siune, *New Media Politics* (London: Sage, 1986); and W. Phillips Davison, "The Media Kaleidoscope," in Harold D. Lasswell, Daniel Lerner, and Hans Speier, eds., *Propaganda and Communication in World History*, vol. 3 (Honolulu: University of Hawaii Press, 1980).

10. Anthony Smith, *Television and Political Life: Studies in Six European Countries* (New York: St. Martin's, 1979), p. 37. See also the troubled record of the subservi-

"Objective" Media Messages

Presumably, not all media communications are designed to control an audience. Some entertain. Do some simply inform? No, not "simply" inform, for even news and other ostensibly "objective" informational communications show a pattern of defending elite advantages. How they do so is familiar and warrants only a brief summary. The media usually offer conventional interpretations of events.[11] Conflicts of interpretation appear, and the commentator may proudly call attention to them; but those reported fall within a narrow range, as in broadcasts that report differences between major political parties but do not often report interpretations that lie outside that range. On political and economic affairs, interpretations diverge less than on fashions, the arts, and life-styles.

As is also familiar to those who have studied the media, aside from media attention to strikes, riots, and other dramatic disturbances, reporting of the activities of dissenting groups is weak.[12] It also appears that the more politically dissenting the group, the less favorable is its treatment in news and in other ostensibly objective media messages, and the more frequently the media denies it access.[13] In the U.S., even labor unions face great difficulties of media coverage.

Since media "impartiality" or "objectivity" usually means media conventionality or conformity with dominant opinions, the media are not impartial between, say, advocacy of communism or *dirigiste* authority and that of capitalism, or between revolution and gradualism, or even between advocacy of legal street demonstrations and advocacy of political action restricted to voting. Although professionalism in mass communications tends to rule out the more extreme distortions of the news and related ostensibly objective communications, it brings messages into convergence around modal opinions of the audience.[14]

In news and other ostensibly objective communication, the sta-

ence of British broadcasting to the state in Paddy Scannel, "A Conspiracy of Silence," in Gregor McLennan, David Held, and Stuart Hall, eds., *State and Society in Contemporary Britain* (Cambridge: Polity Press, 1984).

11. Louis Martin, "The Role of the Media in the Political Process," *Communication et information* 2 (Autumn 1978).

12. Terence H. Qualter, *Opinion Control in the Democracies* (London: Macmillan, 1985), p. 198.

13. On this point, see Pamela J. Shoemaker, "Media Treatment of Deviant Political Groups," *Journalism Quarterly* 61 (Spring 1984), esp. p. 70.

14. Louis Martin, "The Role of the Media in the Political Process," *Communication et information* 2 (Autumn 1978).

tus quo orientation of the media with respect to politics and economics is also familiar. A study of press and broadcast news in the U.K. with special attention to industrial relations as a conflict area significant for testing the character of reporting concluded that "at its most basic, the organizing principle . . . is that the normal workings of the particular economic system are never treated as if they might themselves generate serious problems. Rather, the causes of economic problems are sought largely in the activities of trade unionists who reject the priorities and purposes of the dominant group. . . . [Presented is] a highly selective account of the nature and workings of that economic order."[15]

Consequently, the media move their audiences toward conformity of thought on basic political and economic institutions. "As a form of adult socialization," a survey concludes, "the media are seen as guarantors that a body of common ultimate values remain visible as a continuing source of consensus."[16] This despite the fact that in politics journalists stand somewhat to the left of the general public, think more critically, show more desire for change.[17]

Because press and broadcast journalists hunger for inputs and cannot afford the time and expense of extended inquiry on most issues, they seek input from public officials and other persons in positions of authority. As a consequence, the opinions of such persons often come to circulate as fact.

The news media also often establish a common agenda of issues on which people then focus their political attention: that is, the media are "stunningly successful" in telling people what to think about and what not to think about.[18] Media norms of what is or is not worth communicating to some degree come to be accepted by the audience, although influence runs in both directions. Aside from media conformism and conventionality, the media play up the visual and the dramatic.[19] But, again, all these characteristics the media display in

15. Glasgow University Media Group, *Bad News*, vol. 2 (Boston: Routledge & Kegan Paul, 1980), p. 112.

16. Warren Breed, "Mass Communication and Sociological Integration," in Lewis Anthony Dexter and David Manning White, eds., *People, Society, and Mass Communications* (New York: The Free Press of Glencoe, 1964), p. 187.

17. For differing views, see S. Robert Lichter and Stanley Rothman, "Media and Business Elites," *Public Opinion* 4 (October–November 1981); and Peter Dreier, "The Corporate Complaint against the Media," in Donald Lazere, ed., *American Media and Mass Culture* (Berkeley: University of California Press, 1987).

18. Shanto Iyengar and Donald R. Kinder, *News that Matters* (Chicago: University of Chicago Press, 1988).

19. Qualter, *Opinion Control in the Democracies*, pp. 103, 164. See also, on several of the above points, Elihu Katz and Tomás Szecskö, eds., *Mass Media and Social Change* (Beverly Hills, Calif.: Sage, 1981).

their most objective or impartial roles. In the service of advertising and politics, the media are for hire and design their messages to suit their clients.

CONTEMPORARY ELITES IN BUSINESS AND STATE

There may remain some doubt as to whether at this late date in the history of democracy business and political elites can and do still deeply engage in defending their advantages. That they can and do seems reasonably clear on the evidence. Even in Sweden, where elites have accepted a relatively high degree of economic equality, elites selectively resist further moves in that direction.[20] They continue to defend the status quo, their advantages in political participation and authority in both state and the business enterprise, and existing political and economic institutions. They also continue to endorse a general passivity or docility in popular attitudes and political behavior.[21] In most of the other democracies, elites resist almost all movements away from old inequalities, in so doing resisting alteration of any of the society's fundamental situations. I shall try to hurry through the familiar parts of the story.

Business Elites

Corporate executives and other business people often find themselves fighting each other on some issues.[22] On a number of issues about political and economic life, however, big business approaches unanimity, a research study concludes, on "a strong acceptance of the

20. Sidney Verba et al., *Elites and the Idea of Equality* (Cambridge: Harvard University Press, 1987), chap. 7.

21. "Swedes exhibit a well-developed deference to public officials, who are accorded high status and generally allowed to go their own way in pursuing their 'expert' solutions to public problems" (Thomas J. Anton, *Administered Politics: Elite Political Culture in Sweden* [Boston: Martinus Nijhoff, 1980], p. ix; see also pp. viii, 162, 167, 215). See also Verba et al., *Elites and the Idea of Equality*, pp. 30f; and Hugh Heclo and Henrik Madsen, *Policy and Politics in Sweden* (Philadelphia: Temple University Press, 1987), pp. 9, 18f, 21–23, 27f, 39, 315, 324, 330–332.

One wonders if Swedish elites have traded generous economic benefits to the citizenry in exchange for its continued acceptance of obligations of political passivity and deference to authority. Elites may have thrown into the bargain a commitment to take initiatives in discovering, formulating, and solving social problems, in exchange for which the Swedish citizen desists from interest-group participation other than the formality of membership. See Anton, *Administered Politics*, pp. 14, 38, 73f; 112f, 120ff.

22. On differences among them in the U.K. and the U.S., see Michael Useem, "Business and Politics in the United States and United Kingdom," *Theory and Society* 12 (May 1983); and Useem, *The Inner Circle* (New York: Oxford University Press, 1984).

fundamental elements of capitalism—private property, employer dominance, economic stratification—and it is never challenged."[23] For all business people, except in some small proprietorships, one hardly requires research to establish their high degree of agreement on the naturalness and necessity of existing economic inequalities; the indispensability of private property in a free and dynamic society; the ethical merit and efficiency of the existing distribution of property; the appropriateness of hierarchal forms of social organization together with accompanying differences in status, rank, and prestige; the merits of the market system; at least lip service to the merits of democracy in its present form; the claim that democracy has already been largely realized; the indispensability to democracy of markets and private enterprise; the readiness of business enterprises to respond to new public needs; and the frequent incompetence of government officials.[24] In all these respects one finds "very pronounced tendencies for the economic elite to deny the influence of factors that question and to affirm the influence of factors that support the legitimacy of their highly privileged position."[25]

Again, the impairing effects follow both from a lopsided competition of ideas on these positions, causes, beliefs, attitudes, or messages, and from the methods used by business in sales promotion, in institutional advertising, much of which contains a political component, and in outright advocacy on public issues. Despite the straight-faced attempts of a few public-relations practitioners to deny it, these methods embrace massive attempts at obfuscation, misrepresentation, and deceit. Their appeals are designed to shortcut or undermine probing.[26] They consist of "communications designed to convey images and symbols rather than argument, scenes rather than speech, actions rather than words, emotions rather than thoughts. 'Ad' spots

23. The quotation is on U.S. business executives (Maynard S. Seider, "American Big Business Ideology," *American Sociological Review* 39 [December 1974], pp. 811f). His conclusion is derived from content analysis of almost five hundred executive speeches.

24. Francis X. Sutton, Seymour E. Harris, Carol Kaysen, and James Tobin, *The American Business Creed* (Cambridge: Harvard University Press, 1956); and Sidney Verba and Gary R. Orren, *Equality in America* (Cambridge: Harvard University Press, 1985).

25. James R. Kluegel and Eliot R. Smith, *Beliefs About Equality* (New York: Aldine de Gruyter, 1986), p. 252.

26. See T. J. Jackson Lears, "From Salvation to Self-Realization," in Richard Wightman Fox and T. J. Jackson Lears, eds., *The Culture of Consumption* (New York: Pantheon, 1983), pp. 22 and 27; and on these and related issues, Michael Schudson, *Advertising: The Uneasy Persuasion* (New York: Basic Books, 1984).

have the capacity to achieve these objectives by catching the attention of ear and eye with fast cuts, sound overlays, striking visual techniques and virtually complete control of the content."[27] Research on business communication on public affairs finds that it is often designed to "sow the seeds of confusion," which is all the easier because business more often engages in blocking new policy moves than in advancing them.[28]

In none of the contemporary democracies do speakers other than political elites match the voices of business elites or rival their capacities for exerting other impairing influences like intimidation.[29] In some of the democracies it superficially appears that labor unions speak with no less powerful a voice than business managers. But the most that can be said to support such a belief is that in traceable election campaign expenditures, union and business contributions in some countries may be roughly equal.[30] "Laundered" or otherwise hidden corporate expenditures to influence elections deny any such equality.[31] Nor do such estimates take into account the great advantage that business has over labor unions in influencing the public from day to day on issues other than choice of party or candidate—in communications to influence the probing of citizens and officials on specific issues of policy or to confirm support for existing social institutions. Nor do union officials rival business managers in their capacity to impair, not through mass messages to influence public opinion, but through intimidations and coercions such as those that managers exercise, often without being aware of doing so, to induce obedience to workplace authority, say, or to threaten a town with a plant closedown. The disparity between business and labor in capacities to impair is reflected in the great disparity between the two groups in all the democracies in assets and receipts: for example, for the U.S.,

27. Paul E. Corcoran, *Political Languge and Rhetoric* (St. Lucia, Queensland: University of Queensland Press, 1979), p. 161.

28. Several such research studies are cited with comment in Thomas Milan Konda, "Political Advertising and Public Relations by Business in the United States," Ph.D. diss., Department of Political Science, University of Kentucky, 1983, p. 32.

29. On religious elites, see the appendix to this chapter.

30. See, for example, Michael Pinto-Duschinsky, *British Political Finance, 1830–1980* (Washington, D. C.: American Enterprise Institution for Public Policy Research, 1981).

31. On how expenditures are hidden, see Sidney Verba and Gary R. Orren, *Equality in America* (Cambridge: Harvard University Press, 1985), p. 16; Steven D. Lyndenberg, *Bankrolling Ballots: Update 1980* (New York: Council on Economic Priorities, 1985), pp. 19–31; and Philip M. Stern, *The Best Congress Money Can Buy* (New York: Pantheon, 1988), chap. 10 and p. 39.

three to four billion dollars for unions compared to two to four trillion dollars for corporations.[32] In Britain, for another example, the ratio is about the same, a thousand to one.[33]

The voice of organized labor, even when heard, constitutes no general challenge to the business voice. On many issues, the two voices share a concern for the profitability of business enterprises, a concern that makes both union and management preoccupied with maintaining existing institutions and hostile to probing them. In most of the democracies, management also speaks on the full variety of issues facing the society, unions on a small number of issues of industrial relations and wage and price policy, though both also speak through political parties. The character of the evidence on business advantage is detailed in an appendix to this chapter.

Business people themselves deny the magnitude of their influence on contemporary thinking—they see themselves as under constant attack. But the constancy of the attack on them—and they correctly perceive it—is a consequence of the advantages that a historical movement hostile to inequality seeks to take away from them. A defense of elite advantages is, of course, defensive—and implies advantages, the existence of which is confirmed rather than denied by the defense of them.

Business people and some social scientists also deprecate the business influence on contemporary thinking by alleging only a narrow range of influence: selling goods and services. But selling is only the most conspicuous effort at control that business elites attempt. Their less obvious communications and other influence work quietly through the schools and through repeated reinforcement of endorsements of the status quo, existing equalities of income and wealth, authority, political docility, and the other common virtues of contemporary societies. Many—probably most—of their messages have no explicit political content. An example: corporate assurances on American television in the 1970s that the petroleum industry could cope with the oil shocks by energetically prospecting for new petroleum sources, without requiring new policy initiatives from Washington. The messages dramatically displayed off-shore oil rigs with a splendid technology and promised a more abundant supply of oil, but contained no explicit reference to any issue of public policy. Most of us do

32. Edward S. Herman, *Corporate Control, Corporate Power* (Cambridge: Cambridge University Press, 1981), p. 384.

33. For U.K. corporate assets in 1980, see Central Statistics Office, *U.K. National Accounts* (London: Her Majesty's Stationary Office, 1987), table 13.7, p. 96. For U.K. union assets in 1980, see Arthur Marsh, *Trade Union Handbook*, 3d ed. (Aldershot: Gower, 1984), pp. 24–25.

not stop to recognize the constancy of business influence on our probing implied in such a statement as this from a West German business
leader: "[Politics] is not an alien world to the entrepreneur; it is his
own. At stake for him is the leadership of the state."[34] And much of
business influence on contemporary thinking is hidden from view as
a distinct source of influence for the very reason that past successes
of elites have created a structure or pattern of public opinion such
that business messages seem to assert nothing but only register an
agreement with what others already believe.

In trying to demonstrate their inefficacy in the competition of
ideas, business people also point to frequent cinematic depictions of
business executives as clowns or villains. This fact points to a variety
of explanations, of which one is that corporate executives are seen as
powerful people, intensely interesting subjects for speculation. Politicians are also often pictured as clowns or villains—and because of
their power, not in denigration of it. As evidence of the strength of
business influence on thinking, I sense—though data are lacking—
that in the U.S., and perhaps elsewhere as well, generalizations categorically disdainful of politicians (popular at least since Mr. Dooley
and Will Rogers) are entirely permissible in discourse, while comparable categorical disdain for corporate executives is not. The former
stimulates a smile; the latter an anxiety that the speaker means something subversive or radical. Consider the frequency of generalized
regret for the characteristic spinelessness, equivocation, and incompetence of politicians with the insistence in much discourse that an
errant business executive is only one rotten apple.[35]

Political Elites

The answer to the question of whether contemporary elites are
still motivated to continue the struggle to defend their existing advantages seems less obvious in the case of political elites. For although
political elites, like everyone else to some significant degree, pursue
their own private purposes and possess extraordinary opportunities
to benefit themselves at the expense of everyone else, still they do

34. Heinz Hartmann, *Authority and Organization in German Management*
(Princeton: Princeton University Press, 1959), p. 229.
35. One would think that on business influence on contemporary thinking one
could tap into a long line of research. This is no so in any country. Instead, research is
somehow deflected from the fundamental question of the influence to
such questions as what business people think about their power, whether large firms
are more active or influential than smaller firms, and whether business influence,
whatever it amounts to, is rising or declining. See, for example, David Vogel, *Fluctuat-
ing Fortunes* (New York: Basic Books, 1989).

accept some legal and moral constraints and at least intermix a commitment to public purposes with their contrary pursuits.[36] Just how much room does this leave for attempts they might make to defend their own advantages?

No one can fathom the magnitude of impairment at the hands of political elites without first acknowledging that the state or government, though a necessary institution, is not a very benign one. While accomplishing tasks that confer benefits on most of the population, it has always offered some people advantages at the expense of others. Coercion and extraction mark its history; "the state-makers only imposed their wills on the populace through centuries of ruthless effort."[37] Over the centuries, it has perhaps been more conspicuously a destroyer and killer than an instrument of betterment.

Nor in democratic societies does the malignancy of the state recede into a distant past. A species of the genus state—or perhaps a domesticated variety—democracy has shown itself capable of waging murderous wars of dubious justification, of treating minorities inhumanely, of harassing dissenters, and of denying individual rights. Democracies often attend to humane purposes only weakly and fitfully.

Democratic politics seems removed from advantaging and exploitation when it establishes nearly unanimous common purposes like national defense, resource conservation, or education for the young. But even for these purposes it falls away immediately into a politics of advantaging because participants load the costs of these common purposes on some rather than others, or give a particular character to these programs so as to advantage some rather than others, or put the control of the programs into the hands of officials sympathetic to some people or groups rather than to others.

Democratic governments or states sometimes appear to intend a higher degree of control of the citizen's mind than do nonauthoritarian states that can rely more heavily on such forms of repression as incarceration, exile, discharge from job, and terror. If control of the mind or coerced obedience in behavior stand as alternatives, democracy has to choose the former.[38] In early democracy, we saw, elites

36. As emphatically argued recently in Steven Kelman, *Making Public Policy* (New York: Basic Books, 1987); and Robert B. Reich, ed., *The Power of Public Ideas* (Cambridge, Mass.: Ballinger, 1988).

37. Charles Tilly, ed., *The Formation of National States in Western Europe* (Princeton: Princeton University Press, 1975), p. 24.

38. See David Apter, *Choice and the Politics of Allocation* (New Haven: Yale University Press, 1971), pp. 138–148. On the relative influence of indoctrination and repression in authoritarian societies, see James C. Scott, *Weapons of the Weak* (New Haven: Yale University Press, 1983), chap. 8. On the efforts of South Africa's National

took up this task of "winning men's minds," a frequent euphemism for impairing them. Earlier elites frankly acknowledged the task of winning minds. Bagehot wrote: "Our statesmen . . . have to guide the new voters in the exercise of the franchise; to guide them quietly, and without saying what they are doing, but still to guide them."[39] Yet in the twentieth century, elites sometimes dare express the same intent: "If we understand the mechanism and motives of group mind, it is now possible to control and regiment the masses according to our will without their knowing it."[40] Political elites inundate citizens with messages designed to shape, inhibit, or slow their demands while maintaining their support for the regime.

The most familiar examples of obfuscating messages from political elites appear in election campaigns. Campaigns routinely oversimplify and misrepresent—indeed, almost everyone seems simply to accept as normal their various obstructions to probing. In recent decades, campaign obfuscations have multiplied at the hands of inventive practitioners of the techniques used to sell consumer goods.[41] As a result, organized political discussion of parties and candidates may now do more to obstruct probing than to assist it. In both campaigns and other arenas, a study of the history of political discourse from Athens to today concludes: "Political rhetoric has virtually become a barrier to communication." It intends "not to persuade, but to control; not to stimulate thought, but to prevent it; not to convey information, but to conceal or distort it; not to draw public attention, but to divert or suppress it."[42] Our everyday experience with it confirms that political communication conveys "images and symbols rather than argument," and emotions rather than thoughts. It appeals to the "elusive and fugitive" listener or reader "with evocative imagery."[43]

If information and analysis disappear in this kind of rhetoric, they also disappear when officials and agencies deliberately conceal. Concealments extend from security issues to others that suit the con-

---

party government to develop a new ideology capable of appealing to the black majority as their capacity to control that majority by coercion declines, see Stanley B. Greenberg, *Legitimating the Illegitimate: State, Markets, and Resistance in South Africa* (Berkeley: University of California Press, 1987), esp. pp. 171–201.

39. Walter Bagehot, *The English Constitution* (Ithaca, N.Y.: Cornell University Press, 1966), introduction to the second edition (1872), p. 274.

40. Edward L. Bernays, *Propaganda* (New York: Liveright, 1928), p. 83.

41. Robert Westbrook, "Politics as Consumption," in Richard Wightman Fox and T. J. Jackson Lears, eds., *The Culture of Consumption* (New York: Pantheon, 1983).

42. Paul Corcoran, *Political Language and Rhetoric* (St. Lucia, Queensland: University of Queensland Press, 1979), pp. 175, xv.

43. Ibid., p. 161.

venience of officials who wish to protect themselves.[44] "In the Western democracies generally," an observer concludes, "a blanket of official secrecy and obfuscation, going beyond the legitimate demands of security and good government, is a more serious threat to traditional liberal concepts than persuasive, blatant propaganda."[45]

In addition to the impositions of concealment and of obstructive messages, heavier-handed impositions of intimidation and coercion by political elites are commonplace in nondemocratic societies and persist, though on a smaller scale, in the liberal democracies. Every democracy has a record of crippling popular dissenters by such tactics as withdrawing their passports or intimidating employers to discharge them. "There has probably never been a government, no matter how tolerant and benign, that has never expelled or imprisoned some citizens for espousing alternatives to the status quo."[46] Even execution is practiced now and then, through capital charges brought against dissenters who appear to be prosecuted, however, less for the announced charge than for the dissent. In the U.S., Federal Bureau of Investigation practices, many of which are illegal, include disruption of political meetings, domestic espionage, and personal harassment.[47]

In all political systems, elites compete with each other. And democracy opens up a freer competition among elites in which masses

44. Jonathan Aitken, *Officially Secret* (London: Weidenfeld and Nicolson, 1971), p. 2.

45. Terence H. Qualter, *Opinion Control in the Democracies* (London: Macmillan, 1985), p. x.

46. Robert Weissberg, *Political Learning, Political Choice, and Democratic Citizenship* (Englewood Cliffs, N.J.: Prentice-Hall, 1974), p. 3.

47. For a brief account of historical uses of such tactics in England, see Francis Hearn, *Domination, Legitimation, and Resistance* (Westport, Conn.: Greenwood Press, 1978), pp. 96–99. On FBI harassment, see Herbert Mitgang, *Dangerous Dossiers* (New York: Donald I. Fine, 1988); and Richard L. Criley, "The Cult of the Informer Revisited," *Crime and Social Justice* 21–22 (1984). On intimidation of dissenters generally in Europe and the U.S., see Robert J. Goldstein, *Political Repression in Nineteenth-Century Europe* (London: Croom Helm; Totowa, N.J.: Barnes and Noble, 1983), and his *Political Repression in Modern America* (Cambridge, Mass.: Schenkman, 1978). See also John Gaventa, *Power and Powerlessness* (Urbana: University of Illinois Press, 1980); Frank Donner, *The Age of Surveillance* (New York: Knopf, 1980); and Bud Schultz and Ruth Schultz, *It Did Happen Here* (Berkeley: University of California Press, 1989). On recent security police interventions in Canadian political activities, see Edward Mann and John A. Lee, *The RCMP versus the People* (Don Mills, Ontario: General, 1979), pp. 25–66, 107–121; and Richard Frence and André Beliveau, *The RCMP and the Management of National Security* (Montreal: Institute of Research on Public Policy, 1979), esp. pp. 19–34. On Japan, see Beverly Smith, "Democracy Derailed: Citizens' Movements in Historical Perspective," in Gavan McCormack and Yoshio Sugimoto, eds., *Democracy in Contemporary Japan* (London: M. E. Sharpe, 1986).

48. Adolf Sturmthal, *The Tragedy of European Labor, 1918–1939* (New York:

of people can choose among the competitors. But, as many observers of democracy will grant and as the evidence and argument of these chapters maintain, on many fundamentals of political and economic organization—on many issues on which convergences develop—they compete weakly or not at all, just as corporations, however intensely competing for sales, do not compete in the many ways in which they influence people on convergences.

Conflict among political elites makes them on some points a less monolithic influence on the competition of ideas than business elites are on the desirable role of government enterprises. For in some countries socialists and communists play important roles within the political elite. Rising in the political elite—specifically, moving from membership in the opposition to membership in the government—puts great pressure, however, on communists and socialists in the liberal democracies to dampen their radicalism, both to win votes and to conduct a successful government if elected.[48] Witness the pressure on Mitterand to modify his socialism both to win office and to hold it. Witness also the domestication of Italian communists.

As a result, although some members of political elites maintain a drumfire of dissent, their far more numerous political colleagues join in much the same messages as businessmen. Indeed, the interchange of business and political elites becomes so close that the two cannot be separated. If a Republican Herbert Hoover could say, "The sole function of government is to bring about a condition of affairs favorable to the beneficial development of private enterprise,"[49] a Democratic John F. Kennedy could say many decades later, "This country cannot prosper unless business prospers. . . . So there is no long-run hostility between business and government."[50] Kennedy's statement is precisely correct, for no market-oriented society can prosper unless business prospers. Members of the political elite, even a Mitterrand, know that and act accordingly. In their places in the competition of ideas the two elites do not come together wholly on business's terms. Governments exercise formidable powers; hence

---

Columbia University Press, 1943); Ralph Miliband, *Parliamentary Socialism* (London: Allen & Unwin, 1961); and Frank Parkin, *Class Inequality and Political Order* (New York: Praeger, 1971), p. 135.

49. Quoted in Stephen L. Elkin, "Capitalism in Constitutive Perspective" (xerox, 1988), pp. 18–19; on Hoover's beliefs concerning the appropriate economic role of the state, see the essays by Ellis Hawley (esp. pp. 4–6 and 11–15) and Gerald Nash (esp. pp. 99–102) in Ellis W. Hawley et al., *Herbert Hoover and the Crisis of American Capitalism* (Cambridge, Mass.: Schenkman, 1973).

50. Quoted in Alan Wolfe, *America's Impasse* (New York: Pantheon, 1981), p. 67.

the two elites move reciprocally toward their agreements.[51] They do so because of the dependence of each on the other and for other reasons as well—among them, common backgrounds and education.

One final word on how both business and political elite make use of the media. The democracies have not made their principal forms of institutional communication into methods of enlightenment. The media are designed primarily to enable communicators to control audiences—specifically, to believe something, buy something, or do something. Hence, the democracies, like authoritarian societies, have made the obfuscation of probing into an industry—an industry with the immediate task of capturing the minds of members of that society in large part through kinds of communications that misrepresent and in other ways obstruct informed and thoughtful probing. They have made a business of impairment.

In the history of humankind there is nothing quite like this institutionalization of deliberate, planned, carefully calculated impairment through sales promotion, institutional advertising, and the use of the same techniques in campaigning and political advocacy. In many societies, clergy have enjoyed comparable freedom to impose but have been far less well financed to do so. Not even exploitative political authority has given such focused and sustained attention to addling the minds of its subjects as have those engaged in these contemporary institutions of impairment.[52]

APPENDIX 1: RELIGIOUS ELITES

Although organized religion achieves an access to many juvenile minds that impairs because it is not challenged in a crippled competition of ideas—for in many families neither parents nor the schools take up such a challenge—the more important point to make about impairment through organized religion concerns the content of many of the communications, both for children and adults. A number of religions and sects not only do not acknowledge the validity of the kind of probing discussed in this book, they are explicitly hostile to it. On those issues that concern them, they discourage skeptical inquiry

51. An extraordinarily hard-headed and fair-minded formulation of the government-business relation in the liberal democracies, one that displays as well an excellent command of the relevant literature of controversy on the topic, is the Elkin paper cited in note 49.

52. Here is an opportunity to try to falsify my analysis: show that media managers, business executives, and government officials do not enjoy large advantages in the communication of information and ideas or that, even if they do, they do not converge on such attitudes and beliefs as I attribute to them.

and instead call on their audiences to accept what they hear on faith. They are hostile to demands for evidence, to challenge and counter-challenge, to openness of inquiry, and to individual attempts at some significant degree of autonomy of thought. In short, they impair. They contrast with other religious elites who are more committed to open inquiry, evidence, and challenge.

Shall I try to demonstrate the correctness of my characterization of these religious elites opposed to probing? The audience for such a demonstration is composed of two parts. One part is already persuaded. The other part is persuaded by other methods of "knowing" either that the characterizations are incorrect or that, even if correct, they show not impairment but virtue. Nothing I can say will reach and persuade the latter. For neither group, therefore, is there any point in an attempted demonstration.

Is there a third group somewhere between these two? Perhaps they are the practitioners or advocates of science, of open inquiry, and of skepticism rather than faith, among them scientists and social scientists on university faculties, who nevertheless have walled off in their minds a corner or subdivision in which impairments of these religions or sects survive or even flourish as moral virtues, their inconsistency with what is in the rest of the mind simply ignored. It is unlikely that members of this third group would find any persuasiveness in a demonstration that must question, inter alia, so curious a partitioning of their minds. For purposes of this book, I think it advisable to let that sleeping dog lie. I note, however, without further comment the institutionalization of religious impairment in many rituals of universities that are ostensibly committed to the reduction of impairment. If for many people of religious faith their impairment is enormous, I shall not press the point. Aside from the futility of doing so, it is considered discourteous, bad form, even unethical to engage in reason on this subject (a fact that is in itself a monument to impairment).

APPENDIX 2: BUSINESS IN POLITICS

In societies ostensibly committed to a competition of ideas, one might suppose that the volume of resources that various parties throw into impairing or enlightening attempts to influence popular opinion and the thinking of government officials would be well researched. It is not. Even for the U.S., better studied than other nations, research is fragmentary. What estimates and judgment there are, however, for opinion-molding activities of business managers and labor union officials leave no doubt about the existence of an extremely large advantage for business managers. For bits and pieces of the evidence, see Lindblom, *Politics and Markets* (New York: Basic Books, 1976), chaps. 13–15. The following bibliography is organized by country:

FRANCE

Peter Hall, "Economic Planning and the State," in Maurice Zeitlin, ed., *Political Power and Social Theory*, vol. 3 (Greenwich, Conn.: JAI Press, 1982).

William Safran, *The French Polity*, 2d ed. (New York: Longmans, 1985), pp. 105, 254 f.

Vincent Wright, *The Government and Politics of France* (New York: Holmes and Meier, 1978), p. 193.

WEST GERMANY

Gerard Braunthal, *The Federation of German Industry in Politics* (Ithaca, N.Y.: Cornell University Press, 1965), chap. 3.

Lewis J. Edinger, *Politics in West Germany*, 2d ed. (Boston: Little, Brown, 1977), pp. 223–227.

Peter J. Katzenstein, *Policy and Politics in West Germany* (Philadelphia: Temple University Press, 1987), p. 26.

Andrei S. Markovits, *The Politics of the West German Trade Unions* (Cambridge: Cambridge University Press, 1986), pp. 28, 30, 423.

Frank Vogl, *German Business after the Economic Miracle* (London: Macmillan, 1973), chap. 6.

SWEDEN

Victor A. Pestoff, "The Politics of Private Business, Cooperatives and Public Enterprise in a Corporate Democracy—The Case of Sweden," *EUI Colloquium Papers* 1988 (a mimeo by the University of Stockholm Department of Business Administration, prepared for The European University Institute, Florence, Italy), pp. 45–83.

Bo Rothstein, "State and Capital in Sweden" Report 18, English Series, of *The Study of Power and Democracy in Sweden* (Uppsala, March 1988), p. 12.

Michael Micheletti, "The Involvement of Swedish Labor Market Organizaitons in the Swedish Political Process," Occasionai Paper 18 of Business and Social Research Institute (Stockholm 1984): a statistical comparison of union expenditures, not with employer expenditures but with employer association expenditures.

JAPAN

Ronald Hrebenar, "The Money Base of Japanese Politics," in Hrebenar, ed., *The Japanese Party System* (Boulder, Colo.: Westview Press, 1986), pp. 57f, 71, 194.

UNITED KINGDOM

Julian Friedmann, *Review of Security and the State* (London: Julian Friedmann Books, 1978), pp. 135–145.

On interpretation bearing on union spending, see Ralph Miliband, *Capitalist Democracy in Britain* (Oxford: Oxford University Press, 1982), chap. 3.

Michael Pinto-Duschinsky, *British Political Finance, 1830–1980* (Washington, D.C.: American Enterprise Institute for Public Policy Research, 1981).

Richard Rose, *Influencing Voters* (New York: St. Martin's, 1967), p. 171 and appendix.

UNITED STATES

Ronald Brownstein and Maxwell Glen, "Money in the Shadows", *National Journal*, March 15, 1986, p. 634.

Thomas Milan Konda, "Political Advertising and Public Relations Advertising by Business in the United States," Ph.D. diss., University of Kentucky, 1983, p. 94.

Steven Lyndenberg, *Bankrolling Ballots: Update 1980* (New York: Council on Economic Priorities, 1981), Appendix A.

Phyllis McGrath, *Redefining Corporate-Federal Relations* (New York: The Conference Board, 1979), pp. 37, 44, 48.

Don A. Mele, "Organizations Seeking to Influence Tax Policy," *Tax Notes*, September 21, 1981, p. 629.

Nutrition Action 15 (September 1988), p. 8.

Mary Ann Pires, "Fertile Fields," *Public Relations Journal* 42 (November 1986), p. 41.

Linda Cordillo Platzer, *Annual Survey of Corporate Contributions* ed. (New York: The Conference Board, 1987), p. 42.

Mike Ryan, Carol Swanson, and Rogene Buchholz, *Corporate Strategy, Public Policy, and the Fortune 500* (Oxford: Blackwell, 1987), p. 72.

K. L. Schlozman and J. T. Tierney, *Organized Interests and American Democracy* (New York: Harper & Row, 1986), p. 67.

Leo Troy and Neil Sheflin, *Union Sourcebook: Membership, Structure, Finance Directory* (West Orange, N.J.: Industrial Relations Data Information Services, 1985), pp. 4–6.

Neil Ulman, "Companies Organize Employees and Holders into a Political Force," *Wall Street Journal*, August 15, 1978, pp. 1, 15.

Sidney Verba and Gary R. Orren, *Equality in America* (Cambridge: Harvard University Press, 1985), p. 16.

CHAPTER 8

Convergences as Evidence

of Impairment

One final and unusual analysis of the impairing influences of elites and other advantaged groups bears both on the magnitude or general severity of impairment and on the specific additional hypothesis that one major pattern of impairing influences takes the form of defense of advantages.

Setting aside impairments that produce a diversity of incompetences, I continue to examine convergences of attitude, empirical belief, value, and volition in order to lay the ground for and then propose a hypothesis that forges another link between such convergences, usually attributed to the socialization process discussed in chapter 5, and impairment arising from defense of advantages.

I preface the hypothesis by first asking how such convergences among large numbers of people on complex social issues can be explained if not by impairment. Certain kinds of pragmatic agreements—in contrast to the convergent volitions under discussion here—are easy to explain. When, for example, legislators perceive the need to form a majority so that a legislative decision can be taken on an issue, their transitory pragmatic agreement is hardly puzzling. Similarly, we can understand why people come to agree on a common language: although they do not deliberately decide to create one, their practical needs for communication with each other induce each of them to exploit commonalities in sounds and signs; and over enormously long periods of time, languages consequently develop.[1] Setting aside what might be called urgencies—practical desires for agreement in order to accomplish a purpose in mind—the question posed here is: why do convergences develop on volitions on complex social issues? On such issues, agreement on volitions is not obviously urgent or necessary, as in the case of the legislative decision. Even when on policy issues the society decides for or against higher taxes, a military attack on a neighboring nation, or a program for energy conservation through a vote or authoritative decision that imposes an outcome, underlying volitions can remain divergent. Hence, if instead of remaining divergent they themselves converge, an explanation is required.

EXPLAINING CONVERGENCES

How to explain the convergences? This is a question that some people never ask, for they simply take it for granted that people in any society think alike in some respects. Looking at fashions in dress, taste for music, or items of folklore, they see some degree of likemindedness as normal, natural, to be taken for granted. But I press the question: how does it come about on complex social issues? Even if such likemindedness appears simply as normal, natural, or taken for granted, it nevertheless needs explaining.

Social scientists have often written about the benefits of likemindedness without explaining its causes. They say that it is necessary to organized, stable, and peaceful social life. Perhaps so. If so, it is all the more significant to ask, How is it achieved? Many political scientists say that it is also necessary to democracy, for without likemindedness only a coercive government could survive.[2] Perhaps so. If so, all the more important again to know how achieved. Its necessity to social stability or to democracy does not explain how it comes about. Anthropologists and sociologists say that shared ideas constitute a culture. Perhaps so. But why do people share rather than differ

1. This is not a functional explanation. I do not say that language is functional and that its necessity is the cause of its creation. I say only that people who wish to communicate with each other will be motivated to seize upon sounds and signs that carry agreed meanings.

2. For this argument and evaluations of it, see James Piereson, John L. Sullivan, and George Marcus, "Political Tolerance: An Overview and Some New Findings," in John C. Pierce and John L. Sullivan, eds., *The Electorate Reconsidered* (Beverly Hills, Calif.: Sage, 1980).

over some ideas? Even if one defines a society as a collection of people joined by shared attitudes and beliefs, values, and volitions, one needs an explanation of how or why a collection turns into a society.[3] Some people dismiss the convergences as nothing more than the mainstream of thought in a society. But must a mainstream exist instead of competing streams of thought? If a mainstream, why? What are its sources and causes?[4]

Explanations Rejected

A common biological imprint explains very little convergence. We are all likeminded in forming volitions to satisfy biological drives like hunger. Perhaps we are also likeminded in less obvious ways— say, in a common desire to enjoy the protection of a father figure or in a disposition to seek revenge. But if biology explains why we all wish to eat, it does not explain why in some societies people eat dog meat and in others do not. It largely fails as an explanation of complex social attitudes, beliefs, values, and volitions. It explains relatively little about why some societies believe in witchcraft, shaking hands, euthanasia, labor unions, corporations, legislatures, torture, or Christmas trees.

A common proffered explanation of convergence is tradition. "Tradition," however, refers not to the origins of a belief, attitude, value, or practice, but to "whatever is persistent or recurrent through transmission."[5] If so, tradition can just as well explain how a society inherits not convergences but a great diversity of attitude, belief, value, and volition. Nor does a reference to tradition explain

3. See, for the one but not the other, Geert Hofstede, *Culture's Consequences* (Beverly Hills, Calif.: Sage, 1980). An interesting attempt to trace what I call volitions to their origins in culture that, like other references to culture, does not explain convergences is Aaron Wildavsky, "Choosing Preferences by Constructing Institutions: A Cultural Theory of Preference Formation," *American Political Science Review* 81 (March 1987).

4. Although social scientists interested in the contribution of convergences to social stability and democracy have not well studied the causes of convergence, others have. In social psychology and sociology, one can find, as noted in chapter 5, an interest in convergences running through the classics of political philosophy, to which one can add recent scholarship at least since Ross, Cooley, and Mead. This work on the causation of likemindedness has not often been brought to bear on the literature on likemindedness as a source of stability and democracy. Moreover, work has been largely occupied with formative influences that operate within small-group relations—that is, what might be called microcausation to the neglect of macrocausation. In addition, it does not ask a question fundamental to the present inquiry: what is the relative significance in formation of attitude and belief of external influences that edify or illuminate and those that impair? For a history of these studies, see Albert Pepitone, "Lessons from the History of Social Psychology," *American Psychologist* 36 (September 1981).

5. Edward Shils, *Tradition* (Chicago: University of Chicago Press, 1981), p. 12.

how the transmission occurs. If through misrepresentation, intimidation, blind obedience to authoritative teaching, or obfuscation of issues, then the resulting convergence, even if apparently explained by tradition, traces to impairment.

The same difficulty obstructs common explanation of convergences as attributable to socialization. In an earlier chapter I noted that socializing can be either nonconformist or conformist. If conformist, how is the conformity produced?[6]

Others try to explain convergence through culture transmission: for example, increasing communication through trade or war. But why would people who trade or fight with each other think alike rather than create out of their conflicts a diversity of thought? Still another answer alleges that ideas tend to spread. If so, then many ideas would move about in contention with each other. How does one explain why some ideas drive out others?

Or one might seek an explanation of likemindedness in such a process as some social scientists call "state formation," and thus in such developments in a geographical area as political hegemony responding to a common culture or imposed by invaders. But if a common culture, from what causes or origins does it arise? How the commonalities develop remains unanswered. If they are imposed by invaders, the convergence—whether of form of government, of language, or of economic organization—presumably is imposed with a good deal of coercion. Such a case then looks like a clear instance of elite impairment.

Some say that people become likeminded because they instinctively like to attach themselves to leaders and then take on the attitudes, beliefs, and values of their leaders.[7] If so, innumerable groups, each attached to its leader and each internally likeminded, would differ in thinking from group to group. Similarly, if people instinctively desire to be like each other, such a desire would lead to like-

6. A thoughtful reading of two surveys of a good deal of the literature on socialization will show that it, like the reviewers, largely pursues concerns with the benefits of socialization, apparently does not find the question of causes significant or interesting (as indicated not by explicitly rejecting causal analysis but by ignoring it), and goes no further than to acknowledge "instances," not followed up as indicative of broader causal factors, of "dysfunctional" methods of socialization. See Victor Gecas, "Contents of Socialization," and Diane Mitsch Bush and Roberta G. Simmons, "Socialization Processes over the Life Course," both in Morris Rosenberg and Ralph H. Turner, eds., *Social Psychology* (New York: Basic Books, 1981). For further discussion of the literature on socialization, see chapter 12 below, where I offer the literature as itself an example of impairment of social science. See also note 4 above.

7. As described in Wilfred Trotter, *Instincts of the Herd in Peace and War* (London: Unwin, 1916).

mindedness within groups small enough to permit conversation, observation, and reciprocal display rather than constitute a strong push toward uniformity in the impersonal relations of millions in a nation-state or region of the world.[8]

Perhaps convergence or likemindedness simply grows out of common life circumstances? People think alike because they live alike. But they do not live alike, for differences in income, work situation, hence of standard of living and pattern of consumption, differentiate people—and all this on top of frequent ethnic and religious differences. In any case, as already observed, each person does not so much observe the world as read and hear interpretations of it. How then do the interpretations converge?

Perhaps, then, people think alike simply because they do not think much—at least about complex social issues. But if they think little about them, why would not the superficiality of their thought produce differences among them, even eccentricities, rather than convergences? Perhaps—to try another explanation—they are incapable of thinking about unfamiliar institutions and practices. Again, a failure in explanation. For they do not converge simply in not thinking about the unfamiliar. They converge in thinking about the familiar—family, government, unions, authority, and the like—instead of developing competing beliefs and volitions about them. Perhaps, then, they think alike to escape cognitive dissonance. Again, this is no explanation, for reconciling dissonances calls for coherence or consistency in each mind but no similarity between minds.

Finally, one might suggest that people think alike because on complex social issues they think only incrementally, that is, about small changes in existing policies, and that they must do so because the political system can ordinarily cope with no more than incremental policy proposals. But why can the political system not cope with a wider range of possibilities? Because neither officials, nor other political functionaries, nor citizens think more broadly. If so, the explanation has become circular.[9]

KNOWLEDGE AS A VALID BUT LIMITED EXPLANATION

The only general alternative to impairment as an explanation of convergent thinking is knowledge. People converge in the belief that

8. On the former, see Aaron Wildavsky, "Choosing Preferences by Constructing Institutions," *American Political Science Review* 81 (March 1987).

9. As well as for several other conclusive reasons. See the appendix to this chapter on incrementalism.

the earth is a sphere. People agree that trees are not made of styro-foam because there exist "out there" things classified as trees that various observers can observe and put to test; and since all the observers examine the same category of things, they come to an agreed conclusion. If a real world exists "out there," then knowledge about it will lead thinking about it to converge. For present purposes it is enough to define knowledge as well-probed belief, whether empirical or evaluative.[10] Since even the best probing remains fallible, knowledge is sometimes false. But the error stems from shared perceptions and interpretations among multiple observers all examining and interpreting the same objective reality "out there." A presumed tie of some kind between an external reality and a proposition about it lies behind the concept of knowledge.

Knowledge explains not only convergence on propositions excellently tested—that water consists of H_2O, that some diseases are spread by viruses, that money talks in politics, and that Western Europeans are richer than the Bangladeshi—but also convergences tested less conclusively: for example, that military deterrence avoids, or at least postpones, war; or that commerce can flourish only on some at least minimal degree of honesty and trust among participants. Highly "verified" propositions go by the name of fact; less "verified" ones by the name of judgment.

Compelling Observations

The category of beliefs on which convergence might be attributable to knowledge includes an in-between set of beliefs resting on what might be called a compelling or seductive empirical observation.[11] The observable flatness of the earth apparently once compelled or seduced people to agree on its flatness. They regarded their observations as conclusive, as constituting a sufficient probe. Presumably, some of contemporary knowledge derives from compel-

10. Obviously, not everyone confirms his own observation that the earth is spherical, or much of anything else he claims to know. But he knows that the earth is spherical because he knows that some others have so observed and, a few eccentrics aside, are not challenged by other observers. To explain how he knows that others have observed requires another round of the same kind of explanation.

Whether a belief is well enough probed to be called knowledge will be answered differently by different people depending on what they think is essential to good probing. That something is known is never more than a disputable claim. There is no neutral detached position from which any observer can adjudicate disputes over whether a belief does or does not constitute knowledge.

11. It would not disturb the developing argument to make a separate category of the compelling or seductive observation, so long as one takes account of it one way or another.

ling observations common to most or all people or to most or all scientists.

If seductive or compelling direct observations may pull people toward agreement on some beliefs, they do not go far to explain convergences on complex social issues. Attitudes and beliefs about complex social issues derive, as noted, from interpretation of a social world in the absence of a compelling or seductive observation. For a complex issue, no one can observe a resolution (except after the fact). No one can derive a belief in private property or about many of its empirical effects, the Protestant work ethic, the certainty of retribution, or the value of self-discipline from any compelling observation. Hence, belief in them is either well probed—and constitutes knowledge—or is impaired.

Yet the concept of a seductive or compelling observation helps to explain two phenomena crucial to the present line of analysis. Masses of people can and do observe many kinds of social inequality—in income and wealth, power and other influence, status, accorded deference, and the like. Observing these empirical phenomena, they are strongly drawn to hostility to many of them. They cannot *observe* that the inequalities are unjust or unwarranted, for observation cannot decide such a question. But it is easy to understand that the observation of the inequalities themselves would give rise to many attacks on them and many convergences hostile to them. Hence, even though inegalitarian lines of thought and attitude enjoy the advantages of elite advocacy, some conspicuous egalitarian convergences develop, especially highly abstract convergences that coexist with inegalitarian convergences at a lower level of abstraction. So the egalitarian convergences, resting as they do on a hostility to observed inequalities rather than on careful probing of issues about inequality, again represent the result of impaired inquiry. But impairments in this case derive from seductive observations rather than elite influences.

Similarly, elites can observe—correctly or by seductive observation—both that they hold advantages and that the advantages can be employed to defend the advantages. Money, other economic assets, prestige, various forms of power and influence can all be employed in the defensive struggle. That elites consequently converge in attitudes and beliefs defensive of their advantages and in using them as instruments of their own defense is hardly puzzling.

Hence, some degree of knowledge mixed with some degree of seductive observation produces some convergences among egalitarians and among inegalitarians. Neither group probes the merits of various institutions and policies with any satisfactory degree of competence.

Remaining to be explained, however, are those convergences that concern these chapters—on authority, deference, hierarchy, political docility, and many explicit forms of political, social, and economic inequality. That they are shared not solely by elites but by masses of people, contrary to the attitudes and beliefs that might be anchored in popular seductive observations, calls for an explanation other than seductive observation.

Convergences that Knowledge Cannot Produce

Granted all these possible ways to explain convergence as a consequence of knowledge, knowledge falls short as an explanation for convergence on the kind of beliefs, attitudes, values, and volitions on complex social issues that have been discussed in this chapter. No one knows that a presidential system is superior to a parliamentary system, or vice versa. Yet American volitions converge on the one, and British on the other. Even on complex factual questions, empirical knowledge is usually inadequate.

Everywhere people confuse intense belief with knowledge (well-probed belief). They believe firmly in—and mistakenly claim to know—answers to questions both of fact and value: for example, that the nuclear family makes for social stability. Perhaps so, but no one *knows*. No one has well probed other possibilities, and experience has been too narrow to test the belief. Intensity of belief rests on something, but not knowledge.

That does not say people know nothing about the nuclear family or about its alternatives. They know a great deal, and it accounts for some reduction in their potential disagreement. But their knowledge falls short. They do not know as much as they agree to. Knowledge even of the most learned does not explain the narrow range of belief and attitude on the nuclear family. For another example, many people agree that a substantial reduction in wage differentials will reduce employees' incentives to work. On that proposition, intense, even dogmatic belief is apparent; but no available knowledge can settle the issue. Formal economic theory offers an "it depends" answer that provides no warrant for the convergence in many societies on sweeping and often confident "empirical" assertions that reductions would impair productivity. One must look elsewhere for the factors that produce the convergence in thought.

Similarly, empirical knowledge does not exist as a sufficient basis for convergences on such issues as arranged marriages, religious faith, the Protestant work ethic, individual versus collective values and responsibilities, the desired pace of progress, most rules for social interchange, and social and political inequality. And that the convergences on such issues vary from society to society calls even more loudly for some other explanation than knowledge.

A striking evidence that knowedge does not explain such convergences on complex social questions appears in the frequent inverse relation between convergence and knowledge, as in the example of economists' openness to a wider range of positions on incentives than laymen take. In many cases, the more knowledgeable the opinions, the less the convergence. It seems reasonably clear that social scientists entertain a wider variety of positions on many social questions than do ordinary citizens, who have probed social questions less. In Western democracies, although neither professional social scientists nor ordinary citizens endorse drastic constitutional reform, the range of inquiry and positions among the former appears broader than among the latter, as also for issues about equality, new forms of corporate organization and control, responses to stresses on family solidarity, or methods of coping with racial conflict. In addition, new bursts of research on an issue frequently produces even greater diversity.[12] Knowledge on sufficiently complex social issues explains—perhaps surprisingly—diversity better than convergence.

In chapter 2 I rejected the idea that probers who are wise enough will eventually converge on a description of utopia, for, as I also argued, there exist many different ways to live and to organize societies. Instead of uncovering a single blueprint, probers create, form, choose volitions. That is, of course, a fundamental reason for believing that not even in principle or hypothetically could knowledge produce convergence on great questions about society.

On all issues, knowledge suffices to rule out some positions and some peripheral issues. Even in the days when economists disagreed among themselves more than they do now on the merits and faults of market systems, their knowledge (in the form of probed empirical judgment) effectively disqualified some propositions, such as, for example, the foolish popular claim that market systems are "chaos" or that making money and performing a useful public service are wholly antagonistic to each other.

12. More on this in chapter 10 below. For evidence and argument on social science divergence, see David K. Cohen and Michael S. Garet, "Reforming Educational Policy with Applied Social Research," *Harvard Educational Review* 45 (February 1975); and David K. Cohen and Janet Weiss, "Social Science and Social Policy," *The Educational Forum* 41 (May 1977).

Might a Society Know Even If Individuals Do Not?

Attempts to find a larger role for knowledge as an explanation of convergences sometimes claim a kind of collective mind that knows what no individual knows—some kind of cumulative social wisdom. "Neither genetically transmitted nor rationally designed," these convergences result from an evolutionary process—social, not biological—by which, in a kind of survival of the socially fittest, intelligent rules, practices, attitudes, beliefs, and values drive out less intelligent ones.[13] As Friedrich A. Hayek has written, "The ultimate decision about what is good or bad will be made not by individual human wisdom but by the decline of the groups that have adhered to the wrong beliefs."[14] But if some groups survive and others decline, why? Groups do not compete with each other through rounds of seminars. As a critic of the survival-of-the-fittest thesis puts it, often "cultural groups decline, not because their beliefs are false or their traditions maladaptive, but simply because political power is used to suppress them or their culture."[15]

Against confidence in the benign rationality of each society, one recoils in incredulity. As noted at the outset of the preceding chapter, human interchange consists not so much of mutual education as of mutual impairment. Each society emerges as a product of a history that combines some attempts by some of its ordinary people and functionaries to bring to bear both inevitably inadequate knowledge and unending exercises in coercion and other intimidations, obfuscations, disorientations, and suppressions of information.[16]

13. *Law and Legislation, and Liberty*, vol. 3 (Chicago: University of Chicago Press, 1973), p. 155.

14. Friedrich A. Hayek, *The Constitution of Liberty* (Chicago: University of Chicago Press, 1960), p. 36. See also Richard A. Posner, *Economic Analysis of Law* (Boston: Little, Brown, 1972).

15. John Gray, *Liberalism: Essays in Political Philosophy* (London: Routledge, forthcoming).

16. When, as F. A. Hayek put it, "the ends of the successful group become the ends of all members of the society" (*The Constitution of Liberty* [Chicago: University of Chicago Press, 1960], p. 36), he appears to acknowledge that the result may be achieved by coercion, intimidation, and other harsher forms of social interchange that deny to the result the intelligence claimed for it.

Lurking behind some versions of the survival-of-the-fittest argument is the assumption that there exist objectively fit and unfit sets of attitudes, beliefs, values, and volitions, and an objective distinction between the two. That can be the case only if preferences, wants, and needs as indicators of welfare are taken as facts to be observed rather than as volitions to be formed, chosen, or willed. Thus, everything I said in chapter 2 on these concepts is an objection to the survival-of-the-fittest doctrine.

THE HYPOTHESIS: CONVERGENCE ITSELF AS EVIDENCE OF IMPAIRMENT

Now the hypothesis promised at the chapter's opening: On complex social issues on which people do not know but only believe, patterned impairment is necessary to explain their convergent thinking, the pattern being supplied by defense of elite advantages.

Compare it with the earlier argument. The preceding three chapters offered a variety of evidence of impairment, together with evidence and analysis to support the thesis that advantaged groups impair probing by distorting it to favor institutions and practices that protect the advantages of the advantaged. They do so both by misleading, obfuscating, and intimidating, and by enjoying advantages in communication that weaken and narrow a competition of ideas, as evidenced in convergences. The additional thesis now adds that on complex questions on which people cannot *know* answers and are not seduced by a compelling observation, convergences in themselves constitute evidence of impairment by elites and other advantaged groups. That is to say, even if one could not point to schools, family life, media practices, and the details of influence at the hands of business and state elites, the fact that convergences exist cannot be explained otherwise than by reference to an impairing defense of advantages.

A physician takes certain characteristic small facial scars to be evidence of an earlier affliction with a certain infectious disease. When? He cannot say. Does the disease always cause scars? No. Was the underlying cause perhaps a nutritional deficiency that raised vulnerability? He does not know; it might have been. The source of the infection? Not known; there are many possible sources. How long ago did the infection occur? He does not know; it is either early or recent. All he knows is that if there are scars, then clearly the disease must have caused them.

An audacious proposition, it does not command a high level of probability. Yet perhaps more care has been lavished on its presentation than anyone has given to the contrary thesis. A proposition of weight, it would seem to deserve thoughtful consideration and continuing debate.

The hypothesis offers the methodological advantage that it permits one to identify impairment without falling into the trap of judging a belief or attitude impaired because it differs from one's own or because it differs from those of educated people, taken as a standard. It also permits one to consider the possibility of impairment even when one cannot for the time being locate the specific impairing practices that cause it. Convergence itself supplies the evidence, irrespective of content or method.

The thesis does not say that the impairments revealed by convergences are necessarily the most severe of all impairments. Those that produce divergences, including eccentric divergences, might—nothing in our analysis denies it—be more severe. The thesis does, however, add to the weight of evidence on both of two lines of analysis pursued in this and the preceding chapters: the one on the severity or magnitude of impairment, the other on its particular pattern.

Although all of us long ago knew that impairment exists, we have easily deprecated its frequency, intensity, and significance by regarding it as peripheral and also by treating it as a given phenomenon—like, say, the Himalayas—rather than man-made and alterable. To see it now as the other side of the coin of much-prized social agreement is to acknowledge that it is not at all peripheral. It becomes central to our understanding, which we must as a consequence reconsider, of how a society or polity holds together. We turn from celebrating agreement, consensus, and harmony as sources of social order, social peace, and democracy, to facing up to them no less as cripplers of minds and obstructions to using them for human betterment. We are also confirmed in knowing that impairment is man-made, hence within some limits alterable. Influences that impair people's thinking becomes a fundamental social phenomenon and problem; coping with it, a daunting task.

The thesis has made allowance for practical or urgent agreements as on a common tongue, for seductive or compelling observation, for biologically imprinted agreements, for knowledge, and for elite-patterned impairment. Might there exist another alternative so far missed? I cannot find one, but the invitation is open to anyone who cares to try.[17] In the absence of another alternative, the limitations of each of the above explanations other than patterned impairment—and the limitations of each have been specified—leave patterned impairment as a powerful general explanation of convergences on complex social issues. Hostile as many minds will be to such a conclusion, they should not find it surprising or improbable, for the preceding chapters provided abundant evidence of impairments in a pattern of defense of elite advantages; and, more than that, it is now, if it was not always, clear that all people live in a sea of impairing influences. Culture is a society's way of swimming in it. What people feel,

17. Here, then, to be very specific, is another opportunity to try to falsify my analysis: produce an explanation of convergence that I have overlooked.

think, and do follows from their impairments as well as from their knowledge.

I have no objection to providing for one empty box to set beside the five that contain explanations. If one could find content for it, it would, at one extreme, weaken my hypothesis, or at another extreme destroy it—all depending on whether the additional explanation promised, at the one extreme, to cover only a few unusual cases or, at the other, to cover a very large number of cases. Some critics of the hypothesis might offer the incest taboo as an example of what belongs in a sixth box, for convergence on it seems unexplainable by any of the explanations so far acknowledged as at least sometimes operative. How to account for convergence on the incest taboo, I do not know. Possibly some deeply buried biological imprint can account for it, improbable as it seems. Possibly it can be traced back to primitive elite impairments, but that also seems improbable. The taboo remains a reminder that there are ragged edges to the cloth being woven, though by no means as ragged as an argument that would deny significance to convergences that elites produce through their impairing influences.

Once again, it is no valid objection to the hypothesis to declare that convergences are important elements in culture. Of course they are; but to say so says nothing about their origins or causes, nor does it deny their impairing influences, for a culture is in large part an assortment of impairments, along with some insights, skills, and effective practices. Nor is it a valid objection to the thesis to declare that some or many convergences support social stability or democracy. Whether they do or not (a question to be examined in a later chapter), their origins lie in large part in impairments, and that is a significant fact about them, however uncomfortable.

IMPAIRED UNDERSTANDING OF IMPAIRMENT

If social impairment is as broad and severe as claimed in these four chapters, no one can see it fully, not even on familiar issues. A colleague writes to me with some irritation to deny the efficacy of impairing influence in defense of elite advantages: "How and why have some priests and bishops become egalitarians if they are indoctrinated and impaired? American universities by all accounts do not have an inegalitarian influence but just the opposite. Nor do social scientists or people in the humanities. How did they escape? Reporters in the major media, whose influence has grown, are far more egalitarian than the rest of the population. Nor are the last few years' movies defenders of established inegalitarian social relations."

His implicit logic is defective. That social scientists, some clergy, and professional journalists tend to be less inegalitarian than most people does not mean that their thinking does not defend inequalities, nor does it indicate that they have escaped impairment. It does not mean that they object to the inequalities of corporate organization, to inequalities of wealth and income, or to the political inequalities of those political systems classified as democratic. It only means that they dissent in some degree from the stronger inegalitarian thinking of others. And their limited dissents reach audiences infrequently in comparison to the frequency and amplification with which the advocacy of continuing organizational, political, and economic inequalities, on which they join, finds expression. My colleague takes modal thinking in the society as a norm, departures from which indicate biases. But the norms themselves are impaired.

APPENDIX: CONVERGENCES FROM INCREMENTALISM?

An incrementalist explanation for narrowness in probing proceeds in four propositions. First, narrowness is a consequence of a disposition of citizens, policymakers, and social scientists to constrain probing, discussion, and policy-making to policy alternatives that are only incrementally different from the status quo—in short, to discard drastic, highly unfamiliar, or "big" solutions. Second, such a disposition narrowly concentrates probing, discussion, and policy-making on issues on which, because they are familiar, people can think and act more competently than if they were not familiar. Third, people are aware that such a narrowing improves their competence. Fourth, hence they choose narrowness to improve their competence, and their narrowness is thus not evidence of impairment.

Of these four propositions, only the second is probably true; and the explanation as a whole consequently fails. As for the first, narrowness of belief, discussion, and policy-making is not generally—this we have already seen—a consequence of discarding big solutions in favor of incremental ones. Such a pattern of discarding is frequent, no doubt; but the range of policies thought about, discussed, and acted on is a narrow range even within the array of incremental possibilities. For example, there is almost no discussion in the U.S. of more than a few incremental changes to grapple with a continuing informed dissatisfaction—itself little discussed—over near exclusive profit-seeking use of broadcast bands, a "resource" ostensibly in the public domain. Nor does sporadic discussion of ways to induce citizens to communicate with their representatives in Congress embrace so modest a proposal as postage-free letters. Thus, something narrows belief, discussion, and policy to a much narrower band than an incremental disposition can explain.

Then, although the second proposition is granted, the third does not follow: not everyone is so sophisticated as to understand that incrementalist thinking on many complex issues improves competence. The third proposition assumes an extraordinarily perceptive and self-disciplined body of citizens, as against a society in which, on the whole, people rarely raise issues about their own competence in social problem solving and how it might, through an appropriate strategy, be raised. Similarly, the fourth proposition strains credulity. Assuming that citizens want many things from social life and from policies, it is impossible to believe that they would foreswear belief, discussion, and action on many issues simply out of an obligation to raise their competence.

The argument that incremental thinking is commonplace in the liberal democracies, as well as in many other societies, is a strong one. So also is the argument that, other things being equal, it raises competence.[18] But why people think and act incrementally as often as they do is not explained by any of these propositions. Insofar as incremental thinking and acting constitute one form of narrowness, they, like the other forms of narrowness, require an explanation. How does that narrowness come about? How is it inculcated in a population? Who or what does what to whom, as a result of which thinking, discussion, and action are narrowed?

18. On the frequency of incrementalism and on the case for it (but not on an explanation of its sources), see Charles E. Lindblom, "Still Muddling, Not Yet Through," *Public Administration Review* 39 (November–December 1979).

PART III

The Social Science

Contribution

CHAPTER 9

What Can Social

Scientists Do?

If one seeks to understand probing, some impatient critics might here interject, one ought to look at the social sciences. The consequential probers, they might say, consist of the professionals: economists, sociologists, and other social scientists. Some critics go so far as to toy with the possibility that capacities for the professional production and organization of information and analysis bring into sight at last the scientifically organized society.[1]

Social scientists have indeed become specialist armies of inquirers, in themselves an industry.[2] They include academic social scientists, ranging from ivory-tower theorists to policy analysts; so also those attached to research institutes, as well as many attached to government agencies, business enterprises, and other organizations, some of whom pursue only modest inquiry. All professional social investigators make sustained inquiries into society with some spe-

1. See the opening of chapter 13 below on persons holding such a vision.
2. Because definitions of *social scientist* and *researcher* are not agreed upon, and for other reasons as well, good estimates of their numbers are not available. In the U.S., unusually well supplied with social scientists, it has been estimated that in 1981 there were about 100,000 social scientists, including psychologists with doctoral degrees (U.S. National Science Foundation, *Characteristics of Doctoral Scientists and Engineers in the U.S.* [Washington, D.C.: Government Printing Office, 1987]).

cialized competence and ostensibly in pursuit of some such goal as truth or wisdom.[3] Some journalists count as social scientists, but not those limited to superficial inquiry or to entertaining an audience. A difference between a professional investigator and a probing citizen or functionary is that the latter typically move to volitions, the former as often do not. Some social scientists define their task as stopping with understanding; they think it inappropriate for a social scientist, qua social scientist, to proceed to a volition.

One characteristic of social science makes an assessment of its contributions extraordinarily difficult and always leaves open the possibility that its admirers overestimate them: the absence of undeniable evidence, which is plentiful for natural science and engineering, of its indispensability. Although science may overreach itself in genetic engineering or some other heady ambition, the whole world continues to need science and engineering for one task after another: building bridges, protecting the fertility of soils, and harnessing energy, among others. Not simply helpful, they are indispensable and unmistakably so. Without science and engineering, there would be no heart bypass, no moon shot, no high-speed organization and retrieval of information, and no nuclear destruction.

Not so for social science. The centuries have given it abundant opportunities. Practiced as long as natural science, it goes back at least to ancient Greece. In the last century thousands of social scientists trying to practice methods much like those of the natural sciences have swarmed over institutions and social processes to try to extract propositions hidden to the lay mind. For all that effort and for all its presumed usefulness, I cannot identify a single social science finding or idea that is undeniably indispensable to any social task or effort.[4]

Not even one, I suggest. A few disputable cases can be argued. Some economists would claim that new insights in macrotheory are indispensable for achieved reductions in the recurring bouts of unemployment since World War II. Probably, but not unmistakably or undeniably so. For perhaps the economy stabilized because of institutional changes—among them, for example, unemployment compensation that automatically feeds new spending into the economy when it slackens.

Social science offers help even if not undeniably indispensable to

3. For a more detailed listing, see Charles E. Lindblom and David K. Cohen, *Usable Knowledge* (New Haven: Yale University Press, 1979), pp. 7–9.
4. Perhaps the closest one can come to an undeniable claim of social science indispensability to a social task or effort is its statistical methods.

many of the ventures embarked on by individuals and collectivities. A highly plausible case can be made that economics has indeed helped dampen economic fluctuations, that political science has thrown some helpful light on administrative organization, that psychology has improved the teaching process and perhaps made psychotherapy more effective, that sociology has made the treatment of deviants more humane and perhaps more constructive, and that anthropology has raised the level of intelligence with which industrialized societies deal with primitive and other nonindustrial cultures. Other examples of presumably helpful contributions are plentiful from each discipline.

Yet the troubling possibility persists that with no or only a few exceptions, societies could perhaps continue to go about these and other activities if social scientists vanished, along with their historical documents, findings, hypotheses, and all human memory of them, or if the likes of Plato, Hobbes, Adam Smith, Marx, Freud, Weber, Keynes, and a few thousand others had never lived. The disappearance would presumably in some ways render social tasks more difficult, but perhaps in no case render any existing social task impossible, as would the disappearance of any one of many contributions from natural science and engineering. The value of social science to social problem solving remains clouded to a degree that should shake any social scientist's complacency.[5]

One can easily find other grounds for caution about the consequentiality of social science. Consider, for example, that the U.S. employs many more professional investigators than does the U.K. and spends much more on social research than does the U.K. (Its expenditures are twenty to thirty or more times U.K. expenditures.) It systematically and routinely draws on social scientists to a degree not institutionalized in the U.K. For two societies sharing many common intellectual and political traditions, the difference in reliance on professional inquiry is great.[6] It is not clear that the U.S. copes with its

5. Perhaps the idea of a "task" or "venture" demands too much from social science. Perhaps instead it has produced some orienting or deeply illuminating ideas without which the world would clearly be different. Perhaps there would have been no French Revolution without the philosophers, no Soviet Union or Communist China without Marx. One cannot be sure. The idea of a market system first appeared in lay thinking, not in Adam Smith; the idea of class conflict and economic determinism in lay thinking, not in Marx; the idea of the unconscious in lay thinking, not in Freud; the idea of the achievement of economic recovery through spending in lay thinking, not in Keynes; and various new understandings of emerging bureaucracy in lay thinking, not in Weber.

6. For a discussion of the differences, see L. J. Sharpe, "The Social Scientists and Policy Making: Some Cautionary Thoughts and Transatlantic Reflections," in Carol H. Weiss, ed., *Using Social Research in Policy Making* (Lexington, Mass.: D. C. Health, 1977).

social problems better than the U.K. What superiority, if any, does the U.S. buy with its expensive support for professional social research? The example proves nothing; it only suggests again the vulnerability of professional inquiry to skeptical appraisals of it.

In the light of caution, this group of chapters sets out to locate social scientific inquiry within the broader social process of probing, examining such questions as the degree to which social scientists undertake kinds of investigations that lie beyond the competence of ordinary probers, whether social science as a set of specialized techniques restricts itself to a narrower range of inquiries than those of the ordinary or lay prober, how much it engages in confirming or disconfirming lay knowledge, and whether it contributes greatly to reducing impairment. This chapter begins with a quick and admiring look at what at the best social scientists do.[7] For example, familiar accounts say that they explain and predict. It will quickly become apparent that they do more.

EXPLANATION AND PREDICTION

Explanation and prediction, in the eyes of some methodologists, define science, including social science. "Scientific explanation" often passes as a synonym for "scientific method." Clearly social scientists engage in it. For the most part social scientists retreat, as often do natural scientists, from strict invariance in hypothesized or discovered relationships to probabilistic relations, and in the case of social science often very loose ones, such as: if the price of a good rises, the

---

7. The chapter examines concrete activities rather than abstractly investigating forms of knowing, as, for example, in the classical Greek distinction between *techne* and *episteme*. Social science inquiries can of course be classified in many different ways. Different from yet in some ways similar to our listing (see note 3 above) is that of Robin Williams, "Sociology in America," in Charles Bonjean, Louis Schneider, and Robert Lineberry, eds., *Social Science in America* (Austin: University of Texas Press, 1976), p. 98.

See also Louis M. Smith, David C. Dwyer, and John J. Prunty, "Observer Role and Field Study Knowledge" (mimeo, St. Louis, Mo.: Washington University, Graduate Institute of Education, 1980), p. 8, in which they classify some of the less obvious kinds of social science and locate them in the social science literature: thus "portrayals," R. Stake, "Description versus Analysis," in D. Hamilton et al., eds., *Beyond the Numbers Game* (London: Macmillan, 1977); "thick description," G. Ryle, "What Is 'Le Penseur' Doing?" in G. Ryle, *Collected Papers* (New York: Barnes and Noble, 1971); C. Geertz, *The Interpretation of Cultures* (New York: Basic Books, 1973); and E. Eisner, "Thick Description," in Hamilton et al., *Beyond the Numbers Game*; "grounded theory," B. Glaser and A. Strauss, *The Discovery of Grounded Theory* (Chicago: Aldine, 1967); and problem redefinition, analogies, and new metaphors, M. Rein and D. A. Schön, "Problem Setting in Policy Research," in Carol H. Weiss, ed., *Using Social Research in Public Policy Making* (Lexington, Mass: D. C. Heath, 1977).

quantity bought will decline, depending on circumstances and some exceptions.

When social scientists practice explanation and prediction, they practice a variety of kinds of inquiry not limited to conventional scientific explanation—as often modeled on theoretical physics.[8] Consequently, they differ on whether to dispense with mentalistic or subjective variables like thoughts, intentions, reasons, motives, and purposes and to anchor explanation directly in an observed behavioral regularity. Most employ mentalistic variables. The entire corpus of economic theory is full of reference to intentions, motives, and states of mind: it describes people as calculating, weighing alternatives, pursuing gain.[9] In psychology, attribution theory explains by reference to the working hypotheses held in the minds of the people whose action it explains.[10] For that matter, whenever social scientists take for granted—as does everyone—that people often design practices or institutions for various benefits to be had from them—armies for national defense or schools for educating the young—they incorporate intention and purpose into their explanations.

Human beings maintain institutions and patterns of social interrelationships under the influence of a vast variety of social controls, including those of information and persuasion, intimidation, threat, and reward. Almost every control (other than actual physical constraint such as incarceration or binding) that influences a person is processed by the influenced mind.[11] Faced, say, with a threat of job

For a classification by method, see the table of contents of Paul Diesing, *Patterns of Discovery in the Social Sciences* (Chicago: Aldine, 1971).

8. For extended discussion of alternative methods of explanation, see Robert Brown, *Explanation in Social Science* (Chicago: Aldine, 1963); and George Henrik von Wright, *Explanation and Understanding* (Ithaca, N.Y.: Cornell University Press, 1971). Just what conventional science or social science *is* in our time is not clear, since prescriptive theory about scientific method is now and has long been in flux. Theory aside, in the actual practice of professional inquiry, a wide variety of investigatory methods are employed in tandem with both positivist methods and expressed deference to positivist percepts, which to a degree cripple the other employed methods; and it is that kind of practice that I call "conventional." Yet that kind of social science has been under attack for roughly one hundred years, as detailed in H. Stuart Hughes, *Consciousness and Society* (New York: Knopf, 1961), chap. 2.

9. To complete such "rational economic man" explanations, it is necessary to supplement them with auxiliary assumptions or findings; see Herbert A. Simon, "Human Nature in Politics," *American Political Science Review* 79 (June 1985).

10. Lee Ross, "The Intuitive Psychologist and His Shortcomings," in L. Berkowitz, ed., *Advances in Experimental Social Psychology* (New York: Academic Press, 1977).

11. H. A. Simon and Allen Newell, *Human Problem Solving* (Englewood Cliffs, N.J.: Prentice-Hall, 1972), p. 788–789. See pp. 874–878 for some idea of the earlier (American) behavioralist tradition that rejected this view.

loss, what one will do depends in large part on what goes on in one's head—how the mind processes the threat. It may lead one to a vigorous search for a new job, or to a collective effort with similarly threatened fellow employees to take over management of the enterprise. Understandably, then, attempts at explanation repeatedly turn to an examination of mentalistic and subjective variables in addition to examination of statistical regularities in observed behavior.[12]

At the extreme, practitioners of interpretive or hermeneutical social science intend not at all to explain behavior and action in ways parallel to the "scientific explanation" of naturalist and positivist science, but to interpret: to examine how people both see and fail to see themselves and the world about them; what people think, mistakenly or not, that they are doing, and what purposes they pursue in their actions. Interpreters see the whole social world as a product of man's perceptions or ideas about it.[13]

Presumably, the longtime dominance of positivist prescriptions in the philosophy of science has induced many social scientists to make special efforts to enlarge positivist elements in their explanations. But only rare social scientists ever limited their practice strictly to what the positivist (or naturalist) preached. None of the examples above of explanation in social science—economic theory or attribution theory, for example—score high on positivist or naturalist standards, all corrupted or enriched as they are by explanatory elements prized by interpretists and hermeneuticists.[14]

Some social scientific explanations successfully veer away from conventional scientific explanation in other directions. For example,

12. The question of what kinds of variables are appropriate for social science continues to be disputed. It has been argued, for example, that any observed probabilistic regularity in relations among variables must be explained by the powers or tendencies of things—structures and mechanisms—to act or exert influence in particular ways. "The ultimate objects of scientific understanding are neither patterns of events nor models but the things that produce the mechanisms that generate the flux of the phenomena of the world" (Roy Bhaskar, *A Realist Theory of Science* [Atlantic Highlands, N.J.: Humanities Press, 1978], p. 66). See also, on causal powers, Paul F. Secord, "Explanation in the Social Sciences and in Life Situations," in Donald W. Fiske and Richard A. Shweder, *Metatheory in Social Science* (Chicago: University of Chicago Press, 1986), pp. 202f.

13. The different kinds of variables used in social science research are greatly clarified in Roy G. D'Andrade, "Cultural Meaning Systems," in Robert C. McAdams et al., eds., *Behavioral and Social Science Research*, part II of a report of the National Research Council Committee on Basic Research in the Behavioral and Social Sciences (Washington D.C.: National Academy Press, 1982); and in Paul F. Secord, ed., *Explaining Human Behavior* (Beverly Hills, Calif.: Sage, 1982).

14. Despite their own methodological strictures frequently hostile to the use of subjective variables in social scientific explanation, it may be that social scientists' reference to such variables is far more frequent than their references to nonsubjective

genetic explanations in social science resemble history more than science, and sciences like paleontology and geology more than physics and chemistry. They assert no empirical regularity, no causal law. They make a contribution by outlining a temporal sequence of events with plausible links: for example, some psychological explanations of human maturation through stages of physical, cognitive, or moral development or explanations of economic or political modernization.[15] Social scientists also engage heavily in functional "explanation." Certain witchcraft practices are alleged to maintain social stability among the Navahos.[16] Markets are alleged to be necessary for efficient resource allocation. Agreement among political activists on fundamental rules of the game is alleged to be necessary for stable democratic government.[17] Linked with feedback from function performed to observed process, functionalism becomes a useful kind of cybernetic explanation.[18]

Even in one social scientist's work, several methods of explanation usefully mix. Some social scientists attempt to reconcile elements of conventional "scientific explanation" that rely on invariances or probabilistic relationships among behavioral variables with elements like reasons and purposes, so that they describe an action as the result of choices of persons constrained by an environment of external physical forces and external social controls.[19] Or, while

variables. Much of survey research, for example, studies perceptions, attitudes, and beliefs. See the mountainous evidence of social science reliance on subjective variables in the many contributors to Charles F. Turner and Elizabeth Martin, eds., *Surveying Subjective Phenomenon*, 2 vols., (New York: Russell Sage Foundation, 1984), which includes (p. 8) their explicit distinction betwen the two kinds of phenomena.

15. For example, Jean Piaget, *The Moral Judgment of the Child* (Glencoe, Ill.: Free Press, 1948). Examples from other areas: Alfred Grosser, *Das Deutschland im Westen: Eine Bilanz nach 40 Jahren* (Munich: Carl Hanser Verlag, 1985); and James R. Beninger, *The Control Revolution* (Cambridge: Harvard University Press, 1986).

16. Clyde Kluckhohn, *Navaho Witchcraft*, Peabody Museum Papers, vol. 22 (Cambridge: Harvard University, 1944). This kind of explanation, including Kluckhohn's use of it, is scrutinized in Francesca M. Cancian, "Varieties of Functional Analysis," *International Encyclopedia of the Social Sciences*, vol. 6 (New York: Macmillan, 1968).

17. J. Roland Pennock, *Democratic Political Theory* (Princeton: Princeton University Press, 1979), pp. 247–253.

18. Jon Elster, *Explaining Technical Change* (Cambridge: Cambridge University Press, 1983), p. 57; and Georg Henrik von Wright, *Explanation and Understanding* (Ithaca, N.Y.: Cornell University Press, 1971), p. 17.

19. For illustration, see Gabriel Almond and Stephen J. Genco (and their references to John Bennett, Isidor Chein, Donald Campbell, and Lee Ross), "Clouds, Clocks, and the Study of Politics," *World Politics* 29 (July 1977). On explanation by reference to unique combinations of circumstances, see Albert O. Hirschman, "The Search for Paradigms as a Hindrance to Understanding," *World Politics* 22 (April 1970), pp. 341–343.

methodologists dispute whether inquiry should focus on unique events, social scientists in fact do both. Keynes, for example, explained recurrent patterns of business fluctuation in *The General Theory* and the unique consequences of a unique event in his *Economic Consequences of the Peace*. While methodologists also dispute whether social scientists should attempt nomothetic propositions or only more modest propositions tied to unspecified time and place, social scientists insightfully pursue both, producing nomothetic propositions on the incest taboo or on the moral rule of reciprocal obligation, on one hand, and propositions about politics and economics that do not hold for any specified domain but may be true, say, for the Western democracies in the twentieth century. They also practice, despite methodological controversy over the relation of prediction to explanation,[20] conditional predictions (if x, then y) that are often regarded as equivalent to explanatory propositions, as well as unconditional predictions of results of elections, or of fluctuations in gross national product, and intermediate types such as Schumpeter's insightful though qualified predictions on the decline of capitalism.[21]

Social science inquiry embraces the same variety of explanations that ordinary people construct for themselves and exchange with each other.[22] Not at all distinctive to social science, the explanatory methods constitute the ways in which we all try to make sense of the world and go about the pursuit of our own purposes, the solutions to our own problems. In their efforts at explanation, social scientists and researchers only try to do much better what everyone else does.[23] Relatively little explanation in social science closely approximates the model of scientific explanation in which an event is explained by subsuming it under a specified, carefully articulated

20. For example, Roy J. Howard, *Three Faces of Hermeneutics* (Berkeley: University of California Press, 1982), p. 47; Brian Fay, *Social Theory and Political Practice* (London: Allen & Unwin, 1975), pp. 33–40; and Harry Redner, *The Ends of Science* (Boulder, Colo.: Westview Press, 1987), pp. 297ff.

21. Joseph A. Schumpeter, *Capitalism, Socialism and Democracy* (New York: Harper, 1942).

22. Concretely illustrated in case studies in Bernard Barber, *Effective Social Science* (New York: Russell Sage Foundation, 1987).

23. Again, this is not a study of epistemology. It is a study of how people—ordinary people, functionaries, government officials, policy experts, and social scientists—attack their problems, which they always do fallibly. While they do so, students of epistemology continue to debate problems of verification and validity of knowledge and belief. Their epistemological inquiries are peripherally of great importance to everyone else's probing, especially that of professionals; but no one else stops his own investigations while waiting for a definitive disposition of epistemological issues. To put the point in another way, in this study I do not ask how in principle we can achieve truth or firm validity, but how in practice we cope.

general law. And the continuation of the hoary dispute over whether social science can ever produce more than a scattered few general laws itself provides evidence that it does not yet do so, more than two thousand years after Plato and Aristotle.[24]

ALTERNATIVES TO EXPLANATION AND PREDICTION

By no means constituting all of social science, explanation and prediction probably do not even count as the most frequent methods of social science inquiry.

Reporting

A great deal of social science that one might think explanatory or predictive—much statistical work, for example—is neither. It simply reports.[25] "The special task of the social scientist in each generation is to pin down the contemporary facts."[26]

The natural sciences have always considered reporting to be a respectable, important task, some tendencies of social scientists to picture natural scientists as all engaged in theoretical explanation to the contrary. They report on the size of the planets, the mineral composition of soils, and the life span of elephants. Among prominent works in social science in roughly the last half century, many have offered valuable reports describing an existing state of affairs or trend—independently of any other kind of analysis they accomplish: Myrdal's *American Dilemma*, Stouffer's *American Soldier*, Butler and Butler's *British Political Facts, 1900-1985*, Inglehart's *Silent Revolution*, and Campbell's *Sense of Well-Being in America*.

LePlay's nineteenth-century quantitative reports on three hundred working-class families in Europe and Asia was an early landmark in reportorial social science. In addition to practicing such reportorial methods as census, time series, and field survey, social scientists continue a constant flow of reports on every aspect of social life: for example, on how lawyers defend clients against white-collar crime charges,[27] or on changes in class mobility.[28] Commenting on

24. On the dispute, see Robert Brown, *The Nature of Social Laws* (Cambridge: Cambridge University Press, 1984).

25. All reports rest on a theory, often a hidden one. But the report is not the source of the theory, and the theory is usually of lay origin.

26. Lee Cronbach, "Beyond the Two Disciplines of Scientific Psychology," *American Psychologist* 30 (February 1975), p. 126.

27. Kenneth Mann, *Defending White-Collar Crime* (New Haven: Yale University Press, 1986).

28. John H. Goldthorpe, Clive Payne, and Catriona Llewelyn, "Trends in Class Mobility," *Sociology* 12 (September 1978).

knowledge needs and social science response to them in the accelerated American social welfare programs of the 1960s, a sophisticated participant-observer found the main contribution of social science at the time in reporting. "We now have much more detailed and usable knowledge about who is poor or sick or inadequately educated."[29] Reports may or may not combine with explanation or other kinds of inquiry; clearly they do not simply preface other kinds of social science inquiry.[30] For immediate tasks of problem solving, one can hardly overlook the importance of reports on such questions—say, for educational policy—as: What are our children learning? What abilities do they display?[31] How do they compare with children abroad?[32] Do some groups of children conspicuously lag?[33] For other purposes the population as a whole seeks answers to such questions as: Are things getting any better?[34] How are relations of parents to children changing?[35] How do elderly people think about death?[36]

29. Alice Rivlin, *Systematic Thinking for Social Action* (Washington, D.C.: Brookings Institution, 1971), p. 9.

30. For extended discussion with many examples of reporting and description (with a terminology more refined than ours), see W. G. Runciman, *A Treatise on Social Theory* (New York: Cambridge University Press, 1983), esp. chap. 4, "Reportage in Social Theory."

31. Examples: T. S. Barrows, S. F. Klein, and J. L. D. Clark, *What College Students Know and Believe about Their World* (New Rochelle, N.Y.: Change Magazine Press, 1981); Ajit K. Mohanty and Mamata Mohanty, "Intellectual Abilities of Children in an Early Education Programme," *Psychological Studies* 30 (July 1985); and C. Brainerd, *Children's Logical and Mathematical Cognition* (New York: Springer-Verlag, 1982).

32. Example: H. W. Hogan, "German and American Authoritarianism, Self-estimated Intelligence, and Value Priorities," *Journal of Social Psychology* 111 (June 1980), pp. 145–146.

33. Examples: Lyle V. Jones. "White-Black Achievement Differences: The Narrowing Gap," *American Psychologist* 39 (November 1984), pp. 207–213; and S. Kagan, G. Zahn, and J. Gealy, "Competition and School Achievement among Anglo-American and Mexican-American Children," *Journal of Educational Psychology* 69 (August 1977), pp. 432–441.

34. Example: Reynolds Farley, *Blacks and Whites* (Cambridge: Harvard University Press, 1984).

35. Examples: F. Hurstel, "Les changements dans la relation père-nourisson en France: Qui sont les pères que paternent?" *Neuropsychiatrie de l'enfance et de l'adolescence* 33 (February–March 1985); Norma Radin and Rena Goldsmith, "Caregiving Fathers of Preschoolers," *Merrill-Palmer Quarterly* 31 (October 1985); Glenn F. Ross, "Styles of Discipline: Reported Responses to a Variety of Child Behaviors," *Australian Journal of Sex, Marriage and Family* 5 (November 1984); and David Cramer, "Gay Parents and Their Children," *Journal of Counseling and Development* 64 (April 1986).

36. Erdman Palmore et al., *Normal Aging* (Durham, N.C.: Duke University Press, 1985).

Evaluation

Even the strictest empiricist will, in choosing a research project, evaluate its potential worth in comparison with alternative possible projects. "If we decided to examine the universe objectively in the sense of paying equal attention to portions of equal mass, this would result in a lifelong preoccupation with interstellar dust, relieved only at brief intervals by a survey of incandescent masses of hydrogen—not in a thousand million lifetimes would the turn come to give man even a second's notice."[37] Choosing what to investigate is, however, only the beginning of an investigator's evaluative tasks.[38] Who any longer doubts that evaluation inescapably shapes (or warps) ostensibly value-free empirical analysis? A social scientist can describe the political "education" of children as socialization or as impairment, the first concept casting the process as benign, the second not. No less familiar, many statements cannot be unambiguously classified as either factual or evaluative, as, for example, the statement to a skater "The ice on the pond is thin today."[39] Evaluations often take the form of prescription. Economists tell us what to do about balance of payments deficits; psychologists, how to rear children;[40] sociologists, what to do about drug dependency; and political scientists, how to reform parliamentary procedures. Anthropologists tell us in the "advanced" nations how not to treat people in "primitive" societies.[41]

Social scientists evaluate particular policies, "policy evaluation" now being a well-recognized subfield in social science with its own

37. Michael Polanyi, *Personal Knowledge* (Chicago: University of Chicago Press, 1958), p. 3.

38. For a succinct account of normative or evaluative elements in Plato, Aristotle, Machiavelli, Hobbes, Tocqueville, Durkheim ("the very model of a positive social scientist"), and Weber, as well as in a sample of contemporary social scientists differing in their own awareness of evaluative elements in their thought, see Robert N. Bellah, "The Ethical Aims of Social Inquiry," in Norma Haan et al., eds., *Social Science as Moral Inquiry* (New York: Columbia University Press, 1983).

39. For illustraiton and specification of inescapable evaluation in what is often intended to be value-free analysis, see Charles Taylor, "Neutrality in Political Science," in P. Laslett and G. Runciman, eds., *Philosophy, Politics and Society*, 3d ser. (Oxford: Blackwell, 1967).

40. Example: C. J. Anderson, D. B. Sawin, "Enhancing Responsiveness in Mother-Infant Interaction," *Infant Behavior and Development* 6, no. 3 (July 1983), pp. 361–368.

41. The social science commitment to evaluation denies the charge that it pursues only "technical" questions, that is, positivist questions about empirical connections between mean and end, the end somehow given or provided by others so that the social scientist need not evaluate it. Many social scientists show some veneration for such a division of labor between empirical and evaluative inquiry, but few practice it. For discussion of technical or means oriented social science, see Edward Shils, *The*

literature, including professional journals. On the other hand, they also attempt valuable broad evaluations of whole social systems: thus an unending procession of intellectually ambitious social scientists: among them, to indicate their diversity, Adam Smith, Mill, Keynes, Weber, Durkheim, Michels, and Pareto, along with contemporary system evaluators like Galbraith, Friedman, Horvat, Kornoi, Lindbeck, and Kothari, all of whom practice both empirical and evaluative analysis.[42]

Given the character of evaluation, social scientists can hardly escape it.[43] As I noted in chapter 3, evaluative analysis employs empirical propositions that many social scientists regard as their stock-in-trade.[44] Evaluation is not quite an alternative to empirical analysis but a way of incorporating empirical analysis into a larger analysis ending in a formed volition, commitment to a value, or judgment about worth.[45]

In evaluation, social scientists might be looked on as usurping the domain of philosophers. Philosophers, however, have tended to

---

Calling of Sociology and Other Essays on the Pursuit of Learning (Chicago: University of Chicago Press, 1980); and Robert N. Bellah, "Social Science as a Practical Reason," in Daniel Callahan and Bruce Jennings, eds., *Ethics, the Social Sciences, and Policy Analysis* (New York: Plenum Press, 1983).

Yet the attack on technical social science can be broadened to parallel a good deal of the analysis of some of the present chapters. See, for example, Nicholas Maxwell, *From Knowledge to Wisdom* (Oxford: Blackwell, 1984).

42. Milton Friedman, *Capitalism and Freedom* (Chicago: University of Chicago Press, 1962); Branko Horvat, *The Political Economy of Socialism* (Armonk, N.Y.: M. E. Sharpe, 1982); János Kornai, *Overcentralization in Economic Administration* (Oxford: Oxford University Press, 1959); Rajni Kothari, *Politics in India* (Boston: Little, Brown, 1970).

43. And they do not often lapse into such muddled thinking as from a committee of the National Science Foundation: "The aim of the social sciences (in common with all sciences) is to seek knowledge and provide understanding, not to determine the nation's values. This is an important point. When social science knowledge contributes to the improvement of social programs that flow from widely shared values, there is little likelihood that political controversy will occur. But when social science knowledge suggests that values should change, or that implicit values should be examined and made explicit, political controversy will almost surely arise" (Report of the Special Commission on the Social Sciences of the National Science Board, *Knowledge into Action* [Washington: National Science Foundation, 1969], pp. 19f). Social science often contributes to debate on society's values. That its contribution sometimes stimulates controversy is hardly a reason to discourage the contribution in societies dependent on a competition of ideas.

44. On this point, see Max Weber, "The Meaning of Ethical Neutrality," in Weber, *The Methodology of the Social Sciences* (N.Y.: Free Press, 1949), pp. 20f.

45. Among countless possible examples: David Schweickart, *Capitalism or Worker Control?* (New York: Praeger, 1980); and Peter Koslowski, ed., *Individual Liberty and Democratic Decision-Making* (Tuebingen: J. C. B. Mohr, 1987).

become methodologists, perhaps on the whole less interested in evaluative questions about society than are social scientists, many of whom show established competences at least in distributive ethics[46] and in the ethical attributes of key social processes like markets or hierarchies, on which processes their competences exceed those of philosophers.[47]

Chapter 3, "Probing", acknowledged that ultimate or end-of-the-line values or volitions pose special problems to probers that they often attack by temporarily—only for the analytic task at hand—treating any one ultimate value or volition as a means to some other value treated, for the moment, as more ultimate end. By thus rotating various ultimate ends in and out of their positions as ultimates, thus also in and out of their positions as means, a prober gives a whole structure of values a kind of coherence test. Social scientists do the same. In addition, a social scientist can draw on a variety of studies that differ with respect to which values they position as ultimates and which as means. That is, social scientists grapple with ultimate values not simply by exercises in their own minds but by observing which ends seem to survive evaluation across a spectrum of studies differing in how means and ends are transitionally positioned.[48]

Some heroic attempts at escape from evaluation continue in social science. Some social scientists have tried to use cost-benefit analysis in this way. In cost-benefit analysis, analysts propose to excuse themselves from taking a position on values by simply adding up the positive and negative values attached by others to a policy, institution,

46. For example, Amartya Sen, *Ethics and Economics* (Oxford: Blackwell, 1987); Douglas Rae et al., *Equalities* (Cambridge: Harvard University Press, 1981); Duncan MacRae, Jr., *The Social Function of Social Science* (New Haven: Yale University Press, 1976); George Barjas and Martin Tienda, eds., *Hispanics in the U.S. Economy* (Orlando, Fla.: Academic Press, 1985); Michael Harrington, *The Other America*, (New York: Macmillan, 1962); and Guido Calabresi and Philip Bobitt, *Tragic Choices* (N.Y.: Norton, 1978).

47. Frank H. Knight, *The Ethics of Competition* (New York: Harper, 1935); Samuel Brittan, *The Role and Limits of Government* (London: T. Smith, 1983); and R. E. Lane, "Market Justice, Political Justice," *American Political Science Review* 80 (June 1986) and his related papers cited in his bibliography.

48. For example, equality of opportunity, an end in democratic theory, is treated as such in Robert E. Haveman, *Poverty Policy and Poverty Research* (Madison: University of Wisconsin Press, 1987), esp. chap. 2, "The War on Poverty and the Great Society: Motivation, Social Spending, and Results." But equality of opportunity is often treated as a means to other ends, notably efficiency. See, for example, Victor R. Fuchs, "Toward a Theory of Poverty," in Task Force on Economic Growth and Opportunity, *The Concept of Poverty* (Washington, D.C.: U.S. Chamber of Commerce, 1965) and Robert E. Haveman, "New Policy for the New Poverty," *Challenge* 31 (September-October 1988), pp. 27–36.

or sequence of events. Thus, they take existing popular evaluations somehow aggregated, whether well probed or not, as the values by which policies, institutions, processes, and events should be evaluated. In so doing, they have not escaped evaluation but have plunged deeply into it in one bold move. Moreover, in toting up popular values, users of cost-benefit analysis pick and choose among possible values, accepting some kinds and rejecting others. Shall they count as a benefit, for example, such pleasures as some people take in abusing others—for example, the pleasures of wife battering?

Analysts who invoke the criteria of Pareto efficiency or Pareto optimality sometimes claim value neutrality. Quite aside from the limited possibility of applying the criteria—since it permits analysts to say that a second alternative is superior to a first only if the second is of a character that, compared to the first, benefits some (at least one) persons without harming any other—it is not at all neutral. As between two policy proposals, each differing from the status quo, one of which helps some people at no cost to others and the other of which helps a larger number of people more greatly but at some cost to others, one is not being neutral to choose the former.

The status quo is marked by—indeed, is maintained by—a pattern of impositions. To set as a criterion for any movement away from the status quo that it must not create any new impositions or deprivations is to treat existing impositions and deprivations as always more acceptable than new ones. Such a criterion is clearly not neutral on values.[49]

At the same time, efficiency is positioned as a means in the analysis of various alternative policies meant to reduce poverty. See, for example, Gary Burtless, "Public Spending for the Poor: Trends, Prospects, and Economic Limits," chap. 2 of Sheldon H. Danziger and Daniel H. Weinberg, *Fighting Poverty: What Works and What Doesn't* (Cambridge: Harvard University Press, 1986); and Charles A. Murray, "The Two Wars against Poverty: Economic Growth and the Great Society," *Public Interest* 69 (Fall, 1982), pp. 3–16.

Recently proponents of the "welfare reform" movement have positioned the reduction of the cost of welfare programs—rather than the more abstract volitions such as poverty reduction, reduction of inequality, or even efficiency—as the ultimate end of their probing. See, for example, Mickey Kaus, "The Work Ethic State: The Only Way to Break the Culture of Poverty," *The New Republic*, July 7, 1986, pp. 22–34. In contrast, however, other professional probers position poverty reduction as an end, but regard equality of education and training as necessary and prior means to equality of opportunity and efficiency. See, for example, Sarah K. Gideonse and William R. Meyers, "Why 'Workfare' Fails," *Challenge* 31 (January–February 1988), pp. 44–49.

49. A superb extended analysis of buried value commitment in cost-benefit analysis and use of Pareto criteria is Laurence H. Tribe, "Policy Science: Analysis or Ideology?" *Philosophy and Public Affairs* 2 (Fall, 1972).

Concepts and Cognitive Organization

Like everyone else, social scientists can inquire into the world only through invented shared concepts (both empirical and evaluative) and through their organization into a structure of concepts.[50] They consequently engage heavily in conceptualization and cognitive structuring: among many examples, Weber's concept of legitimacy; Freud's concepts of id, ego, and superego; and Hayek's concept of catallaxy.[51]

Much of Keynes's general theory consisted of cognitive restructuring. So also much of the theory of rational expectations in economics. In psychology, an earlier stimulus-response model gave way to a restructuring of the human animal as an information processor, much like a computer.[52] Other social scientists who have invested their energies substantially in conceptualization or cognitive structuring include, among many who might be listed, George Homans and Peter Blau on social relations as exchanges, B. F. Skinner on behaviorism, and Radcliffe-Brown on functionalism in anthropology.[53] Perhaps some of the greatest works in social science have been of this kind: those of Machiavelli, Hobbes, Locke, and Rousseau, for example.

Checklists and Scenarios

A cliché in social science—"We may not know the answers, but we know the questions!"—irritating when offered as an alibi, contains more than a kernel of truth. Not uncommonly, the principal contribution of a social science lies in a list of questions to be asked, issues worth raising. If, for example, one wants to know the possible consequences of an exchange-rate devaluation or to form a volition on devaluation, the economist's list of possible linkages between devaluation and its many possible results has become an impressive accomplishment, a long cumulation of insight into economic processes. It

50. Stephen Toulmin, *Human Understanding*, vol. 1 (Princeton: Princeton University Press, 1972), p. 35.
51. Friedrich von Hayek, *Law, Legislation and Liberty: The Mirage of Social Justice*, vol. 2 (Chicago: University of Chicago Press, 1976), pp. 107–132.
52. H. A. Simon and Allen Newell, *Human Problem Solving* (Englewood Cliffs, N.J.: Prentice-Hall, 1972); and George A. Miller, E. Galanter, and K. H. Pribram, *Plans and the Structure of Behavior* (New York: Holt, Rinehart and Winston, 1960).
53. George C. Homans, "Social Behavior as Exchange," *American Journal of Sociology* 62 (May 1958); Peter Blau, *Exchange and Power in Social Life* (New Brunswick: Transaction Books, 1986); B. F. Skinner, *Beyond Freedom and Dignity* (New York: Knopf, 1971); and A. R. Radcliff-Brown, *Structure and Function in Primitive Society*, (London: Cohen & West, 1952).

does not permit a firm prediction of consequences, not always even a firm set of alternative explanations of possibilities. No more than a checklist or set of possible scenarios but valuable on that count alone, it helps "demonstrate the existence of apparent forces hitherto not appreciated by showing simply that some possibility does indeed exist."[54] One can, of course, view such a checklist or set of scenarios as a loose explanatory model, sketch of a model, or a preliminary loose structuring of explanatory hypotheses.

As just noted, much of economic theory constitutes a checklist or set of scenarios. The other social sciences have gone less far. Yet the centrality of the ideas of unanticipated consequences and of functionalism in sociology and anthropology reveals the interest of these disciplines in tracking possible interconnections, even if not generalized as fixed or probable interconnections. Neomarxists now often recast earlier and no longer defensible Marxist predictions into alternative possible scenarios, especially with respect to the "autonomy" of the state.[55]

Some social scientists have, in their reaction against positivism, abandoned the conventional explanatory function of social science in favor of a view of social life as an array of possible scenarios designed by human beings who are more autonomous than those envisaged in positivist theory—people who autonomously then choose from the array. "In their coping, humans create the social future." And "by analyzing the factors that guide the choice of strategies, one gains knowledge of the possibility and direction of change."[56]

Meaning

Some social scientists claim to make a contribution to understanding through a kind of synthesizing analysis or conceptualization that gives "meaning" to social phenomena. I say "a kind of" in quotation marks to indicate discomfort with the allegation. Not because I regret it but because precisely what it itself "means" stirs controversy and lies beyond my powers to clarify. In one form of the allegation:

The important issue is not the determination of the facts, but rather the ordering of them. Social theorizing, then, is often a

54. Stanley Lieberson, *Making It Count* (Berkeley: University of California Press, 1985), p. 220.
55. Claus Offe, "Challenging the Boundaries of Institutional Politics," in Charles S. Maier, ed., *Changing Boundries of the Political* (Cambridge: Cambridge University Press, 1987), pp. 63–105; and James O'Connor, *The Meaning of Crisis* (Oxford: Blackwell, 1987).
56. John W. Bennett, "Anticipation, Adaptation, and the Concept of Culture in Anthropology," *Science* 192 (May 28, 1976), p. 847.

search for the meaning of the personally real, that which is already assumed to be known through personal experience. Basing itself on the imputed reality of the ordinarily experienced, much of theory-work begins with an effort to make sense of one's experience. Much of it is initiated by an effort to resolve unresolved experience; here, the problem is not to validate what has been observed or to produce new observations, but rather to locate and to interpret the meaning of what one has lived.[57]

Perhaps such a statement, as well as similar statements by advocates of an "interpretive" social science, makes much the same point as already made: that social science engages in cognitive organization of both empirical and evaluative elements in thought.

Synthesis and Design

Any social scientist can give full time to any one of the kinds of investigatory activities just outlined, ignoring the others. But many social scientists try to bring the various aspects of social science together. They can bring them together in the formulation of a standing volition—a volition, say, for a general structure of society. Or for an action volition—a volition, say, for a withdrawal of one's country from NATO. Evaluation itself—specifically of volitions—can integrate or synthesize, as already noted by Adam Smith, Mill, Keynes, Weber, Durkheim, Michels, and Pareto, along with contemporary large-system evaluators like Galbraith, Friedman, Horvat, Kornai, and Kothari.[58] On a small scale, the whole subdiscipline of "policy analysis" often operates as an integrating subdiscipline, not, as has been proposed, for integrating the disciplines generally but for synthesizing or integrating the various specific inquiries that social scientists and researchers undertake in examining any one problem.[59]

Social scientists sometimes accomplish a synthesis or integration of various kinds of social science inquiry in a different way. They undertake complex institutional design or invention, distinguishable from evaluation, to which, however, it usually attaches.[60] Synthesis

57. Alvin Gouldner, *The Coming Crisis of Western Sociology* (New York: Basic Books, 1970), p. 484.

58. Cited above, p. 146.

59. How far it might go is discussed in James C. Charlesworth, ed., *Integration of the Social Sciences through Policy Analysis* (Philadelphia: American Academy of Political and Social Science, 1972).

60. Examples: Martin Weitzman, *The Share Economy* (Cambridge: Harvard University Press, 1984); Rudolf Meidner, *Employee Investment Funds* (London and Boston: Allen & Unwin, 1978); Oskar Lange and Fred Taylor, *On the Economic Theory of*

aside, taken by itself design is sometimes a significant accomplishment, as, for example, the design of the reverse income tax. Synthesis and design, however, perhaps more often come from outside social science and research—from original or thoughtful minds anywhere in society, political functionaries, and interest groups, among others.

Methodology

Finally—and obviously—professional investigators engage in the study of professional investigation itself; how it is done and how to do it better. One can so classify their efforts at conceptualization and organization. Innumerable other efforts include studies—to indicate their variety—of statistical method, field survey techniques, appropriate disciplinary boundaries, fact-value relations, ethical questions in research design, relations between the methods of history and those of social science, feasibility of attempting nomothetic generalization, comparisons of natural and social sciences, postpositive reconstructions of social science, and all the issues raised in the present study. Examples seem unnecessary: books on statistical methods alone number in the thousands, and on survey research methods at least in the hundreds.

Is Social Science Scientific?

In calling attention to the variety of inquiries that social scientists make in addition to the most conventional scientific explanation, I may seem to imply that the social sciences are usually not sciences, an implication that I do not intend. Whether social science is scientific is an empirical question not about terminology but about standards and procedures; the answer depends on the criteria used. For example, some scientists would say that a science requires: "well-articulated hypotheses and their systematic testing"; "precise measurement and operationalization of concepts"; "careful observation by publicly checkable methods"; "sophisticated and rigorous conceptual structure, and great insight"; and "shared paradigms."[61] By that set of criteria, many social scientists clearly will score high as scientists. No less clearly, others will not because they are in default on one or more criteria. They include Weber, Durkheim, Radcliffe-Brown, Malinow-

Socialism (Minneapolis: University of Minnesota Press, 1938); Phillipe Herzog et al., *Un chemin pour sortir de la crise* (Paris: Messidor/Editions Sociales, 1985); and Christopher Hawkins, *Britain's Economic Future* (Brighton: Wheatsheaf Books, 1983).

61. Ernest Gellner, "The Scientific Status of the Social Sciences," in Gellner, *Relativism and the Social Sciences* (Cambridge: Cambridge University Press, 1985), pp. 125f. Implicitly, Gellner identifies science with scientific explanation.

ski, the classical and neoclassical economists, Merriam, and Lasswell, among hundreds of social scientists remembered in histories of their disciplines. Other criteria produce other answers.

SCIENCE FOR CONTROL?

A word may be in order on how social scientists justify or find a purpose in what they do.[62] A question I wish to raise at this point, because the next chapter requires its answer, concerns the parallel justification of natural science as a method of achieving mastery of the physical world and of social science as a method of achieving mastery over the social world.

Like many scientists who followed him, Francis Bacon wanted knowledge or science "to establish and extend the power and dominion of the human race itself over the universe."[63] Helmholtz contemplated "the dominion of man over all the forces hostile to intelligence."[64] In our time one often hears the same aspiration voiced. Even many physical scientists who, like Helmholtz himself, want freedom to explore in any direction without regard to any practical applications of their work, often justify such a policy on the ground that it will epiphenomenally best accomplish human mastery of the physical world.[65] Regardless of their aspirations, the sciences have in fact become, among other things and whatever scientists intend, instruments of human control over the physical world.

That does not deny that scientists and all other people find themselves constrained or controlled by the physical world; in Bacon's words, "Nature to be commanded must be obeyed." It only says that scientific understanding of the physical world makes it possible for human beings to alter, within limits, the impact of the physical world on themselves and to harness physical forces to achieve, again within limits, human purposes. In the controlling relation achieved, the hu-

62. An illuminating history of a British controversy on these issues is in William McGucken, "On Freedom and Planning in Science: The Society for Freedom in Science, 1940–46," *Minerva* 16 (Spring 1978). On contemporary issues, see Jerome R. Ravetz, *Scientific Knowledge and Its Social Problems* (Oxford: Oxford University Press, 1971), chap. 2.

63. Francis Bacon, *Novum Organum* (1620), book 1, aphorism 129, in J. Spedding, R. L. Ellis, and D. D. Heath, eds., *The Works of Francis Bacon* (New York: Garrett Press, 1968), vol. 4, p. 114.

64. Hermann Helmholtz, *Popular Lectures on Scientific Subjects* (New York: Appleton, 1873), p. 29.

65. Thus, science accomplishes something beyond what any scientist himself deliberately attempts. On the distinction, see Solly Zuckerman, *Scientists and War* (New York: Harper and Row, 1977), pp. 140–144.

man beings stand on one side, the inanimate physical world on the other. Insofar as human beings achieve control, they act; and the physical world is consequently in some respects altered.

In parallel, a social scientist declares: "As in other sciences we desire knowledge mainly as an instrument of control."[66] It is a common though not a universal opinion. When, however, human beings exercise control over the social world, human beings act and human beings are consequently altered. People stand on both sides of the relation: controlling or exercising power or influence, and being controlled or yielding to power or influence exercised over them. For every controller, a controllee.

The case sometimes made for human control over the physical world, then, makes no case for human control over the social world. Advocacy of the former does not imply that anyone should succumb to another's will or behave as another wishes. Advocacy of the latter does. Social control includes the possibility of human subjugation and raises ethical questions about acceptable and unacceptable kinds of control.

One can to a degree soften the distinction between physical and social mastery. Because nature to be commanded must be obeyed, the manipulation of the physical world entails backfire consequences for behavior, personality, and social institutions. In the eyes of some students of science and technology, the pursuit of physical mastery of the world has on some counts dehumanized human beings and is also threatening on other counts.[67] To that degree, human beings appear both as controller and controllee in any attempt at controlling the physical world. Moreover, many controls over the physical world— damming a river, for example, or vaccinating a population to prevent an epidemic—require simultaneous exercise of social controls ranging from organizing the work force for the task at hand to dealing with the social consequences of an inundation of inhabited land above the dam. All attempts at control of the physical world imply effects on, thus influences or controls over, the social world. Understandably, then, in the natural sciences "the deeper practical problems of responsibility and morality are . . . beginning to be grasped,"[68] and

66. Wesley Mitchell in Guy Alchon, *The Invisible Hand of Planning* (Princeton: Princeton University Press, 1985), p. 114.

67. On dehumanization, see, among others, Herbert Marcuse, *One-Dimensional Man* (Boston: Beacon Press, 1984); and Jacques Ellul, *The Technological Society* (New York: Knopf, 1964). On other threats, see Watson Fuller, ed., *The Biological Revolution* (Garden City, N.Y.: Anchor, 1972).

68. Jerome R. Ravetz, *Scientific Knowledge and Its Social Problems* (Oxford: Oxford University Press, 1971), p. 417.

natural scientists retreat from an earlier, untroubled conception of their sciences as instruments, as Bacon wrote, of "enlarging . . . the bounds of Human Empire to the effecting of all things possible."[69]

It makes no sense, then, to conceive of social science as trying to facilitate, enlarge, or implement social control. Reflecting widespread confusion on the point, a social scientist declares both that "the central tendency of social science is rather to increase man's capacity to manipulate his own social environment," and that "nothing in the social sciences increases the capacity to manipulate an individual against his will"![70] That is heads without tails, controllers without controllees.

A better statement would specify blocking no less than facilitating social control. The functions of social science include the examination of possible structures of mixed effective and blocked controls, thus facilitating not social control or a maximum of it, but a discriminating mix of its use and its frustration.[71] Exploration of the possibilities has always engaged social scientists: Rousseau, Adam Smith, Max Weber, Karl Marx, Emil Durkheim, among innumerable others. Less ambitious social scientists also study the mix when they examine, for example, processes by which governments induce obedience from citizens—such as policing, tax administration, regulation of business, criminal law, public education, and military conscription—and processes by which citizens protect themselves from governmental controls—such as protection of civil liberties, the use of rights of property to constrain governmental regulation of business, and other constraints on the authority of governmental officials.

Of the two sides of social science interest in social control—achieving it and thwarting it—perhaps the first has been more prominent, from Plato through Charles Horton Cooley to many con-

---

69. Francis Bacon, *The New Atlantis* (1627), in J. Spedding, R. L. Ellis, and D. D. Heath, eds., *The Works of Francis Bacon* (New York: Garrett Press, 1968), vol. 3, p. 156. For a useful summary of criticism of science, both historical and current, see J. R. Ravetz, "Criticisms of Science," in Ina Spiegel-Rösing and Derek de Solla Price, eds., *Science, Technology and Society* (London: Sage, 1977).

70. Daniel Lerner, "Social Science: Whence and Whither?" in Lerner, ed., *The Human Meaning of the Social Sciences* (New York: Meridian Books, 1959), pp. 30f.

71. The whole argument can be put in another way. Suppose we think of everyone as engaged in controlling others, as indeed they are. Suppose also that we think of anyone's attempt to block a social control over him as one's own exercise of social control. So we drop the distinction between exercising and thwarting social control and envision everyone as engaged in social control. With that reformulation, it is still the case that social science cannot be characterized as facilitating a maximum of social control or man's mastery over man—such concepts hardly make sense. Rather, it is as given to blocking some controls as to facilitating others.

temporary organization theorists. A great many investigators have pursued with fascination the question, still not wholly answered, of how millions of disparate persons of divergent intentions can be harmonized through social controls into an orderly society. Then, too, as critics allege, social science may engage more heavily in the former than in the latter partly because research funding depends greatly on grants from government agencies seeking help in imposing on citizens in order to accomplish the agencies' authorized purposes (on which more in later chapters).

Adaptation to Control

This line of analysis of the relation of social science to the exercise of social control enlarges to take account of still another orientation toward social control. Physical science has studied the weather less for the purpose of controlling it, though attempting that too, than for the purpose of improving human adaptation to it. So also, social research often undertakes studies less oriented to either the exercise or the frustration of social control than to adaptation to control. Psychology displays interests in those processes by which people adjust to their environments. Psychotherapy typically recommends adaptation on the assumption that the individual can neither exercise positive control nor block critical controls exercised over him. Sociology has a long history of investigating adaptation, say, of families to low income, of young people to limited opportunities, or of industrial workers to workplace conditions and authority. Political science and economics study how people can live and solve personal and collective problems within a fixed set of political and economic institutions, thus within a set of established controls.

In short, with respect to social control, social science never has engaged in so monstrous an exclusive project as enlarging human mastery of the social world (and, in any case, the concept does not make sense). But it does study how people do and might better exercise, bend to, frustrate, and adapt to control.

CHAPTER 10

Professional Dependence on

Lay Probing

A social scientist writes: "Most students of human nature and society agree that the common-sense knowledge we have of our lives consists largely of misunderstanding."[1] But in Popper's judgment, "All science, and all philosophy, are enlightened common sense."[2] A political philosopher who has studied the methods of social science says that "what we have to learn from the social sciences as they now exist is how little understanding the social sciences can give us beyond the everyday understanding of social life that we have anyway."[3] But then again Descartes long ago wrote that true knowledge requires an intellectual purge to drive ordinary knowledge out of the mind—presumably a task for professionals, not amateurs.

1. Gregg et al., "The Caravan Rolls On: Forty Years of Social Problem Research," *Knowledge* 1 (September 1979), p. 31.
2. Karl Popper, *Objective Knowledge* (Oxford: Oxford University Press, 1972), p. 34.
3. Alisdair MacIntyre, "The Survival of Political Philosophy," *The Listener* 85 (February 15, 1971), p. 238.

Still an unsettled issue is the relation of social scientific inquiry to lay inquiry. Too sharp a distinction between the two overlooks investigators who lie on a continuum between lay probers at one pole and social scientists at the other: among them, amateur scientists and social investigators whose skills and accomplishments sometimes rival those of the social scientists;[4] journalists whose reporting sometimes matches the quality of social research; and a varied set of investigators like staff analysts whose jobs require them to investigate some phenomenon or problem, sometimes with appropriate skills and sometimes not. Among all these, an important category, itself internally differentiated, is that of the expert, the person who develops special competences for probing not by playing the role of professional scientist or researcher but in discharge of specialized duties, or as a result of specialized training: for example, the administrative official, lawyer, agricultural extension officer, librarian, professional arbitrator, therapist, or apiculturist.

Chapter 3 called attention to the inconclusive character of lay inquiry. It consists of probing rather than proving and always remains "open, never-ending, and inconclusive," less well described as knowledge accumulation than as persistence in inquiry or figuratively as "a kind of energy." On some counts social scientific inquiry looks the same. Inquiries pursued by social scientists range over roughly the same wide variety as those pursued by lay probers. Social scientific inquiry rarely achieves a high degree of conclusiveness, and none at all in evaluative and conceptual pursuits, nor in producing scenarios and designs, for such issues never close. Moreover, when, like ordinary citizens or functionaries, social scientists turn to policy analysis, they cannot complete the task and must at some point give way, for the reasons given in chapter 4, to imposition of a solution. Perhaps social science as actually practiced should be classified as a form of probing, professional rather than lay.

In comparing social scientific inquiry with lay probing, the grave impairments of the latter should not wholly obscure its competences. To describe lay probing as casual, as in the term "casual empiricism," goes too far in deprecating it. In societies with relatively high educational levels, for all its impairments probing often rises to limits of sophistication rarely encountered, say, in probing among the

4. For example, Antonio Gramsci, *Selections from the Prison Notebooks*, ed. Q. Hoare and G. Nowell-Smith (New York: International Publishers, 1971). In the natural sciences early development was usually at the hands of amateurs rather than professionals. The nonprofessional-professional distinction is relatively recent, not valid for an earlier period.

Papuans of New Guinea. Some people sometimes work hard on their inquiries. Some lay probers make self-disciplined hobbies of their inquiries, and some demonstrate unusual talent. Lay probing one might call ordinary, except that some of it is extraordinary. Nor is it well described as common sense, for it is usually educated sense or even uncommonly good sense. Impaired, fallible, often foolish, perhaps some lay probing differs little from professional inquiry.[5]

AMATEUR AND PROFESSIONAL

Social scientists differ from lay probers in ways that call for specification. Often they use specialized professional techniques: those of survey research, experiment, or mathematical modeling, for example. Yet many do not. On incentives, for example, a social scientist concludes: "Symbolic rewards and sanctions are quite adequate for limited, intermittent work."[6] Another reaches a broad conclusion: "In Germany, the authoritarian state was deeply involved in the process of industrialization and was active in the nineteenth century in regulating the social position of the workers."[7] In both cases—as well as in countless other examples—the conclusion rests on no specific formal technique. One must look elsewhere for a more general difference between professional and lay inquiry.

Many have suggested that the defining difference between professional inquiry and lay probing lies in the difference between theoretical and practical knowledge. But despite the elegance of economic theory, much of social science does not even attempt theory; and not even economics is wholly theoretical. And, on the other hand, lay probers frequently invent theories, indeed routinely do so, even if cruder, less ambitious theories than those of professionals.[8] Even if they are no more than generalizations, no one can think without them. If *theory* implies more elaborate constructs of interrelated gen-

---

5. On how incompetent it often is, see, in addition to many of the preceding chapters, David Faust, *Limits of Scientific Reasoning* (Minneapolis: University of Minnesota Press, 1984), in which, however, it is agreed that defects of professional probing parallel those of lay probing. See also Richard E. Nisbett and Lee Ross, *Human Inference* (Englewood Cliffs, N.J.: Prentice-Hall, 1980).

6. Amitai Etzioni, *The Active Society* (New York: Free Press, 1968), p. 371.

7. Morris Janowitz, *The Last Half-Century* (Chicago: University of Chicago Press, 1978), p. 237.

8. On theory content of lay thought, see Richard E. Nisbett and Lee Ross, *Human Inference* (Englewood Cliffs, N.J.: Prentice-Hall, 1980), chap. 6; and Reid Hastie, "Causes and Effects of Causal Attribution," *Journal of Personality and Social Psychology* 46 (January 1984).

eralizations, again both lay probers and professionals cannot think without them and repeatedly manufacture them, even if the crudity of lay constructions often becomes obvious.

Setting aside the troublesome word *theory*, one can say that empirical scientific inquiry seeks "to explain, to establish some relation of dependence between propositions superficially unrelated, to exhibit systematic connections between apparently miscellaneous items of information."[9] If lay probers do a great deal of it for themselves, the valid contrast is that professionals push harder, with more sustained and skilled effort, toward systems of relations among variables than do nonprofessionals.

Empirical scientific inquiry attends more carefully than lay probing to its limits. It seeks to specify the conditions in which an explanatory proposition does and does not hold. Social scientific empirical inquiry usually goes less far than natural science in this attempt, as in demography, criminology, economic theory, and even in cognitive theory. Yet for complex propositions professional social inquiry does better than nonprofessional and in many cases treats the problem of specifying the conditions of validity as a major task, as nonprofessionals usually do not.

Scientific inquiry tests scientific knowledge in various areas for mutual consistency to a degree that nonprofessional inquiry does not. It also aims for more precision than does ordinary inquiry. Finally, it is the "deliberate policy of science to expose its cognitive claims to the repeated challenge of critically probative observational data, procured under carefully controlled conditions."[10] In the natural sciences, that might be offered as the core, pivotal, or most critical feature of empirical scientific inquiry. In social scientific empirical inquiry, it has been more an ambition than an actual practice. Yet in comparison with lay inquiry the ambition is distinctive: professional social inquiry contrasts with nonprofessional in its respect for test and counterclaim and the vigor with which it pursues and institutionalizes debate.

The list, it seems, identifies not distinctive techniques, directions, or kinds of inquiry that professionals alone undertake but empirical investigatory activities in which professionals simply do better than lay people.[11] They push harder for connections, for consistency, for probative data, and the like. In inquiry into values, con-

9. Ernest Nagel, *The Structure of Science* (New York: Harcourt, Brace and World, 1961), p. 5.
10. Ibid., p. 14.
11. I have adapted this list from Nagel's *Structure of Science*, pp. 5–14.

cepts, cognitive structures, designs, and scenarios, distinctions between professional and lay inquiry diminish. On a broad view, as in the preceding chapter, of what social science actually consists of, it is all the more apparent that professional social inquiry covers the whole range of lay probing and can stake a claim not to some defining set of techniques but to more skill.

PROFESSIONAL INQUIRY A SUPPLEMENT TO LAY PROBING

From the observation that professional inquiry consists for the most part of lay inquiry done better, some inferences follow, each able to stand on its own feet, all of which cast professional inquiry in a role supplementary to lay inquiry. That does not mean an unimportant role but an adjunct role. Professional inquiry does not constitute a separate stream of inquiry parallel to and largely independent of lay probing. For several reasons, not even in the future will the societies of the world possess, as some social scientists seem to hope, two comprehensive bodies of knowledge, the one lay, the other professional.[12]

Limited Scope of Professional Inquiry

Lay probers undertake most by far of the tasks of inquiry. Not professional but lay inquiry informs you that war has broken out or that your party has won an election. Ephemeral as such knowledge may be, because it consists of "knowledge of the particular circumstances of time and place," it is essential to individual or collective problem solving as well as to the efficacy of scientific knowledge in social problem solving.[13]

About social patterns of behavior and action rather than about particulars of time and place, lay inquiry has produced more lasting empirical knowledge:

> Long before the beginnings of modern civilization, men acquired vast funds of information about their environment. They discovered the uses of fire and developed skills for transforming raw materials into shelters, clothing, and utensils. The invented arts

12. For the natural sciences at least, some scientists and methodologists apparently envision a hypothetical future in which all common-sense concepts have been displaced by the concepts of professional scientists (for example, Paul M. Churchland, *Scientific Realism and the Plasticity of Mind* [Cambridge: Cambridge University Press, 1979], pp. 25–36). But even that remarkable hypothesis does not deny that the route to such a future lies in "incremental" improvement of lay concepts (*ibid.*, p. 36).

13. Friedrich von Hayek, "The Use of Knowledge in Society," *American Economic Review* 35 (September 1945), p. 521.

of tilling the soil, communicating, and governing themselves. Some of them discovered that objects are moved more easily when placed on carts with wheels, that the sizes of fields are more reliably compared when standard schemes of measurement are employed, and that the seasons of the year as well as many phenomena of the heavens succeed each other with a certain regularity.[14]

Lay inquiry did not end with the rise of science, did not restrict itself to the physical world, and today massively explores the social world. From it people have learned that prices usually move in response to supply and demand; that many third-world nations lack a corps of competent and motivated entrepreneurs; that bodily posture reveals attitudes; that a smile sometimes expresses hostility; that in many political systems incumbents resist yielding office; that nations violate treaties in some circumstances but not in others; that many societies divide on ethnic lines; that educational responsibilities in many societies have moved from family to school; that parental authority declines in many societies and subcultures; that people emulate other people, that seashells serve as money among some people; that the Mauryan Empire endured for over 150 years; and that the Ming dynasty sought to remove Mongol influences from China. All this knowledge comes from lay probing.

Beyond empirical knowledge, why is there widespread belief in the practice of honesty, return of favors, and avoidance of cruelty? And whence the belief that democracy and dictatorship serve as useful concepts for distinguishing forms of government, that humankind for many analytical purposes needs classification by age and gender, and that one can usefully distinguish a world "out there" from people's impressions of it?

Professional inquiry is a scarce resource, even in a wealthy U.S., never abundant enough to permit study of all important social phenomena and problems, even if the entire adult population became social scientists.

To the supplementary character of professional inquiry some people turn a blind eye because they have come to define knowledge as that which professional inquiry produces. It is lost to them that everyone engages in the pursuit of knowledge and that knowledge constitutes a vast store ranging from their street addresses or their sense that they are in good health to their incomplete understandings

14. Ernest Nagel, *The Structure of Science* (New York: Harcourt, Brace and World, 1961), p. 1.

of the effect of credit expansion on prices. Such a misperception appears in an extraordinary and unbelievable claim, from a social scientist, that "although some knowledge is generated spontaneously or even accidently, under contemporary circumstances it more typically results from a conscious activity like research and development or experimental innovation." That is not how the world first learned of the accident at Chernobyl, of urban blight, of apartheid, or that man had landed on the moon. The only way to make the statement true would be to define knowledge to exclude every kind other than scientific knowledge, and a particular kind of scientific knowledge at that.

Consider a team of government officials contemplating a decision. Have they estimated the costs of the proposed policy with sufficient accuracy? Only for a few very costly projects can they ask for supplementary professional help on estimates; on most decisions the expense and delay prohibit doing so. Can they trust their information about contingencies? They revolve on the uncertainties of potential reactions of other agencies and the responses of people targeted in the decision. On very few of the contingencies will professional investigators have as much insight as the team itself does, nor, again, do time and expense permit a professional investigation. For the decision, only one of a dozen to be made during the day, required probes are multifold, the team's dependence on lay inquiry great; and social science inquiries can play a role no more than supplementary to the lay inquiries of the team and others.

Empirical studies on how policy makers use the results of professional inquiry confirm its supplementary character. An observer of the interplay among social scientists, other experts, administrators, and politicians on issues of rent control in the U.K. describes one of many patterns:

> Research workers could not present authoritative findings for others to apply; neither could others commission them to find the "correct" solution to policy problems; they are not that kind of problem. Those in the four fields from which experience had to be brought to bear contributed on equal terms. Each was expert in a few things, ignorant about most things, offered what he could, and generally learnt more than he could teach.[15]

Generalized from 204 interviews with high-level executive branch officials in the U.S. government, a research group concludes, with respect to the executive:

15. David Donnison, "Research for Policy," *Minerva* 10 (October 1972), p. 526.

He must augment his reliance on "soft" knowledge (nonresearch based, qualitative, and couched in lay language) with new information examined and applied more formally. Such "hard" knowledge (research based, usually quantitative, and couched in scientific language) once retrieved, may or may not prove crucial to the outcome of a particular decision situation, but it may be called on to serve as a check on the validity of a pre-existent belief as well as to provide new information in its own right.

They go on to say: "Much of the importance of . . . an idea [derived from professional inquiry] for the policy maker lies in its ultimate integration into his entire perspective on a problem." And "much of the relevant information under consideration is already known [before its supplementation by professional information]."[16]

In another study resting on interviews with 155 high-level officials in American federal, state, and local mental health agencies, other researchers reached the same conclusion. Among the testimony of the respondents: "I tend to integrate knowledge that's obtained in the [research] articles into my own thinking." And from another: "It is a continuous awareness and stratification of several kinds of information—TV, newspapers, scientific articles, a book. All of these things overlap." On which the authors of the study comment with respect to the respondents: "It [social science] was auxiliary to their own first-hand experience."[17] And further: "It [social science] is not a beam of light in a dark room. It is more like a candle in a lighted room. . . . It supplements what they already know."[18]

Another follow-up study of twenty U.S. national health program evaluations (sixty interviews of evaluators and of users of the evaluations) comes to similar conclusions, the typical impact of professional inquiry being "additional pieces" of information, that is, additional to lay knowledge.[19]

Professional Tasks Set by Lay Incompetences

Social scientists play a supplementary role again in taking their tasks largely from the inadequacies of lay investigation. They begin

16. Nathan Caplan, Andrea Morrison, and Russell J. Stambaugh, *The Use of Social Science Knowledge in Policy Decisions at the National Level* (Ann Arbor: University of Michigan Institute for Social Research, 1975), pp. 18f.

17. Carol H. Weiss, "Knowledge Creep and Decision Accretion," *Knowledge* 1 (March 1980), pp. 390f.

18. Carol H. Weiss with Michael J. Bucuvalas, *Social Science Research and Decision Making* (New York: Columbia University Press, 1980), pp. 170f.

19. Michael Q. Patton et al., "In Search of Impact," in Carol H. Weiss, ed., *Using Social Research in Public Policy Making* (Lexington, Mass: D. C. Heath, 1977), p. 145.

with a lay belief that requires scrutiny, followed by amendment, rejection, acceptance, or further study. They do not ask the question What is the social world like? but instead respond to such implicit questions as Have we been mistaken in thinking that . . . ? or Perhaps I can improve my understanding of . . . ? Sometimes, of course, they tie their inquiry to a questionable finding, judgment, or conclusion of earlier professional inquiry; but the chain quickly traces back to an attempt to correct, refine, or somehow test lay knowledge; and only rarely, as in economists' search for a formal statement of the conditions of a stable market equilibrium, is the chain a long one. In so esoteric a research venture as that, they may lose sight of the origin of their inquiry, which is not in an attempt to construct an across-the-board substitute for lay knowledge of how markets operate but in difficult questions about markets for which lay answers are absent or inadequate.

Methodological Dependence on Lay Probes

The methods of professional inquiry depend heavily on lay probes. For the most part—that is to say, except on selected points of departure—professional inquiry makes use of the language, concepts, cognitive structures, concerns, questions, and beliefs employed in lay investigation. When, as is sometimes the case, social scientists wish to challenge or replace some of them, they find an additional dependence of professional inquiry: that "while the appropriateness of some presumptions can be probed singly or in small sets, this can only be done by assuming the correctness of the great bulk of other presumptions,"[20] which derive largely from lay probing.

To some degree professionals do break away from lay concepts, presumptions, and frameworks. Social scientists find more satisfactory concepts, say, of democracy than the loose conceptions employed by laymen. Yet they cannot go far in that direction, for both professional and lay inquiry must at least roughly respond to widespread concerns.

> In relying for its own interest in the antecedent interest of its subject matter, science must accept to an important extent the pre-scientific conception of these subject matters. The existence of animals was not discovered by zoologists, nor that of plants by

20. D. T. Campbell, "Qualitative Knowing in Action Research," in M. Brenner, P. Marsh, and M. Brenner, eds., *The Social Contexts of Method* (London: Croom Helm, 1978), p. 185. For comment, see Michael Mulkay, "Three Models of Scientific Development," *Sociological Review* 23 (August 1975).

botanists, and the scientific value of zoology and botany is but an extension of man's pre-scientific interest in animals and plants. Psychologists must know from ordinary experience what human intelligence is, before they can devise tests for measuring it scientifically, and should they measure instead something that ordinary experience does not recognize as intelligence, they would be constructing a new subject matter which could no longer claim the intrinsic interest attached to that which they originally chose to study. Admittedly, the pursuits of biology, medicine, psychology and the social sciences, may rectify our everyday conceptions of plants and animals, and even of man and society; but we must set against any such modification its effect on the interest by which the study of the original subject matter had been prompted and justified.[21]

In addition, professional explanations derive largely from lay hypotheses, in a kind of dependence sometimes also found in the natural sciences.[22] Thus lay hypotheses of an ice age—specifically, hypotheses that glaciers had deposited the granite boulders of Swiss alpine valleys—inaugurated scientific discussion through the Swiss Society of the Natural Sciences.[23] Professional social inquiry similarly takes hypotheses from lay hypotheses, for example, on frustration, aggression, school racial segregation, educational achievement, the effects of taxation on investment, or dependence of election results on the state of the economy.

Professional methods depend on lay inquiry in another way. When social scientists seek to understand, for example, how business managers decide on new investments, or how parties in a multiparty legislature construct coalitions, or how taxpayers exploit loopholes in their favor, they frequently ask the managers, legislators, or taxpayers. The social scientists thus transform lay knowledge into a professional finding. They will usually supplement the collected lay knowledge with some increments of insight, finding, for example, a pattern in their respondents' behavior of which the respondents themselves are unaware.[24]

21. Michael Polanyi, *Personal Knowledge* (Chicago: University of Chicago Press, 1958), p. 139.
22. On this point, see E. A. Shils, "Social Science and Social Policy," in Elizabeth T. Crawford and Albert D. Biderman, eds., *Social Scientists and International Affairs* (New York: Wiley, 1969), p. 39.
23. Jonathan Weiner, "The Grimsel Glacier and Other Oft-Told Geological Tales," *The Sciences* 25 (March–April 1985).
24. As an example, see Douglas E. Rosenthal, *Lawyer and Client: Who's in Charge?* (New York: Russell Sage Foundation, 1974).

Professional testing commonly depends on propositions drawn from nonprofessional inquiry. "If we are told that the Puritans successfully discouraged men from remaining single by taxing bachelors very heavily . . . we take for granted a causal relationship between an activity which is financially penalized and avoidance of that activity."[25] But that causal relation escapes professional testing; it simply draws on a long history of lay probing on the point.

If professional inquiry has not created and cannot create a structure of knowledge independent of lay investigation, not even to the limited but significant degree to which theoretical physics has done so, at its most powerful it operates like an earthmover reshaping the contours of a mountain of impaired and otherwise defective lay knowledge. Again, not to belittle professional inquiry but to understand its specific contributions do I outline its supplementary character. The capacity of professional inquiry to supplement lay probes in order to improve them forbids its deprecation. Among tests of its capacity, one is that corporations and governments will often pay hundreds of thousands of dollars for a professional supplement to lay knowledge.

LAY AND PROFESSIONAL EMPIRICAL "VERIFICATION"

In two empirical tasks, reporting and explanation, one might think that social science moves far from lay investigation, given the fallibility of the latter and the disciplined character of the former. But the assertion that professionals verify and amateurs cannot does not hold water.

Impossibility of "Verification"

Scientists and methodologists now largely set aside as impossible empirical verification as once conceived. Instead, science seeks propositions or models that can survive professional debate, thus survive attack and defense of great variety.[26] Such a test calls not just for a lively intellectual exchange but for employment of "critically proba-

---

25. Robert Brown, *Explanation in Social Science* (Chicago: Aldine, 1963), p. 23.
26. W. Quine, *From a Logical Point of View*, (Cambridge: Harvard University Press, 1961), p. 43; Imre Lakatos, "Falsification and the Methodology of Scientific Research Programmes," in Lakatos and Alan Musgrave, eds., *Criticism and the Growth of Knowledge* (Cambridge: Cambridge University Press, 1970), pp. 119f; Jerome R. Ravetz, *Scientific Knowledge and Its Social Problems* (Oxford: Oxford University Press, 1971), pp. 132–135; and Mary Hesse, "In Defense of Objectivity," Annual Philosophical Lecture, *Proceedings of the British Academy* 58 (1972), p. 280.

tive data, produced under carefully controlled conditions."[27] The specifics of the required employment, however, command much less agreement than they did a few decades ago; and to some degree methodologists fall into two camps: the one searching for a codified set of practices with respect to the specifics of testing; the other debating the tests themselves simultaneously with debate on the findings they have produced or challenged.[28]

Scientists have also largely abandoned the positivist attempt to achieve fairly directly a matching of each empirical proposition to reality. There exists a reality—or so most methodologists seem to postulate—grasped or understood only by concepts and cognitive structures created in the human mind, and the truth value of a report or explanation consequently turns on its fit into a complex coherent cognitive structure. The test of the structure itself lies in its capacity to survive professional debate.[29]

On both counts, testing for empirical "truth" becomes a social process.[30] The close interactions among professionals that permit and encourage them to debate propositions, models, and cognitive structures often breed premature or doctrinal likemindedness, with the result that such agreement as scientists achieve with respect to propositions and models never escapes suspicion.

Accepting the impossibility of "verification" specified in earlier formulations of the scientific method, social scientists look for acceptable degrees and kinds of what they once called verification, where "acceptable" means sufficient to warrant their making a commitment to a proposition or model as a working hypothesis. An empirical proposition becomes scientifically acceptable when social scientists have debated it, usually in the absence of "critically probative data, produced under carefully controlled conditions," and have largely agreed—usually tacitly—on a commitment to use it in their thinking and acting. In some cases, carefully produced probative data enter into the debate, but they often refer to so limited a phenomenon

27. See above, chap. 9.
28. Compare Frederich Suppe, Afterword, in Suppe, ed., *The Structure of Scientific Theories*, 2d ed. (Chicago: University of Illinois Press, 1979), esp. pp. 706–708, with Thomas Kuhn, "Reflections on My Critics," in Imre Lakatos and Alan Musgrave, eds., *Criticism and the Growth of Knowledge* (Cambridge: Cambridge University Press, 1970).
29. See again references in preceding note.
30. Karl Popper, "The Logic of the Social Sciences," in T. W. Adorno et al., *The Positivist Dispute in German Sociology* (New York: Harper and Row, 1976), pp. 95f; and Jerome R. Ravetz, *Scientific Knowledge and Its Social Problems* (Oxford: Oxford University Press, 1971), p. 82.

of particular time and place as to be disqualified other than as illustrative of a possible scenario.

Given the complicity of the social world and the impossibility of strict verification, inconclusiveness becomes a conspicuous attribute of professional inquiry. Every social scientist can find matching examples like the following, and many have come to a weary acceptance of their typicality: "Most researchers report that alienation is highest in the working and lower classes or that it declines as status increases. [Then follow citations to twelve studies as illustrative of even more studies so finding.] Thus the class-alienation relationship is among the best documented in this literature."

But then: "Even here, however, there is apparently some need for caution. First, small local samples again preponderate, and the national surveys included in the list are dated. Second, at least one study has found 'virtually no relationship between indicators of social advantage such as education, occupation, and income [on one hand] and political trust [on the other]' . . . , and there is another study whose evidence suggests that alienation *increases* with social status. . . . Finally, research [reported in still another cited study] suggests that the strength of the relationship may have waned over time."[31]

Judgment, Not Test

Professional testing consequently does not greatly differ from lay testing in that both finally rest on judgment rather than some conclusive technique. Compared to lay judgment, professional judgment often excels in quality of information, analysis, and cognitive discipline. It will often employ special techniques like statistical analysis of variance. But both professional and lay tests finally reduce to judgments, to a subjective weighing of considerations, and to giving reasons not in the form of conclusive evidence but often in the form of ad hoc replies to challenges. For example, empirical beliefs of political scientists on corruption of government officials, capture of regulatory agencies by their clients, or critical political factors in economic growth in the third world all rest on large components of judgment. And many are accepted in the absence of any other distinctive forms of testing envisaged in models of scientific method.

One might regard it as a curious feature of the judgments that both social scientists and lay investigators make that they take the form not of judgments on the truth or validity of each of various well-

31. James D. Wright, *The Dissent of the Governed* (New York: Academic Press, 1976), pp. 67f.

defined propositions but of ad hoc judgments on constantly shifting propositions, concepts, cognitive organizations, and other elements in inquiry. As a consequence, identifiable articulated tested scientific propositions about the social world remain relatively infrequent; and a person's empirical understanding of the social world emerges not in the form of articulated tested facts or theories but in the capacity of that person to appraise judiciously, to form and express shifting judgments about, the confronted confusing social world.

This appears to be the case even for those inquiries that best lend themselves to experiments, simulations, survey research, or other specialized scientific method. For example, decades of well-financed research have employed the analysis of variance to sort out and weigh candidate charisma, economic conditions, or articulated campaign issues as factors accounting for how voters vote. But the propositions they establish as scientifically acceptable are highly restricted. They often refer only to a particular election studied. Instead of extracting from the analysis a scientifically acceptable specification of voting patterns, they achieve an improvement in judgment, which some leading practitioners of voting characterize as follows: "There is beginning to be empirical reason to make the intuitively plausible links between the sharpness of policy differentiation between parties and their candidates and the degree to which voters are influenced by policy concerns. . . . In any event, the continued study of voter behavior . . . has become increasingly helpful in understanding the range of colorations that may be detected in popular voting."[32] The revealing words are "beginning to be empirical reason," "intuitively plausible links," "increasingly helpful," and "understanding the range of colorations," the latter indicating that sometimes not testing at all but the elaboration of scenarios counts as the accomplishment.

For an example from psychology, a review of research accomplishments of the last fifty years takes care to acknowledge the rarity of acceptable scientific propositions. The review comments on experiments and observations by Piaget and Vygotsky that display "deficiencies" in children's behavior. Do the observed deficiencies

32. Philip E. Converse, Heinz Eulau, and Warren E. Miller, "The Study of Voting," in Robert McAdams et al., eds., *Behavioral and Social Science Research*, part 2 (Washington, D.C.: National Academy Press, 1982), p. 53.

33. Katherine Nelson, "Cognitive Development in the First Years of Life," ibid., p. 518. The McAdams volume is a collection of reviews of areas of research that have achieved "significant breakthroughs or that show promise of such breakthroughs" (pp. 1f), but throughout it is difficult to find them; and the reviews are instead rich in discussion of concepts and method. The same is to be said for Karl W. Deutsch et al., eds., *Advances in the Social Sciences, 1900–1980* (Lanham, Md: University Press of America, 1986).

establish any propositions about thought patterns? The reviewer will go no further than to say that psychologists "thought" that the behavioral deficiencies indicated deficiencies in juvenile thought.[33] Then, commenting on recent work on human memory, the reviewer again shrinks from a claim that any propositions survived a test. Instead, the work has "challenged our assumptions."[34]

Many such psychological studies, only a few of which achieve a tested generalization, result in a revised set of general understandings that represent the best judgment of the profession. Thus the reviewer continues: "Collectively, this work [of the 1930s, 1940s, and 1950s] has changed our view of the infant from a passive, unorganized insensitive, unsocial, unaware, incompetent, unknowing organism to an active, sensitive, exploratory, social, and increasingly organized, knowledgeable, and competent organism."[35] And, again sounding an appropriate tentative note: "Most researchers now believe that the human infant engages in quite complex information processing."[36] The emphasis falls on psychologists' "views," "beliefs," or judgments rather than their propositions.

Political science provides similar evidence in the detailed testimony of a distinguished scholar on the accomplishments of the social scientific study of political development in the third world. From the 1950s on into the early 1980s, the study of political development attracted some of the best minds in the discipline, attracting as well participants from the other social sciences. In a meticulous and extraordinarily informed review with citations to roughly two hundred studies, he responds to critics from the left by laying out evidence of the solidity and fruitfulness of mainline research on political development. His review consequently provides examples of the strongest claims made for work in the field.[37]

About half the paper offers evidence and argument to the effect that dependency theory, the principal challenge in these years to mainline inquiry, erred or remained inconclusive. Its important claims were not adequately tested. Then, turning to the impressive cumulation of mainline research, he characterizes the accomplishments of the many studies reviewed by thoughtfully claiming—and I do not deny the validity of the claims—that they "illuminated," "were concerned with," "gave special emphasis to . . . ," "developed insights, hypotheses, and analytical categories," "codified," "stressed the im-

34. McAdams et al., *Behavioral and Social Science Research*, pp. 520f.

35. Ibid., p. 512.

36. Ibid., p. 322.

37. Gabriel A. Almond, "Comparative Politics and Political Development" (mimeo, Stanford University, February 20, 1985).

portance of . . . ," "examined the significance of . . . ," "placed in the context of . . . ," "treated variables theoretically," "produced good work," "were fruitful," "applied concepts and models to . . . ," "vastly improved our understanding," "dealt with," and "increased the level of rigor."

Significantly, these phrases claim improvements in judgment, but do not claim that this rich body of work produced acceptable scientific propositions or approximations to them. On only a few points does the review claim positions that survived a significant testing.[38]

In the studies surveyed, hypotheses, even testable hypotheses, are frequently noted; what is rare is their survival of testing. Studies succeed, however, in undermining hypotheses. That constitutes a significant accomplishment and obviously a help to what was once called verification. Indeed, in some of the natural sciences, "falsification" of some one pivotal hypothesis becomes a powerful though only partial method of testing a rival hypothesis (although a claim that a proposition has been falsified itself requires testing). Given, however, the large numbers of possible rival hypotheses in every field in social science, attempts at disconfirmation, although valuable, often do not even reach a half-way house on the route to acceptance of a rival proposition.

Familiar special obstacles to testing obstruct the social sciences: among others, the complexity of the social world and incessant change in it. And when inquiries themselves lead people to alter their behavior—for example, research on sexual behavior leading to changes in that behavior—then testing becomes all the more difficult for social science.

One more obstacle to testing in the social sciences arises from the fertility of professional probing in producing scenarios. In many circumstances, professional probing uncovers complexity, displays new possible linkages between phenomena. Seventy years ago, Thorstein Veblen observed that "the outcome of any serious research can only be to make two questions grow where one question grew before."[39] A contemporary social scientist concludes that "sociology's functions are primarily those of complicating and undermining received opinions on social life."[40] Professional probing often moves

38. On those infrequent cases, see ibid., pp. 23–26 and 38.
39. *The Place of Science in Modern Civilization* (1919; New York: Russell and Russell, 1961), p. 33.
40. Nathan Glazer, "The Ideological Uses of Sociology," in Paul F. Lazarsfeld, William H. Sewell, and Harold L. Wilinskey, eds., *The Uses of Sociology* (New York: Basic Books, 1967), p. 76.

toward divergence rather than convergence,[41] toward identifying a bevy of possible scenarios rather than one or a few propositions that social scientists might judge to have won a degree of acceptability. It discards some beliefs as untenable but adds more than it subtracts. In the U.S., a vast professional literature on the relation between educational attainment, race, home environment, and school in large part provoked by the "Coleman reports" produced very little professional agreement but a diversity of new hypotheses to take account of the variety of scenarios the research disclosed.[42] A long debate in political science and sociology on the structure of power similarly has produced a diversity of new and more precise insights into possibilities but very little tested generalization.[43]

Weak as social science is in empirical testing, it employs an enormous structure of fairly well tested empirical knowledge. Paradoxically, that knowledge has grown, for the most part, out of lay probing. A methodologically meticulous and demanding economist writes of his own field: "The 'facts' of economic life are all around us. Hence much of the factual background of economics can be presupposed without extensive examination or discussion."[44] Lay probing correctly establishes that money circulates; that business enterprises are formed, hire labor, purchase other inputs, turn out products; and that market-oriented economies are unstable to varying degrees.

Any other disciplinary field offers countless similar examples of facts important to professionals that can be "presupposed without extensive examination." Human beings speak complex languages; in some societies people live in nuclear families, in others in extended families; and people exercise influence and power over each other in many ways. The point is not simply that many or most probes are lay

41. The divergence thesis is developed in David K. Cohen and Michael S. Garet, "Reforming Educational Policy with Applied Social Research," *Harvard Educational Review* 45 (February 1975); and David K. Cohen and Janet Weiss, "Social Science and Social Policy," *The Educational Forum* 41 (May 1977).

42. James S. Coleman et al., *Equality of Educational Opportunity* (Washington, D.C.: Government Printing Office, 1966); Coleman, Sara D. Kelly, and John A. Moore, *Trends in School Segregation, 1968–1973* (Washington, D.C.: Urban Institute, 1975); Coleman, Thomas Hoffer, and Sally Kilgore, *High School Achievements* (New York: Basic Books, 1982). A summary of the controversy is in Duncan MacRae, Jr., *Policy Indicators* (Chapel Hill: University of North Carolina Press, 1985), pp. 118–131.

43. For a sample, see Robert A. Dahl, *Who Governs?* (New Haven: Yale University Press, 1961) and Steven Lukes, *Power* (New York: Macmillan, 1974). A summary of the controversy is in David M. Ricci, *Community Power and Democratic Theory* (New York: Random House, 1971), pp. 265–275.

44. Tjalling Koopmans, *Three Essays on the State of Economic Science* (New York: McGraw-Hill, 1957), p. 131.

rather than professional, a point made and illustrated earlier in this chapter. It is that lay probing suffices to establish "facts," which is to say that they suffice to test observations.

The vast structure of lay knowledge no one rejects as error even if everyone knows it contains an unknown number of falsehoods. Countless lay findings are as true as statements about the social world ever are. Professional testing can add almost nothing to their "verification." It cannot make people more confident that banks and corporations exist, that people buy and sell, feel anger, learn to speak beginning in infancy, become excited and depressed, form likes and dislikes, take bribes, and so on and on.

The acceptability of none of these lay observations turns on the testimony of any one person, and many not even on the testimony of one generation or one society. They are tested by testimony of millions of persons in a wide array of conditions in space and time, to a degree that professional testing cannot match. They have survived the possibility of challenge by professional probers; but the professionals agree on them as a result of their lay probing, not because they have professionally tested them.

Professional inquiry cannot claim more conclusive testing than lay probing. Its distinctiveness is in other directions: level of generality and precision, among others. But more generality and precision are gained at the price of inconclusiveness. As inquiry moves from the most firmly tested propositions of lay inquiry to the ostensibly more refined, precise, and ambitious propositions of professional inquiry, it typically moves to lower and lower levels of scientific acceptability. The argument holds for the natural sciences too. "The uninitiated believe that the result of a scientific experiment is distinguished from ordinary observation by a higher degree of certainty. They are mistaken, for the account of an experiment in physics does not have the immediate certainty, relative easy to check, that ordinary non-scientific testimony has. Though less certain than the latter, physical experiment is ahead of it in the number and precision of the details it causes us to know: therein lies its true and essential superiority."[45]

45. Pierre Duhem, *The Aim and Structure of Physical Theory (1914)* (New York: Atheneum, 1977), p. 163.

CHAPTER 11

Professional Help for

Lay Probing

Clearly, the results of professional social inquiry steadily seep into lay probing. In contemporary industrialized societies, the educated—and many less educated as well—have taken into their own thinking contributions from professional inquiry, drawing, aware or unaware, on classical Greek thought, Hobbes, Rousseau, the classical economists, Darwin, Freud, national income accounting in its juxtaposition with Keynes, the results of survey research in many directions, organizational theory, stratification theory, abnormal psychology, and residues from learning theory, to indicate a few of numberless possible examples. "Our knowledge is through and through suffused with the effects of past and present philosophy, science, and other intellectual disciplines."[1] Lay investigators have also come increasingly to respect and to intend deliberately to use the results of professional inquiry.[2]

1. Harry Redner in correspondence, 1988, expressing judgments that permeate his *Ends of Philosophy* (Beckenham, England: Croom Helm, 1986) and his *Ends of Science* (Boulder, Colo.: Westview Press, 1987).

2. Burkhart Holzner and John H. Marx, *Knowledge Application* (Boston: Allyn and Bacon, 1979), pp. 23–25.

The methods of scientific inquiry have also pervasively affected—serve as a model for—lay inquiry, especially that of the most educated.[3] In contemporary "knowledgeable societies," more than ever before, some people, following scientific canons,

> (a) inquire into the basis of their beliefs about man, nature, and society; (b) are guided (perhaps unconsciously) by objective standards of veridical truth, and, at the upper levels of education, follow scientific rules of evidence and inference in inquiry; (c) devote considerable resources to this inquiry and thus have a large store of knowledge; (d) collect, organize, and interpret their knowledge in a constant effort to extract further meaning from it for the purposes at hand; (e) employ this knowledge to illuminate (and perhaps modify) their values and goals as well as to advance them.[4]

No one can say for sure, but professional inquiry may achieve its influence not so much in accumulating specialized social science knowledge that is largely removed from lay knowledge, but in constantly revising lay knowledge and redirecting lay inquiry. Of its effects on lay probing, the most conspicuous and familiar appear in demonstrations from time to time that apparently well-established, popular, and expert lay belief on a point is in error.[5] But professionals influence lay probing in many other ways as well: through reconsideration, redirection, refinements, amendment, and confirmation of lay probes and in setting guidelines on how to probe.

For these reasons the influence of social science on lay probing appears to be great even if less than the influence of the natural sciences on lay probing. One can hardly doubt the influence of Newtonian mechanics on lay thought, an influence that came to pervade, though not without distortions and misrepresentations, the thinking of educated and uneducated alike. It seems also difficult to doubt a lesser yet nevertheless prodigious and widespread influence of relativity theory. As comparable examples of impact of professional inquiry into the social world, one might offer, say, John Locke or Adam Smith. Yet against those who would confidently offer them as examples stand those who claim for both that they only excellently articu-

3. Marx W. Wartofsky, *Conceptual Foundations of Scientific Thought* (New York: Macmillan, 1968), p. 3.

4. Robert E. Lane, "The Decline of Politics and Ideology in a Knowledgeable Society," *American Sociological Review* 31 (October 1966), p. 650.

5. See Paul Lazarsfeld's dramatic demonstration of many instances of the contradiction of "well-grounded" ordinary knowledge through professional research in "The American Soldier," *Public Opinion Quarterly* 13 (Fall 1949).

lated pivotal lay ideas of educated people of their times. No trivial accomplishment, it nevertheless suggests a reciprocal influence between lay and professional inquiry, rather than a powerful unilateral effect, that creates an uncertainty about the social science impact.

The opening pages of the preceding chapter suggested another ground for uncertainty about social science influence: specifically, the absence of undeniable examples of the indispensability of social science for any of humankind's social or collective ventures. That reason for caution in appraising the social science contribution to lay investigation points to another.

No Invisible World

Professional social inquiry has not empirically discovered, as has natural science, an invisible world possible to know only through professional inquiry. The natural sciences have made such a discovery, a world of particles and waves, of black holes, of continental drift, of nerve synapses. Ordinary people did not discover such a world and, now knowing that it exists, still cannot probe it. Its existence establishes a domain in which professional inquiry moves, even though still dependent methodologically on nonprofessional inquiry, into a world largely of its own—specifically, one in which almost every finding is exclusively professional, both in origin and in method of testing. And to describe it requires a supplementary vocabulary in large part invented by professional scientists.

No counterpart of so invisible a world exists for professional social inquiry. For the most part, professional investigators of the social world observe much the same phenomena that nonprofessionals observe. They have achieved entry into no world private to them. Their professional propositions are largely no more than refinements—however valuable—of nonprofessional propositions about familiar phenomena. And social science professionals "use, by and large, the same concrete concepts and thought-models which were created for activistic purposes in real life."[6]

But Marx wrote of a world of reality lying hidden behind a world of appearances, Adam Smith of a hidden hand, sociologists of latent, in contrast to manifest, phenomena or "functions," and psychiatrists of an invisible world of impulses, motives, and censors. Did each find an invisible world?

When Marx says that a world of exploitation lies invisible, except for his efforts to disclose it, behind a visible world of production

---

6. Karl Mannheim, *Ideology and Utopia* (1936; New York: Harcourt, Brace, Jovanovich, 1960), p. 45.

or of resource allocation, he does not in fact uncover phenomena that are invisible to the nonprofessional eye, beyond analysis except through professional inquiry, and impossible to discuss except with a new vocabulary. Class, exploitation, conflict, value, poverty, money, commodity, capitalism (Marx's word, but for familiar institutions), dialectic, and materialism—all these circulated as familiar concepts and terms, to which he gave some restructuring. The real world that he claimed to find behind the world of appearances was a world of familiar phenomena, invisible only to classical economic theory, to which he opposed his understanding of economy and society. There exist at least two real worlds, both visible: one, Marx's world of exploitation and oppression; the other, the classical world of resource allocation and a cooperative division of labor. One has been neglected by classical and contemporary mainline theory, the other by Marxism.

Adam Smith did not in fact claim the existence of a hidden hand. He claimed instead that the complex market actions of countless people achieved, in specific familiar ways that he pointed out in familiar language, unanticipated consequences "as though by" a hidden hand. His argument depended on a figure of speech to show his readers important intricacies of a familiar visible world.

The sociological distinction between "manifest" and "latent" distinguishes, variably, between the ostensibly and the actually operative, the anticipated and the unanticipated, the intended and the unintended, and the superficially diagnosed and the more deeply diagnosed, all distinctions open to and common to lay probing. They disclose no world describable only with a core of new concepts and vocabulary such that professional inquiry moves a world away from nonprofessional. Eldridge Cleaver, an activist of the troubled late 1960s, needed no special instruments of observation of phenomena invisible to anyone but a professional to add his profound "If you aren't part of the solution, you're part of the problem" to our understanding of latent and manifest functions.

One of Freud's accomplishments was to bring into the world of professional inquiry some ideas about obscure motives, passions, censors, and patterns of behavior found in the nonprofessional literary probing of Shakespeare, Poe, and R. L. Stevenson, among others. In that respect, he pushed further in the exploration of an aspect of a world already roughly perceived in lay probing. Although making a number of terminological innovations—id and superego, for example—his analyses largely employed familiar concepts and vocabulary;

and, indeed, very few lines of professional inquiry have become so intertwined with lay probing as has psychoanalysis, a "vulgar" psychoanalytic discourse having become a popular pastime among many educated lay probers in the West.

From Freud, professional inquiry has, with help from other sources, moved into further study of cognitive processes as well as pharmaceutical controls over behavior. In these lines of inquiry, it moves into the edges of an invisible world, like the world of theoretical physics, and may soon move more deeply into such a world, a world in which the brain is analyzed with concepts and language as esoteric as those of theoretical physics. Here, then, may appear to the professional eye another invisible world impervious to lay probing, but only if the inquiries go to the natural world of biology, physiology, and medicine. Professional inquiry into patterns of social interaction, purposive behavior, social process, and social institutions shows no promise at all so far of carving out an invisible world from which lay probing is excluded by its weak eyes.

One can say, of course, that any new insight, professional or not, into the social world brings something formerly invisible into visibility. More precisely, then, the difference between natural and social science pivots on a critical difference in the character of the things they study. Given that all objects of both professional and nonprofessional inquiry consist of "intellectually constructed things and events," in theoretical physics and some other branches of natural science the intellectual constructs of the professionals differ greatly from those of the nonprofessionals (except as nonprofessionals learn from the professionals). Professional inquiry into the social world took over and remains committed to intellectual constructs close to those that had emerged from lay inquiry. It can find no others.

Natural scientists sometimes broke into invisible worlds because they developed and used special technologies of observation. Beginning with the invention of microscope and telescope in the seventeenth century, scientific probes have, with an ever improved technology, been able to see, hear, ascertain the shape of, or measure the influence of variables either obscured or invisible to the observer who lacks the technology. Today, with scientific inquiry through such devices as nuclear accelerators, electron microscopes, and radio and other waves, professional and lay inquiry into the physical world move far from each other.[7]

7. For detail on the impact of technology for scientific investigation, see Harry Redner, *The Ends of Science* (Boulder, Colo.: Westview Press, 1987).

Yet Newtonian physics did not much depend on a specialized technology of observation, nor did many of the discoveries of nineteenth-century biology. And, on the other hand, the accomplishments of data aggregation in social science—for example, of survey research, census, and national income accounting—rest on special social and mechanical technologies beyond the capacity of laymen—tasks of social organization of teams of observers themselves and of data processing. Even so, professional social inquiry finds no invisible world.

PROFESSIONAL EFFECTS ON LAY IMPAIRMENT

Given both the strengths and limits of social science contribution to lay probing, what can one say specifically about its contributions to the reduction of impairments in probing of ordinary people and functionaries? The question hides no hypothesis, not even a suspicion, that ideally social science supplies "the" answer to the problem of impaired lay inquiry. Whatever its contribution, it is now and forever limited, because at any time everyone's probing suffers not only from ignorance and analytical incapacities that social science can presumably reduce, but from social controls, influences, or powers that constrain everyone's freedoms to think, inquire, and discuss.[8] If one's peers take a dim view of independence of thought or the state and its schools enforce conformity of thought, social science can make only a slow-moving and indirect contribution to reducing impairment, one that is perhaps at best very weak.

Setting that limitation aside, insofar as social science can help people reduce current impairing influences, I suggest four reasons—each to be discussed—for something short of a vote of confidence. First, social scientists do not regard the activity of lay probing and the processes of its impairment in the pattern described in earlier chapters as major phenomena to study. Second, they attend less to the information and analysis needed by ordinary people in their investi-

8. Quite aside from the question as to whether professional inquiry produces the kinds of knowledge that laymen, whether ordinary citizens or functionaries, need is the question of whether the results of professional inquiry are sufficiently well disseminated to laymen. In some circles, the problems of supplying social science useful for social problem solving are often now routinely classified into two main categories—production and distribution—so large do dissemination problems loom. Well analyzed and familiar as the dissemination problem is, we shall not discuss it further. In later chapters, however, we shall consider ways to reduce the problems of dissemination. It is possible that better products would greatly ameliorate the dissemination problem.

gations than to the needs of officials and other functionaries. Third, insofar as they meet citizens' needs, they do so less effectively for their standing volitions, the most severely impaired, than for action volitions. That is to say, they help citizens more on tax policy, current issues on space exploration, or toxic waste disposal than on persisting issues in perception of society, social philosophy, and ideology, issues that are both important in themselves and to improved formation of action volitions. Fourth, they frequently try to displace rather than improve lay probing of both citizens and functionaries. Instead of assisting impaired lay investigators to solve a problem, social scientists both preempt and paralyze lay investigating by offering their proposed solutions as a substitute.

Inattention to the Phenomenon of Impairment

In the opening of the chapters on impairment, I noted a variety of kinds of social science inquiry into defective probing: studies of indoctrination, public-opinion formation, voter ignorance and inattention, cognitive failures, among others, as well as older scholarly references to defects in thinking from Plato to Marx. One can hardly allege, then, that social scientists wholly ignore the phenomenon of impairment.

But, as I also observed earlier, many kinds of studies of ignorance and irrationality treat them as somehow fixed, hence ignore their social causation.[9] Citizens simply do not bother to probe—but why should they? They are interested instead in jobs and "happy families."[10] Thus is dismissed the study of social causation of the defects. Or social scientists treat causation in a curiously distant way. They describe people as investigating no better than they do because of their place in society, their level of education, their socioeconomic class, and other similar influences all regarded as exogenous.[11] That identifiable social processes, including elite influences, have formed their place in society, their level of education, and their class affili-

9. Cognitive psychologists do not see cognitive performance as fixed and have explored ways in which it can be improved. But they do not give much consideration to reducing social impairments or to social influences on performance. The lines of improvement they explore consist largely of teaching people better ways, say, to organize knowledge or avoid illogic. See, for example, Richard E. Nisbett and Lee Ross, *Human Inference* (Englewood Cliffs, N.J.: Prentice-Hall, 1980), chap. 12.

10. Aaron Wildavsky, *Speaking Truth to Power* (Boston: Little, Brown, 1979), p. 253.

11. An illustration of the tendency in social science to regard cognitive limitations as personal attributes understandable with little regard for their social sources is a collection of papers by twenty psychologists and political scientists: Richard R. Lau and David O. Sears, eds., *Political Cognition* (Hillsdale, N.J.: Lawrence Erlbaum Associ-

ation—that, in short, they have been deliberately or inadvertently induced or caused to probe badly rather than well often gets no more than a formal acknowledgement rather than study.

Consider, for example, how a distinguished social scientist accounts for voter incompetence. It is, he says, a "motivational" problem: voters, whom he appears to regard as autonomous rather than influenced, are "engrossed" in other affairs, paying scant attention to social issues. He does not mention social influences on their motivations, such as, for example, draw their attention from one interest to another made more engrossing. And in considering the availability of information to voters, he finds it normally sufficient—but without a word on the possibility that misinformation creates a problem for them, some of it systematic and deliberate in intention to obfuscate or confuse.[12]

Impairing influences at the hands of elites still lack systematic study, despite the history of references to them in political philosophy from Plato to Marx. Only a small number of important attempts to push the analysis of how elites impair appear in the social science literature,[13] and the difficulties of the pursuit appear so great as to persuade a number of social scientists to advise aborting the pursuit—on the dubious ground that it cannot be scientifically pursued—rather than undertake it.[14] Even recent mainline democratic political theorists—just those social scientists who might suspect its relevance to their models of democracy—appear to see it as a phenomenon only secondary to their theoretical tasks.[15]

---

ates, 1986). Or see Stephen Earl Bennett, *Apathy in America* (Dobbs Ferry, N.Y.: Transnational, 1986). Bennett's search for the causes of apathy turns to such factors as gender, education, and age—even education being seen as an attribute rather than as a result of influences brought to bear on people by others around them.

12. Philip E. Converse, "Perspectives on the Democratic Process," *Michigan Quarterly Review* 27 (Spring 1988).

13. Examples are: Peter Bachrach and Morton S. Baratz, "Two Faces of Power," *American Political Science Review* 66 (December 1962); Stephen Lukes, *Power* (New York: Macmillan, 1974); John Gaventa, *Power and Powerlessness* (Oxford: Oxford University Press, 1980); Stuart Ewen, *Captains of Consciousness* (New York: McGraw-Hill, 1976); Larry Spence, *The Politics of Social Knowledge* (University Park: Pennsylvania State University Press, 1978); Nicholas Abercrombie, S. Hill, and B. S. Turner, *The Dominant Ideology Thesis* (Boston: Allen & Unwin, 1980).

14. For example, Nelson W. Polsby, *Community Power and Political Theory*, 2d ed. (New Haven: Yale University Press, 1980).

15. V. O. Key, *Public Opinion and American Democracy* (New York: Knopf, 1961); J. R. Pennock, *Democratic Political Theory* (Princeton: Princeton University Press, 1979); Robert A. Dahl, *Polyarchy* (New Haven: Yale University Press, 1971); Giovanni Sartori, *Democratic Theory* (New York: Praeger, 1965).

Many social scientists deny the elite pattern of impairment; but, even if correct, they do not possess the required evidence, so scanty is it, either to affirm or deny the pattern. The efforts made in the chapters on impairment to establish the fact of its existence themselves constitute evidence of social science neglect of the phenomenon, for those efforts could call on very little previous sustained study of it. Recall, for example, the remarkable paucity of statistical evidence with respect to the volume of business and government spending to influence public opinion—for all countries, including a data-rich U.S.—a mammoth phenonemon the measurement of which is not even attempted.

Some Examples of Professional Inattention to the Phenomenon of Impairment

A few dissenting scholarly voices aside, political science and economics avoid much of the phenomenon of impairment when in democratic theory and market theory they make do with the inadequate and impairment-hiding concept of preferences and then postulate preferences as given. Thus, in their modeling of democracy and market, they simply bypass the formation of citizen and consumer preferences by some mixture of enlightenment and impairment.

Economists frequently defend this inattention by arguing that the assumption of given preferences simplifies: without so simplifying an assumption, the powerful analytical apparatus of economic theory could not have been constructed. The argument does not deny the inattention; it attempts to excuse it.[16] Whether a good excuse or not it confirms the allegation of neglect. Neither does it explain the paucity of empirical studies of preference formation independent of theory formulation.

Nor does any discipline broadly study the normative aspects of impairment. Because no one citizen or functionary can probe all issues—no one has the time and energy to turn every thought or observation into a probe—everyone at best has to live with a significant degree of inadequacy and error in probing. Aside from obvious forms of coercion, what other kinds of impairing influences under what circumstances by any standard count as unacceptable? That absolutely fundamental question rarely emerges for sustained analysis in contemporary social science. Lawyers and judges confront it in some of its manifestations. A few social scientists raise specific issues rel-

16. A sampling of such occasional questions as economists raise about preferences is in Steven E. Rhoads, *The Economist's View of the World* (Cambridge: Cambridge University Press, 1985), pp. 148–158.

evant to it—for example, in discussing limits on campaign spending and sales promotion. The critical theorists of the Frankfurt School give it some theoretical attention. I do not deprecate these contributions in saying that the discussion is thin.[17]

However deep the impairment of probing of such alleged fundamental virtues as loyalty, trust, cooperation, acceptance of group norms, respect for authority and faith, one looks far to find in professional probing anywhere in the social sciences sustained and diverse normative analysis that is helpful to these probes.[18] Despite their frequent personal or nonprofessional sympathy for or identification with dissenters, sociologists have only slowly escaped from a tendency to label dissenters, noncooperators, or agitators as deviants, regrettable figures in social life worth studying only from an interest in correcting their deviance, thus assuming their moral inferiority rather than examining the ethics they question.[19] With little inquiry, many political scientists have embraced the allegation that political activism quickly reaches—or has in fact reached—a level at which it threatens to overload government or to create dangerous political cleavages.[20] Historical studies aside, no social science discipline systematically probes with care the consequences of both too much as well as too little respect for authority, of too much as well as too little trust, and of too little as well as too much dissent.

All the social sciences join history in deploring bloody historical excesses of religious faith; but that the religious faith of contemporary Protestants and Catholics, say, in the U.S. constitutes a powerful force in American politics social scientists professionally consider only with respect to conspicuous political issues: for example, Catholicism on birth control or mobilization of the Moral Majority. That religious faith may chronically conflict with political skepti-

17. Recently enriched by Paul Corcoran, *Political Language and Rhetoric* (St. Lucia, Queensland: Unversity of Queensland Press, 1979).

18. Although, again, empirical study is frequent: for example, Margaret Mead, *Cooperation and Competition among Primitive Peoples* (New York: McGraw-Hill, 1937); Harold Guetzkow, *Multiple Loyalties*, Publication no. 4 of the Center for Research on World Political Institutions in the Woodrow Wilson School of Public and International Affairs (Princeton: Princeton University, 1955); and Morton Deutsch, *The Resolution of Conflict* (New Haven: Yale University Press, 1973).

19. For an analyzed example, together with comments on it, see James B. Rule, *Insight and Social Betterment* (New York: Oxford University Press, 1978), p. 15.

20. David Easton and Jack Dennis, *Children in the Political System* (New York: McGraw-Hill, 1969), pp. 55, 66. Michael Crozier, Samuel Huntington, and J. Watanuki, *The Crisis of Democracy* (New York: New York University Press, 1975).

cism, dampen probing, and consequently obstruct democracy—such underlying possibilities as these draw little attention from social science.[21]

An Inattention Especially Obstructive to Popular Probing

Social science inattention to the phenomena of probing and impairment leaves both functionary and citizen without understandings that would presumably be potentially valuable to them. But it would appear that consequent deficiencies in understanding obstruct citizens more than functionaries. For many elites and functionaries, the less said about popular probing and impairment, the better. But for citizens, an understanding of their own impairments is indispensable to reducing them. One might even go so far as to suggest that no social science neglect of citizens' needs so greatly obstructs as the neglect of the study of the phenomenon of impairment itself. Thus, in the above example, economics' inattention to the role of elite impairing influences in the formation of consumer preferences, and political science's inattention to elite influences in the formation of citizen preferences, undermine citizen capacities to cope with manipulation by elites and functionaries. More than that, such studies of influences on consumer and citizen preferences as social sciences undertake often intend to facilitate functionary control over citizen and consumer, as in market research, public opinion research, and voting studies. Routinely, such studies are used to sell products, candidates, and parties, less often to tell consumers and citizens how to cope with the impairments visited on them by functionaries and elites.

Similarly, in the study of behavior in formal organizations, especially the factory or other work organization, social psychology and sociology seek to learn how members of an organization can be induced or otherwise controlled so as to do what organizational leadership wants them to do. They have done little—though a counter movement is now developing—to explore how ordinary members of the organization might bend the organization to their volitions, rather than accede to those of management, except to treat that possibility as "dysfunctional". Nor have they explored the evaluative question of how far and in what ways managerial objectives for the organization

---

21. Defaulting in favor of philosophers, who, however, for all their insights, lack the social scientist's competence on institutions. For an excellent philosophical discourse on religious faith and probing, see Hans Albert, *Treatise on Critical Reason* (Princeton: Princeton University Press, 1985), chap. 5.

might require modification in the light of the standing and action volitions of ordinary members.[22]

No example, however, better illustrates social science's inattention to the study of impairment as well as its confusion than the study of socialization of children and adults, a confusion arising out of the impairments of social science itself. In that confusion, impairment drops out of sight. That illustration will be saved for the next chapter, on the impairments of social science.

A Benign Neglect?

Social science's inattention to what the citizen needs to know about impairment deserves a defense, one might believe, because citizens would not use attentive studies if offered, would not read the relevant publications, would not understand much if they did. Until a later chapter, I set aside that or any other justification of the inattention in order to make the point here that, for good or bad, social science gives little attention to the phenomena of impairment. At best, transmission of professional analysis and findings to citizens proceeds slowly and indirectly; through journalists, popularizers, and opinion leaders at various levels from chief executive or campaigning candidate to an informed workmate or neighbor. On the subject of impairment, professionals provide little input for such a subsequent transmission, for good or bad, wisely or not.

Policy-Making

In social science attempts at more immediate contributions to social problem solving—that is, when it undertakes analyses of specific social problems, often also proposing and appraising possible solutions—inattention to citizens' needs becomes even more apparent.

Consider governmental problem solving in the Western democracies as it necessitates the following probes (mixed with one another in actual practice):

1. *Officials probe to form their action volitions on governmental policy.* These probes are the closest of all probes to decisions or outcomes. Officials intend to formulate action volitions that are appropriate to their own standing volitions and in varying degrees to the standing volitions of their constituents. Only to a lesser degree do they seek to formulate action volitions that are appropriate to the action volitions of

22. For comment, see Charles Perrow, *Complex Organizations*, 3d ed. (New York: Random House, 1986), esp. chap. 3.

constituents, for their constituents may not have formulated action volitions, or the officials may be willing to override constituents' action volitions for any of many reasons, including the possibility that the officials find constituents' action volitions on an issue inconsistent with constituents' standing volitions or their other action volitions.

To accomplish this task, officials must therefore:

2. *probe in varying degree to discover the standing and action volitions of their constituents;*[23]
3. *probe their own standing volitions.*

In addition:

4. *constituents probe their standing volitions,* and, on a small proportion of government policies, *their action volitions.* (They do so in interchange with officials and under substantial influence from them.) These probes are the most distant from decision or outcome, but the volitions of a large, inactive set of constituents set limits to the actions possible for the officials, leaving some policies beyond the pale.

As I noted in chapter 3, one can test an action volition better than a standing volition, because its appropriateness to standing volitions becomes in part an empirical question, less the case for the appropriateness, validity, or acceptability of the standing volitions themselves. Hence, impairment becomes more severe for people when they examine standing volitions than when they examine action volitions, even if it is severe in both cases. Impairment will be most severe, therefore, in probes of standing volitions 3 and 4 above. But professional probing instead focuses largely on tasks helpful to probes 1 and 2, with their emphasis on active volitions. Professional probing attends overwhelmingly to probe 1, attentive to the needs of officials rather than of citizens. (Among various reasons, officials can pay professionals for their services, as well as reward them with influence and recognition.) Professional inquiry attends mostly to officials' need to develop action volitions that take standing volitions as given, no matter how impaired. Yet insofar as it comes to the aid of anyone's impaired probing of his standing volitions, it does so largely for officials. Thus on two counts—attention to action rather than more deeply impaired standing volitions, and attention to officials rather

23. Officials will also probe how to manipulate rather than ascertain constituent volitions, but for our immediate purpose that can be disregarded.

than constituents—it fails to strike deeply and broadly at impairment of the probing of masses of citizens.

Consider a parallel but not identical schema for market problem solving, in which the same pattern appears.

1. *Business managers probe their action volitions for the enterprise.* Again, these probes are the closest of all probes to production decisions or outcomes. Managers intend to formulate action volitions appropriate to their own standing volitions and to the action volitions of their constituents (customers and suppliers). In market problem solving, unlike governmental problem solving, constituents form innumerable action volitions (for buying and selling), and these volitions, rather than their standing volitions, are the concern of managers (in contrast to official concern with standing volitions in governmental problem solving).

To do this:

2. *Managers probe to ascertain the action volitions (volitions to buy or sell) of their constituents.*[24]
3. *Managers probe their own standing volitions.*
4. *Constituents probe their action volitions.* They probe what to buy of countless products and services, these volitions being innumerable in market problem solving, as is not the case in governmental problem solving. They intend to formulate action volitions appropriate to their standing volitions.
5. *Constituents probe their standing volitions*: life-styles, career aspirations, family responsibilities, opportunities and obligations as citizens, political participation, all of which carry implications for market action volitions to buy, sell, save, invest, and so on.

In this pattern of problem solving, constituents' standing volitions share the usual impairments of standing volitions generally. But all-pervasive sales promotion additionally impairs both standing and action volitions of constituents. Hence, impairment of people broadly rises to its greatest severity in probes 4 and 5 and, for managers, in probe 3. Not to these severely impaired probes, however, does social science normally bring assistance. Instead, professional probers attend to probes 1 and 2. Probe 2, for example, encompasses a great deal of market research to find and exploit consumer demand.

24. Managers will also probe how to manipulate rather than ascertain constituents' volitions.

Evidence of relative inattentiveness to citizens' needs lies in the development of "policy analysis" for functionaries, especially in the U.S., as a specialization within the social sciences and as a profession for training in which numerous graduate schools offer master of arts programs and for which specialized journals and instructional materials abound.[25] Several nations now follow the American lead. None, including the U.S., give comparable explicit and specialized professional attention to the needs of citizens engaged in probing.[26] Wisely or not, a special social science subject labeled policy analysis attends to the needs of functionaries, not of citizens.

A social science preoccupation with policy problems seen from the functionary's position to the relative neglect of citizen as investigator emerges also in many explicit social science attempts to examine the possible contributions of research to governmental policy-making. For example, a component study of the U.S. National Research Council's Study Project on Social Research and Development tries to identify all important avenues leading from research to better policy-making. Public opinion is identified as one, thus presumably opening up for consideration the contribution of research to public attitudes and knowledge that will subsequently influence policy. In fact, however, the study makes no further reference to citizen need or use for information and analysis. From that point on, it simply assumes that research and development is for officials, not citizens.[27] Commenting on the need for, uses of, and design of studies of policy, another social scientist simply assumes without argument: "The goal of policy analysis is to inform policy makers about the likely consequences of alternative policy choices."[28] Citizens do not seem to exist.

In recent years, a frequent explanation of social science's attention to the needs of functionaries rather than of ordinary people de-

25. For details, see John Friedman, *Planning in the Public Domain* (Princeton: Princeton University Press, 1987), pp. 433–435; and Stuart S. Nagel, *Contemporary Public Policy Analysis* (University: University of Alabama Press, 1984), pp. 1–6.

26. Despite specialized and institutionalized social science help to functionaries, individual professionals do not wholly neglect citizens' needs for policy analysis: see, for example, Duncan MacRae, Jr., and James A. Wilde, *Policy Analysis for Public Decisions* (North Scituate, Mass.: Duxbury Press, 1979); Kenneth Fox, *Metropolitan America* (Jackson: University Press of Mississippi, 1986); and Victor R. Fuchs, *Who Shall Live?* (New York: Basic Books, 1974).

27. Larry E. Lynn, Jr., ed., *Knowledge and Policy* (Washington, D.C.: National Research Council, 1978).

28. Mark H. Moore, "Social Science and Policy Analysis," in Daniel Callahan and Bruce Jennings, eds., *Ethics, the Social Sciences, and Policy Analysis* (New York: Plenum Press, 1983), p. 273.

clares that the positivist influence on social science and consequent preoccupation with cause-and-effect relations pushes social science toward the study of how people can be manipulated, which means, for the most part, how functionaries can manipulate masses.[29] Why study cause and effect if not to locate a cause sufficient to produce a desired effect? But the allegation that the study of cause and effect is necessarily oriented toward social control goes too far. For ordinary people, not just functionaries, need to understand cause-and-effect relationships—for example, the causes of unemployment or the causes of various kinds of family discord—for their own tasks in problem solving, sometimes simply to understand their options. One cannot thoughtfully form either standing or action volitions without cause-and-effect knowledge. Conventional scientific explanation, or even positivist science, is not necessarily manipulative, only often so; and social science's inattention to the needs of citizens in favor of the needs of functionaries would require a more complex explanation.

PROFESSIONAL PREEMPTION OF PROBING

The fourth and last explanation of social science's relative inattention to lay impairment is that, instead of assisting citizens and functionaries in their inquiries, social scientists often propose to take the task of inquiring away from them, although they of course require lay consent to do so. If solutions to social problems were anchored in wants, preferences, or interests regarded as "there" and empirically discoverable, social scientists might do better than ordinary people in the task of discovery. But if anchored instead in formulated, decided-upon, willed, or created volitions, then roughly everyone must probe and resist preemption by social scientists.

The social science attempt at preemption, when it occurs, seems deliberate and clear—indeed, often undertaken with professional pride—when a policy analyst, say, on contract with a government agency as a client, proposes to solve the client's problem for him. The analyst proposes first to reexamine and redefine the problem, then seeks possible solutions, and finishes the task with a recommended solution offered to the client. Such a preemptive analyst does not ask the client to identify the parts of his problem on which the client needs help, in contrast to the parts within the client's own competence. Nor does the analyst encourage the client to reconsider the

29. Brian Fay, *Social Theory and Political Practice* (London: Allen & Unwin, 1975), p. 41; and Herbert Marcuse, *One-Dimensional Man* (Boston: Beacon Press, 1964), pp. 158, 166.

relevant volitions. Analyst does it all for client. This textbook model of policy analysis as commonly taught in many recently inaugurated schools may or may not constitute a good method of social problem solving; but it leaves no room for, makes no contribution to, reduction of the client's impairment on the issues at hand.[30]

Aside from "policy analysis" as institutionalized in textbooks and schools, published social science with an orientation to policy often displays the same tendency to preempt. At least for simplicity's sake or, more specifically, to minimize difficult ethical and other aspects of public policy problems and focus quickly on the empirical aspects of it, social scientists often hurry to fix targets, goals, or governing values early in their analysis, so that the values can for the remainder of the study rest quietly as given.[31] That reduces to a low level the possibility that social scientists can contribute to social problem solving by engaging their own minds and those of their audiences on the evaluative aspects of the problem. They leave a pool of impairment, not even stirred.

If for all the reasons noted in this chapter, social science makes only a greatly limited contribution to the reduction of lay impairment, its own impairment further reduces its capacity to assist, as I will show in the next chapter.

30. For further discussion, see chap. 15.
31. Some regrettably strong tendencies in this direction appear in Robert A. Dahl and Charles E. Lindblom, *Politics, Economics and Welfare* (New York: Harper and Brothers, 1953), as can be seen by an inspection of its table of contents.

CHAPTER 12

Professional Impairment

Everyone is a defective investigator, social scientists not excepted, even though they struggle to discharge professional obligations to discipline themselves: to practice skepticism, to disclose their methods, to provide evidence and analysis in defense of whatever claims they make, and to remain open to challenge.

The defects that leave social science vulnerable to skeptics have given rise to a voluminous literature in recent decades and years. Although differing on the severity of various afflictions, perhaps social scientists will agree to some such list as the following, evidence of the agreement lying in the absence from professional literature of attempts to deny the charges categorically. I shall hurry through it as a preface to more consequential observations about the frequent impairments of social science.

Like natural scientists, social scientists find it difficult to remain open to new ideas that challenge key beliefs; their resistance to them goes beyond their need for fixed points from which inquiry can move.[1] Sometimes fundamental new ideas enter a discipline only

1. For a diagnosis, see M. J. Mulkay, "Sociology of the Scientific Research Community," in Ina Spiegel-Rosing and Derek de Solla Price, eds., *Science, Technology and Society* (Beverly Hills, Calif.: Sage, 1977), pp. 119–123.

with the death of one generation and its replacement by another.[2] Again like natural scientists, they often hide information from each other, and the intensity of their competition with each other seduces them into hasty work.[3] Some of them lie and practice other kinds of fraud.[4] Often pretentious, they erect elaborate unnecessary and even obstructive conceptual and theoretical structures.[5] They often mix useful precision in terminology with obstructive jargon. They fall under suspicion of inventing an excess of institutionalized subfields to insulate themselves from competition.[6] Many social scientists ape the methods of theoretical physics, despite their inappropriateness for the study of society.[7]

Many practice obscurantism, protecting themselves from criticism by sowing uncertainty as to just what they have said or pretending to ascend into esoterica where lesser minds cannot follow.[8] They often permit available research methods to decide the direction of their work, like the fabled drunk who on a dark night prefers to look for his lost keys under a streetlight rather than in the unilluminated spot where he lost them. They often indulge in an excessive and uncritical practice of statistical quantification, that is, beyond what is appropriate or defensible.[9] Some critics charge social science with "mindlessness," for pursuing research that is "poorly thought through."[10]

Quality control through peer review is often erratic, superficial, designed to avoid offense, and in other ways inadequate.[11] Social scientists take advantage of the autonomy that democratic societies confer on them to practice various kinds of self-indulgence, including

2. Max Planck in M. J. Mulkay, "Three Models of Scientific Development," *Sociological Review* 23 (August 1975), p. 512.

3. M. J. Mulkay, "Sociology of the Scientific Research Community," in Spiegel-Rosing and De Solla Price, *Science, Technology and Society*, pp. 117–119.

4. W. Broad and N. Wade, *Betrayers of Truth* (New York: Simon and Schuster, 1982).

5. For a diagnosis, see Albert O. Hirschman, "The Search for Paradigms as a Hindrance to Understanding," *World Politics* 22 (April 1970).

6. Warren O. Hagstrom, *The Scientific Community* (New York: Basic Books, 1965), p. 18.

7. As outlined in Duncan MacRae, Jr., *The Social Function of Social Science* (New Haven: Yale University Press, 1976), chap. 1.

8. Distinguished social scientists as far apart as Harold Lasswell, empiricist, and Leo Strauss, political philosopher, have been accused of obscurantism.

9. As outlined in William Alonso and Paul Starr, eds., *The Politics of Numbers* (New York: Russell Sage Foundation, 1987).

10. Herbert A. Gans, "Sociology in America," *American Sociological Review* 50 (February 1989), p. 10.

11. Laurence E. Lynn, Jr., *Knowledge and Politics* (Washington, D.C.: National Academy of Sciences, 1978), p. 6.

bypassing troublesome research topics in favor of easier ones—easier because they are well financed, or not likely to endanger their reputations, or intellectually more manageable.[12] They only infrequently display the doggedness and willingness to bear tedium and take risks that a good investigative journalist shows. In their treatment of classes, occupations, and ethnic groups, they discriminate in ways that appear to lack a scholarly justification.[13]

Social scientists are faddish[14]—witness the rise and fall of the "behavioral revolution" in political science or of learning theory in psychology. Each of the disciplines pursues an agenda in large part taken, with insufficient critique, from the internal intellectual traditions of the discipline rather than from a view of the social world with its challenges to understanding. And when it turns to the social world for guidance on its agenda, it turns mercenary; research follows money, especially governmental and corporate money. It may not have become, however, as "industrialized" as the natural sciences.[15] Social science practices a self-deceiving, fraudulent neutrality,[16] also a timid narrowness or avoidance of big issues.[17] Often frivolous, it lauds new findings or ideas not as significant but as "exciting," as though social science were a hobby, game, or other divertissement.

For such a list as this, no end comes into sight, for all the ordinary imprinted or socially acquired human attributes obstructive to probing appear in social scientists: among them, carelessness, wishful thinking, self-deceit, vulnerability to intimidation, self-righteousness, cowardice, defensive prevarication, and low cunning. And technically poor execution of research also belongs on the list. Using a number of specified criteria, a study rated half of all reviewed research projects (in a research field chosen for investigation) as of low rather than of

12. Todd Gitlin, "Media Sociology," *Theory and Society* 6 (1978); and Charles Sykes, *Profscam: Professors and the Demise of Higher Education* (Washington, D.C.: Regnery Gateway, 1988).

13. Irving Louis Horowitz, *Professing Sociology* (Chicago: Aldine, 1969), p. 165.

14. Alfred J. Kahn, "From Delinquency Treatment to Community Development," in Paul F. Lazarsfeld, William H. Sewell, and Harold L. Wilensky, *The Uses of Sociology* (New York: Basic Books, 1967), p. 485.

15. On "industrialization" in biology, see Martin Kenney, *Biotechnology* (New Haven: Yale University Press, 1986). On industrialization in science as a whole, see Jerome R. Ravetz, *Scientific Knowledge and Its Social Problems* (Oxford: Oxford University Press, 1971), chap. 2; and David F. Noble, *America by Design* (New York: Knopf, 1977).

16. Charles Taylor, "Neutrality in Political Science," in P. Laslett and G. Runciman, eds., *Philosophy, Politics and Society*, 3d ser. (Oxford: Blackwell, 1967).

17. Stanislaw Andreski, *Social Sciences as Sorcery* (London: André Deutsch, 1972).

medium or high quality of execution. The authors observe that five other reviews of the field reached the same conclusion, the other reviews describing the research each surveyed in such terms as "methodologically inadequate," "poorly conceived, poorly executed," "seriously deficient," and "weak in design and methodology."[18]

Is social science reformist, leftist, radical, or subversive?[19] Only in comparison with lay probers who are not;[20] and lay positions do not represent a benchmark of truth, validity, or good sense. If, for example, social scientists differ from lay people on the probabilities of AIDS infection from sneezes or the merits of free speech, the differences do not demonstrate a social science error, misjudgment, or bias. Frequent charges that because social scientists are more egalitarian than populations as a whole, they consequently hold an egalitarian bias, are invalid. For all the above criticisms of social science, it can be spared this one.[21]

SOCIAL SCIENCE IMPAIRMENT

An examination of the listed defects will show both biological and social limits on social science capacities to probe. Setting aside the biological limits, as throughout the study, one can roughly distinguish two kinds of socially caused defects, or impairments: common or shared, on one hand, and those distinctive to the profession, on the other. Clarifying them becomes the task of this chapter.

Common Impairments

Since social scientists do not begin as professionals, it is clear that early years immerse them in all the influences that impair everyone's capacity to probe: among others, family, school, church, peer pressures, obfuscations and indoctrinations of the communications media, governmental and corporate secrecy, threatened barriers to

18. Ilene Nagel Bernstein and Howard E. Freeman, *Academic and Entrepreneurial Research* (New York: Russell Sage Foundation, 1975), p. 102. The studies surveyed were all examples of evaluation research on governmental policies and projects.

19. See Eva Etzioni-Halevy, "Radicals in the Establishment," *Journal of Political and Military Sociology* 14 (Spring 1986).

20. S. M. Lipset and E. C. Ladd, Jr., "The Politics of American Sociologists," *American Journal of Sociology* 78 (1972), p. 71. Confirming evidence on this point can be found in Harold Orlans, *Contracting for Knowledge* (San Francisco: Jossey-Bass, 1973), pp. 1–14.

21. To allege a deep conservative, rightist, or status quo bias, a vast and varied literature is available. It includes the works of Marx; Karl Mannheim, *Ideology and Utopia* (New York: Harcourt, Brace, Jovanovich, 1960); Stephen Jay Gould, *The Mismeasure of Man* (New York: Norton, 1981); Henry J. Aaron, *Politics and the Professors*

employment or promotion—a long and familiar list. When they take up careers as social scientists, they do not wholly remove themselves from earlier and continuing impairing influences common to all. The ivory tower sits in the public square, its windows without panes or shutters.

Evidence abounds that most professional probers hold to the religion, political party, and ideology of parents and childhood, even though to a declining degree over time. Perhaps even more impressive as evidence of common impairments: within liberal democratic societies, differences among social scientists in conception of liberal pluralism follow national lines, revealing that, say, French society forms its scholars as firmly as American society forms its own. Or consider as evidence the way in which psychoanalytic theory comes to differ from nation to nation.[22] Even on so relatively simply a question as safe highway speeds, experts—sheeplike—disagree from nation to nation in ways not explained by national differences in characteristics of vehicles or highway design.[23] Impairment seems clear.

Impairment Distinctive to Professional Probers

Beyond sharing the impairments of the whole society, their profession subjects social scientists to distinctive impairing influences. Research often depends on unusual access to data or other information often denied by governments, corporations, and other organizations. Sources of funds grant or withhold them in order to control the direction of research, an influence by no means necessarily impairing

(Washington: Brookings Institution, 1978); Sidney Fine, *Laissez-Faire and the General-Welfare State* (Ann Arbor: University of Michigan Press, 1964); Ellen W. Schrecker, *No Ivory Tower* (New York, Oxford University Press, 1986); Irene L. Gendzier, *Managing Political Change* (Boulder, Colo.: Westview Press, 1985); William Appleman, *The Great Evasion* (Chicago: Triangle Books, 1964), Michael Shapiro, *Language and Political Understanding* (New Haven: Yale University Press, 1981); and any of various works by Jürgen Habermas.

It is illuminating to place social scientists not only against popular belief and attitude as a benchmark but against social critics, such as those that appear in Michael Walzer, *The Company of Critics* (New York: Basic Books, 1988). In that comparison, they appear to be conventional, cautious, conservative, highly oriented to the status quo.

22. As traced in Edith Kurzweil, *The Freudians: A Comparative Perspective* (New Haven: Yale University Press, 1989).

23. Geert Hofstede, *Culture's Consequences* (Beverly Hills, Calif.: Sage, 1980), p. 180.

but often so. These and other familiar impairing influences need no elaboration. More important to explore, even if only briefly, is the effect, both liberating and impairing, of the professional commitment to the canons and conventions of science and discipline and to those of each discipline.[24]

As is familiar, social scientists find themselves in scientific communities in which shared judgments specify the requirements of membership and criteria of success. Without shared judgments among professionals, scientific advance seems impossible. The requirements and criteria they specify make professionals out of amateurs, providing a necessary training and discipline. Yet although they greatly raise competence in several dimensions, they reduce it in others. Just as they make one more meticulous, say, about evidence, require that one submit to criticism and always stand ready to "give reasons" for any position taken, they also guide training and research so that one explores some topics but not others, uses some concepts but not others, stands open to some new lines of thought but not others.[25] Such a process of closing off some inquiries concentrates the firepower of professional inquiry but also retards other kinds of topics of investigation.

Since professional inquiry, a limited resource, cannot examine everything and must make choices, impairment of some lines and styles of thought follows as inescapable and acceptable. The degree to which professional impairments of this kind obstruct social science and social problem solving depends on such factors as the direction, pattern, and rigidity of the process by which inquiries are closed off. In lectures in 1912 and in the publication in 1915 of his *Die Entstehung der Kontinente und Ozeane*, Alfred Wegener presented with an extraordinary display of evidence a theory of continental drift that is today recognized as a foundation for contemporary scientific thought on continental drift and plate tectonics. But most of his scientific

24. Distinctive commitments and controls being a characteristic of all the professions. On the organization of professions, see Eliot Freidson, *Professional Powers* (Chicago: University of Chicago Press, 1986).

25. M. J. Mulkay, "Sociology of the Scientific Research Community," in Ina Spiegel-Rosing and Derek de Solla Price, eds., *Science, Technology and Society* (Beverly Hills, Calif.: Sage, 1977); Paul Diesing, *Science and Ideology in the Policy Sciences* (New York: Aldine, 1982); W. O. Hagstrom, *The Scientific Community* (New York: Basic Books, 1965), pp. 10f; and Donald T. Campbell, "A Tribal Model of the Social System Vehicle Carrying Scientific Knowledge," *Knowledge* 1 (December 1979).

colleagues ignored or rejected Wegener until after World War II. As a geologist-historian of the plate tectonics revolution in geology puts it, "Orthodoxy would have its day." One might dismiss scientific hostility to Wegener's thesis as an example of inevitable and acceptable closing off, except that the historian goes on to say: "Much of the criticism [of Wegener] was in fact logically indefensible, but history is replete with examples of purely emotional attacks on bold theorists like Wegener. . . . Many of the strongest critics displayed abysmal command of their own materials."[26] One suspects that the resistance stemmed not from a defensive concentration of firepower on other lines of inquiry but from indefensible impairments. Resistance to Wegener perhaps then stemmed from an unnecessarily rigid scientific orthodoxy in which scientists had been trained, enforced because it was used as a criteria for scientific competence, hence for recruitment, promotion, and allocation of research funds.

The Wegener rejection is not unusual. The history of science abounds with such cases.[27] Probably more common in the social sciences than in the natural sciences, their identification is difficult, for the inconclusiveness of social science makes it impossible to find as unambiguous an example of impaired hostility and subsequent acknowledgement of error as in the many examples from the natural sciences. In the social science disciplines, impairing processes operate in such subtle ways that they sometimes elude identification and appraisal. The training of economists provides an example. For many young minds, grasping the concept of a market system becomes an overpowering influence on their intellectual development. In absorbing the idea of a market system, they come to understand for the first time in their lives the intricacy of social organization, the possibility of unintended order, the potential precision of unplanned resource allocation, the idea of general equilibrium, and the possibility of tracking links in an endless chain of causation. Never before in their lives have they learned so much, so fast, and with such elegant techniques, nor been so persuaded of the staggering importance of their intellectual acquisitions to an understanding of the social world—a "thrill which, alas, no one can experience twice."[28] But their illumination, like a powerful beam of light, leaves in lesser light things no

26. William Glen, *The Road to Jaramillo* (Stanford, Calif.: Stanford University Press, 1982), p. 5.
27. Many can be found in David L. Hull, *Science as a Process* (Chicago: University of Chicago Press, 1988).
28. Paul A. Samuelson and William D. Nordhaus, *Economics*, 13th ed. (New York: McGraw-Hill, 1989), p. xl.

longer seen at all or only intermittently. During their years in graduate training, their incoming communications—from reading, teachers, and fellow students—do not much challenge the adequacy of their exciting new view of the world, for almost all share the same view. As a result, economics becomes the most distinctive, the most differentiated, perhaps the most analytically powerful, and also the most provincial of the social science disciplines. Economists may pay—perhaps even pay too much—for their insights with impairments of cultishness, inbreeding, and narrowed vision. I have gone through the whole process myself, at one time overwhelmed by it; ever since struggling to see both the market system and adjacent shadowed terrain clearly. But the impact of my early years in graduate training was, as for many of my colleagues, a seductive influence from which I can never wholly recover.

Similarly, each of the other social science disciplines constrains.[29] Hence, kinds of explanations of behavior that are accepted in one discipline are rejected in another. The constraints of the disciplines, not the facts of the social world, account, say, for persistent differences between economists and sociologists in explaining the same phenomena, such as recidivism or agricultural innovations in peasant societies.[30] As in the natural sciences, the constraint operates through methods of recruitment into the profession, through graduate training programs, and through the use of certain orthodoxies in thought as tests of competence, as well as through conventions in the editing of scholarly journals and in the organization of scholarly conferences.

Like convergences in thought in the population as a whole, convergences in scientific thought derive from a mixture of knowledge and impairing influences. A poll of economists showed that only 3 percent disagreed with the proposition that "tariffs and import quotas reduce general economic welfare." Evidence to support the belief is "obscure to the point of darkness", and "no study has shown . . . that high tariffs in America during the 19th century on balance hurt Americans."[31] Presumably, impairment mixes with softer forms of knowledge to account for the near unanimity.

29. See Campbell on "tribal" science: "A Tribal Model of the Social System Vehicle Carrying Scientific Knowledge," Knowledge 1 (December 1979).

30. Brian Barry, Sociologists, Economists, and Democracy (Chicago: University of Chicago Press, 1978), chap. 1.

31. Donald N. McCloskey, The Rhetoric of Economics (unidentified xerox), pp. 10f. See also his Rhetoric of Economics (Madison: University of Wisconsin Press, 1985).

If social scientists never wholly escape from the common impairments of their societies, then the impairments originating in defense of elite advantages become their impairments too, though perhaps less severely impairing than for others in the population. In that sentence, the cautious "perhaps" takes account of two special conflicting influences on social scientists. One comes from their self-disciplined and mutually reinforcing struggle to break out of impairments, on which, futile as an only weak struggle is for some of them, many make headway. The other and opposing influence, widely documented and discussed, consists of those social processes by which social scientists, like all scientists, become dependent on elite grants, take employment with elites, seek acceptance by elites, identify with elites, or even pass into the ranks of economic or political elites.[32] The phenomenon of elite cooptation, whether deliberate or not, of scientists and scholars would deserve its own chapter as one explanation of their impairment were it not already so familiar a phenomenon.

For this reason, but also because social scientists from birth share common impairments, many of the impairments that appear distinctive to the disciplines turn out to be differentiated manifestations—yet manifestations nevertheless—of the impairments of the population as a whole. Many convergences distinctive to a single discipline fall into a pattern of defense of advantages.

Because disciplinary conventions and traditions of many kinds, as well as standardized textbooks and methods of training, also produce convergences independent of or distant from those influences that produce convergences in defense of advantages, one must proceed cautiously in sorting them out. On the occasion of receiving a professional award from his disciplinary colleagues, a distinguished social scientist reminded his audience of colleagues that for violating a dominant set of beliefs and attitudes among them they, a little more than a decade earlier, had subjected him to "a tortured period of intellectual isolation."[33] The conformity for the alleged violation of which

32. For a careful book-length documentation of these phenomena in the case of the discipline of industrial psychology, see Loren Baritz, *The Servants of Power* (Westport, Conn.: Greenwood Press, 1960). See also a set of Swedish conference papers: Ron Eyerman, Lennart G. Svensson, and Thomas Söderqvist, eds., *Intellectuals, Universities, and the State in Western Modern Societies* (Berkeley: University of California Press, 1987). Among many other sources is, of course, Karl Mannheim, *Ideology and Utopia* (New York: Harcourt, Brace, Jovanovich, 1960).

33. James Coleman, "Response to Section on Sociology of Education Award," *Footnotes* 17 (January 1989), pp. 4f.

they had sought to punish him was an egalitarian conformity, an antagonism to elite advantages rather than a defense of them. In our times, social scientists often display conformities in support of various specific forms and degrees of equality—and often display intolerance in so doing. But I offer some illustrative cases to show that strong central tendencies in disciplinary traditions continue to constitute inegalitarian convergences of the pattern outlined in earlier chapters.

Marx pointed to a class bias in specialized professional probing. Mannheim's *Ideology and Utopia* explored a variety of distinctively professional impairments and their sources in society at large. Critical theorists of the Frankfurt School have alleged a powerful specialized preoccupation of social scientists, many among them unaware of their preoccupation, with social control, hence with the achievement of domination of masses by elites. Gouldner has argued at length, with meticulous attention to the details of his evidence, that structural-functionalism, especially at the hands of Parsons and the thousands of social scientist he appears to have influenced, turns the ever-present irrationality, coerciveness, inhumanity, and ugliness of many social processes into a picture of benignity, thus bringing into professional inquiry the impairments of lay probing.[34] Spence has argued a hierarchal bias anchored deeply in popular impairment and mirrored in professional probing: an inability of professionals to overcome presumptions in favor of hierarchical forms of social organization in family, school, work organization, and politics.[35] In the light of such theses, the illustrative cases take on all the more significance.

Economists on the Functions of an Economy

A standard statement, such as opens many textbooks in economics (in the neoclassical, Keynesian, and post-Keynesian tradition dominant in the U.S., the U.K., and Western Europe), declares that the functions or accomplishments of an economic system are represented by some such list as resource allocation, capital accumulation, and income distribution, together with other closely related, useful functions that differ from one economist's formulation to another's.[36] Presumably, these claims express a desire of professional

34. Alvin W. Gouldner, *The Coming Crisis of Western Sociology* (New York: Basic Books, 1970).

35. Larry D. Spence, *Politics of Social Knowledge* (University Park: Pennsylvania State University Press, 1978).

36. For example, chaps. 2 and 3 of Paul A. Samuelson and William D. Nordhaus, *Economics*, 13th ed., (New York: McGraw-Hill, 1989).

economists to call attention to these beneficial consequences of economic organization.

One of several possible alternative views might hold that the function or accomplishment of an economy is to permit a relatively small segment of the population to enjoy disproportional income and wealth and to permit a small segment of the population to direct the productive activities of a less qualified mass. In all economic systems elites do in fact live better than the masses, and small groups exercise powers of direction and coordination over the masses.

Persons accustomed to the first of these two views of the functions of an economic system will spring to its defense. They will say that the functions they cite represent functions of value to the whole population. The dissident's functions represent functions of value only to a minority. But that is no defense at all. In every economic system, some gains are shared by all: some increases in production will raise the standard of living for all. Yet in every economic system, groups conflict with each other; the pie has to be divided, with the result that what one group gets another does not; and individual persons and groups struggle to take advantage over others. To understand an economy, one must explore conflicts as well as achievement of objectives like resource allocation that everyone might be construed as sharing.

The economics tradition under discussion has made and continues to make a choice: choosing both to study an economic life as a benign process and not to study it as an advantaging process through which some groups achieve advantage over others. It does not do both; it silences or closes off one inquiry. The conventional interpretation even seduces some Marxist economists, although the conventional Marxist view neglects benign interpretations in favor of malign. A competition of ideas on the issue hardly exists, nor have many economists integrated two such interpretations. In many countries the one interpretation largely silences the other.

Political Scientists on the Nature of State and Politics

Parallel to the described impairment of economics runs an impairment of political science. Some interpretations of the state and politics from a sampling at various dates of American political scientists of excellent professional reputation, leaders of the discipline in recent decades, will disclose it.

A political scientist writes about democratic politics: "Political parties are basic institutions for the translation of mass preferences into public policy."[37] The statement does not, for example, acknowledge that parties are also basic institutions, say, for party control of citizens. And it stands as a kind of axiom without evidence or argument to support it. Patently, party functionaries often try to bring citizens around to their volitions, perhaps more often or more characteristically than they adapt public policy to citizen volitions. Any thoughtful nonprofessional or professional prober who knows that parties often engage in rigging elections, misrepresenting issues to citizens, obfuscating, suppressing information, building political machines to insulate functionaries from genuine electoral control (all of which political scientists study), sometimes giving little or none of their energies to "translation of mass preferences into policy," might wonder how a distinguished scholar can anchor analysis of parties, as in the work cited, in so incomplete or misleading an interpretation of them, as though the contradictory evidence deserved rejection as anomalous. A benign interpretation of politics, one must call it remarkably benign except that it is not remarkable, for a similar convergence on benign interpretations pervades the discipline.

Another example: "Politics has the function of coordinating the learning processes of the whole society."[38] Again, a narrow, benign interpretation of politics, it washes away the many processes, as noted in the preceding chapters on impairment, by which elites and others impair the probing of citizens and obstruct their learning. Coordination of learning is "the" function, not one of many.

Another example defines a political community as "a group of persons who seek to solve their problems in common through a shared political structure."[39] It appears to deny the existence of interest groups seeking advantages for members even at the expense of other groups in the community—to win, say, tariff protection, agricultural price supports, or higher wages. One does not need professional qualifications to find the interpretation benign and incomplete to the point of naivete.

Other political scientists claim that people "erect governments to maintain order, further mutual goals, and promote general well being."[40] Again, the context rules out or deprecates other motives for

37. V. O. Key, Jr., *Public Opinion and American Democracy* (New York: Knopf, 1967), p. 432. The examples and analysis are taken from Lindblom, "Another State of Mind," *American Political Science Review* 76 (March 1982).

38. Karl Deutsch, *Politics and Government* (Boston: Houghton Mifflin, 1980), p. 19.

39. David Easton and Robert D. Hess, "The Child's Political World," *Midwest Journal of Political Science* 6 (August 1962), p. 233.

40. Kenneth M. Dolbeare and Murray J. Edelman, *American Politics*, 3d ed. (Lexington, Mass.: Heath, 1981), p. 7.

erecting governments: for example, to subjugate, exploit, tyrannize, promote one group's welfare over that of others, or promote not general but private or segmental well-being. Because the long history of political philosophy abounds with references to subjugation, exploitation, tyranny, conquest, and repression, none unfamiliar to contemporary political science, the benign interpretations suggest an impairment bordering on mindlessness. Commenting on the origin of the state, another political scientist says—again, as a categorical fundamental: "Communities search for ways of adjusting conflicts so that cooperation and community life will be possible and tolerable."[41] Do none—to alter his phrase—search for ways of adjusting conflicts so that subordination of groups to other groups, or repression, or stratification will be possible?

That such a claim protects the advantages of the advantaged need not be spelled out again. Frequency of professional criticism of government, I suggest, does not deny these evidences of impairment. For the criticism largely assumes the fundamental benignity of those states or governments called democratic. Indeed, it appears that the distress of critics of contemporary democracies reflects a gap between an implicitly postulated norm of benignity and actual practice. Were they to take a less benign view of democracy, the aberrations they identify would hardly be classifiable as aberrations.

Social Scientists on Socialization

In the professional literature on socialization, the same benignity of interpretation appears again. As I noted in chapter 5, a conventional presentation of the phenomenon calls attention to two aspects of it: socialization as personal development, that is, acquisition of skills and competences which no child possess at birth and which everyone must acquire through social interchange; and socialization as learning to conform to social norms, the presumption of social scientists being that only through conformities can a society perpetuate itself.[42] For democratic societies, both of these processes are presented as benign: obviously, it seems, persons should develop competence and, no less obviously, democratic societies should perpetuate themselves. Yet many of the social interchanges of life, even in ostensibly democratic societies, obstruct the development of competence

41. Robert A. Dahl, *Democracy in the United States* (Chicago: Rand McNally, 1972), p. 5.
42. Outlined in Viktor Gecas, "Contexts of Socialization," in Morris Rosenberg and Ralph H. Turner, eds., *Social Psychology* (New York: Basic Books, 1981), pp. 165f. See also chap. 5 above.

and inculcate acceptance of systems, regimes, political elites, or parties the perpetuation of which might be regrettable. The arguments I advanced in part 2 on the pervasiveness of impairments are hardly necessary to demonstrate that in many circumstances, even in the democracies, socialization does not deserve to be regarded as benign to the neglect of its contrary aspect, which receives bare acknowledgment. A review article, for example, on socialization goes no further than to acknowledge "instances" in which socialization is "dysfunctional," benefiting "the group" at the expense of the individual,[43] an inadequate recognition of ubiquitous obstructions of socialization to individual development. And its reference not to many conflicting groups but to "the group" also misses the degree to which socialization does not in any case benignly preserve the society but instead protects some groups at the expense of others.

Impairment of professional thinking on socialization also appears in the infrequency with which conflict between the two allegedly benign aspects of socialization is faced and analyzed rather than overlooked.[44] Developing the competences of young people may be deeply at odds with inculcating conformism to shared norms. Indeed, one can be confident that the two kinds of socialization will often oppose each other; and, again, that conclusion does not require the arguments of part 2 on impairment. Any thoughtful observer can find examples of conflict, for example, between independence of thought, the development of analytical skills, and self-confidence on one hand, and acceptance of commonly held values, attitudes, and beliefs on the other.

In chapter 5 I observed that social scientists (and others) who value socialization as necessary either to individual development or to perpetuating the society often—perhaps typically—fall into an indiscriminate, implicit defense of social interactions on the ground that they socialize. The chapter favored a more discriminating position distinguishing at least in principle between all interactions on one hand, and those that socialize on the other. The distinction permits a clear-headed examination of the possibility that some interactions do not at all socialize and perhaps impair. Because the distinction is little cultivated in the sociological and social psycho-

43. Diane Mitsch Bush and Roberta G. Simmons, "Socialization Processes over the Life Course," in Morris Rosenberg and Ralph H. Turner, eds., *Social Psychology* (New York: Basic Books, 1981), p. 135.
44. In the Gecas paper above in which the two aspects of socialization are presented, I find only incidental reference to peripheral conflict between the two. As a major issue about socialization, it is absent from his review of the literature.

logical professional literature on socialization, a host of impairing interactions are by default classified as processes of socialization of benefit to individual and society.

That same chapter also drew a distinction that almost everyone will accept as valid in principle between two ways of influencing a child or adult: on the one hand, education, information, enlightenment, and persuasion; on the other hand, authority, intimidation, deceit, and coercion. Either can be used to socialize, but the choice presumably makes a great deal of difference to individual development and the character of the society. The social science literature on socialization makes almost no use of so fundamental a distinction.[45]

The impairments of social science on the subject of socialization appear in yet another way. "The concept of socialization refers to the ways in which individuals learn skills, knowledge, values, motives and roles appropriate to their position in a group of society."[46] But since from some positions in society everyone would wish to escape and since some are themselves impairing in the ignorance or other disadvantages they impose on those who occupy them, then it follows that socializing persons into those positions may constitute a method of obstructing their development. The very idea of predetermined or unquestioned positions to which socialization adapts people itself raises questions about the benignity of the socialization process, to which, again, social scientists on the subject of socialization frequently appear blind.

The term *learning* runs through much of the socialization literature. But "learning," like "socialization," can refer either to processes through which persons develop skills in perception, analysis, and evaluation—thus in probing—or to the influences on the mind that reduce these very competences, as when a person "learns" a falsehood, or learns that he is destined to fail in anything he attempts, or learns from an abusive parent to trust no one. These two kinds or effects of learning—one benign, the other not—intermix in uncritical research in socialization.

Another example of scholarly impairments on socialization: a study takes note of the possibilities that the process of socialization teaches citizens to curb their demands. Intent as the study is on soci-

45. An examination of the sources cited above and below will confirm the observation.
46. Diane Mitsch Bush and Roberta G. Simmons, "Socialization Processes over the Life Course," in Morris Rosenberg and Ralph H. Turner, eds., *Social Psychology* (New York: Basic Books, 1981), p. 135.

etal benefits for all, it observes only that these taught self-restraints help to prevent system overload.[47] Quite possibly they do. But that the constraints may obstruct thinking and might also stop legitimate demands from reaching the political system, they largely ignore.[48]

A distorting preoccupation with benefits of socialization appears also in the finding that working-class children accept the norms of their class superiors. "The social scientist would suggest, on the basis of the preceding findings, that there is a potential for introducing 'modernizing' norms to the lower classes by way of heterogeneous class environments."[49] No doubt. But the study singles out the benign potential for modernizing norms to the exclusion of other dubious potentials, such as teaching the disadvantaged not to probe their disadvantages. Or consider, finally, the striking example of survey researchers who in dozens of studies have asked respondents some such question as: From what sources do you obtain your political information—friends, newspapers, radio, or television? It never occurs to them to ask, From what sources do you obtain your misinformation? From what sources the obfuscations that leave you uncertain about your political positions? The benign view of society deeply obscures the understanding of socialization.

Social Scientists on Causation and Responsibility

Some years ago, the Australian government took note of high infant mortality among aborigines by undertaking an official inquiry into its causes. Aborigines are seminomadic; health care facilities are fixed in location; the result is a mismatch between location of demand and location of supply of health care facilities. How did the inquiry diagnose the cause of the problem? It pointed to the seminomadic life of the aborigines, not to the fixity of health care facilities.[50]

In Western economies in recent decades, an excess of aggregate spending often appears as the cause of inflation. Consumer, business, and governmental spending add up to too large a figure. How do economists identify the cause of the problem? Typically by pointing to

47. David Easton and Jack Dennis, *Children in the Political System* (New York: McGraw-Hill, 1969), pp. 55, 66.
48. In the same way, a benign view of socialization misses important issues in Dennis's later "Major Problems of Political Socialization Research," in Jack Dennis, ed., *Socialization to Politics* (New York: Wiley, 1973).
49. Kenneth P. Langton, *Political Socialization* (New York: Oxford University Press, 1969), p. 138.
50. Michael Shapiro, *Language and Political Understanding* (New Haven: Yale University Press, 1981), pp. 186f.

excessive government spending, not excessive consumer or business spending.

In these three cases, and many more like them that abound in the literature of social science inquiry, social scientists proceed selective in their choice with respect to causation and responsibility. Not driven by the facts to their choice, they choose under the influence of conventions shared with a public impaired in its probing. We do not argue that they make the wrong choice, for the opposite choice in each of the two cases would be no more correct. The evidence of their impairment lies in the absence of their recognition of arbitrariness or conventionality in attributing causality and responsibility, in the constraining orthodoxy that plays up one interpretation to the neglect of others.

In this connection, much professional inquiry finds causation and blame in individual persons rather than in the social system. Authors of a study of sixty-nine abstracts of articles in professional journals of psychology dealing with black Americans came to these conclusions: "Although our categories are admittedly a crude way of measuring fairly complex phenomena, the picture that emerges is one of psychologists investing disproportionate amounts of time, funds and energy in studies that lend themselves, directly or by implication, to interpreting the difficulties of black Americans in terms of personal shortcomings. . . . We see that 82 percent . . . of the research . . . is of this sort. . . . It overlooks the importance of other kinds of forces." And, they add, "Psychologists should not be singled out for criticism on this point, since until recently the standard sociological works on 'social problems,' 'deviance' and the like, have also focused to a large extent on individuals."[51]

Stimulated by this study, another group of social scientists studied a sample of 698 research articles for the years 1936, 1956, and 1976 taken from a variety of disciplines and subdisciplines, dealing with alcohol and drug problems, suicide, delinquency, job satisfaction, rape, and race relations. For all the years studied, they found a concentration of research "at the personal characteristic end of the continuum." They also found a failure of research to achieve an integration of personal and systemic factors in social problems. "In addition, the concentration of inquiry at the personal characteristic end of the continuum does not just create a benign imbalance; it mys-

51. Nathan Caplan and Stephen D. Nelson, "On Being Useful," in Irving Louis Horowitz, ed., *The Use and Abuse of Social Science*, 2d ed. (New Brunswick, N.J.: Transaction Books, 1975), pp. 145f.

tifies the whole social world, concealing larger institutions behind intra-psychic obfuscations."[52]

Social Scientists on the Burden of Proof

A final example of professional impairment: social scientists often load a burden of proof on professional dissent, especially when dissent carries radical implications for society. Such a load on a dissenter makes sense in circumstances in which the agreed or conventional professional belief has emerged from well-conducted professional inquiry, often the case in the natural sciences. Anyone who in 1900 proposed to challenge Newton might well have been required to carry a heavy burden of proof; so also one who joins contemporary efforts to discredit evolutionary biological theory. Frequently, however, in the social sciences, established agreement has never been processed in that way and may itself represent an untested, impaired professional agreement. Professional agreement in the U.S. on a presidential system loads a burden of proof on dissenters, just as in the U.K. a high degree of agreement on a parliamentary system loads a burden of proof on dissenters. Those in each country who agree on its present system carry no equivalent burden.

For another example, in contemporary social science outside Marxist circles, anyone who alleges "false consciousness" on the part of ordinary citizens is asked to carry a burden not also carried by those who deny it, despite the paucity of study on which the conventional denial rests. A political scientist admonishes, for example: "I believe that a heavy responsibility rest upon analysts . . . to justify the claim that actors are in fact unaware of what they are doing and are generally misguided by their own lights."[53] But he accepts no burden of proof in his denial of this claim.

For all these examples of professional impairment, I assume their fit into the pattern of defense of the advantages of elites and other advantage groups is apparent in their stress on the benign quality of the social order, their limited examination of human plasticity, their assignment of responsibility and causation, and their hostility to dissent.

---

52. Gary Gregg, Thomas Preston, Alison Geist, and Nathan Caplan, "The Caravan Rolls On," *Knowledge* 1 (September 1979), p. 48 and passim. See the bibliography of other studies of social science preoccupation with individual responsibility on pp. 35–37.

53. Nelson W. Polsby, *Community Power and Political Theory*, 2d ed. (New Haven: Yale University Press, 1980), p. 230.

PART IV

Toward Prescription

CHAPTER 13

Scientific Society and

Self-Guiding Society

It is time now to draw some prescriptive inferences from the foregoing analysis of probing and its impairment. I begin by presenting two prescriptive models, pictures, or visions of how societies can best use knowledge for social problem solving. The first does not fit the preceding analysis, the second does. The first provides a foil for the second, a contrast to give emphasis to the key features of the second. Heuristically formulated, they only roughly capture two currents in history of thought, each appearing historically in diverse versions, even if the first, as here sketched, describes an impossibility.

In the history of thought, the first has the benefit of earlier and better articulation—also of more explicit advocacy—but the day of the second may now have arrived in the liberal democracies. The first is the vision, model, or norm, in one form as old as Plato, of a scientifically guided society. The second still goes without a name or easy identification. I shall call it the self-guiding society. The labels exaggerate the differences between the two but nonetheless serve the need for easy reference. Most models or visions of a scientifically guided society leave some room for guidance by political authorities and also acknowledge that social change in some large part escapes guidance from either science or politics. Intended by no one, it nevertheless happens. Then, too, since scientists are part of society, scientific guidance constitutes to some degree a form of self-guidance. And, on the other hand, the vision of a self-guiding society does not deny a significant formative role to science. Even with these qualifications, however, the two models differ deeply.

The one puts science, including social science, at center stage. In that model, social problem solving, social betterment, or guided social change (regarded as roughly synonymous) calls above all for scientific observation of human social behavior such that ideally humankind discovers the requisites of good people in a good society and, short of the ideal, uses the results of scientific observation to move in the right direction. Social science also of course studies and learns how to go where it has learned society ought to go. In contrast, the model of the self-guiding society brings lay probing of ordinary people and functionaries to center stage, though with a powerful supporting role played by science and social science adapted to the lay role in probing volitions.

Francis Bacon idealized a scientifically guided society in *New Atlantis*. Elements of it appear in Descartes' insistence on proof and rational design and in the Enlightenment's faith in reason, which for some implied a faith in the potential of scientifically informed benevolent despots. Condorcet anticipates the scientifically guided society when he says that "we are approaching one of the grand revolutions of the human race,"[1] and perhaps so does Bentham in his opinion that "knowledge is rapidly advancing towards perfection" and in his deprecation of politics except as politics could itself be made scientific. Saint-Simon counted on science to replace politics with the "administration of things," a recurring expectation in some currents of the positivist tradition in science, to which Saint-Simon greatly contributed. The Webbs rejoice in hope for rule by "a comprehensive knowledge of social facts" and a "Science of Society" that will make possible the "conscious, deliberate organization of society."[2] At least one side of John Dewey concurs: "The questions of the most concern . . . are technical matters, as much so as the construction of an efficient engine for the purposes of traction or locomotion. Like it they are to be settled by inquiry into facts; and as the inquiry can be carried on only

1. Franklin Le Van Baumer, ed., *Main Currents of Western Thought*, 3d ed. (New York: Knopf, 1970), p. 362.
2. Shirley Robin Letwin, *The Pursuit of Certainty* (Cambridge: Cambridge University Press, 1965), pp. 368–389.

by those especially equipped, so the results of the inquiry can be utilized only by trained technicians."[3]

A similar faith in science marks both early-twentieth-century American Progressivism and the most confident of contemporary systems analysts, the "new utopians" who wish to depoliticize social problem solving and to construe problems of social choice as technical problems for experts.[4] And it turns up frequently in professions like medicine, engineering, and law when practitioners extend their claims of competence beyond their professional skills to larger questions of social policy.

> Professionals profess. They profess to know better than others the nature of certain matters, and to know better than their clients what ails them or their affairs. . . . Physicians consider it their prerogative to define the nature of disease and health, and to determine how medical services ought to be distributed and paid for. Social workers are not content to develop a technique for case work; they concern themselves with social legislation. Every profession considers itself the proper body to set the terms in which some aspect of society, life or nature is to be thought of, and to define the general lines, or even the details, of public policy concerning it.[5]

In these respects some contemporary professionals and some systems analysts unwittingly join with Marx, whose "scientific socialism" became the most fully asserted model of the ideal of the scientifically guided society. As many Marxists see—or saw—it, "scientifically based universal calculations" lay down a course for social change.[6]

The alternative model of how to use intelligence for social problem solving, the model of the self-guiding society, remains only partially articulated—often distorted or insufficiently qualified—in the history of thought: perhaps, for example, in Polybius's appreciation of the way in which Rome's accomplishments grew from experience or practice rather than design, more clearly in Hume's skepticism regarding the capacity of government to rule wisely; in Rousseau's legacy to radical democrats, in some anarchist theory, in liberalism's penchant for a competition of ideas, in classical and contemporary

3. John Dewey, *The Public and Its Problems* (1927; Chicago: Gateway Books, 1946), pp. 124f.

4. Robert Boguslaw, *The New Utopians* (New York: Irvington, 1981).

5. Everett C. Hughes, "Professions," *Daedalus* 92 (Fall 1963), pp. 656–667.

6. Jerome M. Gilison, *The Soviet Image of Utopia* (Baltimore: Johns Hopkins University Press, 1975), p. 120.

economics' common commitment to the market system instead of to central planning for fear the central planners cannot achieve a sufficient scientific competence; in Dewey's "reflective intelligence"; in Hayek's insistence on the superiority of undesigned over designed or deliberately constructed social organization;[7] and in contemporary grasping at alternatives to bureaucracy. If theorists often admire the scientific model, politicians and other practitioners of social problem solving take an appreciative even if obscured view of the self-guiding model: compare Marx with Franklin Roosevelt or Jan Tinbergen with Saul Alinsky.[8]

DIMENSIONS OF THE SELF-DIRECTING SOCIETY

What are the specific distinctions between the two models of social problem solving?[9] Outlining them will to a degree recapitulate and to a degree extend the analysis of all preceding chapters.

Probing

The self-guiding model centers of course on lay investigation or probing, a wider variety of inquiries than those of social scientists. The self-guiding model also pictures its wide inquiries as much less conclusive than those of the scientific model. Probing, again, suggests accepts a never-ending inconclusiveness while science pursues closure. As for ends—usually standing volitions—the self-guiding model neither takes any as given, as in some versions of the scientific model, nor regards them as discoverable. For no one can dis- or uncover a volition; and instead people form, chose, decide upon, or will. This they do through a mixture of empirical, prudential, aesthetic, and moral probes. Among more numerous lesser questions, probing pursues great existential and moral questions, working answers to which join with the unexpected to shape people and society.

Social Science in Aid of Probing

Consequently, the self-guiding model rejects social science as an alternative to ordinary inquiry and sees it instead as an aid, refiner, extender, and sometime tester of it, always a supplement, never

7. Friedrich Hayek, *Law, Legislation and Liberty*, vol. 2 (Chicago: University of Chicago Press, 1976), chap. 10.
8. Conflict between the two visions or models appears, though it is not explicitly articulated, in contemporary studies of planning: for example, John Friedman, *Planning in the Public Domain* (Princeton: Princeton University Press, 1987).
9. The distinctions revise an earlier list in C. E. Lindblom, *Politics and Markets* (New York: Basic Books, 1977), pp. 249–260.

broadly embarked on a program to displace or replace it. No less present in the self-guiding model than in the science model, social science pursues an adaptive strategy in the former instead of trying to set out on its own course as in the latter. Even on most empirical questions, problem solving in the self-guiding model remains more often dependent on lay inquiry than on scientific investigation.

Lay Learning

In the science-guided model of social problem solving, for every social problem sufficient analysis can almost certainly find at least one solution. The other model makes no such assumption. Given certain institutions, social processes, established patterns of behavior, a problem may be beyond hope of solution or amelioration. Acknowledged problems—say, prison reform, some forms of juvenile delinquency, or environmental decay—for which knowledge of appropriate techniques for solution lies at hand, persist because neither political functionaries nor ordinary citizens will bear the costs of remedy. For such problems, all solutions remain closed off unless and until people experience sufficient distress to induce them to reconsider the institutions, social processes, or behavioral patterns up to that moment regarded as parameters. Expert opinion and social research on policies for such problems come to nothing in the absence of a reconsideration of volitions, nor can social scientists or experts of any other kind themselves accomplish the reconsideration. If achieved, it comes as an outcome of a diffuse social process in which at least politically active citizens examine their relevant volitions. Consequently, lay probing as a social process can cope with problems intractable to social science.

Sensitivities

As I noted in chapter 3, statistics on unemployment do not make it a problem, and it does not become a problem except to those who for some reason care, are disturbed, or feel badly about it. That the origin of problems lies in sensitivities, feeling, or affect continues to be an embarrassment to the model of a scientifically guided society, for such a model aspires to more objective indicators of the existence of problems and to analyses of problems that can be stripped of sentiments, feelings, or emotions. The self-guiding society model takes for granted that no escape from feeling can be found. If people do not feel an aversion to a situation or state of affairs, they cannot formulate it as a problem, nor will they seek to escape from that state of affairs, nor is there any reason why they should or would. Even a person who sees inefficiency as a problem and claims to be coldly analytical in analyzing it cannot make it into a problem without some feeling of aversion to it or to its results.

No Correct Solutions

In some forms of the scientific model, by a good solution one means, in principle, an approximation to the correct solution, even if in practice one cannot determine correctness. One regards "best," "ideal," and "correct" as synonymous. The assumption that complex social problems have correct solutions has a long history.[10] When Rousseau says that under appropriate circumstances, the "common good will then be everywhere evident," he may intend an assumption that there exists a common good and a correct order of society.[11] The Webbs often made such a claim explicit, and some social scientists still dare to make it: for example, Maslow in seeking a scientific ethic.[12] In Marxist thought it appears frequently. Thus the Chinese Communist party achieves "correct policies, and the Constitution of the Communist Party of China declares the Party to be great, glorious, and correct."[13] Or a Soviet writer offers Soviet science as "the only correct approach."[14]

Among advocates of the self-guiding model, the claim seems naive. Except for solutions to extremely simple problems, any such claim to correctness would have to assume that volitions are in principle empirically discoverable rather than created, an assumption which the self-guiding model rejects. In the self-guiding model, the usual test of a good solution is instead that it has been well probed. Competent opinions will differ on whether it has. Judgments about the quality of probing will be supplemented retrospectively by examination of the solution's consequences as they in fact unfold. And any one observer's appraisal of the solution will reflect his substantive

10. See the discussion in Alvin W. Gouldner, *Enter Plato* (New York: Basic Books, 1965), p. 281.

11. Jean-Jacques Rousseau, *The Social Contract*, trans. Charles Frankel (New York: Hafner, 1947), p. xviii.

12. See chap. 2, p. 19.

13. Gong Yuzhi, "Deng Xiaoping and Party's Intellectual Policies," *Beijing Review* 27 (March 19, 1984), p. 16.

14. L. V. Golovanov, "Socialism and the Scientific and Technical Revolution," as quoted by James N. Danziger, "Power Is Knowledge," in Kenneth E. Boulding and Lawrence Senesh, *The Optimum Utilization of Knowledge* (Boulder, Colo.: Westview Press, 1983), p. 266.

volitions. One may, for example, regard a solution as unethical or in some other way unacceptable even if those who reached it probed it well. In particular, one may evaluate a solution as unacceptable because it blocks the continued investigation of the problem area, for one may think the preservation of inquiry itself more important than the solution to any given problem subjected to probing.[15]

Learning From Error

In the science model, the problem solver aims for a solution; in the self-guiding model he tries a step toward amelioration, a step very likely containing a significant element of failure but leaving the situation open for another, now better informed step. The one model tries to avoid error; the other feeds on it, engaging in indefinitely prolonged change of course in which both means and ends change in the light of newly informed probes. While the science model always at least hints at aspiration to closure, equilibrium, or stasis, the self-guiding model envisages a constant reconsideration, including endless problem redefinition in which a "solution" forever recedes, like "Neurath's sailors who must rebuild their ship on the open sea without discerning its ideal design."[16]

A Learning from Action

In the model of scientific guidance, problem solving is entirely cerebral. In the alternative model, the acknowledged impossibility of anyone's ever achieving a full grasp of the relevant complexities of society compels action in ignorance. Hence the model counts on strategies like trial and error, in which the trial serves not simply as an action to attempt a solution but provides feedback information to illuminate subsequent attempts. In this model, citizens, functionaries, social scientists, and other experts do what they have learned and then learn what they have done.[17]

Downgrading Elites

For all the foregoing reasons, it goes almost without saying that although the self-guiding model calls greatly on elites for many dis-

15. In advocating in this book a society's commitment to probing, I must weigh heavily a continuation of probing as a condition to be met by any solution to a problem.

16. Laurence H. Tribe, "Ways Not to Think about Plastic Trees," *Yale Law Journal* 83 (June 1974), pp. 1340f.

17. At an extreme is the deliberate social experiment, on the justification of which social scientists as well as lay people differ. See Alice M. Rivlin, *Systematic*

tinctive functions, it assigns far less responsibility and power to elites than does the science model. It in effect transfers a large component of social problem solving away from scientific, technical, political, and economic elites.

In some early-eighteenth-century Enlightenment thought, the world's future appeared to lie in the hands of enlightened intellectual elites joined to benevolent despots. But Montesquieu at midcentury called for the enlightenment of all, and by the end of the century many French thinkers similarly committed themselves to universal enlightenment. In England, the liberal tradition divides on elitism. If early-twentieth-century English and American scholars in that tradition—for example, Barker and Lindsay—advocated a broad competition of ideas or envisioned democracy as "government by discussion," earlier liberals like John Stuart Mill and Walter Bagehot had little confidence in the cognitive capacities of ordinary people and both proposed and hoped that the masses would largely leave government to an able and well-educated elite, not a scientific elite but an elite of merit that included scientists among other educated people. Mill believed that true principles could be discerned only by a sufficiently competent intellectual elite.[18] Burke may have looked less suspiciously on popular participation in democracy, but not on a probing citizenry. Better, he thought, that citizens accepted prevailing prejudices and customs.[19]

If the model of the self-guiding society embraces a more restricted role for elites than does the scientific model, on one line of reasoning it displays positive hostility to intellectual elites. Elites of inheritance, arms, land, or other wealth have historically obstructed the development of a self-directing society, their influence diminishing, however, in the era of political democracy. In part, their diminution follows from growing conflict among them; for example, conflicts between landed elites and rising commercial and industrial elites. Of growing concern in some quarters, however, is the potential for social control by a meritocratic elite insufficiently challenged by

Thinking for Social Action (Washington, D.C.: Brookings Institution, 1971) chap. 5; and Donald T. Campbell, "Reforms as Experiments," *American Psychologist* 24 (April 1969).

18. Walter Bagehot, *The English Constitution* (1867; Oxford: Oxford University Press, 1963), pp. 235–240, 263–272; and John Stuart Mill, *Considerations on Representative Government* (1861; Indianapolis: Bobbs-Merrill, 1958), pp. xxvi–xxix.

19. Edmund Burke, *Reflections on the Revolution in France*, vol. 2 of *Works* (1790; London, 1861), p. 359.

any other elites. The potential lies in the possibility that, in a society of increasing upward mobility, a knowledgeable elite sanctioned by the scientific model may come to possesses everything that knowledge brings with it: wealth, office, deference-inducing status, and dominant influence in publishing, broadcasting, and education. It could become an elite of such dominance as society has never seen.[20]

Downgrading Social Control

The disposition in the science model to envision elites, whether political, expert, or scientific, as guiding social change or problem solving tends to reinforce a misperception of knowledge of the social world as an instrument of social control, parallel to knowledge of the natural world as an instrument of man's mastery.[21] Social science in fact makes contributions not only to control but to blocking attempted controls and to facilitating adaptation to social controls. Outlined in chapter 9, these alternatives seem better appreciated by advocates of the self-guiding model than by advocates of the scientific model.

Politics and Imposition

Many of the thinkers of the Enlightenment intended a radical substitution of reason for power.[22] Saint-Simon looked forward to a society governed not by men but by principles, Proudhon to a government not of man but of fact. The Utopian socialists made no place for politics of power; Marx predicted the withering away of the state; and Durkheim thought that "political questions [had] lost their interest."[23] In some versions of the science model, power represents a regrettable lapse from reasoned problem solving, sometimes a necessary evil, and at best an element in problem solving that should be minimized. The science model frets about power and imposition, without much regard for the limited capacities of reason and the efficiency of imposition discussed in chapter 4.

20. On intellectuals or the intelligentsia as a possible power elite, the literature grows ever larger. See, for example, John Gunnell, "The Technocratic Image," *Technology and Culture* 23 (July 1982); and Alvin W. Gouldner, *The Future of the Intellectuals and the Rise of the New Class* (New York: Seabury Press, 1979). Gunnell's paper takes him into the intertwining of the knowledgeable elite thesis with the "technical domination" thesis now widely discussed, and his bibliography is extensive.

21. See above, chap. 9.

22. Judith N. Shklar, *After Utopia* (Princeton: Princeton University Press, 1957), p. 8.

23. Sheldon S. Wolin, *Politics and Vision* (Boston: Little, Brown, 1960), p. 361.

The self-guiding society displays much less hostility to power; there, authorized power has a necessary and honorable contribution to make to problem solving, even if it often degenerates into playing politics. The model of the self-guiding society recognizes, for such reasons as noted in chapter 4, that probing, discussion, and persuasion cannot take a society all the way to solutions, acknowledges the indispensability of imposition, and probes how to distribute power or the capacity to impose in an appropriate way rather than entertain hopes, inevitably to be frustrated, of minimizing its use.

Democracy

Even within the democracies, some advocates of the science model show uneasiness about or hostility to democracy, although most are in some way committed to it. Accounting for failure in social problem solving often turns quickly to recounting the failures of democratic politics. A commentator notes two currents of thought:

> Broadly speaking, there have been two general accounts of failure. One view, generally that of the economics-influenced analysts, is that the analytic universe is abundantly populated with good ideas (policies), but that the political system (government) somehow manages persistently to overlook them or, if it tries them, constantly botches their translation from the analytical to the political realm. The second view, generally that of political scientists sobered by their studies of implementation, is that many seemingly good and simple ideas turn out to be poor ones on closer inspection, but that the political system, through an excess of naive good will or a shortage of foresight and common sense (or both), often embraces these ideas and tries to put them into practice.[24]

From another angle, advocates of the "overloaded state" thesis display some hostility to democracy, hoping for "leadership less responsive to democratic pressures and demands."[25]

Ever since Schumpeter's vivid conceptualization of democracy

24. Lawrence D. Brown, *Politics and Health Care Organization* (Washington, D.C.: Brookings Institution, 1983), p. 19.

25. The point is made in an analysis of the thesis in David Held, "Power and Legitimacy in Contemporary Britain," in Grogor McLennan, David Held, and Stuart Hall, eds., *State and Policy in Contemporary Britain* (Cambridge: Polity Press, 1984), p. 325.

as "competitive politics," according to which citizens choose from time to time (in elections) among competing prospective ruling elites but otherwise remain generally inactive and ineffective in politics,[26] social scientists have disputed whether such a concept captures democratic practice and/or ideal better than earlier concepts giving more room to citizen activism. In both the science model and some versions of the self-guiding model, citizens may delegate the immediate or proximate tasks of governmental problem solving to elected officials and persons they appoint. A question: do they choose among parties or candidates for office by probing their own standing volitions and a sample of action volitions to compare with candidate's volitions so that their choice among parties or candidates becomes a consequential influence on problem solving? Or do they choose on other grounds? The ideal of the probing society specifies the former. Some versions of the science model specify the latter. Of these, some see democracy as working well enough even if voters do not bother to probe and proceed irrationally or superficially in their evaluations of parties or candidates.[27] Others take their superficiality or irrationality as evidence of democracy's incompatibility with good social problem solving.

Epiphenomenal Problem Solving

The science model society tends to regard society as a formal organization which recognizes problems and then assigns problem solvers to them. By contrast, self-directing societies leave a great deal of room for epiphenomenal problem solving, in which solutions to problems emerge not from deliberation or design but as by-products of people's attention to other concerns or problems. They solve the problem of teaching infants to speak, for example, less by any deliberate attempts at instruction than by the infant's everyday hearing of speech and attempts of those around him to communicate. A self-guiding society does not deliberately design all the intricacies of social organization, nor deliberately seek to solve all problems. Nor does the model regard society as a purposive organization even if countless purposive organizations exist within it, consonant with Whitehead when he says, "Civilization advances by extending the

26. A concept much like several earlier ones, including Walter Lippmann's in *The Phantom Public* (New York: Harcourt, Brace, 1925).
27. A view long shared by many others as well: see, for example, Bernard R. Berelson, Paul F. Lazarsfeld, and William N. McPhee, *Voting* (Chicago: University of Chicago Press, 1954), chap. 14.

number of important operations which can be performed without thinking about them."[28]

Time-bound, Place-bound

The two models offer another choice: between the timeless problem solutions of the scientific model and the time-bound solutions of the self-guiding model. Spinoza "supposes that the rational answer to the question of what is the best government for men is in principle discoverable by anyone, anywhere, in any circumstances. If men have not discovered these timeless solutions before, this must be due to weakness, or the clouding of reason by emotion, or perhaps bad luck: . . . Hobbes . . . equally dominated by a scientific model, presupposes this also. The notion of time, change, historical development, does not impinge upon these views."[29] And a contemporary sees social science as "the chance to escape the obsessions of time and place and to see things in the aspect of eternity."[30] By contrast, advocates of the self-guiding model hold that problem solving "is not the science of setting up a permanently impregnable society, it is the art of knowing where to go next in the exploration of an already existing traditional kind of society."[31] What a people can do about a problem follows as the product of a specific historical experience.

Not a Burkean argument that through historical experience good problem solutions emerge, compete with less good solutions, and survive only because of their merits, the argument maintains only that appropriate or best problem solutions, if found at all, are appropriate or best to a time and a place. In this respect—not in some others—social problem solving looks like biological evolution: "the interplay of local opportunities—physical, ecological, and constitutional—produces a net historical opportunity,"[32] which for human beings consists often of an opportunity for choice. The timeless universal solutions sought in some versions of scientific problem solving do not exist.

Nor is this a Marxist argument that historical changes move in predictable sequences that a science of social change, such as Marx

28. In Friedrich Hayek, "The Use of Knowledge in Society," *American Economic Review* 35 (September 1945).

29. Isaiah Berlin, *Against the Current* (New York: Viking, 1980), p. 87.

30. Charles Frankel, "The Autonomy of the Social Sciences," in Frankel, ed., *Controversies and Decisions* (New York: Russell Sage Foundation, 1976), p. 30.

31. This is what Oakeshott says of politics: Michael J. Oakeshott, *Rationalism in Politics* (London: Methuen, 1962), p. 58.

32. François Jacob, "Evolution and Tinkering," *Science* 196 (June 10, 1977), p. 1,166.

attempted, can capture. Granting that societies share some universal characteristics, and granting too that some aspects of change social science can grasp and predict, the model of the self-directing society postulates a great deal more indeterminacy than does the science model.

Institutions

In the model of the scientifically guided society, political institutions authorize and implement solutions but do not decide on them, for ideally scientific inquiry instead discovers them. Determining a solution requires only the assignment of social scientists to the task. Advocates of the self-directing model see, though often only obscurely, the need for institutions that not only implement but reach solutions. The market mechanism provides the great example. It solves mammoth allocational and distributional problems without their appearing on anyone's desk or agenda, thus discharging the same problem-solving tasks as would be assigned to social scientists in a science-guided society. Similarly, the self-guiding model locates problem-solving tasks in parties, legislatures, cabinets, and courts. Idealized models aside, the two visions differ in the consequentiality they find in institutional, political, and social procedures for reaching problem solutions.

No Holism

At least back to ancient Greece one can trace an aspiration, powerfully revived by Descartes, that "a single system of knowledge, embracing all provinces and answering all questions, could be established by unbreakable chains of logical argument from universally valid axioms."[33] Persisting through the Enlightenment, it eventually ran head-on into the articulation of the fact-value distinction and shrank to become an aspiration, as in Alexander von Humboldt, Lord Kelvin, and T. H. Huxley, among many others, for a comprehensive or unified scientific theory of the empirical world alone,[34] such as gave rise to the later "unity of science" ambitions of the logical positivists. positivists.

Not even theoretical physicists have, however, attempted a comprehensive theory; Einstein is among those whose pursuit of a key segment of it ended in failure. On the state of physical theory he says: "The greater part of physical research is devoted to the development

33. Isaiah Berlin, *Against the Current* (New York: Viking, 1980), p. 3.
34. Shirley R. Letwin, *The Pursuit of Certainty* (Cambridge: Cambridge University Press, 1965), pp. 325f.

of the various branches in physics, in each of which the object is the theoretical understanding of more or less restricted fields of experience, and in each of which the laws and concepts remain as closely as possible related to experience."[35]

In the social sciences, such explicit proposals as Horkheimer's for "theoretical consideration of society as a whole"[36] are uncommon, though they perhaps persist unspoken in the minds of many social scientists. More commonly one hears pleas from both lay people and social scientists for broad and complete analyses of vast phenomena and clusters of problems. Either way, holistic ambitions for social scientists and citizens alike often mark the scientific model of society, ambitions beyond those of the self-directing model both for social scientists and ordinary investigators.

Limited Faith in Reason

Not entirely but in large part, the foregoing differences between the two models turn on a difference in faith in reason to solve social problems. Advocates of the science model have great faith in reason or human cognitive capacity: as already noted in Plato's concept of the philosopher-king, Bacon, Descartes, the Enlightenment, Bentham, the Webbs, Marx, and many of the "new Utopian" enthusiasts of contemporary formal systems of analysis like systems analysis. In Descartes' words, "There is nothing so far removed from us as to be beyond our reach, or so hidden that we cannot discover it." In advocates of the self-guiding model, a contrary sense of human cognitive incapacity dominates: in Hume and Burke, liberal concerns about human fallibility, and liberal advocacy of the market system as a device for reducing the otherwise unbearable burdens of economic planning. To these we can add recent and contemporary explicit argument on human cognitive incapacities from Hayek, de Jouvenel, Michael Polanyi, and Herbert Simon, among many others, as well as mountainous testimony on human cognitive incompetence for complex problem solving displayed in the retreat from over-ambitious economic planning for development in the third world, in the dismal record of city planning in many countries, and in the disrepute of Soviet and Chinese economic planning even in Soviet and Chinese circles. Between the supply of competence and demands for solutions

35. Albert Einstein, "The Fundamentals of Theoretical Physics," in L. Hamalian and E. L. Volpe, eds., *Great Essays by Nobel Prize Winners* (New York: Farrar, Straus & Giroux, 1970), p. 220.

36. Max Horkheimer, *Critical Theory* (New York: Herder & Herder, 1972), p. 4.

lies a tragic discrepancy. Rationality, as social scientists now say, is bounded;[37] the best human minds can cope well only with greatly simplified problems.

A faith in reason can take the form of faith in the capacity of excellent minds to discover inexorable social laws that paradoxically reveal limits on man's capacity to change the social world. Such a faith in reason tells some people that poverty is ineradicable or ordinary citizens forever incompetent in public affairs. But the faith in reason may also take the form of faith in the capacity of scientists, other intellectuals, and experts to discover leverage points in society and thus design and effect solutions to social problems. Hence, the faith in human cognitive capacity opens either the road to powerlessness or the road to social control. It is not possible for both positions to be correct, unless one modifies each to approach the other in an appreciation of what can and cannot be changed in social organization. In the model of the scientifically guided society, the inconsistency between the two forms of faith in reason often embarrasses advocates of the model who want to have it both ways.

Insofar as an advocate of the science-guided society believes that reason can solve problems, just where does he find reason? It might appear in the capacity of millions of reasoning people to live cooperatively with each other with only a hint of the coercions of the state, thus, in a kind of reasoned harmonious anarchy or near-anarchy, as anticipated by many of the figures of the Enlightenment. Or, as other figures of the Enlightenment believed, it might appear in the form of intellectual capacity of no more than an elite, which must then find the authority to effect its reasoned solutions to social problems. Advocates of the self-guiding model need make no such choice. Their vision of society calls neither for harmonious anarchy nor benevolent authority, but for political institutions and leadership, and for a citizenry of investigators who turn again and again to politics to reach problem solutions because of the many conditions in which inquiry, discussion, and persuasion cannot reach a solution without the additional element of imposition.[38]

The Connection between Reason and Democracy

A complex connection joins a greatly limited faith in reason to a belief in democracy in the self-guiding model. Arising in the Enlightenment, one great tradition in liberal democratic theory identified

37. Herbert A. Simon, *Models of Man* (New York: Wiley, 1957), pp. 196–197.
38. See chap. 4 above.

liberal democracy with government by reason instead of authority or coercion, as in the concept of "government by discussion."[39] A now parallel younger tradition identifies, to complete the picture, communism with force, authority, and the suppression of inquiry. Yet from another perspective, not inconsistent with this first perspective, the identification of democracy with reason and communism with force and authority reverses.

However much actual communist societies constrain discussion and inquiry, communist doctrine has continually displayed a faith in elite intellectual capacity in sharp contrast to the troubled concern about fallibility that is characteristic of liberal democratic society as represented in Mill. The liberal democrat's faith in reason looks strong only in contrast with earlier traditionalism and authoritarianism in science, religion, and politics. Compared to the Marxian and communist faith in reason, it looks puny. Marx's scientific socialism was meant to be scientific; the term was not just a slogan.

The version of democracy as "government by discussion" identified democracy less closely with the self-guiding model than with the scientific model. As, roughly coincident with the later Enlightenment, the egalitarian democratic idea emerged in France, democrats were typically admirers of science, rationalist, turning against traditionalism, authority, and superstition. They might believe, as a result of their new faith in rationality and science, in the possibility that they—or even better minds—could find harmony in the universe, each person potentially no longer in conflict with others, the intellect consequently capable of discovering "correct" solutions.[40]

This earlier faith, both in human intellectual capacities and in harmony, has declined for numerous reasons, including, among other intellectual influences, Freud's investigations of human irrationalities. Many thoughtful people also lost faith in reason when they recoiled from the Terror of the French Revolution and the later demands and counter-revolutionary bloodshed of the Paris Commune, a "pivotal event in European political thought."[41]

Thus, a once confident movement of thought that somehow amalgamated enlightenment, science, democracy, and equality, divided. Down one road, liberal democratic thought allied itself with clas-

39. Frank Knight, *Freedom and Reform* (New York: Harper and Brothers, 1947), p. 190. Ernest Barker, *Reflections on Government* (Oxford: Oxford University Press, 1942), p. 40.
40. Carl L. Becker, *New Liberties for Old* (New Haven: Yale University Press, 1941), p. 106.
41. Edmund Wilson, *To the Finland Station* (Garden City, N.Y.: Doubleday, 1947), p. 283.

sical economic thought and became increasingly skeptical of man's capacity to reshape his world. It therefore turned toward institutions that would hold fallible leaders responsible but would not grant them authority to create "correctly" an egalitarian world. Down the other road, the communist movement, armed with Marxian "science," marched behind leaders not held responsible to an inhibiting electorate but granted authority to create by "correct" design an egalitarian world.[42] The earlier tie between science and democracy came loose, and a model of a self-guiding society began to emerge.[43]

The two models present fundamental alternatives in strategies for social problem solving, and with particular respect to the place of social science in the social process as a whole. Almost everyone mixes elements of the two in developing his own picture or way of participating in social problem solving. The choice requires an inquiry—a probe into one's political and social philosophy. That should not, however, call up only the traditional problems in political and social philosophy—of achieving order, authority and obligation, or even distributive justice. It should call up problems in how to use intelligence in social problem solving.

Is it foolish to regard the model of the self-guiding society as a working ideal? Less so, it would seem, than so to regard the science model with its trust in a disinterested intellectual elite and its peripheral hostility to democracy, to say nothing of its other disabilities outlined above. On many counts, contemporary democracies approach the self-guided model in their bouts of hostility to elites, their broad scope for both politics and "politics," their occasional demands for aspirations to greater popular participation, and their intermittent veneration of the popular will. Not on these points can the self-directing model be dismissed as foolishly utopian. It is its postulate that masses of people probe and can greatly improve their probing that stirs disbelief in some quarters.

To that disbelief, John Dewey replied in commenting on judgments of citizens in political life: "Until secrecy, prejudice, bias, misrepresentation, and propaganda as well as sheer ignorance are replaced by inquiry and publicity, we have no way of telling how apt for judgment of social policies the existing intelligence of the masses may be. It would certainly go much further than at present. In the

42. J. L. Talmon, *The Rise of Totalitarian Democracy* (Boston: Beacon Press, 1952).

43. Five paragraphs have been taken almost verbatim from Lindblom, *Politics and Markets* (New York: Basic Books, 1977), pp. 252f.

second place, *effective* intelligence is not an original, innate endowment. No matter what are the differences in native intelligence (allowing for the moment that intelligence can be native), the actuality of mind is dependent upon the education which social conditions effect."[44] Improving the quality of inquiry by citizens and functionaries does not rest on improbable or improbably successful positive efforts to promote better probing—strained proposals, for example, for neighborhood or workplace forums, new adult education programs, or new pressures on citizens to read serious books. It rests on what might be called negative reforms—reducing impairment, getting the monkey of impairment off the citizen's back. Societies do not need to urge citizens to probe; they need only to permit them to do so. They need only to reduce the disincentives to probe, the diversions and obfuscations that muddle or dampen probing, the misinformation and indoctrinations that misdirect it, and the intimidations and coercions that block it. If none of that looks easy, none is impossible nor, in the long future, even unlikely.

44. *The Public and Its Problems* (Chicago: Gateway Books, 1946), p. 209.

CHAPTER 14

Multiplism, Pluralism, and

Mutual Adjustment

A self-directing society requires the customary civil liberties of a democratic regime: free inquiry, assembly, and speech, among others.[1] That leaves open, however, further questions about the social organizations of inquiry. By inference, all the preceding chapters strongly suggest some answers.

In any democratic society, the quality of probing should, it would seem, satisfy certain conditions set forth below. (In effect I ask readers to examine them to see if in the light of the analytical chapters, they would form volitions like mine.) If poorly satisfied, social problem solving remains correspondingly poor; if better satisfied, correspondingly improved.

All those who vote directly on policy, as in initiatives and referenda, carefully probe the preferred policies, as well as probe problem identification, definition, and formulation; or they

1. A more precise and general statement would be that the customary liberties are required for those, in any collection of people, whose volitions are to count—thus roughly, in what is ordinarily called a democracy, all adults, but otherwise some restricted class or elite.

probe to appraise advisors or informants who do some of their probing for them.

All those who vote for parties or candidates carefully probe them both before and after elections. They do not, however, necessarily probe the various issues on which the contestants will take action during their incumbency, but probe such questions as their qualifications and volitions, the degree to which decisions by them need supervision by citizen scrutiny and political agitation, and the cumulating reasons for prolonging or cutting short the incumbencies.

At least as many probe (and vote) as are required for the viability of democracy (despite broad disagreement among observers as to what number is thus required).

The number of probers is not reduced by legal or informal social prohibitions such that persons who wish to probe social problems do not in fact probe. Nor is the number reduced by government or other institutional failures to facilitate probing: at least a free press and public education, among other requirements.

Significant inequalities in opportunity to probe—for example, inequalities of education, availability of information, or available time—do not reduce the number of probers and quality of probing.

There exists no significant number of persons who fail to probe or probe well because, as a consequence of prohibitions or lack of easy facilitation, they have not probed the case for probing them.

The number of probers is great enough to sweep many profoundly innovative probers, always a small proportion of the whole, into the process.

The number who probe is large and varied enough so that non-probing members of every group whose circumstances might be expected to produce volitions different from those of any other groups can locate and receive relevant communications from those in their group who do probe. This requirement implies that numerous probers—indeed, very large numbers in large, heterogeneous societies—be active in each ethnic, racial, religious, geographical, ideological, gender, and age group, subgroup, and sub-subgroup. Any distinction in biological imprint or circumstances of life that would probably predict a distinctive quality to some of the volitions of that group when compared to other groups calls for many active probers in that group.

It seems reasonably clear, despite much room for disagreement on the magnitudes implicit in each listed condition, that probing of social problems requires the participation of vast numbers of people, most of whom bring significant though greatly limited competence to their inquiries, and many of whom bring educated and experienced competences to the task. Call such a state of affairs multiplism. Multiplism requires pervasive sustained inquiry at many levels of competence broadly distributed in the society. Because formal organizations— interest groups and business enterprises, especially—tend to crowd individual participants out of activism in the political system,[2] multiplism not only becomes essential but in fact needs a revival.

Although open to great vigor of participation, multiplism does not call for the extremes of popular participation in public affairs called for in many versions of participatory democracy. As a concept, multiplism is intended to call up a picture of a society not unfamiliar—one that is not populated by high-minded guardians of the public interest, nor by people who are engaged in incessant political discussion, or who are all people of goodwill and cooperation—yet one that is significantly different from present societies in the frequency and quality of inquiries into social problems. This is possible because of reductions in impairing influences.

PLURALISM

The model of the self-directing society requires not only multiplism but pluralism, although not the earlier English pluralism of sovereign organizations denying the sovereignty of the state, but the pluralism of later and contemporary, largely American, political thought.[3]

By probing problems, people in one of several ways identify themselves as members of, supporters of, or sympathizers with each of many groups of persons. Each group is to a significant degree internally likeminded with respect to some collective issues or social

2. Robert H. Salisbury, "Interest Representation: The Dominance of Institutions," *American Political Science Review* 78 (March 1984).
3. For a brief history of pluralism in its various forms, see R. Jeffrey Lustig, "Pluralism," in Jack P. Greene, ed., *Encyclopedia of American Political History*, vol. 2 (New York: Scribner's, 1984). For a more extended yet still brief analysis, see Peter Self, *Political Theories of Modern Government: Its Role and Reform* (London: Allen & Unwin, 1985), chap. 4.

problems. They may go no further than identifying themselves with reference groups. Some think of themselves, for example, as peasants and consequently take on some of the volitions that they attribute to peasants. Or some may go further to engage in a high frequency of intercommunication with others in some group: workmates, members of their church or union, or fellow hobbyists. Into some such groups every person is born, say, as a Protestant or a black. With other groups people may only inattentively identify themselves, choosing to do so but never quite realizing that they have made a choice: they gradually become racial bigots, for example, or advocates of the Common Market. Other groups they deliberately choose, deciding, for example, to join a veterans organization, or to take a position on disposal of toxic wastes and engage in communication with others of a similar position.

Second, groups of this kind represent their volitions to the state in such a way as to influence government policy. They often do so through formal organization of the group or segments of it. Formal organizations of this kind not only urge desired policies and definitions of problems on government officials, but also invest money and energies in appeals to both nonmembers and their own members, often only loosely attached to the organization.

Third, each of large numbers of specialized policy-making government officials, each playing a distinctive role in policy-making, exercise some significant autonomous influence on problem definition and outcomes, not wholly subordinated to higher directives. Bureau chiefs and the like, often as well as members of the legislature, cabinet, or parliament, constantly interact in problem areas in which they converge. Foreign aid policy, for example, may emerge from interaction of somewhat autonomous officials from the ministries of foreign affairs, defense, finance, and trade, all of whom have a stake in the outcome.

Officials in position of authority over government agencies make of their own agency an organized "group" participating in policy-making in much the same way, though often more immediately and powerfully, as does a formal group composed of likeminded citizens.

What is here called pluralism—and identified as necessary to the self-guiding model—consists of neither more nor less than that just specified: people in likeminded groups exercising influence on government policies and somewhat autonomous, specialized governmental officials (both elected and appointed) having multilateral influence on each other. Groups inevitably form, though not always formally, unless repressed. Many of them will seek political influence unless they are repressed. Consequently, a substantial degree of pluralism appears in all societies that do not employ control mechanisms to destroy it. The pluralist picture depicts a society other than the sometimes idealized society of a homogeneous citizenry, ethnically alike, holding to the same religion, united by language, custom, and folklore.

For reasons now so often recorded in the literature of social science and public affairs as to need only the briefest reference here, people cannot probe well without group identifications.[4] They cannot think successfully about their volitions if they regard themselves as unique. Instead, they look for clues in the situations, attitudes, and beliefs of others whom they regard as like themselves. They deal with problems of rearing their children by reflecting on how other parents that they regard as like themselves deal with their children. Similarly, on social problems, their questions implicitly—indeed, often explicitly—take the form not of What do I think ought to be done? but of How do people like me think about this problem? Even if they dissent—that is, develop some elements of uniqueness in their analysis—they dissent from group thought and identification, which constitutes their starting points.

Nor can they make their volitions generally politically influential in social problem solving without group influence on the state. Governments cannot respond to millions of diverse volitions. On that ground alone, problem solving requires that people move their volitions toward clusters of agreement. These agreements are an early step in a long process by which an impossible diversity of volitions reduces to so few that a cabinet or legislature can make a political choice. Perhaps many of us overlook this reason for the indispensability of group organization for efficacy in social problem solving in our frequent preoccupation with a more obvious need for group organization: organizations have bigger muscles and louder voices than one person alone.

Those versions of the scientific model of problem solving in which scientific observers of society rather than citizens set policy goals and fashion instruments for their achievement, abandon these first two aspects of pluralism along with the multiplism on which they rest. Even in a modified version of a scientifically guided society in which "the people make demands, the state responds by providing

<hr />

4. Eleanor Singer, "Reference Groups and Social Evaluations," in Morris Rosenberg and Ralph H. Turner, *Social Psychology* (New York: Basic Books, 1981).

answers, the people (now pacified) accept the state's authority, and the state builds a consensual basis for its politics,"[5] little room can be found for these two aspects of pluralism or for multiplism.

As for the third aspect of pluralism—policy-making interaction among officials, each having some significant degree of autonomy— only an authoritarian regime fearful of losing its authority would wish to repress it entirely. On all other grounds, some autonomy for each of many participants in official problem solving is everywhere endorsed as a method of drawing on information and capacity beyond the competence of the very highest authority; or—more simply—it is endorsed as a necessary way of achieving the benefits of specialization, of a division of problem-solving labor. On how much autonomy is desirable, disagreement runs in many directions; and perhaps most American political scientists would say that officials have too much in the American system.

An endorsement of pluralism as here defined follows from the analysis, both empirical and normative, of the earlier chapters. But "pluralism" draws fire, many thoughtful critics deplore it, and their oft-repeated reasons for doing so, though now thoroughly familiar, ask for attention.

The Critics

Pluralist problem solving or policy-making, its critics say, wherever found in the world is in actual practice highly inegalitarian, going so far as to exclude some groups from political influence and in any case giving some people much more influence than others.[6] Granted. Given the commitment of this study to at least a very rough equality of deservingness among persons, so serious a charge against pluralism cannot be swept under the rug.

In many societies, pluralism also fastens the attention of citizens and leaders on the segmental or subsociety volitions that separate people from each other rather than on widely sharable volitions that might otherwise be formed.[7] The consequences: social problem solving neglects volitions that, if pursued, would benefit almost everyone, society suffers from various disturbing forms of divisiveness, and policy-making limps.

5. John Friedman, *Planning in the Public Domain* (Princeton: Princeton University Press, 1987), p. 8. It is a version of problem solving that Friedman does not himself accept.
6. William E. Connolly, "The Challenge of Pluralist Theory," in Connolly, ed., *The Bias of Pluralism* (New York: Atherton Press, 1969), pp. 3–34.
7. Theodore Lowi, "The Public Philosophy: Interest-Group Liberalism," in Connolly, *The Bias of Pluralism*, pp. 81–122.

The formal organizations of a pluralist society typically become too large and too bureaucratic to serve as arenas for discussion helpful to inquiry; in addition, governing bureaucracies or other elites within such organizations often manipulate the members more than respond to their needs. Even unorganized likeminded groups fall under elite manipulation. Moreover, pluralism in fact sometimes becomes a kind of corporatism: government by negotiation among leaders of large groups—labor, business, agriculture, for example—in which leaders escape appropriate responsibility to members, in which they nevertheless gain a kind of formal status in government, and in which, because the groups greatly differ in numbers of members, equality among organizations undemocratically displaces equality among citizens as a normative principle.[8] Again, the allegations are almost certainly correct.

Another flaw in existing pluralist systems—a profound one—is that the diversity of volitions expected of multiplism and pluralism appears only for a restricted set of issues.[9] On many issues, multiplist and pluralist controversy never appears, or only so weakly as to fall far short of a competition of ideas. Pluralism, the critics would say, operates on secondary issues of current policy but not on more fundamental issues of social, political, and economic structure that the influence of social class or some other elite influence silences. Again, a valid criticism. The allegation that pluralist contention rages over only a limited set of issues and falls far short of a competition of ideas on many more issues finds confirmation in the preceding chapters on impairment, especially chapter 8 on convergence.

Implications of the Critical Allegations

These powerful objections to pluralism appear in another light if one asks what might be done about them. Do they establish a presumption or case for repressing group identifications, for forbidding citizens to draw on interchange with likeminded people, for prohibiting formal organizations representing likeminded people, or for forbidding such organizations as exist from exercising any political influence? It seems clear that they do not. As already observed, probing cannot proceed without interchange within groups. In democratic societies, it also seems out of the question to try to forbid people to

8. On this group of allegations, an excellent analysis and survey of the literature is Andrew S. MacFarland, "Recent Social Movements and Theories of Power in America" (Washington, D.C.: Resources for the Future, 1979 [mimeo]).

9. Peter Bachrach and Morton Baratz, "Two Faces of Power," in Connolly) The Bias of Pluralism, pp. 51–64.

band together in organizations to mobilize resources to communicate with each other, to acquaint government officials with their volitions, to mobilize persuasion of other people to join with them on policy issues, and to use the vote and other avenues of communication and representation to further the implementation of their volitions.

As for the last-named objection to pluralism, it declares pluralism at fault because it does not extend to certain large and important issues. One might infer then that pluralism ought to be extended, not rejected.[10]

In short, the objections raised against existing pluralist practices do not seem to constitute a reason for abandoning pluralism as here defined. Instead, these objections turn attention to the possibilities of restructuring or otherwise improving pluralism. Prospects for reforms adequate to reduce the force of the objections to pluralism seem slim in view of the effective political opposition by advantaged groups. Yet there exists no alternative, given the necessity of multiplism and the dependence of multiplism on group identifications and affiliations. The reforms might well include attempts to dampen some group identifications and to restructure the relations between organized groups and branches or agencies of the state. But the core of the reform has to reconstitute pluralism, not eliminate it; nor should reform in any way impede either the citizen's search for interchange with potentially likeminded people or the maintenance of open avenues to communication with agencies of the state, including the use of formal organizations to do so.

No alternative? Perhaps, in fancy, a nonpluralist, elite-led, revolutionary democratic overthrow of the entire political system. Even supposing the success of such a revolution, the postrevolutionary order, if it intends democracy, has no alternative but to let multiplism and pluralism flourish. What about other opportunities for more drastic or fundamental problem solving than pluralist systems can normally exploit—say, opportunities opened up by some catastrophe? The answer remains the same. If after the catastrophe citizens are to probe, they require multiplism; and, if multiplism, then pluralism, both made more genuine.[11]

Subsequent chapters will indicate further possibilities for cop-

10. See, however, the argument of William E. Connolly, "The Challenge to Pluralist Theory, " in his introduction to *The Bias of Pluralism*. Like some other critics of pluralism, he argues that, because not only pluralist theory but the actual practice of pluralism on only a restricted set of issues obscure an indefensible process of class or elite domination in politics, pluralism should be deplored.

11. The issue discloses another objection to pluralism that is held in some quarters but usually only tacitly argued: as a set of norms or as a prescription, pluralism

ing with the inequalities of pluralism, its excesses of attention to segmental volitions rather than those shared by whole societies, the bureaucratic and often elite inversions of the appropriate relation between group members and leaders, and the elimination of many issues from multiplist and pluralist competition of ideas. Before that, a third process necessary to a self-directing society requires attention. In addition to multiplism and pluralism, a self-directing society calls for a great deal of both stimulation and coordination through mutual adjustment among its citizens and among its leaders. Indeed, mutual adjustment lies half-implicit in both multiplism and pluralism.

MUTUAL ADJUSTMENT

Every society has to move by some combination of inquiry and imposition, as discussed in chapter 4, from a multiplicity or plurality of volitions to an operating set of decisions or outcomes. The process of transforming diverse volitions into a collective choice would be difficult enough for problems nicely segregated one from the other, so that choosing a course of action, say, on energy sources for electric power did not intertwine with choosing one, say, on taxes. But problems intertwine. No society wisely decides whether to use nuclear energy sources for the production of electric power without considering questions about utilizing its own coal or petroleum, about threats to health and safety, about foreign exchange and trade, about the state's regulatory role in markets, or about the physical location of electric generating facilities and of energy-using industrial enterprises. Hence, the number and variety of volitions that must be transformed into one or a few choices go well beyond what first appears.

How to move from diversity of volition to collective choice or outcome? Voting provides only an occasional possibility, for no more than a few of the thousands of governmental decisions made each week. Sometimes rules or routines suffice. In by far the largest number of cases, however, only two possibilities are open. Either some central decision-making official or organization chooses among the diverse volitions (or makes a decision that disregards them), or various persons acting without a central decision maker mutually control and adapt to each other to reach an outcome.

---

fails to give guidance on how to create or exploit a political paroxysm without which significant social change and advance in problem solving is impossible. An example may be John Manley, "Neopluralism: A Class Analysis of Pluralism I and Pluralism II," *American Political Science Review* 77 (June 1983).

Some pluralists opt for centralism because they envision government as a referee adjudicating among the contending pluralist groups. At an extreme, others cast government into a participatory role like that played by any other participants in mutual adjustment.[12] A commitment to multiplism and pluralism leaves open the question: centralism, mutual adjustment, or what mix of the two?

In contrast to the highly unilateral exercises of power that define central decision making, mutual adjustment embraces all forms of highly multilateral exercises of influence and power, including but by no means limited to bargaining. It includes cases in which two persons reciprocally influence each other, as well as cases in which, although no two persons reciprocally influence each other, many persons interlock in multilateral controls, each exercising control over some of the others. Like central decision makers, participants in mutual adjustment may control through persuasion or through any of other common forms of power and influence, including threats, contingent payments or other offers of benefits, suppression of information, deceit, and even highly coercive methods such as assassination. (Obviously, the merits of mutual adjustment and central decision will depend heavily on the methods employed by participants in them.)

When participants come together to reach an explicit resolution of their differences, say, through discussion, one might label their mutual adjustment as joined. When, without so doing, they influence each other—A discharges B from his job for carrying out certain activities opposed by A, as a result of which C, in another organization, hires B to continue in those activities—then one can label their mutual adjustment as disjoined. In the give and take of joined mutual adjustment, every participant both controls and adapts to other participants in it. In disjoined mutual adjustment, a person's relation with any other given persons will often be almost wholly adaptive or wholly controlling. In the example given, B adapts to A and to C but controls neither, both of whom exercise control over B.

A central authority may be an organization rather than a person, in which case the organization's decisions may emerge from internal mutual adjustment among persons within it. In that way and many others, centrality and mutual adjustment mix.

As an institutional mechanism for good problem solving, for wise decisions, or for social "rationality," mutual adjustment remains

12. See the distinction between "area" pluralism and "umpire" pluralism in Connolly, The Bias of Pluralism, pp. 8ff; and between "vector-sum" and "referee" pluralism in Robert Paul Wolff, The Poverty of Liberalism (Boston: Beacon Press, 1968), pp. 128ff.

under a cloud, while the merits of centralism seem intuitively obvious. Yet mutual adjustment can claim accomplishments that compel a rethinking of its merits. Languages are created—epiphenomenally, we saw in chapter 4—by mutual adjustment. Moral codes have typically emerged from mutual adjustment.

By several criteria, the most elaborate mutual adjustment process in the world flourishes in the form of market systems. Of many millions of people in any one society or in the world at large, each holds volitions for a variety of goods and services far beyond the much smaller number of volitions that production can satisfy. They also hold job volitions that available positions cannot satisfy—not everyone can find employment, for example, in the cleanest, safest, or most enjoyable lines of work. In the absence of central determination of who gets what, market buying and selling constitutes a mutual adjustment process through which these volitions are reduced. The production of goods and services responds to money offers, and job choices to vacancies and wage offers. A potentially impossible variety and number of conflicting volitions reduce to feasible outcomes. The intricacy of decision making and the reductions of conflicting volitions achieved through mutual adjustment in the market system go far beyond what is achieved anywhere in the world by any centralists.

In the political arena one recognizes a historically conspicuous example of explicitly designed mutual adjustment in the American constitutionally designed separation of executive, legislative, and judicial powers, as well as a specification of a bicameral legislature and division of authority between the federal government and the states. (The design, however, reflected not an ambition to facilitate a broad problem-solving competence in American politics but to "preclude the exercise of arbitrary power.")[13] Yet, even without constitutional design of separation of powers, mutual adjustment in politics appears everywhere. Of the British, French, and Italian systems, though often described—and probably correctly—as more centralist than the American, observers speak of decisions "arrived at by a continuous process of mutual adjustment between a plurality of autonomous policy makers operating in the context of a highly fragmented multiple flow of influence."[14]

If one then takes account as well of nonmarket mutual adjustment in the political arena—outcomes reached through exchange of political favor, negotiation, committee work, incurring and discharg-

13. Justice Brandeis in Myers v. United States, 272 U.S. 52,293 (1926).
14. Jack Hayward, "National Aptitudes for Planning in Britain, France, and Italy," *Government and Opposition* 9 (Autumn 1974), p. 399.

ing political obligations, reciprocal exercises of authority, preemptive strategic moves, and many other forms of reciprocal and mutual influence and deference—it seems clear that a great deal more social problem solving proceeds through mutual adjustment than through centralism. That does not deny that, like centralism, mutual adjustment through the market system and elsewhere is plagued by distinctive defects.

Mutual adjustment also largely accounts for the international order and for such prospects as the world has for coping with worldwide problems of energy depletion, ocean and air pollution, deforestation, and overpopulation. It seems impossible to anticipate a world state in the foreseeable future; and, for that matter, the peoples of the industrialized world and the third world alike, though for different reasons, would almost certainly oppose one if it became a lively issue. But if so, then nothing except mutual adjustment can accomplish the required collective action.

Mutual Adjustment in Politics

Mutual adjustment specifically in politics operates at three, deeply intertwined levels. Citizen mutual adjustment of many kinds constitutes one layer: intimidations, coercions, but also the exchange of information and analysis in probing. "He who walks in the crowd," wrote Montaigne, "must step aside, keep his elbows in, step back or advance, even leave the straight way, according to what he encounters."[15] This first level accomplishes a large part of the task of transforming diverse volitions into a course of action.

Mutual adjustment among representatives of likeminded groups and of formally organized pluralist groups constitutes the second layer. They do not wish to waste their energies on agitation for policies that will incur avoidable opposition from other groups, and they wish active allies when possible. They shape their policy positions accordingly, doing so often with more explicitness and formality than do ordinary citizens, as when leaders of groups talk with each other to work out a political strategy.

At these two levels central decision making is, by any reasonable standard, wholly unacceptable—and even difficult to imagine. Yet the largest part of all transformation of conflicting volitions into outcomes takes place at these two levels. At these two levels—among individual citizens and among group leaders—the efficacy of mutual adjustment in moving toward outcomes successfully resists any chal-

15. *The Complete Works of Montaigne*, trans. Donald M. Frame (Stanford, Calif.: Stanford University Press, 1957), vol. 3, p. 758.

lenge, since mutual adjustment in a democratic society is undeniably indispensable.

Mutual adjustment among government officials constitutes the third layer: specifically, mutual adjustment among government officials between and within all levels and between officials and interest group leaders. Here one finds the kind of mutual adjustment in which in the U.K., for example, ministers "come briefed by our departments to fight for our departmental budget, not as Cabinet Ministers with a Cabinet view."[16]

This third level of mutual adjustment many people look on askance, and I am not going to argue that it is generally or universally superior to centrality. For some tasks, centrality will appear indispensable or superior; for others, mutual adjustment or some mixture of the two. A priori, neither practicing politicians nor social scientists can generalize much about when one is superior to the other. But the role for mutual adjustment is not, a priori, any less than the role for centrality.

The Core Argument for Heavy Use of Mutual Adjustment

The principal reason for a large role for mutual adjustment at all three levels in a self-directing society is its indispensability for permitting, encouraging, and giving fullest possible effect to multiplist and pluralist inquiry and for reducing impairment.

The core supporting argument would be as follows: to move from a diversity of volitions to decisions or outcomes requires one or more of the following methods or practices: (1) impairments of probing that will lead to convergences; (2) adjudication so that decisions or outcomes respond to some volitions but not others or to some aggregation of them; or (3) a further probing of the volitions that moves them toward reduction of conflict among them.

Rule out the first for a probing and self-directing society. The second becomes necessary when continued reconsideration of volitions becomes for any reason impossible or too costly; but it is often otherwise regrettable as a premature termination of inquiry and, in addition, often leads to paralysis of decision making. The third, when time and energy allow, excels for all the reasons that inquiry, multiplism, and pluralism are desirable. Central decision making largely practices the second of the three methods. Mutual adjustment practices the third.

16. A former minister, as quoted in Grant Jordan and Jeremy Richardson, "The British Policy Style or the Logic of Negotiation," in Richardson, ed., *Policy Styles in Western Europe* (London: Allen & Unwin, 1982), p. 83.

Central authorities choose the second method for several reasons, one of which is their frequent relative isolation from citizens and their group functionaries, in contrast to the relative closeness of relationship between participants in governmental mutual adjustment and their various constituents. Moreover, central decision making lacks firm ground unless it takes citizen volitions largely as fixed for the moment, while mutual adjustment makes headway typically only on further reconsideration of relevant volitions, since no participant can simply unilaterally impose his decision on others.

Good social problem solving requires that citizens and functionaries recognize that the inadequacy of their current volitions requires their unending reconsideration and reformulation so as to move toward agreeing well enough to permit the imposition of a solution by appropriate political authority. Although, for expediency's sake, political decisions often have to adjudicate among existing volitions rather than encourage reconsideration of them, the fundamental, lasting, ever-present, long-term requirement for good problem solving is advance toward well probed society-wide, group-wide, or class-wide agreements to create—not to discover, but to create—opportunities for collective action that did not exist before.[17]

Probing ought therefore to remain open as long as time and energy permit, and interchange between functionaries and citizens should continue uninterrupted. Mutual adjustment will also often maintain a lively interchange between citizens and functionaries, each influencing the volitions of the other, while central decision makers find that their isolation prevents it.

Some refinements of this core argument, as well as objections to it, are presented in the appendix to this chapter.

MUTUAL ADJUSTMENT IN THE HISTORY OF THOUGHT

Perhaps because of the ties in intellectual history between mutual adjustment and epiphenomenal problem solving, the neglect of the former has logically followed the almost equally severe neglect of the latter. The idea that systematic betterment, including "solutions" to states of affairs that could be conceived of as problems but are not, can occur epiphenomenally, that is, without an intention to better or to solve, is perhaps still not broadly appreciated in social science. And those who do appreciate that idea or possibility may not push their

17. But, as I pointed out in chapter 4, imposition has its place. Moving in the direction of well-probed agreement is an ideal, but agreement itself is not.

thinking further to ask questions about the specific epiphenomenal mechanisms by which decisions or acts systematically produce betterment or solutions intended by no one. If they do, they will find a large part of the explanation in mutual adjustment. The connection stands out clearly for the market system, in which epiphenomenal results derive from mutual adjustment among buyers and sellers. But social science has not much generalized from market to other arenas.

Social thought confused the two phenomena from earliest times, and perhaps one stretches a point to find any appreciation of mutual adjustment at all in texts that show at least some explicit appreciation of epiphenomenal problem solving. A hint of appreciation of both, but only a hint, appears in Polybius's observation that the Roman constitution was a product of "many struggles and troubles" rather than of explicit design.[18] Nor are other examples unambiguous. They appear to refer to mutual adjustment as a method of betterment or problem solving, though not with those words.

Montaigne observes: "Whatever position you set men in they pile up and arrange themselves by moving and crowding together, just as ill-matched objects, put in a bag without order, find of themselves a way to unite and fall into place together, often better than they could have been arranged by art."[19] In loose formulations largely implicit, Montesquieu grants a fundamental place to mutual adjustment. Writing, for example, of a harmonious policy, he says "it results from the same sort of process as that of the universe whose parts are connected by the action of some and the reaction of others."[20]

Kant's view of mutual adjustment seems anchored in a concern with controlling excesses of power, but there he also suggests a concern with wise or intelligent policy. "It is only necessary to organize the state well . . . and to direct these forces against each other in such wise that one balances the other. . . . Consequently the result for reason is as if both selfish forces were nonexistent."[21]

Adam Ferguson observes: "In free states . . . , the wisest laws are never, perhaps, dictated by the interest and spirit of any order of men: they are moved, they are opposed, or amended, by different hands; and come at last to express that medium and composition which con-

18. *The Histories* 6.10, trans. W. R. Paton (Cambridge: Harvard University Press, 1923).

19. *The Complete Works of Montaigne*, vol. 3, p. 730.

20. *Considerations on the Causes of the Romans' Greatness and Decline*, chap. 8, as cited in Melvin Richter, *The Political Theory of Montesquieu* (Cambridge: Cambridge University Press, 1977), p. 161.

21. C. J. Friedrich, ed., *The Philosophy of Kant* (New York: Random House, 1949), p. 452.

tending parties have forced one another to adopt."[22] Similar insights little developed appear in Democritus, Machiavelli, Hume, and Burke, among others. Michael Polanyi's 1941 characterization of mutual adjustment not to control excesses of power but for rationality may be the first wholly explicit description of the phenomenon generalized and not limited to the market.[23]

Most references to mutual adjustment do not clearly distinguish between mutual adjustment among citizens and among functionaries, on one hand, and mutual adjustment among government officials, on the other. Some appreciation of the former one can find in Aristotle, Aquinas, and Locke, among many others; but mutual adjustment within the state itself, instead of highly unilateral decision making, goes beyond what they had in mind, except, again, in frequent appreciation of separation of powers as a defense against tyranny. How sharply others just quoted or cited visualized both popular and official mutual adjustment remains obscure.

Anthropologists and sociologists have, however, made some headway in bringing mutual adjustment out of obscurity. Grappling not with problem solving or decision making but with such a question as what holds a society together,[24] they have looked at the depth and breadth of interaction among ordinary people. Some have tried to show that all human interaction constitutes a form of exchange.[25] Others, without fastening on any one core concept like exchange, have meticulously examined forms of interaction and their consequences. Of those, many and perhaps most have sought to clarify the way in which interaction produces governing norms in society, especially moral codes but also rules governing specific activities like speech.[26] Thus, they see "a process of crystallization of different norms and frameworks which takes place through a series of ex-

22. *An Essay on the History of Civil Society*, ed. D. Forbes (1767; (Edinburgh: Edinburgh University Press, 1966), p. 128.

23. "The Growth of Thought in Society," *Economica* 8, n.s. (November 1941). My own flawed *Intelligence of Democracy* (New York: Free Press, 1965) appears to have done relatively little to lift mutual adjustment from its continuing obscurity in many circles.

24. Roger Keesing and Felix Keesing, *New Perspectives in Cultural Anthropology* (New York: Holt, Rinehart and Winston, 1971), p. 226.

25. George C. Homans, "Social Behavior as Exchange," *American Journal of Sociology* 63 (May 1958).

26. For example, Talcott Parsons, *The Structure of Social Action*, 2d ed. (Glen Coe, Maine: Free Press, 1961); Elman R. Service, *Primitive Social Organization* (New York: Random House, 1962), esp. p. 41; and Roger Keesing and Felix Keesing, *New Perspectives in Cultural Anthropology* (New York: Holt, Rinehart and Winston, 1971), esp. pp. 231f.

changes between people placed in different structural positions."[27] In making that advance, they neglected patterns of interaction that organize human society without the intermediary effect of norms or rules. That neglect has been partly remedied by the work of Goffman and that of Garfinkel, who explore the variety of ways in which interactions serve, independently of governing rules, as social controls.[28] But almost none have asked questions about how these studied interactions constitute mechanisms of social problem solving or social betterment, either through the state or other social processes (again, aside from well-studied market interactions). They have tended to stop with questions about interpersonal influence and social order rather than continue into questions about social change and especially those changes that will be evaluated, by some people, as betterment. A significant exception is organization theory, in which problem-solving mutual adjustment within formal organizations is well recognized.[29]

Quietly rejecting mutual adjustment in politics as a method of betterment or problem solving, the more dominant intellectual tradition draws on Plato's centralist as philosopher-king, Bodin and Hobbes on the necessity of central power for social order, Saint-Simon, Lenin, and Mao, and large numbers of recent and contemporary social theorists, as well as policy analysts, many of whom, except for the market, see mutual adjustment as a largely regrettable intrusion of "politics" into rational problem solving.[30] While many people grant the usefulness of diffusion of power and of mutual adjustment for preventing excesses of power, they resist doing so for wise, intelligent, or informed problem solving.

Centralist Bias

Curiously, they make no explicit case for central coordination in problem solving, and it does not seem to occur to them that their faith in it requires one. There exists in the literature of social science

27. S. N. Eisenstadt, "The Study of Processes of Institutionalization, Institutional Change, and Comparative Institutions," in Eisenstadt, ed., *Essays on Comparative Institutions* (New York: Wiley, 1965), p. 22.

28. Erving Goffman, *The Presentation of Self in Everyday Life* (Woodstock, N.Y.: Overlook Press, 1973), esp. pp. 8–16; and Harold Garfinkel, *Studies in Ethnomethodology* (Englewood Cliffs, N.J.: Prentice-Hall, 1967).

29. W. Richard Scott, *Organiztions* (Englewood Cliffs, N.J.: Prentice-Hall, 1981), pp. 194–196.

30. For example, Samuel Brittan, "The Economic Tensions of British Democracy," in R. Emmett Tyrrell, Jr., ed., *The Future that Doesn't work* (Garden City, N.Y.: Doubleday, 1977).

no justification of centrality over mutual adjustment, the favoritism shown to it more habitual than reasoned. Rational decision making, as both many lay people and professionals see it, is simply what a rational mind does with a problem, and a centralist has a rational mind. That a centralist's mind alone achieves rationality denied to interacting people they simply assume. Their mistake derives in part from their view of problem solving as wholly cognitive, not also social; thus they habitually speak of the "decision maker" rather than of interacting participants. They remain blind to the fact that centralists do not necessarily think their way through to a solution but instead impose one by exercise of authority. While centralism, as they see it, reaches solutions with brain instead of brawn, mutual adjustment they regret as all brawn, no brains.

There are elements of this taken-for-granted view of central coordination in, for example, Max Weber, Herbert Simon, Elton Mayo, Erich Fromm, A. A. Berle, and Jürgen Habermas; but it lodges, and with fewer qualifications, in the minds of hundreds of social scientists who, although assuming the value of centralism, say nothing at all about it because their commitment to it is only with difficulty raised to a conscious level. They throw a burden of proof on advocates of mutual adjustment that they as tacit advocates of centrality have never carried. Among social scientists the favoritism may derive in part from careless inferences. They see themselves as "centralist" problem solvers when they attack their own professional intellectual problems. That is to say, each takes a responsibility for thinking through and solving a problem at hand. If this is appropriate for a scholar's intellectual problem, it would seem—but here the mistake—that a central mind is appropriate when society tackles a social problem. That mutual adjustment among a plurality of participants might better solve it is foreign to the scholar's own methods.

Bias in favor of centrality arises for another reason—in the minds of both lay people and social scientists. They can imagine an omniscient central mind; but, except for models of the market system, they cannot conceive of an omniscient mutual adjustment process. On the contrary, every imaginable kind of mutual adjustment suffers from easily observable defects. But how well a centralist can inform himself and comprehend a problem is an empirical question not settled by the characteristics of an idealized model. The relative perfection of two models says nothing about actual performance levels.

Another curious bias works against an appreciation of mutual adjustment specifically in politics: the belief that central decision making, because designed, can be restructured to improve its performance when defective but that mutual adjustment, because spontaneous rather than designed, cannot. In fact, human beings created both and can restructure both; and a defect of mutual adjustment will often call more appropriately for redesigning the character of the mutual adjustment rather than moving toward centrality.

A report of an American presidential commission illustrates the common and elementary confusion between generic mutual adjustment and frequent badly structured forms of mutual adjustment.[31] The commission followed the conventional diagnosis of American politics: pointing to fragmentation of policy-making power as an obstacle to the pursuit of the common good. Nowhere in the report can one find an indication that it occurred to any members of the commission that just as the market system can be organized well or badly—and calls for frequent restructuring—so also can the mutual adjustment of multiple participants in government. At least one conspicuous structural feature of political mutual adjustment in the American system might have stimulated a consideration of altered structures: the widespread dissemination of veto powers to participants in mutual adjustment, a structure of mutual adjustment in which unanimity is often required for action, while any one participant can alone stop it.

If all social theorists and practical men in public life acknowledge at some level the indispensability of both central and mutually adjustive transformation of diverse volitions, a great cleavage separates those who rely largely on centrality from those who rely largely on mutual adjustment. The conflict between the two positions poses a fundamental issue about social organization, and thus for the future of humankind.

31. President's Commission for a National Agenda for the Eighties, Report of the Panel on the Electoral and Democratic Process (Washington, D.C.: Government Printing Office, 1980).

APPENDIX: MORE ON MUTUAL ADJUSTMENT

Mutual Adjustment and Conflict

It is sometimes said that, on a view of political life as fundamentally cooperative or consensual, one chooses centralism, while on a view of political life as fundamentally conflicted, one chooses mutual adjustment.[32] On the contrary, Hobbes would say that centralists are required for conflict resolution; and Adam Smith would say that mutual adjustment is required for prodigious tasks of social cooperation in a world-wide market system.

Indeed, it seems as though much of the conventional endorsement of central decision making might trace back to fear of conflict: specifically, to the desire of advantaged members of society to protect their advantages against the challenges of social disorder. Central authority, by definition, is highly unilateral. Mutual adjustment disperses authority, and some forms of it disperse it throughout society, as in the fragmentation of authority in some pluralist democracies, or its extreme fragmentation in the market system. Thus, an argument for mutual adjustment is that it might be structured to permit challenges to the advantaged or to possibilities of smuggling social change into a society to which its institutions for central decision making were opposed.

Coordination

Often it is argued that centralism is required for coordination. But nothing coordinates the world's many millions of economic decisions more effectively than the mutual adjustment of the market system, defective as it is; and nothing coordinates a team of soccer players more effectively than their mutual adjustments, even if in both cases the coordination is not perfect, nor wholly unassisted by central authority.

Coordination is only one among competing values and can be overdone—by central and mutually adjustive problem solving alike. In the market system, bankruptcies are evidence of failures of coordination: someone has tried to sell a product for which demand turns out to be insufficient. But too low a rate of bankruptcies is as regrettable as too high a rate. Vigorous innovation requires scattered failures and is often worth the failures it costs. So also in politics, new ideas, programs, solutions—and, always, reconsidered volitions—are desir-

32. On the consensus-conflict distinction, see John Horton, "Order and Conflict Theories of Social Problems," in James Curtis and John Petras, eds., *The Sociology of Knowledge* (New York: Praeger, 1970).

able even at some cost in poor coordination. It is often the defect of central coordination that it seeks coordination and nothing else. Mutual adjustment, by contrast, is motivated not solely by desires for coordination but by desires of its participants to remove obstacles to new achievements and to give effect to reconsidered volitions. In mutual adjustment, a political functionary maneuvers to adapt his proposal to soften opposition to it and to win allies not because he wants coordination but because he wants his proposal to succeed.

Again, as elsewhere in this study, a choice is posed between intellectual and administrative tidiness, on one hand, and flexibility for innovation, on the other. It is one of the many facets of the distinction between being right and probing well, or more precisely, between failing to be right and probing well, for on complex social problems no one can be right and can at most only probe well.

Broad Vision

It is claimed that only the centralist sees the problem as a whole; that participants in mutual adjustment see only their corner of it. But, as I argued in chapter 3, there is no whole problem; all social problems are fragments, and probably all of them are also residues of older, not wholly solved, problems. So a centralist coordinator in a city planning department confronts problem of the physical layout of the city, while problems of economic growth of the city are in other hands, as are the city's problems, say, in public education and sanitation. Each ostensible centralist calls his fragment of the city's problems his whole problem, but, then, so also can each participant in mutual adjustment call his fragment his whole problem.

Are the concerns of participants in mutual adjustment necessarily narrower than those of centralists? Many interest-group leaders take a broad view of the whole society, no less so than any ostensibly central problem solver. Environmentalists, for example, often place their concern for the environment in a model of a good society, while, on the other hand, a centralist may be narrowly occupied with an assigned function. When environmentalists as would-be or actual participants in mutual adjustment try to persuade the sanitation department to change its disposition of wastes, who is likely to take the broadest view of the problem?

In fact, there never is any one problem; there are always many intertwined problems. Finding new markets for agricultural producers, for example, raises closely related questions of foreign policy. Officials in the ministry of agriculture may be as incompetent about, and as little interested in, foreign affairs as officials in the foreign affairs ministry are about agriculture. Mutual adjustment offers the possibility that both problems will be seen in their interconnections, hence more broadly examined than in the absence of mutual adjustment.

With few exceptions, if any, every central decision maker is in fact largely a participant in mutual adjustment with other decision makers over whom his central authority does not extend. He is actually a centralist only with respect to some island of decision making in a sea of mutual adjustment. Even the chief executive of a nation on his large island is in large part engaged in mutual adjustment with officials of other nations. And in his attempts to exercise unilateral authority within his island, he is typically confronted with other officials who can, even if he appointed them, exercise influence over him. Whether he calls up a "wholer" view of any problem than do those with whom he participates in mutual adjustment between his island and theirs and with others on his own island is an empirical question the answer to which will vary from situation to situation. But it will often be his engagement in mutual adjustment, both between islands and on his own, that compels him to face up to the interlocking of some problem of his with many others.

A study of economic planning in France, Japan, the Netherlands, and Sweden shows that ostensible central coordinators of economic policy simply cannot grasp the entirety of their task. As coordinators they fail; but they appear to succeed instead as advocates of economic growth in their mutual adjustment with others within the state outside their own planning departments or organizations.[33]

Centralists find that each of many possible solutions to any given problem produces distinctive repercussions for the solutions to other problems, thus for volitions other than those that first concerned them. By engaging in mutual adjustment, they are often more likely to be motivated to take account of relevant volitions earlier thought irrelevant and to try to influence them. To the extent that they can withdraw into an exercise of unilateral authority as centralists, they lose many of their opportunities to respond to and take part in a broad reconsideration of volitions.

Cogitational Capacity

Here we come to the most elementary and an ineradicable defect in centralism: the discrepancy between human cogitating capacity and the difficulty of the problem at hand. For complex tasks of social

33. Peter Murrell, "Planning and Coordination of Economic Policy in Market Economies," *Journal of Comparative Economics* 3 (June 1979).

problem solving, no human mind can obtain or process all the relevant information.[34] Even with the aid of electronic computers, no Soviet planning organization has ever approached a complete central mastery of Soviet economic volitions or decisions, let alone a coordination of the economic with volitions and decisions in foreign policy, military affairs, and other aspects of Soviet society. Western city planners exhaust their capacities before they have encompassed all variables pertinent to their aspirations. Nor can any nation's military force in time of war be deployed wholly through central decision; units in the field have to adjust mutually to each other.[35]

Analysis and Imposition

The task of reaching solutions is always more than a cognitive or analytical task, as I pointed out in chapter 4. If various parties conflict over their versions of the common good—in a dispute, for example, that pits the advocates of economic growth against the advocates of price level stability, each held to be the sine qua non of the common good—reducing their conflicting volitions to one that can be acted on calls for a choice which, beyond some point at which discussion is exhausted, must be imposed rather than further analyzed. At that point, central imposition is arbitrary, responding to some volitions, not others. So also are the mutual impositions of participants in mutual adjustment. But the case for centrality vanishes at such a point: its arbitrariness is no better than any other arbitrariness. Often there will be a positive case for reaching a decision or outcome by dispersing the power to impose among participants in a process in which, because each can be imposed on by others, they employ imposition sparingly and gently.

Information Flows

When, however, decision making does pose an analyzable problem, a further defect in centrality—beyond cognitive limits on the human mind—is its characteristic suppression and distortion of information. In a hierarchial structure, the centralist relies on information from below. The subordinates protect themselves by suppressing some information and distorting other communications, a familiar problem in decision making. In mutual adjustment, too,

34. Julian Feldman and Herschel Kanter, "Organizational Decision Making," in James March, *Handbook of Organizations* (Chicago: Rand McNally, 1965).
35. The most explicit arguments on cognitive limits on central decision making are in the work of Michael Polanyi. See his *Logic of Liberty* (Chicago: University of Chicago Press, 1951), chaps. 8–10.

participants hide information and distort it. But they do so subject to challenge from other more or less equally placed participants. If one participant has reason to hide or twist a piece of information, another participant pursuing different volitions is often motivated to dig it up or restate it. The inequalities of unilateral power often lend themselves to obstructed communication more than greater equality of multilateral power.

Moreover, almost everyone experienced in the ways of large organizations knows, though he may fail to generalize from his insight, that organizations cannot function well if all questions about cooperation between persons at any one level have to be passed up to a higher level for approval and then transmitted down to the persons responsible for action. It is too cumbersome, too slow, too imprecise.[36] Direct communication between persons at each level is also required. It permits them to achieve outcomes through their mutual adjustment. This is true for members of a government bureau or department, for executives in a large corporation, and for industrial managers in the Soviet Union who cannot fulfill their assigned output tasks without dealing directly with each other in black and gray markets. In organization theory, it is often also said that informal channels of communication and of exercise of authority are necessary to supplement formal channels of organization.[37] The informal channels are often those of mutual adjustment, the formal channels those of centrality.

Partisanship

It is also claimed that central coordinators are nonpartisan, while participants in mutual adjustment are partisan. But everyone is necessarily a partisan, whether a narrow one or a public interest partisan. Centralists are of both kinds, and even the broad responsibilities of a chief executive of a nation may be in the hands of a narrow partisan. Similarly, participants in mutual adjustment are of both kinds. The American Committee on the Present Danger, mobilized behind a tough policy toward the Soviet Union, and Les Amis de la Terre are motivated by their broad vision of a good society.

A common concern about mutual adjustment is that it encourages participants to focus their probing on their narrow or segmental volitions, ignoring the possibilities that they would do better to form volitions they can share with everyone and thus engage in the pursuit

36. For a discussion and citation on horizontal and vertical relations, see W. Richard Scott, *Organizations* (Englewood Cliffs, N.J.: Prentice-Hall, 1981), pp. 149f, 254–256, 264f.
37. Ibid., pp. 81–84.

of the common good. But no one has made a plausible case that we should even try to be all alike, thus moving away from those volitions on which we diverge and that permit what most people would regard as a desirably diversity in the society, whether a diversity in individual patterns of life or ethnic, religious, geographical, or other cultural diversity. Hence the concern, properly stated, is that, despite the value of narrow or segmental volitions, people invest excessively in them, to the neglect of potentially sharable volitions that could define the common good.

Even that modified claim constitutes no justification for central coordination. For those who make the claim do not contend that centralists should simply declare common values or on their own authority define the common good. Again, as above, if there is a common good it can only emerge from multiplist and pluralist probing. And if there are volitions that can be shared by members of subgroups like social classes, they can emerge, we have argued, only from multiplist and pluralist probing. It is in the mutual adjustment among probers, both citizens and functionaries, that the commonalities emerge, including a widespread volition for probing.

A common structure of decision making that comes to be dominated by narrow interests is actually a form of central decision making easily confused with mutual adjustment. A government official facing a decision invites representatives of various segmental volitions to advise him, he himself assuming that problem solving is nothing more than an aggregation of such narrow volitions. He may therefore extend no similar invitation to participation to any representatives of versions of the common good. The domination of segmental over common volitions in his decision is then a product of his practice of central coordination, not of mutual adjustment, which in fact does not occur.[38] Another practice, perhaps growing in frequency as it extends beyond the United States, is central benefit-cost analysis. It also permits segmental volitions to dominate if, as is common, the calculations identify relatively conspicuous gains and losses to specific subgroups and ignore widespread or common gains or losses that are more difficult to estimate. Many cost-benefit calculations also give heavy weight to segmental or narrow volitions simply because they take market prices or surrogates as measures of value, thus building evaluations around such individual values as are pursued in market behavior and neglecting widely shared or common values for

38. The argument and evidence are in Robert Reich, "Policy Making in a Democracy," in Reich, ed., *The Power of Public Ideas* (Cambridge, Mass.: Ballinger, 1988), pp. 123–156.

which prices or surrogates are not available. The problem, again, is central decision making, not mutual adjustment.

No doubt participants in mutual adjustment do often seize what they can in the process, to the neglect of the formation of more widely shared volitions. But the inference to be drawn is not that a hypothetical—and impossible—nonpartisan centralism can cure the disease; it is instead that the structure of mutual adjustment needs a great deal of improvement. If one would like to see a society move toward a greater pursuit of shared volitions and a diminished pursuit of segmental volitions, the route is often through altering mutual adjustment rather than suppressing it. For an example: given the earlier outlined disproportionate influence of business managers in the democratic politics, I suggest that many other groups rate the possibilities for success of any broad programs they might develop as too low to warrant the attempt. Hence, they fall back on a kind of guerrilla warfare, raiding when they can. Even labor unions, for all their power relative to most groups other than business, are in most countries less interested in joining to develop an incomes policy than they are in grasping what ever monopolistic and other advantages that circumstances offer.

Other structural features of existing political systems may stand in the way of the formation and pursuit of thoughtfully probed common volitions. Informal and formal devices for functional representation in legislatures and bureaucracies may be among them, for·they represent people according to their differing roles as producers, thus suppressing what they have in common. Other obstructive structures may include close ties between administrative agencies and business groups; the often tortured construction of electoral districts and voting rules, and avenues of ethnic or religious influence on governmental officials. Many of these structures are supported by volitions of leaders and politically active citizens and will not be eliminated until those volitions themselves are reconsidered.

CHAPTER 15

Some Questions about

Professional Inquiry for a

Self-Guiding Society

The proposition presented in chapter 10 that social science necessarily supplements rather than replaces lay inquiry carries a prescriptive implication, hardly necessary to spell out, that social scientists might attend carefully to how any work they plan might best adapt to the state of lay knowledge. Or the proposition made in chapter 11 that social scientists allocate, without ever having made a case for doing so, more of their energies to meeting the needs of functionaries than to meeting the needs of ordinary citizens, carries a prescriptive implication, again unnecessary to spell out, that social scientists might wish to reconsider the allocation. Similarly, the proposition that conclusive testing of empirical hypotheses is not a strong suit in social science but that social science accomplishes a variety of other inquiries like the writing of scenarios carries a prescriptive implication, again not necessary to spell out, that social scientists might wish to reconsider their ambitions. All the foregoing chapters point to many such prescriptive implications that are sufficiently clear without elaboration.

Some of them, however, were brought closer to explicit prescriptive formulation in the contrast between the model of the self-guiding society and that of the scientifically guided society. And a few others now warrant further discussion. I acknowledge that the analysis of all foregoing chapters, though full of prescriptive implications for the organization and practice of social science, leaves abundant room for debate on appropriate specific institutional prescriptions. I will go no further than to identify issues to be faced with respect to the organization and practice of professional inquiry and to indicate a direction of inquiry into them. My discussion might persuade a professional investigator to change direction or a foundation to alter its priority in research grants, but it pins neither down to any precisely defined resolve other than, perhaps, to probe professional probing itself.

BENEFICIARIES

Of issues calling for further discussion, one raises the question of the identify of intended beneficiaries of professional inquiry. The question is not for whom a social scientist should work—a university or a government agency, for example—but whose welfare, if anyone's, should guide or constitute the concern of the work.

Perhaps many social scientists believe they need face no such question; that they would be well advised not to face it; and that they will become less than scientific if they allow their research be influenced by an answer to it. Professional investigators, they believe, should pursue productive or fruitful research of quality without regard to the distribution of its benefits. Social scientists who pursue inquiry solely for the pleasures of doing so can perhaps defend that line of argument. But many social scientists and researchers, whether they work on estoric or applied problems, intend their work, sooner or later, perhaps only indirectly and with a long lag, somehow to help society solve its problems. For them, does an estimate of the fruitfulness or productivity of their research constitute a sufficient guide without regard to beneficiaries?

Scholarly communities develop some agreements on less or more fruitful directions of inquiry. But the agreement fails as an inadequate guide for at least two reasons. Not sufficiently precise, agreement leaves investigators with large remaining questions about the direction of their own inquiries. And the agreements themselves need probing, for social scientists have not developed competences on direction of research to match their competence in the methodology of project execution. No literature on project choice matches the literatures, say, on statistical or survey research methods. The agreements reflect not only professional inattention but also the impairments of social science, including both those impairments that social scientists share with laymen and those distinctive to each discipline or scholarly community. Any one professional should look upon the agreement as significant, yet as evidencing some combination of professional competence, inattention, and impairment.

Assume then that, independently of or as a critique of collegial agreement on research priorities, a social scientist tries to make an estimate of the potential productivity or fertility of a proposed line of inquiry. Could one make a defensible estimate without regard to who and how many benefit from the fertility of the work? No social scientist justifies his work on the ground that it will benefit some one member of society. It seems safe to suggest that all social scientists who want their work to contribute to betterment at least indirectly and ultimately believe they should choose projects of fertility or benefit to some large number of people.

How large a number, then? And who? Perhaps everyone more or less equally. Or fellow citizens but not necessarily foreigners. Or the populations of the industrialized world, but not necessarily those of the third world. Or those in power. Or one's own socioeconomic class. It is difficult to see how a professional can justify a choice of research direction without facing up to these questions. If a social scientist claims not to care who or how many benefit from the fruitfulness of social science—claims indifference—it would seem that he does not care about its usefulness at all. Any reason for wishing to be useful would seem to imply a wish to be useful to some number or some category of human beings.

In the physical sciences, often no such question arises because mastery of the physical forces of the world has been assumed—though the assumption is increasingly doubted—to open up potential benefits ultimately available for all: improved crops, energy from petroleum, control of contagious disease, among countless examples. But, as I noted in chapter 9, a gain in mastery of the social world constitutes a gain in someone's control, whether intended or not, over other people, and not necessarily or usually a benefit for all. Social scientists cannot escape the question of what kinds of controls in whose hands they intend their work to facilitate. From the preceding chapters one cannot infer the right answer to these questions, only that every social scientist guides his work according to his probed answers.

Choice of beneficiaries (together with other ethical choices)[1] might seem to compel social scientists to sail in dangerous waters. Choices of these kinds would seem to deprive society of one of social science's distinctive contributions to social problem solving: its relative nonpartisanship, its relative impartiality, when compared with lay probing. Granted the impossibility of strict professional neutrality on value issues, one might believe that a social science aspiration toward a distanced neutrality might serve as a necessary counterweight to the brawling partisanship of lay probers.

The waters are less dangerous than they appear, for social scientists have never sailed in any other waters and are still afloat. They have always been partisan. Perhaps the most obvious evidence of the partisanship of professional social probers lies in their nationalism.[2] All over the world in recent years, economists debate, for example, the merits of "industrial policy," national policies designed to encourage some industries over others, especially in international competition. Merits for whom? With some exceptions, West German social scientists take it for granted that desirable industrial policies consist of those that will serve the government or people of West Germany. So also for the Japanese, American, Soviet, or Indian social scientists: their own nation or its people concerns them. National partisanship becomes even more conspicuous in debates on guest workers or immigration.

What character and degree of partisanship, then, might warrant an endorsement? The kinds of partisanship worth contemplating do not include those that condone misrepresentation in the form of suppressed evidence, cooked statistics—or in any form. They do not challenge the obligation of professional investigators to follow long-standing rules about evidence, disclosure, accuracy, and the like.[3] Yet a place for defensible—indeed, inescapable—partisanship for social scientists can be found in both the common-good partisanship and the narrow partisanship of chapter 4.

1. See chap. 9 above.
2. In which they have been joined by natural scientists. For the erosion of an earlier non-national or international state of natural science, see Sanford A. Lakoff, "Scientists, Technologists, and Political Power," in Ina Spiegel-Rösing and Derek de Solla Price, eds., Science, Technology and Society (London: Sage, 1977).
3. Yet even these have been called into question by contrary norms: secrecy and stubborn commitment, among others. See Ian Mitroff, The Subjective Side of Science (Amsterdam: Elsevier, 1972) and Mitroff, "Norms and Counter-Norms in a Select Group of Apollo Moon Scientists," American Sociological Review 39 (August 1974).

Common-Good Partisanship

As outlined in chapter 4, every intended nonpartisan concept of common good or public welfare favors some groups over others because conflicts among them call for a choice or trade-off. Every concept will similarly respond to some values rather than others or will trade off some values for others, as in the *Federalist Papers*, Myrdal's *American Dilemma*, or Plato's *Republic*. Consequently, although social scientists can escape from premature judgment, narrowness of vision, thoughtless advocacy, and the like, they cannot escape from this fundamental partisanship, however informed or thoughtful. Consider educational psychologists who find some pedagogical methods more effective than others because they raise student examination scores. As soon as they define "effective," it becomes a partisan criterion emphasizing some values to the relative neglect or subordination of others.

Many social scientists need no explicit concept of common good because their work is purely descriptive rather than applied. Even so, social scientists who, for example, simply want to sort out the consequences of tighter and looser forms of classroom discipline face a choice with respect to which effects they intend to trace: order in the classroom, obedience to teacher, or rates of learning of various kinds, among other possibilities. However fair-minded, dispassionate, neutral, and committed to the common good such investigations intend to be, they must choose, and in so doing will express their interest in some values more than others.

Egalitarianism

Social scientists might seem to remain nonpartisan by regarding all persons as of equal worth, equally deserving, or equally entitled to the benefits of social institutions and policies.[4] Since all societies are inegalitarian, such egalitarians become partisans for the disadvantaged. Clearly, their concept of the public interest or general welfare will differ sharply from more conventional concepts such as those used in policy-making in the ostensible democracies, in which public-interest concepts endorse many familiar kinds of inequality.

Egalitarians of this kind differ among themselves on what specific alterations in existing patterns of inequality they seek and on how fast those alterations should come. They differ in both practice and

4. One could take such a commitment to equality among persons as defining nonpartisanship, thus answering the question—but not well—by definition.

theory on the degree to which, if at all, inequalities of one kind—
intelligence, special talents, or physical infirmities—can and ought to
be offset by others, especially by those of income and wealth. They all
consequently become partisans—however fair-minded, informed,
thoughtful, and dispassionate—for one kind, degree, or speed of
movement to equality.[5]

The Dominant View as Concealed Partisanship

Professional investigators concerned with a common good often
try to escape from taking a partisan position by letting dominant
thought in the relevant society define it. In the U.K., for example,
many social scientist would analyze, say, problems of sluggish economic growth in the light of general welfare conceived of as requiring
accelerated industrial growth within a largely unquestioned economic order and set of property rights, and with no more than slow evolutionary change in class relations. By accepting some such
conventional concept of common good, they spare themselves the
partisan task of constructing their own. But the dominant view itself
is already a partisan one, and they make a partisan choice, although
inconspicuously, in accepting it.

Popular, conventional, or dominant general welfare concepts
serve the purposes of much policy-oriented professional probing because solutions to current policy problems normally have to square
with such concepts. But they would seem indefensible in social science generally. Even on policy problems, other proposed solutions
motivated by alternative concepts of common good call for exploration, as do a variety of issues suggested by the alternative concepts.
Such explorations may exercise a long-term effect through gradually
shifting the policy debate and opening up for a distant future some
possibilities now inconsistent with the conventional volitions that
guide policy.

A frequent professional habit of accepting conventional general
welfare concepts both in social science generally and in policy analysis appears to have deprived dissident groups—not wholly but disproportionately—of the help of social science. Hence, a carelessly
partisan social science often fails to come to the help of fresh ideas in
policy and instead joins in discrediting them as partisan. It fails to

---

5. On how far apart advocates of various kinds of equality can be, see Douglas
Rae et al., *Equalities* (Cambridge: Harvard University Press, 1981).

contribute at the potential growing points or innovation opportunities of society.

The choice between conventional and alternative general-welfare concepts sometimes appears as a choice between acceptable and unacceptable clients, say, in policy analysis. Many social scientists accept a government as a client. Working for it does not ordinarily downgrade them in colleagues' eyes, nor label them partisan. They often reject private groups—environmentalists, for example—as unacceptable clients. Working for them often downgrades social scientists, in that their colleagues label them partisan. Even if they can, without injury to reputation, join such groups in their roles as citizens, in their professional or scholarly roles they must, for the sake of scholarly reputation, keep some distance from such organizations. So false a distinction between clients obstructs useful research.

But, one might reply, the state is the state, not a private organization. Many private organizations, however, pursue no less well-probed and no less defensible versions of the common good than the state's—as safe a proposition as any in this book. A private organization may drift or blunder into activities at odds with its own concept of the common good, but so also do states—again, a remarkably safe proposition. A more sophisticated statement of "the state is the state" might run as follows. In every democratic society, some person or organization—a chief executive, party leader, or party organization—is in effect authorized to formulate a governing concept of common good. This authorized version of the general welfare should guide the social scientist. But even if there existed an "authorized" version of the common good so designated, those who formulated it would constantly change it to meet changing circumstances. Hence, at all times alternative concepts of common good would require examination, presumably by a variety of both public and private groups.

A conventional or dominant concept of the common good, one might still argue, derives from majority volitions, which professionals should respect in a democracy. But no thoughtful person would confine inquiry to implementing what observers correctly or mistakenly perceive to be the majority's volitions, poorly probed as they are. On professional inquiry, among other sources, societies depend for innovation. On professional inquiry, again among other sources, societies also depend for advice on the appropriate relations between majority and minority volitions. Even those observers of society who find less impairment of popular probing than found in this study will still find enough impairment to prohibit their taking present majority opinion as a criterion sufficient for defining the common good.

Narrower Partisanship

In addition to social scientists (and other probers) who pursue (their partisan versions of) the common good are those who do not.

The most elementary thinking about the common good leads, inter alia, to an appreciation of the necessity for specialization in social roles. Societies assign special responsibilities, say, for fire protection, or highway construction, to some persons; and others take on valuable tasks of greatest variety: growing food, rearing children, or agitating for social change, among others. Most thoughtful persons would hope that the firefighters attach unusual value to fighting fires, so much so as largely to subordinate or disregard other values when on duty. Similarly they would hope that a parent's obligations to children override certain other obligations levied on parents. In short, specialized partisan roles are everywhere required.

Such partisan specialists would seem to be entitled to the help of social scientists. Indeed, it would seem impossible to find grounds to deny them. And if the efforts of dissenting groups to change society take their place in society's division of labor, social science ought equivalently to be available for their dissenting purposes. In short, social science designed to help each of various specialist partisans—and itself therefore partisan in that specific sense—would seem to be called for whether that specialized group is a nation, ethnic group, governmental organization, business enterprise, family, interest group, or collection of dissenting agitators. Even advocacy of legal status for an illegal group may be a purpose deserving social science assistance.[6]

The Myth of the "Decision Maker" in Policy-Oriented Inquiries

Finally, in accepting and choosing their partisan roles carefully, it would seem that policy oriented professional investigators should free themselves from the myth of the "decision maker." Instead of addressing their studies to one or more of a multiplicity of partisan participants in policy-making, they often fall into the habit of imagining and addressing a single, nonpartisan decision maker. Some of them know better, and say so, but postulate a single decision maker because they are not ready to face up to the complications of bringing professional inquiry to the aid of a multiplicity of partisan partici-

6. For a well-thought-through line of reform on obligations of policy analysts, see Harold Orlans, "Neutrality and Advocacy in Policy Research," *Policy Sciences* 6 (June 1975).

pants in social problem solving.[7] Some propose that policy analysis be imagined as offered, as one puts it, to "the Prince," taking an image of policy-making from Machiavelli rather than from the complexity of democratic politics.[8] Perhaps many policy analysts, influenced by conventional academic canons of research and scholarship, believe they have an obligation to achieve an overview of the problem they study as though from Olympus. The obligation requires that they insulate themselves from the fragmented disorder of politics and bring into their vision more than can be seen by any preoccupied participant. To whom, then, can they speak? Only to a hypothetical or mythical "decision maker," who shares the Olympian perspective of the social scientist. These policy analysts sometimes seem to believe that together, the professional prober and "decision maker" approximate Plato's philosopher-king.

But the mythical decision maker remains a partisan, no less so than the policy analyst. Mt. Olympus is never high enough, and the decision maker is plural. Social problem solving reaches outcomes through interaction among a multiplicity of problem solvers or decision makers, all partisan. There would seem to be more hope for good policy in the contestation of partisan participants, each aided by social science, than in policy-making by an inevitably partisan single decision maker falsely perceived as or postulated as above partisanship.

Scholarly Partisanship

Quite aside from professional investigators' partisanship on public issues, social goals, and other social values and volitions, it would appear that social scientists have to allow some room for scholarly partisanship with respect to competing empirical interpretations of social phenomena. Conclusive testing remaining beyond their capacities, for reasons indicated in chapter 10, the pursuit of testing ought often to give way to pursuit of illumination through an indefinite continuation of contestation among competing empirical hypotheses with no agreement on any one of them in sight. In such a competition of ideas, a strongly partisan—but short of corrupt—advocacy of each of the competitors will often advance understanding, a proposition that can claim a long endorsement in the history of

---

7. As in Edith Stokely and Richard Zeckhauser, *A Primer for Policy Analysis* (New York: Norton, 1978), p. 3.

8. As in Guy Benveniste, *The Politics of Expertise*, 2d ed. (San Francisco: Boyd and Fraser, 1977).

thought.[9] A frequent contrary prescription that social science be "adapted to the pursuit of consensus"[10] is half-blind and dangerous.

PROJECT CHOICE

If social scientists fully acknowledge, among other considerations, the variety of kinds of inquiries among which they must choose, the variable inconclusiveness of their work, the dependence of success on simplifying strategies, the necessity of choosing among rival possible beneficiaries, their role supplementary to lay probing, and their partisanship, they may see the task of choosing among alternative possible inquiries as formidable. Because capacity for professional inquiry constitutes a valuable resource for any society, the allocation of that capacity to any one of many possible studies or lines of work becomes, among other things, an economic choice. A society has a stake not simply in projects that accomplish some new insight or understanding but in projects that achieve as much insight or understanding as possible—in the American vernacular, "the biggest bang for the buck."

If one believes that almost any competently done research will illuminate something, almost any direction for research might appear justifiable. But if research so predictably illuminates, so valuable a resource ought to be allocated with care to its most illuminating uses. And if not always illuminating, then also its allocation calls for careful attention. The selection of directions or projects for professional social inquiry deserves, it would seem, status as a major topic for social science, a line of inquiry the neglect of which is indicated by the degree to which in at least some disciplines incumbent members have been turning away from their own history and track record. Compare also the sophistication and self-consciousness of statistical methods or of laboratory simulations as revealed in a large methodological literature of high quality on methodology with the near absence of a professional literature on what to probe.

9. For a capsule history: "The idea that knowledge can be advanced by a struggle of alternative views and that it depends on proliferation was first put forth by the Presocratics (this has been emphasized by Popper himself), and it was developed into a general philosophy by Mill (especially in *On Liberty*). The idea that a struggle of alternatives is decisive for science, too, was introduced by Mach (*Erkenntnis und Irrtum*), and Boltzmann (see his *Populaerwissenschaftliche Vorlesungen*), mainly under the impact of Darwinism" (Paul Feyerabend, "Consolations for The Specialist," in Imre Lakatos and Alan Musgrave, eds., *Criticism and the Growth of Knowledge* [Cambridge: Cambridge University Press, 1970], p. 211).

10. Charles Frankel, "The Autonomy of the Social Sciences," in Frankel, ed., *Controversies and Decisions* (New York: Russell Sage Foundation, 1976), p. 26.

The problem of choice appears more difficult than in the natural sciences. In some lines of natural science, a sequence of steps necessary to further development becomes evident, hence the races between leading scientists for the required discovery, the discovery of the structure of the DNA molecule being a case in point.[11] No such tight sequences occur in social science.

In addition, as is familiar, because social science knowledge cumulates less than natural science knowledge, social scientists can remove almost nothing from the list of possible social inquiries. In the natural sciences, the circulation of the blood is demonstrated once and for all, the atomic table gradually completed, and Boyle's Law established and understood to apply to gases today as well as gases in 500 B.C. or A.D. 3000. Scientists sometimes overturn some findings, and give many a new more precise formulation from time to time, relativity theory thus for some purposes replacing Newtonian. They dispose of many tasks. In social inquiry, by contrast, almost all inquiries remain at any time inconclusive and unfinished, and consequently continue to compete for attention. Again, unlike atoms and rocks, people learn, with the result that their patterns of behavior forever elude systematic stable description.[12]

In comparison with natural scientists, social scientists also face a more daunting task of choosing because they bring more, more varied, and more competing concerns to their inquiries.[13] Because atoms, rocks, and planets do not think, do not pursue purposes, and do not learn, the number of significant questions possible to ask about them falls far short of the number to ask about human beings in their complex social relations with each other. Social inquiry responds to a wide and changing multiplicity of concerns of both lay people and professionals; consequently, the latter are again well advised against "waiting for Newton."[14]

The difference in number of concerns shows up in differences in

11. Michael Polanyi, *The Logic of Liberty* (Chicago: University of Chicago Press, 1951), p. 51.

12. And of several prescriptive inferences to be drawn, one is that social scientists should temper their inevitably frustrated passion for conclusiveness with the pursuit of many alternative kinds of inquiry. For further questioning of the pursuit of conclusiveness, see Lindblom, "Alternatives to Validity," *Knowledge* 8 (March 1987), pp. 509–520.

13. Natural scientists differ on concepts and concerns only marginally, in sharp contrast to behavioral scientists; see Stephen Toulmin, *Human Understanding*, vol. 1, (Oxford: Oxford University Press, 1972), p. 382.

14. Philip E. Converse, "Generalization and Social Psychology of Other Worlds," in Donald W. Fiske and Richard A. Schweder, eds., *Methatheory in Social Science* (Chicago: University of Chicago Press, 1986), p. 48.

possibilities of agreeing on concepts. Natural scientists usually agree on conceptualization of phenomena. But consider such a concept in social science as democracy. To some social scientists, it refers to a feature of the social structure. To others, it refers only to a political or governmental structure. And for the latter, some will conceive of it as one in which citizens choose top leadership through elections in which almost all adults can vote, while others hold that elections do not sufficiently identify democracy, for it also requires open opportunities for all to enter into candidacy, as well as open discussion of issues. Others will say that even that does not suffice: democracy does not exist unless direct mass participation rises to greatly higher levels than in any existing ostensible democracy. Each concept is suited to a specific concern.

Naively, some critics of social science—a few social scientists, too—suggest that social scientists should simply agree on concepts and thus put an end to the diversity of inquiry that conceptual disagreement supports. But conceptual diversity does not compel a diversity of inquiries. A diversity of inquiries requires a diversity of conceptualizations. That social scientists disagree on concepts only further demonstrates the multiplicity of concerns that they bring to their work.

For another and obvious reason, defensible project choice becomes all the more difficult. Professional inquiry has the effect, whether an investigator so intends or not, of changing the world: of retarding change, influencing its direction, benefiting some groups, harming some groups, and reallocating their various powers over each other. As a consequence, to evaluate either an alleged historical accomplishment of professional inquiry or a contemporary research proposal requires substantial elements of a social or political philosophy. Indeed, to undertake such diagnosis of both lay and professional knowledge as the present study attempts requires constant reference to just such elements of a social philosophy.

How far contemporary practice in professional inquiry falls short of competence in project choice is repeatedly demonstrated in conventional project justifications. Anyone who has read large numbers of research proposals (including proposals for dissertations by doctoral candidates, who learn early that on project choice their supervisors do not expect them to develop professional competence) recognizes the litany. A proposal typically claims three justifications for a topic: it is important, neglected, and feasible. But there exist far more numerous important, neglected, and feasible topics than professional probers can ever pursue. Passing the three tests only clears the deck for serious attention to choice, including its grounding in the investigator's social philosophy.

Taking into account professional inattention to and frequent incompetence in choice of project or research direction, I suggest that, to any proposal for a research project that comes to a social scientist, whether it comes from foundation, colleague, willing sponsor, or self, the most frequently appropriate response is No! Not because a professional should refuse to study anything but because for any given proposal, the overwhelming odds are that its choice has not been well probed. A list of problems—even of the world's greatest social problems—does not constitute an agenda for research.

Of course, no society allows its social scientists complete freedom, if even imaginable, to choose their lines of inquiry.[15] The costs of inquiry give citizens and functionaries a stake in direction and method of inquiry. So also do tendencies toward self-indulgence of any professional group, as do other factors such as the impairments of social science itself. Although beyond the boundaries of this study, questions of how much and what kinds of autonomy social scientists ought themselves to have call for probing in which citizens and functionaries participate along with social scientists.[16]

SIMPLIFYING STRATEGIES

Given the inconclusiveness of social science, skillful inquiry would seem to require strategies. Although for formulating and testing empirical propositions, a familiar complete set of steps once constituted an idealized scientific method, for the investigation of the social world, no social scientist can complete the required steps. The investigator must find shortcuts, surrogates, and approximations. Nor can one complete tasks other than empirical verification. All the more does inquiry call for shortcuts, surrogates, and approximations. Strategies consist of methods sanctioned because conclusiveness is impossible and because the impossible steps to accomplish it do not

15. On external controls over science and social science, see Leonard A. Cole, *Politics and the Restraint of Science* (Totowa, N.J.: Rowman and Allanheld, 1983); Gerald Holton, *The Advancement of Science and Its Burdens* (New York: Cambridge University Press, 1986), chap. 11; and Harry Redner, *The Ends of Science* (Boulder, Colo.: Westview Press, 1987), esp. chap. 1.

16. The question of how much autonomy professionals ought to have is sometimes raised in the form of a question about the appropriate scope of pure as contrasted with applied science. The pure-applied issue does not at all do justice to the larger issues of autonomy vs. social control for professional inquiry, but some further comment on it will be found in the appendix to this chapter.

constitute sufficiently useful guidelines. Without strategies, professional inquiry is more a blueprint than a practice.

In policy-oriented professional inquiry, now-familiar strategies include trial and error, Simon's satisficing,[17] disjointed incrementalism,[18] Etzioni's mixed scanning,[19] and the like. Professionals employ them all, although embarrassment now often distorts their surreptitious use and even if at this late date some of the "theory" of policy analysis resists them. Among policy analysts are many closet strategists. They could do better out in the open.

Many strategies combine action with ratiocination. Trial and error, for example, alternately mixes thought and action, each action, as noted in chapter 13, intended to render subsequent analysis more accurate and better targeted. It would seem that ordinary conventions of science that make little place for thought-action interplay need to be revised.

In professional inquiry of the kind often called pure social science—that is, not concerned with decisions or policies—useful strategies, though no less necessary, have not been equivalently articulated. One such strategy is to substitute an explicit postulate for argument or evidence on points on which the investigator has insufficient time, energy, or competence to persist. Another is to assign an aspect of an intellectual problem to real or fictitious colleagues, especially those in other disciplines, as when an investigator declares that "this aspect I leave to the economists [or the sociologists, etc.]." Another simply terminates a line of inquiry, with or without explicit acknowledgment of incompleteness.

Many social scientists deplore such strategies because they cast doubt on any conclusions reached in the analysis. But inevitable flaws in any analysis of complex social phenomena cast the same doubt. Strategies permit an investigator to choose a flaw in research rather than unwittingly blunder into a worse one.

"POLICY ANALYSIS" AS A TASK FOR SOCIAL SCIENCE

In recent history many social scientists have chosen to encourage the growth of—or themselves engage in—the subprofession of "policy analysis." Having so chosen, they immediately face another

17. Charles E. Lindblom and David Braybrooke, *A Strategy of Decision* (New York: Free Press, 1963).

18. Herbert A. Simon, "A Behavioral Model of Rational Choice," *Quarterly Journal of Economics* 69 (February 1955).

19. Amitai Etzioni, *The Active Society* (New York: Free Press, 1968), chap. 12, esp. pp. 284f. Other strategies are identified in John F. Padgett, "Bounded Research in Budgetary Research," *American Political Science Review* 74 (June 1980), esp. p. 355n.

choice—how best to bring their inquiries to the aid of policy makers. Many choose to ignore the possible analytical contributions of functionaries of various kinds and propose to substitute their vision of scientific problem solving for a cooperative probing in which professional prober—social scientist or researcher—joins with functionary in probing. These policy analysts see their task as solving the decision maker's problem for him—at least formulating recommendations for him—as though he had no competence to join with or dispute the analyst. Much of the methodological literature on policy analysis calls on the analyst to give the client proposed solutions to the problem at hand.[20] One practitioner and student of policy analysis puts it: "A piece of policy analysis is completed when the choice has been given a structure, including alternative actions and relevant possible consequences, and when estimates of the consequences have been made by tracing the causal links between the alternative actions and the consequences."[21]

Perhaps many policy analysts imagine only two choices for a social scientist: academic, discipline-oriented professional inquiry not focused on policy, on one hand, and policy studies that culminate in recommendations, on the other. They overlook the variety of assistance that policy-oriented analysis can offer functionaries who pos-

20. Not only is it a common view of policy analysts, it may be the dominant view among them. It has been widely endorsed over a long period of time. Examples include Jacob B. Ukeles, "Policy Analysis: Myth or Reality?" *Public Administration Review* 37 (May–June 1977); G. Benveniste, *The Politics of Expertise*, 2d ed. (San Francisco: Boyd and Fraser, 1977), pp. 8, 92; Martin Greenberg, Matthew A. Crenson, and Brian L. Crissey, *Models in the Policy Process* (New York: Russell Sage Foundation, 1976), pp. 29f; and Walter Williams, *Social Policy Research and Analysis* (New York: American Elsevier, 1971), pp. 12, 58.

See also, with respect to systems analysis as a paradigm for policy analysis, E. S. Quade's introduction to Quade and W. I. Boucher, eds., *Systems Analysis and Policy Planning* (New York: Elsevier, 1968), p. 2; and Hugh Heclo, "Review Article: Policy Analysis," *British Journal of Political Science* 2 (January 1972). Heclo reviews rather than endorses the work of many policy analysts committed to reaching policy recommendations.

Some students of policy analysis, however, are of two minds. In some of their writing, they appear simply to take for granted that policy analysis is designed to culminate in recommendations (for example, Aaron Wildavsky, *Speaking Truth to Power* [Boston: Little, Brown, 1979], pp. 387–390); yet they have many things to say about it that do not square with such a conception (as in Wildavsky's rich characterization of the dimensions of policy analysis in his first chapter). For other examples, see Stuart S. Nagel, *Contemporary Public Policy Analysis* (University: University of Alabama Press, 1984) and Michael Carley, *Rational Techniques in Policy Analysis* (London: Heinemann, 1980).

21. Mark Moore, "Social Science and Policy Analysis," in Daniel Callahan and Bruce Jennings, eds., *Ethics, the Social Sciences, and Policy Analysis* (New York: Plenum Press, 1983), p. 274.

sesses their own distinctive competences, short of its appropriating (which is what it sometimes amounts to) the whole analysis of the problem and coming up with proposed solutions.[22]

A superior alternative instead asks analysts to choose specific analytical contributions to fit the needs and competences of the functionary.[23] On most of a client's decisions, such analysts would remain silent. On a small number of them they would selectively combine their competence in inquiry with that of their client. On only a small number of the client's problems would analysts proceed with the do-it-all or reach-a-recommendation model that some of the policy analysis textbooks advise. If, as observed in chapter 10, most of the information and analysis required by a functionary in contemplation of a decision in any case necessarily derives from lay probing, including his own, what the functionary specifically needs from a policy analyst depends on circumstances. One might call on an analyst for a missing body of fact; another might call on the analyst for a synthesis of considerations that run beyond the functionary's scope; still another might, for example, ask the analyst to critique pieces of the functionary's own analysis.

In recent years researchers have questioned government officials of many kinds at many levels about their needs for and uses of social science. Clearly, officials do not always want policy recommendations, not even from policy analysts. Often at the opposite extreme they do not want any study tailor-made to their problem at all but instead want information and opinion that social scientists can supply out of their cumulated intellectual capital. Not on a specific study do they sometimes wish to draw, but on the whole intellectual experience of the professional investigator.[24] Even that, along with such special studies as they may draw upon, they use not directly to reach a policy decision but to feed into an emerging understanding of or disposition toward a problem influenced by conversations with colleagues, by the media, and by other sources.[25] Other studies have shown that:

> Rarely does research supply an "answer" that policy actors employ to solve a policy problem. Rather, research provides a back-

22. On the distinctive competences of functionaries to assess, for example, broad impacts of policies, see Gordon S. Black, "A Theory of Professionalization in Politics," *American Political Science Review* 64 (September 1970).

23. A long list of actual examples in U.S. policy-making is in Robert A. Scott and Arnold R. Shore, *Why Sociology Does Not Apply* (New York: Elsevier, 1979), pp, 14–27.

24. David Donnison, "Research for Policy," *Minerva* 10 (October 1972), pp. 526ff.

25. On British experience on this point, see Donnison, "Research for Policy," pp. 526–528; Henry Mintzberg, "Beyond Implementation: An Analysis of the Resistance to

ground of data, empirical generalizations, and ideas that affect the way that policy-makers think about problems. It influences their conceptualization of the issues with which they deal;
it affects the facets of the issue that they consider inevitable
and unchangeable or amenable to policy action; it widens the
range of options that they consider; it challenges some taken-for-
granted assumptions about appropriate goals and appropriate
activities. Often, it helps them make sense of what they have
been doing after the fact, so that they come to understand
which courses of action they have followed and which courses
of action have gone by default. Sometimes it makes them aware
of the over-optimistic grandiosity of their objectives in light of
the meagerness of programme resources. At times it helps
them reconsider the entire strategies of action for achieving
wanted ends (e.g., investment in compensatory education as a
means for altering the distribution of income). In sum, policy
studies—and social science research more generally—have
made highly significant contributions by altering the terms of
policy discussions.[26]

Policy makers count on social science more for enlightenment than
for engineering.[27] Even when provided with a recommended solution,
functionaries may mine the study for information and ideas in the
analysis, rather than the recommendation itself.

A study of decision makers in public health found:

Fifty-seven percent of decision makers reported that they used
social science research and gave illustrations of use. But only
seven percent gave relatively concrete descriptions of the application of research to their work. The other 50 percent talked in
general terms about using research to gain general direction and
background, to keep up with the developments in the field, and
to reduce uncertainties about their policies and programs. They
discussed broad purposes, not specific decisions, specific aims,
or specific content of research studies.[28]

Policy Analysis," *Operational Research '78* (Amsterdam: North Holland, 1979); and on
U.S. experience, see Nathan Caplan, "Social Research and Public Policy at the National
Level," in D. P. B. Kallen et al., eds., *Social Science Research and Public Policy-Making*
(Windsor, England: NFER-Nelson, 1982), p. 40f. See also above, chap. 10.

26. Carol H. Weiss, "Policy Research in the Context of Diffuse Decision-Making,"
Journal of Higher Education 53 (November–December 1982), pp. 620f.

27. On enlightenment vs. engineering, see John Friedman, *Planning in the Public
Domain* (Princeton: Princeton University Press, 1987), pp. 172–178.

28. Carol Weiss with Michael J. Bucuvalas, *Social Science Research and Decision*

The respondents reported social science useful in providing:

- information on need for and distribution of need for mental health services;
- reports on "what works";
- keeping up with the field;
- providing a scientific patina for program and other documents;
- support in argument, legitimation of a position;
- clarification and information for taking a position;
- reduction of uncertainty on positions already taken;
- insights and concepts;
- intellectual perspectives.[29]

From other countries come similar reports.[30]

Adapting to Continuity

Selective contributions rather than a standard do-it-all analytic format respond better to the ever-changing, open-ended continuity of most social problem solving. The do-it-all model assumes a single problem to be defined, then solved, a task with a well-marked beginning and end. In fact problems, year after year, require reexamination and redefinition. A failure at one point redirects subsequent problem solving, often with a new goal or concept of the problem. So also may a partial success. Or new circumstances—change in budget resources, new directives from superiors, or a change in the political climate—change the constraints within which functionaries seek solutions.

The do-it-all format fails especially for such vast problems as averting nuclear war or stimulating economic growth—they go on indefinitely. Even more contained problems continue in endless reshaping: problems like improving the administrative efficiency of local government, reducing waste in the ministry of defense, or

Making (New York: Columbia University Press, 1980), p. 156.

29. Ibid., pp. 158–161.

30. On the U.K., for example, see Martin Bulmer, ed., *Social Policy Research* (London: Macmillan, 1978), esp. chapters by Bulmer, Donninson, and Sharpe. See also, on French, Italian, and West German experience with social science contributions to social problem solving, Peter Wagner, "Social Sciences and Political Projects," in Stuart Blume et al., eds., *The Social Direction of the Public Sciences* (Dordrecht: D. Reidel, 1987).

stimulating educational achievement in primary schools, down to even more contained problems, such as improving traffic flow in an urban center or deciding on suitable sites for public housing. A student of Swedish policy analysis writes: "As I see it, R&D must continue to be aimed at solving problems. What we have to eliminate is the belief—or rather, the expectation—that R&D will provide *the* solution to *the* problem."[31]

With respect to a group of contained problems such as arise in organizational decision making, hence simpler problems than the larger questions of politics, a study concludes that decision processes are

> characterized by novelty, complexity, and open-endedness, by the fact that the organization usually begins with little understanding of the decision situation it faces or the route to its solutions, and only a vague idea of what that solution might be and how it will be evaluated when it is developed. Only by groping through a recursive, discontinuous process involving many different steps and a host of dynamic factors over a considerable period of time is a final choice made. This is not the decision making under uncertainty of the textbook, where alternatives are given even if their consequences are not, but decision making under ambiguity, where almost nothing is given or easily determined.[32]

For the most contained of such problems, analysts sometimes can take a slice out of the chronological continuity of the problem and of sequences of solutions. But studies that do so often lose greatly in their appeal to decision makers, who know the problem has a past and a future not well captured in the study.

When, as typical for a social problem, functionary and analyst both acknowledge that no policy decision will wholly solve it and that it will remain, though in ever-changing form, on the agenda, they may see that selected recurrent aspects of the problem might provide a more suitable focus for inquiry than an analysis of the problem in its most current transitory form. Or they may decide on any one or a few of other various research needs: a history of the problem and of attempts at solution, an appraisal of just what went wrong with a

31. Inger Marklund, "The Impact of Policy-Oriented Educational R&D," in D. P. B. Kallen et al., eds., *Social Science Research and Public Policy-Making* (Windsor, England: NFER-Nelson, 1982), p. 170.

32. H. Mintzberg, D. Raisinghani, and A. Theoret, "The Structure of 'Unstructured' Decision Processes," *Administrative Science Quarterly* 21 (June 1976), pp. 250f; reps. in H. Mintzberg, "Beyond Implementation," in K. B. Haley, ed., *Operational Research '78* (Amsterdam: North Holland, 1979), pp. 106–162.

recent step toward its amelioration, a reconsideration of objectives, a new attempt at measuring progress, an analysis of a particular complexity common to many chronological stages of the problem, or a progress report on related problem solving in another government agency whose activities impinge on the problem solving at hand. Each such discriminating contribution will often provide more help to a decision maker than a conventional do-it-all analysis.

Sometimes problem solving becomes so drawn out, so complex, so much a product of multiple participation that no one identifies himself as making policy. As one study reports:

> The image of decision-making represented by President Kennedy and his group of advisers thrashing out the nation's response to the Cuban missile crisis is inappropriate to most of daily bureaucratic life. Much more commonly, each person takes some small step (writes a memo, answers an inquiry, edits the draft of a regulation) that has seemingly small consequences. But over a period of time, these many small steps foreclose alternative courses of action and limit the range of the possible. Almost imperceptibly a decision has been made, without anyone's awareness that he or she was deciding.[33]

A British prime minister says: "There is just a build-up of big and small events, of big and small factors, and they may not be brought to your notice until the issue has already been decided; and, when you eventually have to decide, it may be in response to the smallest of them all."[34] Under these circumstances, again the conventional do-it-all model of policy analysis does not fit.[35]

THE SOCIAL SCIENCE CONTRIBUTION
TO REDUCING IMPAIRMENT

Social science gives, according to chapter 11, a great deal less attention to the kind of information and analysis that lay people need in their probing than to the needs of functionaries. It also attends less

33. Carol H. Weiss, "Knowledge Creep and Decision Accretion," *Knowledge* 1 (March 1980), p. 401.

34. Henry Fairlie, "Johnson and the Intellectuals," *Commentary* 40 (October 1965), pp. 52f.

35. Although I here expressed criticisms of the do-it-all model of policy analysis, I have not attempted a comprehensive critique of it, nor of its formal variants: cost-benefit analysis, systems analysis, and their several cousins. In the literature, all have been both comprehensively and selectively criticized for many severe shortcomings. Yet they persist—in part because in the right hands, they are of great value. Among

to standing volitions than to action volitions, on that count leaving both citizens and functionaries with slighted help on their most impaired volitions. And it has not taken the study of the phenomenon of impairment very far. Finally, it is itself severely impaired. These propositions about social science carry not conclusive but highly suggestive prescriptive implications, much as the statement "This building is infested with termites!" carries a powerful prescriptive implication.

Again, I refrain from institutional prescriptions, largely because I do not know what institutional reforms deserve advocacy. For the most part, what social scientists do in the future to assist lay probing and reduce impairment they will choose to do as a result of the persuasions (of which this study might be one) and other pressures of their professional lives. As with respect to the beneficiaries they choose and the kinds of partisanship they practice, changes in their habits of inattention to the needs of the ordinary citizen will come about largely because they have probed their practices and have come to be convinced of the merits of change. As for trying to legislate or otherwise impose changes on them in order to step up their attention to the needs of ordinary citizens coping with their impairments, dis-

---

other criticisms: they give undue weight to variables that can be quantified and undervalue others. They treat noncomparables as comparable. In their preoccupation with formally organizing knowledge, they do not sufficiently acknowledge information inadequacy and consequently employ dubious tactics such as treating guesses as facts. They are biased toward the status quo. They do not take account of the sequential, ever-changing open-endedness of policy-making. They pretend to a neutrality that they do not in fact achieve. They overplay analysis of means and underplay analysis of ends. They are often sufficiently esoteric to confuse and intimidate clients. Their appetite for numbers leads them to treat dubious estimates as fact. They assign to the analyst more tasks than he can competently accomplish. They are antidemocratic. They oversimplify. They do not attend to the structure of differentiated ends, values, costs, and benefits, thus falsely homogenizing them. They mistakenly reduce problems of policy choice to problems in resource allocation. They neglect values in the problem-solving process itself. They evade aspects of problems of such complexity as will not fit into their schema. They rest on hidden assumptions critical to their proposed solutions.

For examples of critiques, see Laurence Tribe, "Policy Science: Analysis or Ideology," *Philosophy of Public Affairs* 2 (Fall 1972); Henry Mintzberg, "Beyond Implementation," in Haley, *Operational Research '78*; Peter Self, *Administrative Theories and Politics* (London: Allen & Unwin, 1972), chap. 1; Giandomenico Majone, "The Received View on Policy Science," in Franz-Xavier Kaufmann et al., eds., *Guidance, Control, and Evaluation in the Public Sector* (Berlin: Walter de Gruyter, 1986).

Advocates of these formal techniques do not refuse to acknowledge shortcomings. Their position is that the techniques are sufficiently powerful to warrant their use, despite their shortcomings, which they believe can be corrected for in supplementary less formal analysis attached to the formal methods. For such advocacy, see Edith Stokely and Richard Zeckhauser, *A Primer for Policy Analysis* (New York: Norton, 1978).

cussion—of whether doing so would be a good idea, of what particular impositions, if any, warrant study, and of how to go about them—remains infrequent and thin, except for some useful debate on the abstract issue of more or less autonomy for social scientists. For that reason, no one can claim to have thought through the question of which institutional reforms are appropriate for turning social science in the direction of helping to reduce impairment. Doing so requires an interchange among minds. I would emphasize again that at this junction nothing would seem to be more important for social science than its own probing of lay impairment, its own possible contributions to reducing it, its own professional impairment, and methods for reducing it. Interested ordinary people, experts, and functionaries face the same agenda. Institutional reforms will have to wait until a better understanding brings institutional design within the competence of would-be designers.

One can characterize the situation of ordinary people in a way suggestive for how social science might help them. Like Plato's dwellers in a cave, they are imprisoned. If Plato's cave dweller could not see clearly because imprisoned, they are imprisoned because they cannot see clearly. As a consequence of their impairments of belief, themselves constraining, they accept other constraints, that is, constraints other than on their minds. Both sets of constraints—on what they think and on what they do—imprison them. Some constraints, like the requirements of job, are external. Others have become internal: conscientious obedience to authority, for example.

These people may or may not realize that they live in a prison, may rarely have turned an inquiring eye on their constraints, may never as a consequence have tried to distinguish between just and unjust constraints, and may never have speculated on whether life exists outside the prison or outside their cell or wing, thus offering some hope of less narrower confines. They need help in such probes. They also need help for the time being in making the best of the present situation: avoiding violence at the hands of the other inmates, exploiting such opportunities for freedom as space allows, maintaining some self-discipline as an antidote to the ever present threat of demoralization.

Social scientists and researchers are already helpful on these immediate needs. They ordinarily do not bother to tell the inmates, however, much about the structure of the prison and how their spaces relate to the rest of it. For they have themselves grown up in the same prison. They know its dimensions and attributes better than the ordinary inmates. But some of them do not realize that the structure is a prison, and none knows whether their spaces are a small or large part of the whole prison. So they concentrate on studying the regularities of prison life, venturing too into practical problem solving by making contributions to improved fire protection, policing, comforts of the individual cells, and more humane prison administration. Formed into self-protective groups, they also sometimes build imprisoning cells within the prison.

If the analogy is too dark, change it: regard life as a game. Social science helps in various ways: assists the game officials, and studies the rules of the game, how it might be improved, and how to take care of game injuries. Valuable as this help is, the players need more. They need to know how the game came to be structured as they find it, how they were induced to take for granted that they should play, whether any other game exists, and how they might find and learn to play another game. This is what social science and research still might do for them.

APPENDIX: BASIC? APPLIED?

There must be some reason for the frequency and passion with which scholars return to the question of the difference between basic and applied research.[36] Perhaps their hope is to find grounds for establishing two sets of canons or methodological prescriptions for research: one, the more demanding, for basic research; the other, more forgiving, for the exigencies of applied research or policy analysis. In any case, the distinction, in many of its familiar forms, is over-simple and is not very helpful to our search for guidelines either for sound social science in general or for policy-oriented analysis.

Does the distinction tell us that motivations differ for two kinds of research? Basic research "results from intellectual curiosity, aims

36. On the basic-applied distinction, some endorsing and some rejecting it, see for a sample: Solly Zuckerman, *Scientists and War* (New York: Harper and Row, 1966), pp. 145f; Martin Bulmer, "Social Science Research and Policy-Making in Britain," in Bulmer, ed., *Social Policy Research* (London: Macmillan, 1978), pp. 7–10; James S. Coleman, *Policy Research in the Social Sciences* (Morristown, N.J.: General Learning Press, 1972); David Donnison, "Research for Policy," in Bulmer, *Social Policy Research*, pp. 46–54; Paul F. Lazarsfeld and J. Reitz, *An Introduction to Applied Sociology* (New York: Elsevier, 1975), p. 10; Jerome R. Ravetz, *Scientific Knowledge and Its Social Problems* (Oxford: Oxford University Press, 1971), part IV; and Morris Janowitz, *Political Conflict* (Chicago: Quadrangle Books, 1970).

See also, on recent U.S. history of applied research for government, Richard P. Nathan, *Social Science in Government* (New York: Basic Books, 1988).

at probing the unknown, and has no specific applicational objectives"?[37] According to Marx, "The philosophers have only interpreted the world in different ways; the point, however, is to change it." If revolution is an "applicational objective," then Marx was not engaged in basic research. But if he was not, what social scientist has ever been? An easier example to handle is Keynes, whose "general theory" was as basic as economics ever is, according to many standards. He was motivated, among other motivations, however, by an intention to provide guidance for macroeconomic policy, specifically, government spending and monetary management, to bring the depression of the 1930s to an end.

Professional inquiry will differ significantly from case to case in ways that might possibly call up such words as *basic* and *applied*, but the differences are in many dimensions that can better be itemized than aggregated. Some social scientists will, for example, probe a specific policy problem—say, educational reform—of a particular government at a particular time, while others will probe elements common to educational problems of many times and places. In doing so, they may employ the same analytical techniques, meet the same standards of logic and accuracy of observation. Neither may bring his analysis to a head in a recommendation for policy, preferring instead to illuminate some specific aspect of the problem. On the other, hand both may try to bring their probes to a head in a policy recommendation. In many respects, they do not differ on a basic-applied continuum.

Or one may wish to solve problems that he or his discipline sets, while another chooses to work on problems assigned by a client. But the prober's own choice of problem may be a social or policy problem comparable to a client's choice. He may choose to work on problems, say, of law enforcement or tax reform in ways not distinguishable from those of a colleague with a client. How much a society permits professional probers to set their own problems, and how much it institutionalizes methods for inducing them to work on problems set by decision makers, is an important question, but it is not a choice between two kinds of research, one basic, one applied.

"Applied" is in any case almost always a misnomer. It seems now to be generally agreed that social scientists do not literally apply a stock of basic knowledge to social problems; instead they produce new knowledge, much as engineers long did their probing largely

37. OECD, *Fundamental Research and the Politics of Governments* (1966), p. 15.

independently of physical science.[38] So-called applied social scientists and basic social scientists alike draw on and apply an enormous stock of lay knowledge, we have seen. But basic professional inquiry has not provided much of a stock for applied social science.[39]

We can draw a useful distinction between professional inquiry that is stimulated by academic disciplinary traditions and that which is stimulated by influences outside the academy and discipline.[40] But again that says little about the character of the inquiry. Nor even in the natural sciences does it make the one kind of inquiry more useful, fundamental, less vulnerable to obsolescence, or fruitful than the other, as evidenced in the fundamental accomplishments of Semmelweiss, Pasteur, Lister, and Koch, all credited as basic scientists who nevertheless tackled problems that came to them from outside the scholarly community: anthrax, fermentation, cowpox, surgical and delivery-room mortality.[41]

As for policy analysis, the do-it-all model creates a fundamental distinction between two kinds of research, often called basic and applied: the one searching for empirical generalization, the other for policy recommendations; and the former relatively free from the severe time pressures that constrain the latter. But the selective contribution model of policy analysis evaporates even that distinction. Guided by that model, the policy analyst chooses among possible contributions he might make. He may decide to make no recommendation, to stay with the tasks of reaching conclusions instead. Or he may devote his energies to conceptualization or cognitive organization or to reporting or trend delineation. In so doing he may choose to fashion a contribution to policy choice that he assumes can be made effective only indirectly and with a long time lag. In his "general the-

38. Hendrik W. Bode, "Reflections on the Relation between Science and Technology," in *Basic Research and National Goals*, a report to the Committee on Science and Astronautics of the U.S. House of Representatives by the National Academy of Sciences (Washington: National Academy of Sciences, 1965), pp. 46f; and Thomas S. Kuhn, "The Relations between History and History of Science," in Paul Rabinow and William M. Sullivan, eds., *Interpretive Social Science: A Reader* (Berkeley: University of California Press, 1979), pp. 283–285.

39. Alvin W. Gouldner, "Explorations in Applied Social Science," in Gouldner and S. M. Miller, *Applied Sociology: Opportunities and Problems* (New York: Free Press, 1965), pp. 6f.

40. Philip M. Hauser, "Social Science and Social Engineering," in Elizabeth R. Crawford and Albert D. Biderman, eds., *Social Scientists and International Affairs* (New York: Wiley, 1969), p. 247.

41. Norman Storer, "Basic vs. Applied Research," *Indian Sociological Bulletin* 2 (October 1964), pp. 39ff.; and Joseph Ben-David, "Roles and Innovation in Medicine," *American Journal of Sociology* 61 (May 1960), p. 557.

ory" Keynes made a contribution to policy-making that in the U.S. did not become fully effective for a whole generation. The variety of probes open to a policy analyst in the selective-contribution model is as broad as the variety open to any professional social prober. Hence the basic-applied distinction tends to evaporate; and there seems no reason to fashion two sets of methodological prescriptions.

For all social scientists who want their work to be useful, all professional inquiry is in a fundamental sense applied, yet not necessarily any less basic for that. They will differ greatly in how they intend their probing to become useful—whether on this year's or this century's problem; whether on a French problem or a world problem; whether directly or indirectly; whether soon or later; and whether through reporting, conceptualization, or empirical verification; and so on. Some will achieve broader or more lasting contributions to knowledge than others; but there is no predictable simple relation between the choices they make and their breadth and durability of their contribution. Even a modest study limited in time and place may achieve a broad and lasting contribution denied to a more ambitious explicit venture in broad and stable generalization. The alternatives among which the prober chooses are significantly different, hence worth his study; but they do not reduce to his being basic or applied.

The situation of the policy analysts, applied social scientists, and those who intend pure social science are much alike. What is required of all is, again, that, realizing the inadequacy of any one standard kind of probing, they practice a wide variety of inquiries to achieve some understanding of a social world that always lies beyond their capacity to achieve a high degree of intellectual mastery. They must practice ingeniousness, inventiveness, variety, and strategy. In appreciation of the virtues of indirection, they must only sometimes frontally attack their big problems, and often instead wear them down with modest attacks of greatly limited domain. They must build on the most elementary and solid knowledge of the social world, which is that provided by lay probing, must therefore understand that its refinement for use in specific time and place may accomplish a greater gain in lasting understanding than more conventionally ambitious efforts at explicit broad generalization. Unlike natural scientists, they must acknowledge that the most basically useful understanding they can achieve is an understanding of impermanent—even if only slowly changing—behavior, processes, and institutions, and that an understanding of the eternal elements of an ever-learning and

-changing social world would leave them incompetent to understand the temporary world about them, whose transitory features are of the greatest significance for them. Under these circumstances, almost nothing they do constitutes basic research as it might be defined for physics, nor is anything they do little more than the application of earlier cumulated basic knowledge.

CHAPTER 16

Reducing Impairment

We come finally to the question of what; if any-
thing, aside from such contributions as social science may or may not
directly contribute, to do about impairment. Many millions of people,
including parents and teachers, engage in impairing others, even deliberately, and presumably do not want to desist. Some others, including demagogues and some practitioners of sales promotion and
"public relations," have made an occupation out of impairing. Perhaps
influences on the side of impairment are too strong to resist. Even
aside from the new assaults on reason in an age of television, one
might hold that only a fool would take seriously the possibility of
reducing impairment.

Ideal inquiry requires a society in certain respects ideal.[1] Can a
society move toward such an ideal? Only by probing its way, which it
cannot do well unless the society already is ideal. One may either
throw up one's hands at the impossibility of betterment under those
circumstances or accept the complexities of mutual interaction

1. V. Gordon Childe: "A precondition for the perfection of knowledge . . . is the
realization of the ideal society." Quoted in Larry Spence, *The Politics of Social Knowledge* (University Park: Pennsylvania State University Press, 1978), p. 27.

between improvements in inquiry and improvements in social structure.

The analysis of this study establishes some strong—never conclusive, however—grounds for forming a volition for reducing impairment. Insofar as one can articulate considerations bearing on so complex a choice, the case for trying to reduce impairments comes down to a few key propositions: Not biology but social interactions cause impairments, some intended, some not. If so, people can reduce them. In some dimensions, they have done so. Possibly, they will continue to do so in the future.

A large part of the task of reducing impairment consists of strengthening favorable factors at work within complex processes of unplanned social change: for example, reduction of gender and ethnic inequalities or a reconsideration, repeatedly on public agendas, of educational objectives in the schools. One exploits such opportunities as arise. An outright assault on impairment, if even imaginable, appeals to almost no one and might provoke more resistance than support. Nor can anyone say how a society could carry it off even if the impulse were widely shared. Reduction of impairment will, if possible at all, presumably at best proceed almost imperceptibly.

Again, however, the analysis of the foregoing chapters has not pointed to any need for special exhortation, incentives, or other special stimuli to improve inquiry. It does not envision the conversion of a natural human being into an unnatural prober. A productive line of improvement would appear to call for dampening or removing socially caused positive disincentives and other barriers to inquiry. Instead of cajoling citizens and functionaries into such unlikely efforts as spending an evening or two each week in group discussion of social problems, the reduction of impairment calls for such remedies as a less skewed competition of ideas, less governmental concealment of information, changes in political campaign practices, and less anxious political indoctrination of children in the schools. Although they are difficult enough, they ask for no transformation of human character.

Recoiling from earlier naive ideas that social problems can be solved by education, moral reform, or exhortation, perhaps most of us in our time, when confronted with a social problem, rush in the direction of institutional reforms. But not even the most liberated of societies have probed impairment well enough and long enough to have clarified and created required possible institutional reforms, beyond agreeing on or at least giving lip service to persisting in such policies as raising educational levels, maintaining a free press, protecting civil liberties, and curbing to some small degree the influence of money in politics. All admirable, they reduce impairment to significantly lower levels than prevail under authoritarian regimes, yet leave impairment as severe as here described. If these societies are as severely impaired as here described, they lack competence at present to devise institutional reforms (and so do I). In addition, volitions as they now stand constitute a state of affairs for which institutional solutions are impossible. If anyone could here and now present an array of feasible institutional reforms that would significantly reduce impairment, that is to say, reforms defensible by informed and sustained argument and feasible at least in commanding some endorsement from large groups not dismissed as eccentric, that would in itself be evidence that societies are less impaired than alleged in this study. Turn the proposition around. If the argument on impairment holds, neither expert nor popular discussion has yet achieved the shift of volition required to make design of significant feasible institutional reforms possible.

One might gain some perspective on the possibilities and the present predicament of impairment by considering that no society or subgroup within it ever designed a state or government to make it an effective instrument of social problem solving. Take the American case, in which a constitutional convention and written constitution left a record of intentions. Designed at a time in which "social problem solving" was not even in currency as a concept, the designers of the Constitution entertained no such idea as creating an institutional capacity for general problem solving. They declared their intention to create a government capable of protecting the "general welfare", but protected largely by curbs on state capacity to interfere with private efforts to pursue it. Nor did they intend to create an instrument so that the adult population as a whole could compel agents to do its bidding. Wary of the concept and word "democracy," they instead designed a system to curb popular control over the state and keep control of it disproportionately in the hands of political and economic elites. Since in decades thereafter elites thought it advisable to present their designed constitutional order as a great accomplishment of democracy rather than as a superbly designed halfway house to democracy, American thought has ever since been unable to think clearly about the constitutional order. Various influences arose to displace, through constitutional amendment or judicial interpretation, some of the earlier designed constraints on popular participation; but to this day American thought remains deeply impaired in its capacity to consider how to structure the state for such purposes as solving social problems, facilitating popular inquiry, and reducing impairment.

No general formula for reducing impairment will do. Just as one does not diagnose the problem by saying "capitalism," so one does not identify its solutions by saying "socialism." Nor will any other ism solve it. Early in this study, inquiry or probing was identified as error-prone, self-corrective, ingenious, and open-ended, beginning with the here and now rather than with a priori abstractions from which volitions are deduced. That characterizes the search for ways to reduce impairment, a great and difficult probe. I propose to examine two issues bearing on the reduction of impairment: one on the alleged dangers of reducing impairment, the second on the competition of ideas.

IS A REDUCTION OF IMPAIRMENT DANGEROUS?

Because many people believe that convergences in attitude and belief on fundamentals of social organization maintain both social stability and democracy, a reduction of those impairing influences that provide convergence in thought and attitude, however desirable hypothetically for the use of intelligence in problem solving, may endanger society.[2] Perhaps the use of information and analysis in both lay probing and professional inquiry for social problem solving in the democracies cannot break through a low ceiling. Democratic societies either do not think, or they think their way to disintegration. If so, the democracies already approximate an ideal.

The question here is not whether to aspire to turn everyone into a calculator, philosopher, or a Habermasian truth seeker; the evils of that excess of ratiocination are easy to imagine. The question is whether a significant reduction of socially produced obstructions to probing, not likely to go very far toward the elimination of impairment, would, if achievable, endanger societies. Everything said about impairment demonstrates the difficulty of its reduction; hence, one hardly needs to speculate on a society largely free of it.

2. The thesis can be found in such diverse sources as Talcott Parsons, *Sociological Theory and Modern Society* (New York: Free Press, 1967); Alexis de Tocqueville, *Democracy in America*, trans. Henry Reeve (New York: Colonial Press, 1900), vol. 1, p. 398; and Theodore Lidz and Stephen Fleck, "Schizophrenia, Human Integration, and the Role of the Family," in Don D. Jackson, ed., *The Etiology of Schizophrenia* (New York: Basic Books, 1960), p. 329.

The argument specifically on political democracy can be sampled in Samuel H. Beer, "In Search of a New Public Philosophy," in A. King, ed., *The New American Political System* (Washington, D.C.: American Enterprise Institute, 1978), p. 44; Samuel Huntington, "The Democratic Distemper," *The Public Interest* 41 (Fall 1975), p. 37; Bernard Berelson, Paul F. Lazarsfeld, and William N. McPhee, *Voting* (Chicago: University of Chicago Press, 1954), chap. 14; and Pendleton Herring, *The Politics of Democracy* (New York: Rinehart, 1940), pp. 32ff.

Many social scientists reject the thesis that convergences are necessary to social order or democracy. An anthropologist rejects as a "hoary" assumption the connection between common motives and social stability.[3] A political scientist doubts that democracy requires the "conflict-mitigating influence of homogeneity, consensus."[4] Or social scientists qualify the allegations.[5] "Finally, it is important to remember that the idea of civil association does not require a sense of community or social solidarity. The only shared value necessary to a rudimentary civility is an inner sense of obligation to the law. No other shared experiences are needed, not a common tongue, religion, mores, customs, national purpose or character."[6] A political scientist claims that not everyone but only by "predominant portion of the politically active need share a "consensus on policy,"[7] a view probably now widely shared among political scientists.[8]

No studies of such agreement have been able—and almost none have tried—to demonstrate rather than simply assume the necessity of such agreements for social stability or political democracy.[9] Examples of historical or current disagreements—Northern Ireland, for example—that destabilize society or make democracy impossible come quickly to mind. But that some disagreements in some circum-

3. Anthony F. C. Wallace, *Culture and Personality* (New York: Random House, 1961), p. 29.

4. Eric A. Nordlinger, *Conflict Regulation in Divided Societies* (Cambridge: Harvard Center for International Affairs, 1972), p. 2.

5. An interesting note on the disputed opinions on the issue of both Marx and Durkheim: "In Marx's theory of capitalism, the working class is subordinated because it is excluded from control of the means of production and it is held in subordination because the sheer exigencies of survival in early capitalism make effective protest difficult, if not impossible. In Durkheim's theory, while constraint is recognised, much greater emphasis is given to the co-operative aspects of the social division of labour. There is a very important difference of perspective here, but what is equally important is that neither theory actually *requires* some notion of the normative incorporation of the working class in capitalism" (Nicholas Abercrombie, Stephen Hill, and Bryan S. Turner, *The Dominant Ideology Thesis* [London: Allen & Unwin, 1980], p. 56).

6. Josiah Lee Auspitz, "Individuality of Civility: The Philosophical Imagination of Michael Oakeshott," (MS., November 1975), p. 40. Auspitz here summarizes the arguments of Michael Oakeshott, "On the Civil Condition," in his *On Human Conduct*, (Oxford: Clarendon Press, 1975), see esp. pp. 112–130, 182–184.

7. R. A. Dahl, *Preface to Democratic Theory* (Chicago: University of Chicago Press, 1956), p. 132.

8. For a summary of studies of popular and functionaries' consensus and alienation, see Robert R. Alford and Roger Friedland, *Powers of Theory* (Cambridge: Cambridge University Press, 1985), chap. 3.

9. For documentation of that shortcoming of the research, see Brian Barry, *Sociologists, Economists, and Democracy* (Chicago: University of Chicago Press, 1978), chap. 3.

stances destabilize does not constitute evidence of need for any specific degree or pattern of convergence. One can draw on both empirical evidence and the literature of conflict to argue that social stability and democracy can survive deep social conflict.

Social order—that is, peaceful systematic interchange among people—and political institutions like democracy persist because people behave in certain ways and not in others. People behave as they do because the interchanges of social life, beginning in infancy, amend, curb, direct, or somehow shape the imprinted biological drives or behavioral dispositions that move them. These social influences divide into two categories: those that inculcate in each person a set of concepts, values or norms that through internalization affect behavior, and those external factors that influence or control in other ways: for example, by threatening a penalty, offering benefits, exercising authority, offering or withholding information pertinent to behavior, or offering or withholding resources that would make certain courses of action possible or impossible.[10]

If one asks, then, why people outvoted in a democratic election do not mount an insurrection but instead accept their defeat without disturbance to social stability or the continuation of democracy, one finds an answer in the many external controls exercised over them rather than only in those internalized controls represented by their convergences in thought. Whatever their internalized norms, many people will not turn in defeat to insurrection, sabotage, terrorism, or street violence because they fear, among many external influences that bear on them, the law, the possibility of their own deaths in resulting violence, or their social isolation from their friends.[11] There is probably, therefore, no irreducible minimal requirement for convergence; and for any lack of it appropriate external controls may compensate even in a democracy.[12] In many circumstances not con-

10. For a pertinent short survey of methods of social control, see Morris Janowitz, *The Last Half-Century* (Chicago: University of Chicago Press, 1978), chap. 2. See also Neil J. Smelser, "From Structure to Order," in James F. Short, Jr., ed., *The Social Fabric* (Beverly Hills, Calif.: Sage, 1986), csp. p. 37.

11. For well-argued skepticism on the influence of norms and values, with particular attention to the contrary views of Talcott Parsons, see Brian Barry, *Sociologists, Economists, and Democracy* (Chicago: University of Chicago Press, 1978), chap. 4.

12. For summaries of the debate, see Robert R. Alford and Roger Friedland, *Powers of Theory* (Cambridge: Cambridge University Press, 1985), chap. 3; Claus Mueller, *The Politics of Communication* (New York: Oxford University Press, 1973), chap. 4; James D. Wright, *The Dissent of the Governed* (New York: Academic Press, 1976), pp. 63ff and final chapter; and P. H. Partridge, *Consent and Consensus* (New York: Praeger, 1971).

vergence but leaders or functionaries capable of managing conflict though external controls achieve the required stability.[13]

Do people not need axioms or rules of thumb to guide behavior? Whitehead calls routine the "god of every social system. . . . Unless society is permeated, through and through, with routine, civilization vanishes."[14] Notice that he does not make a claim for agreed routines, only that each person follows some routine, which may be idiosyncratic.

The allegation of tight connection between convergence and stability often rests on an elementary error. Whether a disagreement provokes distabilizing or undemocratic behavior depends on whether people hold divergent opinions intolerantly or not. Some people can disagree on the existence of God, the desirability of democracy, or whether in military service in war they should go on a life-threatening patrol, yet engage in no conduct threatening to stability or democracy when they see decisions going against them. Others will sabotage rather than follow the rules of the game: witness President Nixon's Watergate tactics to insure his reelection, or the history of American white deprivation of black civil liberties. The level of tolerance varies in societies, as the history of the use of religious tolerance in the West makes obvious. Several American studies show significant declines of intolerance toward political radicals among some groups in as short a period of time as fifteen years.[15] Studies have also shown greater tolerance among the better educated and the more politically active,[16] suggesting that if probing increases disagreement, it softens intransigence. Intransigence declines among persons who do not take their volitions from faith but from inquiry, as illustrated by the high levels of intolerance among religious people.[17] A survey of forty years of attitude studies in the West suggests that "the more orthodox followers of [the great] religions today are more compulsive and conformist than they are compassionate."[18]

A frequent fallacy argues a connection between convergence and

13. As argued in Eric Nordlinger, *Conflict Regulation in Divided Societies* (Cambridge: Harvard University Center for International Affairs, 1972).

14. Alfred North Whitehead, *Adventures of Ideas* (New York: Macmillan, 1933), pp. 113f.

15. James Piereson, John L Sullivan, and George Marcus, "Political Tolerance: An Overview and Some New Findings," in John C. Pierce and John L. Sullivan, eds., *The Electorate Reconsidered* (Beverly Hills, Calif.: Sage, 1980), pp. 164–168.

16. Ibid., pp. 160–164; Herbert McClosky and John Zaller, *The American Ethos* (Cambridge: Harvard University Press, 1984), pp. 33–35, 49, 98f.

17. Pierce and Sullivan, *The Electorate Reconsidered*, pp. 171–174.

18. William Eckhardt, "Religious Beliefs and Practices in Relation to Peace and Justice," *Social Compass* 21, no. 4 (1974), p. 466.

stability or democracy without regard to the further expectations that attend defeat on disputed issues. Pluralist thought, however, has often pointed out that a pluralist diversity in lines of conflict over policy promises stability, for a citizen's defeat on one issue does not bode defeat on all issues. Ever-shifting alliances and voting patterns, both in the electorate and in legislatures, hold out to citizens expectations of future victories even on the issue on which they for the moment suffer defeat. The open-endedness of policy-making in a pluralist democracy becomes a major source of democratic viability.[19] The significance of these highly plausible and widely accepted propositions for the convergence argument seems often to have been missed.

One final argument by itself strikes a strong blow at the belief that a general decline in convergences of thought and attitude endangers social stability and democracy. If stability and democracy require convergences at all, those they require consist, by the near unanimous testimony of social scientists who have troubled themselves over the question, of a few selected beliefs and attitudes, as, for example, on some degree of respect for the law or on some critical rules of political behavior. The case for some structure of convergence has never successfully been expanded into a general case for likemindedness or convergence on the many fundamental issues on which earlier chapters found convergence.[20]

Democratic Overload?

One particular formulation of the argument that dissensus threatens order and democracy alleges a "democratic overload."[21] People demand more than government can provide because various groups—employees, blacks, women, the elderly, the poor—ask for larger shares in the benefits of social life, including benefits of power, income, wealth, and status, that encroach on the benefits long awarded to more favored groups in society. Depending on one's sympathies, one can say that divisiveness arises either because the new groups ask too much or because the advantaged yield too little.

19. For a summary statement, see Nicholas R. Miller, "Pluralism and Social Choice," *American Political Science Review* 77 (September 1983), pp. 736f.

20. See above, notes 11 and 12.

21. For a summary (but not an endorsement) of overload allegations, see Colin Crouch, "The State, Capital, and Liberal Democracy," in Crouch, ed., *State and Society in Contemporary Capitalism* (New York: St. Martin's, 1979). See also Clarence N. Stone, "Elite Distemper versus the Promise of Democracy," in G. William Domhoff and Thomas R. Dye, eds., *Power Elites and Organizations* (Newbury Park, Calif.: Sage, 1987).

Advantaged sectors of society have often threatened repression to dampen or resist new demands, and they continue in the present era to make good those threats as, for example, through military coups that displace embryonic democratic regimes in Latin America. Both the challenge against old inequalities and the counterstruggle to protect them appear to be endless and of an intensity that, although they have not brought any stable democracy to dissolution, have blocked the establishment of stable democracy in some societies.

Looking back on the historical struggle, what some observers fear as a "democratic distemper,"[22] others see as "the idea of citizenship being taken more seriously than before."[23] Many observers cannot bring themselves to regret that the democratic movement persists despite the constant threat of instability or of its actual destruction from time to time in some countries. They do not see the price paid for such democracy as has been achieved as too high, nor the risks of divisiveness or of a compelled backward step too great to bear. Whether now and in the future it makes sense to accept the risks calls for a careful probe. The choice is less risky in, say, the U.K. or the U.S., with their long records of elite concession in face of challenge; more risky, say, in France, more risky again by an order of magnitude in, say, Spain; and a deeply perplexing problem for, say, millions of impoverished Brazilians, whom a large risk of repression can hardly deprive of what they in any case go without.

Behind some though not all of the allegations of overload lurks a quite different proposition: that without such convergence as now exists, the present politico-economic order cannot survive. Not an allegation about instability at all—not about violence or a disorderly society, nor about democracy—it alleges that new directions of social change would follow from a decline in convergence on politico-economic fundamentals.

The allegation is probably correct. For the reduction of impairment does not promise volitions that will square in the long run with any existing politico-economic order. Presumably, the world has not yet reached the end or the apex of its ventures in bringing into operation new forms of social organization, possibly some as innovative as the democratic nation-state in its day of entry into history.

22. Michael Crozier, Samuel P. Huntington, and Joji Watanuki, *The Crisis of Democracy* (New York: New York University Press, 1975), p. 106.

23. John H. Goldthorpe, "The Current Inflation," in Fred Hirsch and John H. Goldthorpe, eds., *The Political Economy of Inflation* (Cambridge: Harvard University Press, 1978), p. 204.

Convergence as Ideal

Finally, some anxieties about reducing impairment appear to derive from the notion that, quite aside from problems of stability and democracy, ideal social organization and ideal problem solving call for analyzed and voluntary agreement as a good thing in itself. The belief draws wide endorsement from a variety of perspectives—Rousseau and Mill among others. In chapter 4 I argued to the contrary.[24] For many reasons outlined there, people often wisely turn to imposed rather than analyzed and voluntary agreed policies, practices, and institutions. Often they have no alternative to imposition because of the impossibility of thinking their way through to agreement. Idealizing agreement and voluntarism denies the values of independent diversity and innovation in thought on one hand, and overlooks its limits on the other. An alternative ideal welcomes some thoughtful and informed convergences and rejoices in many continuing divergences that can only be resolved by political procedures that impose outcomes. Idealizing agreement or consensus creates obstacles to those social changes that do not win the assent of the advantaged. It is difficult to see why it should be idealized. Idealization of agreement is perhaps itself a mammoth impairment.

COMPETITION OF IDEAS

Possibly the most effective single way to reduce impairment is to get into circulation a greater variety of messages. Hence, I turn again to the competition of ideas. Not a panacea, an intense competition among too few ideas can easily become a degenerate form of discourse, as illustrated in recent American presidential elections. But as a general program for reducing impairment, an increasingly broad and rigorous competition of ideas can make progress on two fronts: reducing the deceits and obfuscations of any message through the effects of competing messages; and giving voice to ideas that would otherwise be overwhelmed by louder and more frequent mes-

24. Convergence on the value of convergence itself is also evidenced in the moral pressures, which become intense and intolerant and are enforced by discharge and exile, toward conformity of thought in formal organizations, producing the now well-documented but long familiar phenomenon of "groupthink," as in silencing dissent among presidential advisors consulted in advance of the American Bay of Pigs venture in Cuba (Irving L. Janis, *Victims of Groupthink* [Boston: Houghton Mifflin, 1972]). Groupthink is, however, in some part a phenomenon not of a genuine convergence of thought but of enforced conformity in behavior in decision-making interactions.

sages. The competition has to go further than to permit people to listen and read as they wish. If impairing influences have narrowed the range of ideas to which people choose to attend, then their freedom, however prized, to listen and read as they wish will not open them to a competition of ideas, but will leave them impaired.

For all the impairing influences of family, church, and school outlined in earlier chapters, no reforms of them stand out as obviously required to strengthen the competition of ideas. In each of these three institutions, because their impairing influences closely mesh with their educating or enlightening influences, no society has more than a meager competence on how to disentangle the two. Again, therefore, inquiry into impairment and a heightened discussion of it among ordinary citizens, functionaries, social scientists, and other experts stand as prerequisite to any consequential redesign of the institutions. Then again, neither is it obvious that the powers of the state or of any other heavy external influence should be brought to bear to reform two of these institutions, family and church, for each of which a large measure of autonomy seems desirable. On top of these difficulties of and cautions about attacking impairment through these institutions, most people, including highly informed and thoughtful people, hold strong and to some degree well-probed volitions for the use of each of the three for socialization of children and adults through convergence of attitudes and beliefs into acceptable roles and patterns of behavior. Believing that socialization requires impairments of conformity, most people want each of these institutions to continue in their impairing influences.

By the argument of this study, they have not carefully sorted out the convergences necessary to socialization from attendant convergences that simply impair rather than socialize, nor have they probed the possibility that what they call socialization itself needlessly or excessively impairs. Nevertheless, their commitment to what they regard as socialization constitutes an impregnable looking barrier to proceeding in these institutions against the impairing influences of convergence.

In short, a formidable barrier to reducing impairment through any of these institutions consists of impairments that defend existing impairing influences exerted by them: a classical or garden-variety vicious circle that can be broken into perhaps only in fortuitous circumstances. School reform and educational policy questions, for example, repeatedly appear on political agendas; and, when they do, interested persons might seize upon widespread concerns with educational inadequacies to try to give a push to those reforms that might, while attacking the inadequacies, also serve to reduce impairing convergences. That does not call for indoctrinating children to be political activists; it only means considering the removal or reduction of such specific impairing influences toward conformism, as chapter 6 summarized in the discussion of schools. Even so, the prior or first requirement is to make of impairment, even if treated only as a hypotheses, a great and lasting concern of everyone who takes an interest in these institutions, from inside or out—and that includes almost everyone in every democratic society, almost none of whom, however, at this moment wish to abate the impairments they inflict on others.

While changes in church, family, and school may in the long run exercise a greater effect or for widening the competition of ideas, as well as on other paths to the reduction of impairment, than do state, corporation, and communications media, the latter institutions appear more conspicuously as targets of reform—the state or government because it itself constitutes a major and all-purpose lever for social change, the corporation and the media because their conduct stimulates repeated attacks, and because such autonomy as protects family and church from many interventions does not protect them.

But of course the state does not simply serve as a lever or instrument for dealing with a weak competition of ideas but itself constitutes a major source of the weakness. As with the family, there are no easy levers, no buttons to push, to reduce its impairing influences. As with the family, too, what one—a person, group, or government— would wisely do with a lever if available is wholly obscure, so little probed is the state's role in impairment. The democratic state or government on many issues and in many aspects proceeds in constant hostility to inquiry. Every democratic society faces this predicament. To put it more concretely, the same prime ministers and presidents, cabinets, parliaments, legislatures, members of the bureaucracy, and judges who theoretically stand ready to implement a popular desire, if it should arise, for strengthening the competition of ideas, invest their energies in some large part in narrowing and gutting a competition of ideas (in the various ways outlined in chapter 7). And their impairing influences extend to inculcating in citizens such attitudes and beliefs as will leave them without volition or competence for moving the lever. They extend as well to leaving citizens without volition or competence for reforming corporation or media, in which efforts corporate and media functionaries join.

Wholly familiar even if it had not been summarized in earlier chapters, all this again closes off any easy solutions to a weak and narrow competition of ideas. I can, however, sketch out a direction of possible reform of government-corporation-media relations that will illustrate not simply the difficulty of reform, but some favorable factors that might be seized upon, the kinds of issues that especially need to be probed, and the possibilities of advance through indirection. The example may be persuasive on several points: that feasible lines of reform can be imagined and studied; that, like any attacks on impairment, they will stir deep antipathy; but that, although difficult and slow-moving at best, they do not deserve dismissal as hopeless.

Expensive Free Speech

Among the defects of the existing competition of ideas, none seems more impairing or more easily remedied, given the will, than that well-financed communications, whether well-financed by the state, by private organizations, or by wealthy elites, overpower poorly financed ones. Many societies have accepted, at least as a principle, that children should deserve an education whether their parents can afford it or not, and that everyone deserves some forms of life-protecting medical services regardless of ability to pay. But no society has yet grasped the importance of separating rights of communication from ability to pay.

Two alternatives hypothetically lie open for reducing the influence of money on the competition of ideas: some degree of reduction of inequalities of income and wealth, and some degree of insulation of communication from inequalities in the availability of money. The term "some degree" acknowledges the difficulty of doing either, as well as the impossibility, once again, of specifying the ideal or end of the road.

As for the first, those with a volition for it will find it a rough row to hoe. Despite the egalitarian rhetoric of the liberal democracies, redistribution of income and wealth except through social-welfare transfers of income shares within rather than between socioeconomic strata, is, as noted in the chapters on impairment, much resisted. Perhaps popular support for significant moves away from economic inequality in order to alter the competition of ideas has to wait for the very strengthening of the competition for which the moves are sought. Perhaps, that is, only an already less impaired society would form a volition for pursuing a reduction in impairment through redistribution of wealth and income.[25]

25. To sort out various things I have said so far about inequality, which are all too easily confused with one another: In chapter 1 I took a stance, not argued or defended, of regarding all people as roughly equal in deservingness or entitlement for the pur-

Yet if movement on this front faces difficulties, the strength of the long historical retreat from economic inequality has not evaporated. The argument that substantial inequality of income and wealth obstructs a reduction of impairment adds a powerful supplement to historical attacks on those inequalities. Although it rests on an ethical commitment to at least a very rough equality in entitlements, claims, desserts, or opportunities among members of society, taken by itself it constitutes a "technical," nonethical, or empirical argument: specifically that greater equality in income and wealth is necessary—empirically—to a reduction of impairment in probing, whatever its merits and demerits on other counts.

No modest redistribution of income and wealth such as might soon be achieved would greatly alter the influence of ability to pay on the competition of ideas. To cope sooner with that influence, if one wishes to, the second policy—insulation—may be faster, even granting all its own distinctive difficulties. Democratic societies might, for example, greatly limit by law any private or governmental organization's expenditure on certain categories of costly communication to large audiences.

In the case of the state, if one takes seriously the prescription that it should serve the volitions of its electorate, presumably it should not use public funds to mould minds and make popular control circular. That is to say, roughly speaking, citizens decide autonomously what the government should do, and the government does not propagandize, indoctrinate, or "educate" them to endorse what a governing elite has already decided it wishes to do. In fact, constraints to this end, though poorly designed and enforced, operate in the democracies. The volume of public-relations expenditure by governmental agencies indicates the inadequacies of the constraints; but the principle probably commands a wide assent. One might state it as a denial

poses of this study, a volition that is common though not universal among social scientists. Such a volition does not predict a volition against any particular inequalities, such as of influence or income, for one holding it might believe, for example, that, for the good of all considered in their rough equality of deservingness, society should be ruled by an elite favored with power and wealth.

Chapter 6 showed that to protect inequalities of advantage to elites, elites engage in impairing practices. Such a proposition says nothing about whether inequalities are or are not justifiable. The chapters on impairment also argued—and it is distinguishable from the above argument—that many kinds of inequalities cause impairments, as, for example, through a skewed competition of ideas. Taken by itself, that is an argument for less inequality; the chapter did not incorporate it into a general appraisal of the relative merits of inequality and equality.

Nowhere does this study make a general appraisal of that kind or argue the case for less inequality.

that governmental bodies possess any of the "rights" to communicate possessed by persons.

As for private organizations, in light of laws in European nations that prohibit organizations (as well as individual persons) from buying broadcast time for electoral campaigning and of weaker American laws on campaign finance, a broader set of constraints on organizational spending on mass communication, not limited to electoral campaigning, becomes a not-fanciful possibility. Broader constraints such as might prohibit a corporation or any other private organization from spending any large sum of money on political advocacy on any issue raise constitutional issues in some countries. But this very fact underscores the need to probe as deep as the constitutional foundations of society in order to strengthen the competition of ideas.

Because persons have or should have rights to communicate, it does not follow that organizations have or should have them, beyond the individual rights of members of the organization. Poverty and confusion of thought on the difference between persons and organizations perhaps themselves exemplify impairment. In any case, the question of whether "rights" is an appropriate concept for organizations at all needs inquiry. Should corporations have rights that government agencies do not? Should a corporation as a collectivity possess rights to spend organizational funds for political advocacy? One might think, quite to the contrary, that all corporations, like governmental bodies, ought be constrained as instruments of an "electorate," take orders from it, and operate under its control. On those grounds they cannot appropriately claim any of the rights or liberties of a citizen.

Societies might probe even further: into prohibitions or curbs on institutional advertising or, even further, on sales promotion communications. Lines of corporate influence on education and research call for questioning—indeed, the whole scope of corporate philanthropy does.[26] The last entails investigating such possibilities as diverting the equivalent of corporate philanthropic funds, through taxation to the public purse, so that tax exemption could be granted to millions of citizen contributions to philanthropies.

26. Is a general prohibition on corporate philanthropy so far out of the question as to deserve no probing? Does a corporation obstruct the competition of ideas by contributing to an art gallery or orchestra? The pattern of corporate contribution has some effect on the direction of the arts by influencing what can be displayed or performed; but, unlike corporate influence on research, little can be said with confidence about the consequences of such an influence for the impairment of people's probing of their personal or collective problems. Yet raising the question of support for the arts

Inequality in Control, Influence, or Power

Creating a more genuine competition of ideas would also seem to require reductions in those inequalities of control, influence, or power, other than inequalities in communication, that impair inquiry in the ways outlined in the chapters on impairment.[27] The inequalities consist of those in the exercise of authority, intimidation, coercion, threat, deceit, monetary inducement, fines, exchange of favors, among others. For the disadvantaged, severe enough inequalities in the capacity to exercise such controls or in vulnerability to them sap incentives to think, stir fears of doing so, encourage and confuse or warp their capacities to probe.

All this the earlier chapters noted, with particular attention to many familiar inequalities: between parent and child, teacher and pupil, clergy and laity, workplace authority and employee, government official and citizen, male and female, educated and less well-educated, white and black, advantaged ethnic group and disadvantaged, corporate executive and citizen, higher socioeconomic status and lower (at many levels rather than merely bourgeoisie and working class), and, finally, the professional prober and the ordinary citizen.

Not all inequalities in interpersonal control necessarily impair, and some are necessary: between parent and child, teacher and pupil, workplace authority and employee, among others. Yet even the necessary inequality brings with it the potential, some of it always actualized, for impairment. Inequality in capacity to control goes beyond what serves the discharge of the function that justifies some specific inequalities. Authorities in the workplace use their advantages of control to make impositions on employees beyond those sufficient for

and for research sharpens a crucial element in the case for removing corporations from impairing influences on probing. Corporation executives, as a particular category of functionaries, draw on "public" funds—not government yet public, because drawn from consumers. In presiding over that flow of funds, corporate executives can divert some of it into philanthropies. But these philanthropies are not those that might be chosen by the persons whose funds the corporate executives are allocating. They are those that implement the volitions of the executives. There is no adequate method of social control over these philanthropic diversions of funds, and consequently no well-probed rationale for leaving such allocative decisions in the hands of corporate executives, in light of convergences in belief and attitude that guide their grants. See Lawrence W. Levine, *The Emergence of Cultural Hierarchy in America* (Cambridge: Harvard University Press, 1988).

27. Impairing effects of inequalities in control, power, or influence on inquiry again constitute one more argument, among many other arguments long urged, for a reduction of social inequalities. Again not claiming—or denying—validity for historical and traditional arguments for reducing inequalities, I simply add what I have called a "technical" argument: many social inequalities obstruct inquiry.

efficient production. Teachers similarly use their necessary pedagogical authority to impose impairing standards of obedience or docility on pupils. Tax collectors, police, and other members of the state bureaucracy use their authority to harass or intimidate citizens in ways that are not necessary to the discharge of their assigned duties. As Tawney observed over fifty years ago, to functional inequalities many other inequalities adhere.[28]

Not simply residuals of earlier inequalities that policy has neglected to remove, these "attached" inequalities are often energetically rationalized, justified, defended, and enlarged when possible by the advantaged. Hence, sorting out useful from attached inequalities in control becomes subordinated to the struggle of the advantaged to maintain their advantages.

Just such a sorting out constitutes the core of an attack on inequalities of control in order to keep inequality narrowly functional. To the extent to which the attack can succeed, it maintains such specific inequalities between teacher and pupil as facilitates education and removes the inequalities that serve such purposes as inflating the teacher's ego or permitting excessive influence on the child. It gives a government official just that authority necessary to pursue an assigned and constrained task and strips officials of capacity to intimidate—or even to build a political machine through patronage. It also strips from wealth the deference often given it, or from expertise the deference to competence imputed to it on issues beyond its actual competence.

Again, implementation, though difficult, does not require wholly unfamiliar initiatives. Democratic nations have a history of policies to make governmental authority narrowly functional in the sense just described: for example, grants of official authority limited to stated functions and limitations on officials' use of patronage to increase their authority or other powers. The same core strategy appears in fair employment practices, legislation, remedies for sexual and racial discrimination, protection of civil rights, and curbs in labor legislation on the powers of corporate functionaries, from chief executive officer down to shop foreman.

In no society have either ordinary people or functionaries grappled with social problems or their personal problems except under severe impairment. Among their impairments has been an inability to imagine a significantly less impaired society offering substantially im-

28. R. H. Tawney, *Equality* (New York: Capricorn Books, 1961). See also Michael Walzer, *Spheres of Justice* (New York: Basic Books, 1983), p. 19 and passim.

proved prospects for social problem solving. To appreciate the benefits of a reduction of impairment, one needs a substantially new view of less impaired human faculties, a view of inquiring minds in a variety and depth of inquiry such as no society has yet approached. Not a vision of everyone as scholar or even of everyone as devoted good citizen, it acknowledges that even at its best probing will continue to suffer impairment and in any case will often turn in directions other than social problem solving. Consequently, although the required new view appears radical, it cautiously appraises possible modest gains in social problem solving, understanding that the wrongness of the here-and-now does not promise the rightness of the there-and-later. Still, the vision anticipates societies favored by more diversity of volition, ever open-ended inquiry, and a helpful social science to some significant degree reducing the many inequalities that obstruct inquiry—societies for the first time on the edge—no, only the edge of the edge—of a capacity to think straighter about social problems.

The aspiration to improve social problem solving does not follow the spirit of Francis Bacon's advocacy of a cleansing of minds in a "humiliation of the human spirit,"[29] for probing minds do not passively record but actively shape such understandings, all imperfect, as they can. The aspiration follows, however, in the tradition of the Enlightenment: not its frequent expectation that only a few generations would bring society to unheard-of levels of human welfare, but its commitment to inquiry, the exercise of the mind in probing. An aspiration for citizens, functionaries, and everyone, rather than only for a scientific or intellectual elite, it takes sides on that issue, disputed in the Enlightenment. In a degree of retreat from the Enlightenment, it pursues inquiry and the resourceful utilization of its results more than it pursues firm knowledge. Thus, it rewrites Kant's "Dare to know!" as "Dare to inquire!"

The model of the self-seeking society, multiplistic and pluralistic, takes account, as the Enlightenment failed to do well, of the the irrational, nonrational, often tormented side of the human personality that is hostile to inquiry, though incapable of stopping it. It models a society that is successful in reducing impairments to probing, but never removes them. If Freud opened the world's eyes to human irrationality with such disturbing clarity as to have turned many observers of society away from the traditions of the Enlightenment, he did not himself draw any such inference but instead wrote of reason and

29. "The Great Instauration" (1620), in H. G. Dick, ed., *Selected Writings of Francis Bacon* (New York: Random House, 1955), p. 435.

science: "In spite of its incompleteness and of the difficulties attaching to it, it remains indispensable to us and nothing can take its place."[30]

Of the capacity of both elite and mass to probe, Locke believed that "we are born with faculties and powers capable almost of anything, such at least as would carry us farther than can easily be imagined," which one can read as both prescription and expectation.[31] Utopian and foolish? In medieval Western Europe, to return to an earlier example, the idea that rulers, accustomed to vacating their positions of power only on death or by coup or insurrection, might someday be willing to retire on no stronger signal than a count of expressed preferences of some or all of their subjects, must have struck most people as naive. But their descendants now remove their rulers by ballot. Despite their frequent monumental folly, people learn new ways, even if only infrequently do they accomplish so prodigious a gain as in the example of rotating rulers through elections. Mindful of historical demonstration that people learn new ways, I do not wholly despair of the possibility that somewhere along the line descendants of mine may live in a self-guiding society with its characteristic probes, failures, reconsiderations, and endless reformulations of ends.

If they do not perish through catastrophe but work their way to a self-guiding society, they will not do so because professional inquiry has discovered the route to it for them. Given their constant reconsideration of both ends and means, there exists no route to be discovered, only routes they must create. Instead, they will reach the self-guiding society, if at all, by reconsidering, with the help of professional inquiry, their own volitions for what they seek and what they will give up to get it.

30. *New Introductory Lectures on Psychoanalysis* (New York: Norton, 1964), p. 174.

31. *The Conduct of the Understanding* (New York: S. King, 1823), section 4, p. 15.

Index

Aaron, H. J., 195
Abercrombre, N., 61, 74, 84, 182, 288
Agreement, 48. *See* Convergence
Airey, C., 73
Aitken, J., 112
Albert, H., 42, 185
Alchon, G., 154
Alford, R. R., 288, 289
Alinsky, S., 216
Almond, G. A., 59, 72, 73, 96, 141, 171
Alonso, W., 193
Analysis, as alternative to power, 45–48
Anderson, C. J., 145
Andrain, C., 96
Andreski, S., 194
Anton, T. J., 105
Apex values, 37–42
Apple, M. W., 95
Appleman, W., 196
Apter, D., 110
Aquinas, T., 42, 246
Argyris, C., 36
Aristotle, 42, 43, 67, 145
Arrow, K. J., 48
Atilla, 70

Auspitz, J. L., 288
Authority, 73, 74, 83–87, 92–97, 102, 107
Axelrod, R., 54

Bachrach, P., 182, 237
Bacon, F., 62, 153, 155, 214, 226, 301
Bagehot, W., 67, 111, 220
Bailey, F. G., 10
Baratz, M. S., 182, 237
Barbagli, M., 92
Barber, B., 142
Baritz, L., 200
Barjas, G., 147
Barker, E., 51, 67, 220, 228
Barrows, T. S., 144
Barry, B., 199, 288, 289
Basic and applied social science, 279–83
Battistoni, R. M., 95
Baumer, F. L., 214
Becker, C. L., 228
Bedrock preferences, 19–20
Beer, S. H., 287
Beiner, R., 21
Beliveau, A., 112
Bell, D., 11

Niemi, R. G., 59, 96
Nietzsche, F. W., 34
Nisbett, R. E., 60, 61, 159, 181
Noble, D. F., 194
Noelle-Neumann, E., 75, 102
Nordhaus, W. D., 102, 198
Nordlinger, E. A., 288, 290

Oakeshott, M., 38, 223, 288
Objective wants and interests, 18–21, 23–24
O'Connor, J., 150
Offe, C., 150
Oppenheim, A. N., 73, 96
Orlans, H., 195, 264
Orren, G. R., 39, 52, 72, 84, 90, 106, 107, 117
Outcome, distinguished from decision, 7, 275–76
Overloaded state, 222

Padgett, J. F., 270
Page, B. I., 102
Palmore, E., 144
Parents, 97–99
Pareto, W., 146
Pareto efficiency, 148
Paris Commune, 228
Parkin, F., 96, 113
Parkinson, M., 96
Parsons, T., 246, 287, 289
Participatory democracy, 27
Partisanship: anthropologists on, 53–54; benefits of, 264; and common good, 50–54; disguised, 51–52, 262–63; and egalitarianism, 261–62; and language creation, 54; merits of narrow, 52; and mutual adjustment, 254–56; and norms, 53–54; in social science, 260–66; and "the" decision maker, 264–65, three kinds, 51
Partridge, P. H., 74, 289
Pasteur, L., 281
Patrick, J. J., 96
Patton, M. Q., 164
Paul, Saint, 70
Payne, C., 143
Peabody, D., 73
Pennock, J. R., 141, 182
Pepitone, A., 120
Perrow, C., 186
Persell, C. H., 96
Personen, P., 74
Pestoff, V. A., 116

Philosophy, 28, 146–47; conventional concerns of, 5
Piaget, J., 141, 170
Pierce, J. C., 60
Piereson, J., 119, 290
Pinto-Duschinsky, M., 107, 117
Pires, M. A., 117
Piven, F. F., 84, 95, 96, 101
Planck, M., 193
Plato, 42, 43, 62, 137, 145, 155, 182, 226, 261, 278
Plato's cave, 278
Platzer, L. C., 117
Pluralism, 233–39; defects of, 236–37; among government officials, 234; improvements in, 237–40; as indispensable, 237–39
Poe, E. A., 178
Polanyi, M., 145, 166, 226, 246, 253, 267
Policy analysis, 189, 270; adapting to continuity, 274–76; conventional method, 271; defects of, 276–77; to meet variable client needs, 272–74; to reach a recommendation to client, 271
Political strategy, 14, 15
Polsby, N. W., 182, 209
Polybius, 43, 215, 245
Popper, K., 75, 157, 168
Posner, R. A., 127
Pospisil, L., 48
Power: as alternative to analysis, 45–48
Preferences, 17–24, 29; aggregation of, 48; bedrock, 19–20; impossible to discover, 18–19
Preston, T., 209
Pribram, K. H., 149
Probing, 29; and action, 30; as alternative to ideology, 13, 14; biological limits, 61–62; characterized, 9–10, 29–32, 34–35; cognitive organization, 33; and coherence, 37–42; concepts, 33; to define a problem, 36–37; empirical, 32; ethical, 33; evaluative, 32–33, 34; excesses of, 43, 63; ideal impossible to state, 64–65; immanent critique, 42–44; kinds of, 32–36; kinds of probers, 30; limits of, 46–48; and means-ends analysis, 37–42; as method of this book, 16; into methodology, 34; minimum requirements for, 231–33; and multiplism, 231–33; need for pluralism, 233–39; not passive, 33–34; and pluralism, 233–39; and scientific inquiry, 34–35, 40, 63; and social change,

14–15; social science as, 158; strategies, 35; taught capacities, 62; thought and feeling in, 31–32; ubiquity of, 30; and verification, 167–74. *See also* Coherence; Conflict resolution; Impairment; Means-ends analysis; Mutual adjustment; Partisanship; Self-guiding society

Problem: defined, 6; identification, 36–37

Problem solving: and conflict resolution, 7–9; defined, 6–7; as inquiry, 9–10; as probing, 9–10; purposes, 17; scientific, 10–13, 16

Professional inquiry. *See* Social science

Project choice: and beneficiaries, 268; as economic choice, 266; incompetent, 268; in natural and social science, 267; need for social philosophy, 268; problems do not constitute a research agenda, 269; and social control, 268; and social learning, 267

Proudhon, P., 221

Prunty, J. J., 138

Quade, E. S., 271

Qualter, T. H., 101, 103, 104, 112

Quine, W. V., 40, 43, 167

Radcliff-Brown, A. R., 149, 152

Radicalism, 15

Radin, N., 144

Rae, D., 262

Raisinghani, D., 275

Ravetz, J. R., 153, 154, 155, 167, 168, 194, 279

Rawls, J., 39

Real preferences or interests, 19. *See also* Objective wants and interests

Real world, 63; and social construction of reality, 31

Redner, H., 142, 175, 179, 269

Reduction of impairment: absence of motives for, 294; as blocked by impairments, 294; and curbs on corporate philanthropy, 298; and curbs on government, 297–98; and curbs on media and sales promotion, 298; and curbs on private organizations, 298; as dangerous, 287; and democratic overload, 291–93; effect on convergence, on stabilizing leadership, and other stabilizing influences, 289–91; and fears of divergence, 288–91; feasible, 285; by income redistribution, 296–97; and inequality,

299–300; lack of competence, 286; lack of motive, 286; limiting of authority, 299–300; little attempted, 300–301; in school, state, media, corporate and family, 295; strategies for, 284–86; and survival of political-economic order, 292; and tolerance, 290

Reich, R. B., 110, 255

Reichley, J., 60

Rein, M., 138

Reitz, J., 279

Religion, 114–15, 184; and elites, 86–88

Remling, G. W., 99

Renshon, S. A., 33, 96

Reporting, 143–44

Repression, 87, 112

Rescher, N., 18

Residual conflict resolution, 48

Revolution, 15

Rhoads, S. E., 183

Ricci, D. M., 173

Richardson, J., 243

Richter, M., 245

Rivlin, A. M., 144, 219

Roberts, D., 89

Roosevelt, F. D., 216

Rootes, C. A., 74

Rorty, R., 21

Rose, R., 117

Rosenbaum, J., 96

Rosenthal, D. E., 166

Ross, E. A., 120

Ross, G. F., 144

Ross, L., 60, 139, 159, 181

Rothman, S., 104

Rothstein, B., 116

Rousseau, J. J., 62, 155, 175, 218, 293

Rüstow, A., 86

Rule, J. B., 7, 184

Runciman, W. G., 144

Ryan, M., 117

Ryle, G., 6, 138

Safran, W., 116

Saint-Simon, C., 214, 221, 247

Salisbury, R. H., 233

Samuelson, P. A., 198, 201

Sartori, G., 43, 60, 68, 182

Satisficing, 270

Sawin, D. B., 145

Scannel, P., 102

Schattschneider, E. E., 62

Schlozman, K. L., 79, 117

Schön, D. A., 14, 36, 138

202–04; and impairment, 276–79; impairments shared with lay probers, 195, 200–209; inattention to impairment, 181–86; inconclusiveness of, 158; as an industry, 135; interchanging means and ends, 147; interpretive, 139–43; and meaning, 150–51; methodology, 152; multiplicity of concerns, 267–68; neglect of citizens in serving functionaries, 186–90; no invisible world, 177–80; not demonstrably necessary, 136–37; partisan, 260–66; and policy analysis, 270–76; preemption of probing, 190–91; as probing, 158; and project choice, 266–69; as reaching judgments, 169–74; reporting, 143–44; as scientific or not, 152; and scientific socialism, 228; and self-guiding society, 216–17, 257–58; and simplifying strategies, 269–70; and study of policy-making, 186; as supplement to lay probing, 161–67; synthesis and design, 151–52; and "the" decision maker, 264–65; and theory, 159–60; for which beneficiaries, 258–60. *See also* Policy analysis; Project choice
Social stability, 65
Socialization: and convergence, 121; and impairment, 70–72; in schools, 91–96. *See also* Social science
Socrates, 32
Söderqvist, T., 200
Sophists, 43
Southey, R., 92
Spence, L. D., 64, 71, 182, 201, 284
Spinoza, 224
Spiral of silence, 75
Spiro, R., 34, 59
Stacey, B., 95
Stake, R., 138
Stambaugh, R. J., 164
Starr, P., 193
State, 48–50; as cause of problems, 49–50; and cooperation, 49; not benign, 110; as transforming society, 50
State formation, 121
Steinhouse, H., 102
Stern, P. M., 107
Stevenson, R. L., 178
Stokely, E., 265, 277
Stone, C. N., 291
Storer, N., 281
Stouffer, S., 143
Strauss, A., 138

Strauss, L., 43, 193
Strodbeck, F. L., 71
Sturmthal, A., 113
Sullivan, J. L., 60, 119, 290
Suppe, F., 168
Sutton, F. X., 106
Svensson, L. G., 200
Swanson, C., 117
Sweden, 100, 105
Sykes, C., 194
Synthesis and design, 151–52
Systems analysis, defects of, 276–77
Szecsko, T., 104
Szilard, L., 63
Szirmai, A., 84

Talmon, J. L., 229
Taschdjian, E., 24
Tawney, R. H., 90, 300
Taylor, C., 145, 194
Taylor, D. G., 75
Taylor, F., 151
Taylor, S. E., 39
Technology and knowledge, 11–13
Tedin, K. L., 60
Television and broadcasting. *See* Media
Tentler, T. N., 31
Theoret, A., 275
Therborn, G., 74
Tholfsen, T. R., 88, 89
Thompson, D., 66
Three worlds (of Karl Popper), 75
Thucydides, 43
Tienda, M., 147
Tierney, J. T., 117
Tilly, C., 110
Tinbergen, J., 216
Tobin, J., 106
Tocqueville, A. de, 62, 145, 287
Tolstoy, 32
Torgerson, D., 45
Torney, J. V., 73, 89, 94, 96, 98
Toulmin, S., 149, 267
Tradition, 120
Trial and error, 270
Tribe, L. H., 38, 148, 219, 277
Trotter, W., 121
Troy, L., 117
Turner, B. S., 74, 84, 182, 288
Turner, C. F., 141
Tversky, A., 61
Tyack, D. B., 92

Ukeles, J. B., 271